The Fabian Society is Britain's leading left of centre think tank and political society, committed to creating the political ideas and policy debates which can shape the future of progressive politics.

With over 300 Fabian MPs, MEPs, Peers, MSPs and AMs, the Society plays an unparalleled role in linking the ability to influence policy debates at the highest level with vigorous grassroots debate among our growing membership of over 7000 people, 70 local branches meeting regularly throughout Britain and a vibrant Young Fabian section organising its own activities. Fabian publications, events and ideas therefore reach and influence a wider audience than those of any comparable think tank. The Society is unique among think tanks in being a thriving, democratically-constituted membership organisation, affiliated to the Labour Party but organisationally and editorially independent.

For over 120 years Fabians have been central to every important renewal and revision of left of centre thinking. The Fabian commitment to open and participatory debate is as important today as ever before as we explore the ideas, politics and policies which will define the next generation of progressive politics in Britain, Europe and around the world.

Fabian Society
11 Dartmouth Street
London SW1H 9BN
www.fabians.org.uk

First published 2009
ISBN 978 0 7163 4109 3

Editorial Director: Tom Hampson
Editorial Manager: Ed Wallis

British Library Cataloguing in Publication data. A catalogue record for this book is available from the British Library.

To find out more about the Fabian Society, the Young Fabians, the Fabian Women's Network and our local societies, please visit our web site at **www.fabians.org.uk**.

Is Equality Fair?

What the public really think about equality
– and what we should do about it

Edited by Tom Hampson and Jemima Olchawski

About the authors

Louise Bamfield is a Senior Research Fellow at the Fabian Society and is currently on secondment to the Child Poverty Unit at the Department for Children, Schools and Families.

John Denham is Labour Member of Parliament for Southampton Itchen and Secretary of State for Communities and Local Government.

Kate Green is Chief Executive of the Child Poverty Action Group.

Tom Hampson is Editorial Director of the Fabian Society.

Tim Horton is Research Director of the Fabian Society.

Stewart Lansley is the author of Life in the Middle, The Untold Story of Britain's Average Earners, TUC Touchstone Pamphlet, June 2009 and the co-author of Londongrad: From Russia With Cash, The Inside Story of the Oligarchs, 4th Estate, 2009.

Jemima Olchawski is Events Director of the Fabian Society.

Ben Page is Chief Executive of Ipsos MORI.

Zoe Williams is a columnist at *The Guardian*.

CONTENTS

FABIAN SOCIETY

Key points from the Fabian research

This pamphlet examines research undertaken by the Fabian Society which was commissioned and supported by the Joseph Rowntree Foundation. The work looked at some of the values and beliefs that lie behind public attitudes towards economic inequality and welfare policy. It also explored approaches that might be used to build a public consensus for tackling economic inequality in the UK.

The full report, *Understanding attitudes to tackling economic inequality* by Louise Bamfield and Tim Horton, is published by the Joseph Rowntree Foundation (JRF). It is available as a free download from www.jrf.org.uk.

The main findings of this work were:

* Nearly all the participants in the discussion groups placed themselves in **the 'middle' of the income spectrum** and interpreted the 'income gap' as the gap between the 'middle' and the 'super-rich'.

* Most participants believed that **'deserved' inequalities are fair**. They were not opposed to high incomes they perceived to be deserved through high-level ability, performance or social contribution.

- Participants often made assumptions about the **virtues of those with high incomes** in order to justify income inequalities. However, after the start of the financial crisis of autumn 2008, they increasingly questioned whether high salaries were deserved.

- Attitudes towards **those on low incomes** were often more negative than attitudes towards the 'rich'. Two important factors driving these attitudes were widespread beliefs that there are adequate opportunities to earn a reasonable income and beliefs that benefit recipients will not contribute back to society.

- Most participants strongly supported **progressive tax and benefit systems**. When considering evidence about unequal life chances, they were supportive of targeted interventions to improve life chances for the disadvantaged.

- Many participants did not find abstract arguments for greater equality persuasive. They preferred arguments for greater equality framed in terms of **fairer rewards for effort and contribution**.

- Many participants found claims about the possible negative social consequences of income inequality convincing. They showed strong support for a social vision based upon improving quality of life for everyone and were prepared to support certain egalitarian policies in this context.

INTRODUCTION

Jemima Olchawski

Thirteen million people live in poverty in the UK, including one in three children. Anti-poverty campaigners are well versed in the arguments about how damaging that reality is for those who live it and to our society as a whole. Yet, despite all the efforts of campaigners, poverty is in fact rising. Negative stereotypes of the poor pervade the media, and people's beliefs about welfare policy seem to be increasingly hard nosed. Politicians of the left share in this struggle, committed to ending child poverty but fearing that there simply isn't enough money to do it. They also fear public resistance.

So the Fabian research outlined in the next chapter is much-needed. It offers cause for optimism, outlining the areas where there is already public support for action; and it reveals what underlies public opposition to some campaigns so that we can communicate our cause more effectively. The research also flags up some knotty issues that the left simply must engage with, but, equipped with this research, campaigners and policy-makers can tap into existing ideas about fairness and get to the heart of the beliefs that need to be challenged – a much longer term project.

Understanding what people really believe will mean progressives can actually take more radical measures than they might have thought.

The project identified four broad clusters of attitudes – or 'tribes' – which are discussed by Ben Page in chapter 4. The egalitarians amongst us may be disappointed to discover that we are in a minority: only 22 per cent of people are "traditional egalitarians" who understand desert in terms of need and are driven by a vision of a more equal society. However, those on the right should not get carried away either: an even smaller group (20 per cent) are "traditional free marketeers." Around 26 per cent of people make up the "angry middle" (think Daily Mail-style disapproval of those both at the top and bottom of the income spectrum) with the largest proportion of the population (32 per cent) being classed as "post ideological liberals". This group admires the wealthy but are not opposed to taxes on wealth and have more neutral feelings about the poorest.

Looking at people's attitudes in this way it is possible to see where potential coalitions exist and which ideas appeal across the tribes. For instance, the majority of people are actually in favour of tackling wealth at the top, with only the small group of traditional free marketeers truly against such measures. So politicians can afford to be less hesitant about tax rises on the wealthy as a source of revenue and as a measure to deal with Britain's extraordinary wealth inequality.

But there isn't just greater room for manoeuvre in dealing with the top, understanding the public's attitudes also reveals potential support for raising some of the benefits of the poorest. Negative images and stereotypes of the poor are common and Kate Green looks at the asymmetry in the way people treat rich and poor in chapter 3. But the ease with which many people slip into negative stereotypes can lead us to muddle negative attitudes towards 'the poor' with public disapproval of people who are seen to be free loading. The research shows that the public are more than happy to pay taxes to support people, on the proviso that they're 'doing their bit'. This concept of reciprocity underpins much of what the public believe about supporting the poor – most people think of desert in terms of reward for effort, rather than need (as those traditional egalitarians tend to).

As John Denham confronts in chapter 1, the public believe that certain inequalities that result from different levels of effort are deserved and that policies that counteract that are unfair. That creates a longer term problem for the left in challenging ideas about effort and the barriers that many of society's poorest face. But it also means that there was heartfelt support from participants in our focus groups for the in-work poor. Many people were shocked at the levels of income those in the bottom quintile live on and firmly supported a progressive system that gives them a helping hand. The focus groups saw powerful affirmation of a system that redistributes from rich to poor as fair and necessary.

A belief in the importance of reciprocity means people are concerned about contribution and effort and that they have a broad understanding of what that means. The contribution of those caring for children and relatives was recognised as highly valuable by participants. So the blight of poverty amongst our carers is a cause that will really rally public support. The single mum who doesn't work, or who works limited hours to look after her children was actually far less unpopular than might have been predicted, because the public recognises her work in raising her children as important to society and as making a genuine effort.

So, even before trying to change a single mind, there already exists a strong pool of support for tax credits and assistance for the in-work poor, and – in all likelihood – scope to increase these benefits without moralised opposition.

Armed with the knowledge that people are not against benefits to the poor per se, but to benefits to those who they believe are freeloading off the efforts of others, it will be possible to make arguments more effectively.

Campaigners and government should focus on the effort most lower income people make. Using the examples of carers and parents is a good route into challenging casual stereotypes of benefit recipients as scroungers and layabouts. There are widespread myths about the extent of benefit fraud – and the importance people place on contribution and doing your bit makes clear the importance of tackling these in order to gain support for increases in welfare levels.

That belief in reciprocity – in getting something back because you've put your fair share in – points us in the direction of more universal welfare provision. In discussion, participants demonstrated strong support for progressive universalism. Although, when asked directly, people often oppose the idea of redistribution, our research shows that in fact most find the redistributive nature of the tax system unsurprising and appropriate. There was strong opposition to extreme targeting with many concerned about those in the middle who just miss out on government support. This may partly be because most people believe themselves to be in the middle of the income spectrum, as Stewart Lansley discusses in chapter 2. But when asked to design a benefits system themselves, participants tapered the amount received at similar income levels, quite high up the income spectrum, with very small differences in the responses between the more and less well off participants. It reflects a desire to reward the effort of those in the middle.

In the current context of tighter budgets during the recession, the opposition to targeting may seem to present a challenge to those wishing to address low incomes. But the Fabian research suggests that there will be greater willingness to pay and so more in the pot if the way money is paid out is felt to be fairer. This isn't buying off the middle classes but creating a welfare system that reflects reasonable and deeply held beliefs about what is fair.

Those arguing that the recession demands a move toward greater targeting should remember the left's traditional commitment to universalism, a model which treats us all as equal citizens, avoids stigmatising those in receipt of benefits and makes clear that we are all in it together. Introducing benefits and services that are progressively universal would not only have public backing and legitimacy but would help us to make greater strides towards a more equal society.

The single mum who doesn't work, or who works limited hours to look after her children was actually far less unpopular than might have been predicted, because the public recognises her work in raising her children as important to society and as making a genuine effort.

However, this widely-held belief in reciprocity also seriously challenges the left and those working to end poverty. The flip side of sympathy for those the public think are trying their hardest is a considerably tougher position on benefits for the unemployed and economically inactive, people who the public are more likely to see as free riding on the efforts of those in work.

Here, going with the grain of public opinion could have some seriously inequitable consequences and there is an important debate to be had about how to respond to that; where to persuade and where to work with what people believe. Conditionality has been used as a policy tool to reassure the public that those on benefits genuinely deserve them and are contributing their fair share where they can. Going down that route might allow us to do more for these groups and to rebuild the legitimacy of public spending on those who are not working. There is also merit in being explicit about the reciprocal nature of the welfare state, perhaps even opening up discussions about how much those further up the income ladder really put into the pot. But that can only work if we ask the same of all citizens and offer a fair deal to everyone. A tougher approach to those who are out of work might satisfy the public's belief in reciprocity but many on the left will feel that in reality the burden falls far too heavily on the poorest. The long term unemployed, those that resist efforts to support them back into work, those suffering with addiction or mental health problems have not emerged from a vacuum, and many of us will wonder whether we have already asked these people to bear more than their fair share. But that is a story about the impact of our social structures, of poverty and social stigma on individuals that we have yet to find a convincing way to tell the broader public.

To really resolve this, it is clear that campaigners must embark on a far longer-term project to raise awareness of the barriers that people on low incomes often face. The Fabian research shows that one of the most powerful drivers of opposition to anti-poverty policy is a belief that there is enough opportunity for everyone to make it if they try hard enough.

In a country with one of the lowest levels of social mobility of all developed economies that belief may be hard for those on the left to swallow. But as long as that myth persists, the greatest challenge for those wishing to end poverty will be the common belief that those who are at the bottom are there because they simply didn't try hard enough.

RESEARCH FINDINGS

Tim Horton and Louise Bamfield

This research (undertaken July 2008 to February 2009) examines some of the values and beliefs that lie behind public attitudes towards economic inequality and welfare policy. It also explores approaches that might be used to build a public consensus for tackling economic inequality in the UK.

Much research on public attitudes to economic inequality has focused on revealing attitudes rather than exploring what motivates them. This research investigates some of the motivating forces behind these attitudes, and aims to fill in some of the gaps in previous research. It also explores elements around which a public consensus might be built for tackling economic inequality.

One of the key questions for the research was to investigate the 'income gap' paradox revealed by British Social Attitudes Survey data, whereby, despite widespread expressions of discontent about the income gap, people are reluctant to support certain redistributive measures to narrow it.

The view from the 'middle'

Nearly all the participants in the discussion groups placed themselves in the 'middle' of the income spectrum, despite the fact that they came from the full range of socio-economic groups. They interpreted the income gap in terms of the gap between the 'middle' and the 'superrich'. Views about the gap being too big therefore tended to reflect concerns about the pressures that those in the 'middle' were under in comparison with those at the top.

Are high salaries deserved?
Most participants believed that 'deserved' inequalities are fair. They were therefore not opposed to high incomes in general because they tended to believe that these were deserved on the basis of ability, effort, performance or social contribution.

Judgements were sometimes influenced by 'cognitive coping strategies', which generated more positive evaluations of high incomes than might have been expected. In particular, participants would make assumptions about the virtues of those with high incomes to justify existing inequalities. The willingness of participants to use such coping strategies, however, was noticeably affected by the financial crisis of autumn 2008. A tendency to justify large inequalities in pay as being deserved gave way to anger at perceived excess at the top, and people began increasingly to question whether very high salaries really were deserved.

Despite a belief in deserved inequality, in many cases the 'super-rich' and those with very high salaries did attract condemnation – again, more so after the onset of the financial crisis.

Where objections to high salaries were raised, most participants objected on the basis that such salaries were not deserved. A significant minority of more egalitarian participants objected primarily on the basis that they were not needed. Where participants viewed high salaries or extreme wealth as undeserved, however, this did not necessarily lead them to blame the individual concerned or think they should not be entitled to it.

The 'income gap' paradox

The research suggests three reasons why people may be reluctant to support certain redistributive policies, despite apparently widespread unease about inequality.

* It seems that people are interpreting the income gap as that between the very top and the middle, rather than between 'rich' and 'poor' as conventionally understood.

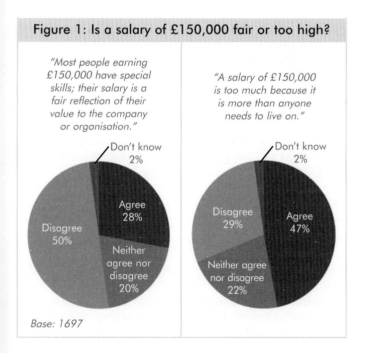

Figure 1: Is a salary of £150,000 fair or too high?

"Most people earning £150,000 have special skills; their salary is a fair reflection of their value to the company or organisation."

Don't know 2%
Agree 28%
Disagree 50%
Neither agree nor disagree 20%

"A salary of £150,000 is too much because it is more than anyone needs to live on."

Don't know 2%
Agree 47%
Disagree 29%
Neither agree nor disagree 22%

Base: 1697

- Concern about the income gap co-exists with a widespread belief that some inequalities are fairly deserved, and this sense of fairness may be violated by some redistributive approaches.

- Even where inequalities are seen as undeserved (for example, inherited wealth), in some contexts there is a sense that an individual is nevertheless still entitled to their resources.

Underlying support for a progressive tax and benefits system

Despite a widespread belief in 'fair inequality', participants strongly supported a progressive tax and benefits system – although they complained that the system is not generous enough towards the 'middle' (that is, where participants placed themselves). Participants therefore often supported highly redistributive policies on grounds of fairness, even if they did not particularly favour the idea of redistribution itself.

Many participants wanted the tax system to treat them differently from those at 'the top'. And, in line with beliefs that the 'middle' are under most pressure, they wanted the benefits system to treat them 'not too differently' from those at 'the bottom'. Nearly all participants were happy for lower-income households to receive more support than those in the 'middle', but many felt uneasy about benefits that were perceived to be very narrowly-targeted.

Of a range of possible distributive strategies, those based on 'progressive universalism' – where people in the middle get something, if less than those at the bottom – were viewed as fair, with suggestions that people would be more willing to contribute to benefits that had wider coverage.

Judgemental attitudes towards those on low incomes
Participants' attitudes towards those on low incomes were often more negative and condemning than their attitudes towards 'the rich'. For example, they placed far greater blame and responsibility on the former for their situation than on the latter.

The research highlighted two especially important factors driving these attitudes:

- a widespread belief in the ready availability of opportunity. Sixty-nine per cent agreed that 'There is enough opportunity for virtually everyone to get on in life if they really want to. It comes down to the individual and how much you are motivated' (with 14 per cent disagreeing);

- a widespread belief that benefit recipients will not go on to make a contribution back to society. Only 25 per cent agreed that 'Most people who receive benefits now will make a contribution back to society in the future, through activities like employment or caring for others' (with 46 per cent disagreeing).

These beliefs seem to exert a powerful influence on support for welfare policy, with beliefs about whether or not benefit recipients will contribute back to society being the most powerful.

When considering evidence about the unequal life chances of those in different socio-economic positions, participants were supportive of targeted interventions to improve life chances for the disadvantaged, even where there would be some cost to the rest of the population.

Building support for tackling economic inequality

A belief in deserved inequality is one reason why many participants did not find abstract arguments for greater equality convincing. Instead, they preferred arguments for greater equality when they were framed in terms of more proportionate rewards for the level of effort and contribution made.

This suggests that any public consensus about tackling economic inequality would have to include an acceptance that certain levels of inequality are fair. Advocates of greater equality might benefit from explicitly acknowledging this, while questioning whether current levels of inequality meet this criterion.

A concern with the quality of life

Evidence was presented to participants about the possible consequences of economic inequality. Many found claims about the possible broader social effects of income inequality convincing and thought that these effects, particularly in areas such as crime and child conflict, were an important reason for constraining inequality.

The life pressures faced by participants were often articulated in terms of the negative consequences of materialism and consumerism. These were also themes in discussions about the effects of inequality.

Most participants were strongly attracted to a social vision founded on improving quality of life for everyone (more so than one founded on explicitly egalitarian objectives, and far more so than one founded on economic growth). Furthermore, most participants showed support for important egalitarian policies when these were considered in the context of improving quality of life.

The four tribes

The research identifies four distinct sets of attitudes to inequality and welfare policy. People falling into these categories are described as follows:

* **'Traditional Egalitarians'** (22 per cent of people) – supporting measures to tackle inequality at both top and bottom. They tend to be older and more heavily weighted towards Labour than the country as a whole; 55 per cent are in socio-economic groups C2DE.

* **'Traditional Free-marketeers'** (20 per cent of people) – opposing measures to tackle inequality at both top and bottom. They are overwhelmingly in socioeconomic groups ABC1 (70 per cent) and are much more heavily weighted towards the Conservatives than the country as a whole.

* **'The Angry Middle'** (26 per cent of people) – supporting measures to tackle inequality at the top, while opposing measures to tackle inequality at the bottom. They are slightly more weighted towards the Conservatives than the country as a whole; 53 per cent are ABC1.

* **'Post-ideological Liberals'** (32 per cent of people) – supporting certain measures to tackle inequality at the top (although they have more positive attitudes towards those at the top than Traditional Egalitarians), without having negative attitudes towards those in poverty or being opposed to tackling inequality at the

bottom (unlike Traditional Free-marketeers and The Angry Middle). Postideological Liberals tend to be younger and less strongly opinioned than those in the other groups, and tend to vote Conservative and Labour in equal numbers; 52 per cent are ABC1.

Conclusion

Participants were generally committed to the idea of 'fairly deserved inequality', whereby certain individuals deserve high incomes because of their superior ability, effort or the contribution they make to society. Participants also defended certain individual rights to wealth, regardless of judgements about whether it was deserved. However, incomes that were perceived as excessively large did often attract condemnation.

Many participants exhibited strongly judgemental attitudes towards people on out-of-work benefits, motivated by beliefs about the ready availability of opportunity and beliefs that those claiming benefits now will not necessarily make a future contribution back to society. This suggests an important route for challenging judgemental attitudes here would be to raise awareness of the barriers to opportunity faced by many people and to highlight the contributions that many of those on low incomes currently make to society and will make in future.

Despite such negative attitudes towards those in receipt of benefits, participants demonstrated strong underlying support for a progressive tax and benefits system – albeit with common complaints that the current system is not generous enough towards the 'middle' (as participants defined themselves). Relatedly, there are signs that the recent financial crisis has opened up space for more radical action on pay and taxation at the top than would previously have appeared feasible.

Most participants were strongly attracted to a social vision framed around improving 'quality of life' for all and demonstrated support for important egalitarian policies when these were considered in this context. This implies that quality-of-life issues could figure as important components in building a public consensus around greater equality – or at least around policies to tackle inequality. It also suggests there is a real desire for a public debate about the social and economic values that guide and direct society, a debate that should provide an important opportunity for advocates of greater equality.

About the project

The research consisted of a series of discussion groups (with 112 participants), including three full-day workshops. These were held between July 2008 and January 2009 in four UK cities, with participants drawn from the full socioeconomic spectrum and a broad range of political affiliations. The work also included a large-scale survey, with data collected and analysed by YouGov, with fieldwork undertaken 28 November–1 December 2008 (2,044 adults) and 3–5 February 2009 (3,316 adults).

This research forms part of a wider Joseph Rowntree Foundation programme on public interest in poverty, which considers attitudes towards poverty and their implications for building public support for action on UK poverty eradication.

The JRF commissioned the study following a review of existing literature on attitudes to economic inequality, which highlighted the apparent contradiction between public dissatisfaction with the income gap in the UK and the lack of support for measures to address it.

Is Equality Fair?

RESPONSES

Is Equality Fair?

1. JUST DESERTS

JOHN DENHAM

*The research found a belief that 'deserved' inequalities are fair. This
meant that our participants were not opposed to high incomes that
they perceived to be deserved (though in many cases the 'super-rich'
and those with very high salaries did attract their condemnation).*

Questions of fairness and equality have defined the
labour movement from the beginning. In the 21st
century our responses will still determine the success or failure of the centre left. The centre left did badly
across Europe in June. Though refracted through many different national cultures and experiences, the same issues –
how to maintain fairness and tackle inequality in a changing world were no less important. On top of the age-old
challenges of fairness in a market economy, relatively new
ones like mass migration – which at first sight appear social
and cultural – are most challenging because they influence
perceptions of fairness: who gets what access to housing,
jobs, benefits and new opportunities.

We all hear "it's not fair" every day, not just out canvassing. "I've paid in all my life but when I needed help there
wasn't much there." People believe that effort and entitlement as well as need should reflect the support you get. The
responsibilities as well as rights should be underpinned. The
behaviour which supports wider society should be encouraged and destructive behaviour discouraged.

Older readers will recognise these as the values New Labour set out in the mid-1990s. There were then, and are now, more than a centre left philosophy. They reflected the deeply held values of the British people – a fairness code.

If we ever give up on the challenges of fairness and equality the centre left will have lost all meaning. The Fabian research on voter attitudes doesn't tell us to give up; it just asks us to think about how we move forward.

Nor have we got everything wrong. Far from it. Statistics heavily skewed by the very highest incomes and the very poorest individuals easily disguise how much progress has been made for millions of poorer families in providing incomes higher relative to the majority of people; incomes far higher than they would have enjoyed if a Labour Government had not acted with determination and conviction. Even more progress has been made in the achievements of the poorest children than for others. The new Equalities Bill is evidence of sustained ambition and commitment.

In recent years Labour has increasingly aligned our approach to fairness with the common sense and deep rooted ideas of what is fair held by the British people.

But it's still worth setting out the key points of this debate. The ground breaking international study 'The Spirit Level', by Richard Wilkinson and Kate Pickett, makes a pretty compelling case for societies that are not too unequal. On Labour's priority issues – school standards, health, community cohesion and social solidarity, fear of crime, and of well being – the societies which are less unequal do better. Ideas of social capital, the importance of 'place', neighbourhood strategies, investment in public space in the most deprived areas, and a focus on the most challenged are all important. They will continue to shape government priorities. But the evidence suggests that the good outcomes are more easily achieved in more equal societies. Unequal societies cannot deal with major social challenges by an isolated approach to the most disadvantaged. This is why Cameron's 'broken Britain' analysis is fatally wrong and the remedies of Iain Duncan Smith's Centre for Social Justice doomed to fail.

But we can't leap from this conclusion to the assumption that all measures designed to reduce inequality are of equal value, or equally likely to get support.

For a start, far more people support the idea of a 'fair' society than support the idea of an 'equal' society. Some measures that would reduce inequality would be seen, widely, as unfair. Taxing people who work to give more to people who don't want to has never had too many takers.

The right have always seen inequality as an inevitable, even beneficial feature of society: a natural reflection of underlying aptitude and ability which enables each of us to find our place. We know that more identifiable forces are at work.

The market economy is the most dynamic, wealth creating and productive economic system humans have created. But the very dynamism of market economies, intensified by globalisation, has powerful tendencies towards greater inequality. Even without crises and recessions, market economies constantly create opportunities for individuals and powerful organisations to accumulate great power, take unfair rewards, and to intensify unfairly the disadvantages of the life chances of different families, different aspirations, and poor education.

If 'progressive politics' still has any meaning, it must be the recognition that that only governments, acting with and on behalf of people, can counter the insistent drive towards greater inequality that markets left alone will produce. In practical terms, this means that government can do a great deal, as Labour has done, to mitigate these pressures. The Tories' rejection of the power of government, whether to intervene in economic management, or to deliver the framework for social change means that they are not even in the real debate about progressive politics. The 'progressive' language they use is unconnected to any progressive policies.

A changing society has changed and challenged ideas of fairness and equality on the left. A mass working class movement wanted a fair deal for people who worked and the post-war welfare state was founded on the contributory principle. Benefits were dependent on – and for a long time directly related to – what you paid in.

Over time, the contributory principle has been eroded, for reasons both good and bad. Contributory systems disadvantaged millions of carers, mainly women, and people who could not work. Giving carers and the unemployed credits into the system made it fairer but weakened the link with earned entitlement. Contributory benefits accumulate value over a long period of time. Governments which wanted to address contemporary poverty and inequality had to use means-tested benefits, which were used to achieve rapid social change. (Labour could, within the same spending, have indexed the basic state pension since 1997, but at the cost of doing far less for the poorest pensioners.) Less benignly, means-tested benefits, though expensive to administer and plagued by problems of take up, were cheaper and less likely prone to claims that taxpayers money is going to those who don't really need it. Social care policy exploded under the Tories because they had insisted that years of work, effort and savings should get no recognition in paying for residential care.

But other ideas were also at work. The most powerful was that need, rather than earned entitlement, should determine what you received. For reasons that are easily understandable, the idea that homelessness automatically trumped years of waiting by those with slightly less immediate need was universally adopted. In these and other areas of social policy, an unholy alliance formed of a left-inspired needs-based view of fairness and a right-wing drive to limit public spending; creating, in the process, systems which many people feel are unfair.

Public opinion can be inflamed if needs-based systems are seen to be leaky or exploitable. The extent to which people manage to fiddle the system to their own advantage is greatly overstated in popular imagination and fed by the tabloid press. But you only need one well documented case to damage confidence.

The cumulative impact of these changes has eroded the link between effort and entitlement which, for all its flaws, was the foundation of the post war welfare state. At the same time we have become more individualistic, more prone to compare individuals with each other, and more willing to question the distribution of rewards. Significant migration has raised new questions about entitlements and how a needs-based approach to welfare reflects a sense of fair entitlement. The one needs-based post-war system in which your rights came as a citizen – the NHS – is sometimes seen to be vulnerable to those whose human needs are in no doubt but whose entitlement to priority is less clear.

A society which saw itself as divided between the mass that were denied a fair return for their efforts and the bosses

The extent to which people manage to fiddle the system to their own advantage is greatly overstated in popular imagination and fed by the tabloid press. But you only need one well documented case to damage confidence.

who took the pickings has become a society much more likely to believe that income reflects effort and ability.

These changes underlie and explain the Fabian research. (Though, through an accident in timing, the research also captured the wider question now rippling through society about whether too many of those doing well – whether bankers, highly paid public sector professionals, politicians and others – were not, in part at least, people whose reward reflected the privilege of their position, not the contribution they make).

Let's be clear. The research isn't telling us that we abandon all notion of need. Just that to get consent to tackle need we have, first, to be sure that our society rewards effort, responsibility and earned entitlement. In choosing and presenting our policies to promote fairness and tackle inequality, they must also pass the test of whether they are seen as fair.

We have reasserted the link between effort, entitlement and reward across our society. We don't have to abandon all notions of absolute need. But we must get the balance right: ensuring that immediate need does not always and unfairly trump earned entitlement.

And we must make clear, in everything we say and do, that these robust, common-sense values of fairness, of rights and responsibilities, underpin everything we do.

It may surprise many – inside and outside the Labour Party – to hear that this is where policy has been going. We've not always said it clearly or put individual policy changes into a strong, consistent story. But we raised the savings allowances for pensioners before means-testing kicks in and Andy Burnham's social care changes would bring a guaranteed payment for care for all pensioners. The new pensions system is explicitly designed to limit the dependence of future pensioners on means-testing. John

Healey's massive investment in new council and social housing was launched, hand in hand, with more freedom for local councils to make sure allocation policy met local needs and priorities fairly. Across the welfare system, the responsibility to work has been enforced (with practical help to do so), and tax credits mean work, not idleness is better rewarded. Migration controls have been tightened and linked explicitly to the ability to contribute, and earned citizenship will ensure that access to the wider benefits of our society are privileges to be won, not taken for granted. Not everyone on the centre-left is comfortable with 'British jobs' or 'British workers' but there's nothing wrong in using public procurement and public investment in skills training to ensure that long term residents have a fair chance of getting the jobs we create.

Our real values, the ones we implement in government, are in tune with the deep-seated sense of fairness of the British people. Tory polices pose a real threat to the ordinary middle Britain families who currently feel society is not fair. If we get that across, and we base future policy on these values, we can not only win the next election, we can make real social progress in tackling inequality and making Britain truly fair.

Is Equality Fair?

2. WE ALL THINK WE'RE IN THE MIDDLE

Stewart Lansley

*The research found that nearly all of the participants in our delib-
erative research subjectively placed themselves in the 'middle' of the
income spectrum, despite the fact that they were from the full range
of socioeconomic groups.*

It is a well-established characteristic of today's society
that most of us have only a poor idea of where we rank
in the income hierarchy. The Fabian research found that
most participants in their focus groups placed themselves
subjectively in the 'middle` of the income spectrum, despite
the fact that they were from the full range of socio-economic backgrounds.

A study of middle income Britain conducted by YouGov
for the TUC also found that the majority of the population
misplaced themselves in the income hierarchy.[1] Participants –
representative of the population's income range – were
asked: "If everyone's income was arranged in order from
lowest to highest, where do you think your income would be
on this scale?" The results are shown in Table 1. All participants have been divided into five income bands (quintiles)
on the basis of their actual income. Each group represents a
fifth of the population. Their *actual* position is then compared
with their *perceived* position.

The final column of Table 1 shows that, on average, respondents tend to understate their true position in the income hierarchy – they think they are relatively poorer than they actually are. Thus, while 25 per cent place themselves in 'the middle`, as many as 60 per cent place themselves 'below the middle` or 'towards the bottom`. Only 12 per cent place themselves 'above the middle` or 'towards the top'.

This tendency to understate is strongest amongst those with the highest incomes. The group that does the best in placing themselves are those in the poorest quintile – with 56 per cent saying they are 'towards the bottom`. A significant proportion of this group – 41 per cent overstate their actual position.

The proportion of each group which accurately position themselves then steadily falls with just over a fifth of median income households placing themselves 'in the middle` while only 7 per cent of the richest fifth of households place themselves 'towards the top`. As many as 60 per cent of the 'affluent and the rich` group place themselves in or below the middle or towards the bottom. Those in the bottom half of the income distribution thus have a much better grasp of the reality of their place in the social hierarchy than those towards the top of the distribution.

There are a number of possible explanations for these findings. Studies have found widespread misunderstanding of the extent of pay and income relativities and that knowledge of the full extent of inequality is very limited.[2] The Fabian study found "a great deal of surprise expressed about the fact that a salary of £42,900 represented the 90th percentile". One participant expressed genuine shock, believing that a quarter of the population earned over this figure.[3] Again, it is those on the highest earnings who appear to be particularly out of touch with reality, especially when it comes to their own pay. A survey by British Social Attitudes found that under a half

Perceived position: 'Where do you think your income would be?'	First quintile 'The poor'	Second quintile 'The lower middle'	Middle quintile 'Middle income Britain'	Fourth quintile 'The upper middle'	Top quintile 'The affluent and the rich'	ALL
Towards the bottom	56	47	26	12	6	28
Below the middle	24	33	45	38	18	32
In the middle	12	13	22	38	36	25
Above the middle	4	3	4	9	31	10
Towards the top	1	0	0	2	7	2
Don't know	3	4	3	1	2	3

Table 1: Comparing people's actual and perceived position in the income hierarchy (percentages). People were asked "If everyone's income was arranged in order from lowest to highest, where do you think your income would be on this scale?" Source: *Middle Income Britain Survey for the TUC, Yougov, January 2009. For details see Life in the Middle, The Untold Story of Britain's Average Earners, TUC Touchstone Pamphlet, June 2009*

of those with earnings that put them in the top ten per cent identified themselves as top earners. They were much more inclined to place themselves towards the middle.

Another explanation may be that different income groups have different reference points. Those on lower incomes may be more likely to compare themselves, their work experience and life chances with those close to their own class and social groupings, making them more realistic in their judgement of their social positioning. There is some evidence that middle and lower earners are content as long as they feel better off than their parents.[4] Perhaps more insulated from the work and pay experience of others on low and middle incomes, there is evidence that the wealthy are more likely to compare themselves not with those below them but with those even richer then themselves, to feel that they are not paid enough. As one survey of bankers and lawyers on earnings of over £150,000 found: "They wanted to compare themselves with richer people, inventing a society in which they are a step or two down from the top. Comparing themselves upwards not downwards, they considered themselves normal, when they are anything but."[5]

It may also be that it suits some of the better off to think they are worse off than they actually are. Downplaying their relative advantage by placing themselves nearer the average may bring a degree of psychological denial about being towards the top of the income league, a form of defence against charges that they should be making a greater contribution to help those with much lower living standards than themselves.

There is another important factor at work which reinforces this process. Social and economic misplacement is part of a much wider phenomenon, a characteristic not just of the better off sections of society themselves but of leading opinion formers as well. In effect, the most affluent sections of society are being subtly redefined – by commentators as well as by themselves – as a group that sits nearer the middle than the top. Alan Duncan somewhat gave it away when he described an MP's salary of £64,000 as 'rations'. It is certainly not a sign of a healthy and well informed society when the rich think, and are encouraged to think, that they are poor.

An objective definition of the term 'middle Britain` would be the social group sitting around the mid-point of the income distribution, the point statisticians call 'the median`. Instead the term 'middle Britain` has come to be commonly used, not least by the political, media and marketing classes, to describe a group that sits in the upper half of the income distribution. Indeed 'middle Britain' has increasingly become shorthand for the professional middle classes. In one report, *Middle Britain in 2008*, by the insurance company AXA, for example, 'middle Britain' was

In just 30 years, Britain has moved away from a 'diamond' towards an 'onion-shaped` society with a few of the very rich, a small group of the affluent and a large bulge below the middle.

described as households with an average income of £62,000, a sum that would have put them in the top 30 per cent.

In 2008 a number of newspapers ran campaigns on behalf of what they portrayed as the victimised middle, a group increasingly 'struggling to make ends meet'. In a three-part series, the *Daily Telegraph* bemoaned the growing problems facing what they dubbed the 'coping classes`: a hard-working, responsible group which, despite earning more than their parents "all feel so damned poor... For while the working class is topped up with family credits, and hedge fund

31

managers cream off millions, it is Britain's beleaguered middle earners who are under siege."[6]

Yet while the *Telegraph* chose to describe the 'coping classes' as typical of middle Britain, the examples they quoted were all of families (priced out of private education, being pulled into the higher rate tax band etc) sitting towards the top of the income distribution. They were in fact referring to the high earning professional middle classes, a group the paper claimed was suffering most from economic and social change. It is a charge echoed elsewhere – as here in the *Daily Mail*: "The obscenely rich are getting richer, while the middle classes, working harder than ever, are becoming poorer."[7]

The evidence, however, does not support this picture of the beleaguered middle classes facing a growing financial squeeze. Indeed, it is top income groups who have benefited most – in work, pay, housing, education and pensions – from the economic and social repositioning of the last two three decades. In contrast, it is the bottom half that has been steadily falling behind the professional middle classes and the rich in both the income and opportunity stakes. Indeed this repositioning has steadily changed the shape of modern Britain.

In the immediate post-war years British society resembled a 'pyramid' with a small and privileged group at the top, a larger but still small and comfortable middle and a large majority at the bottom. By the end of the 1970s, Britain had moved closer to a 'diamond' shape with a small group of the rich and the poor and a much fatter middle. Since then we have seen the rise of a small group of the super-rich together with a much greater concentration of the population by income in the bottom half of the distribution. Indeed, almost two-thirds have an income that is less than the national mean.[8] As a result, in just 30 years, Britain has moved away from a 'diamond' towards an 'onion-shaped' society with a few of the very rich, a small group of the affluent and a large bulge below the middle.

This shift has largely occurred by stealth. Despite its implications, it has been accompanied by little public awareness or political debate. Until the onset of the recession, the rise of Britain's super-rich class generated little interest as a political issue. One study found that despite widening inequality, "people's overall quiescence appeared remarkable".[9] Instead of a rational and well informed public debate about the widening of pay differentials, about fair rewards and the role of merit in the growing wealth and income gap, a series of ill-informed myths have developed. Most people, but especially the most affluent, cannot place themselves with much accuracy in the income hierarchy. Some of our most senior political figures and media commentators cannot distinguish between middle Britain and the professional middle classes. There is limited understanding of the real winners and losers from the social and economic change of the last three decades. Such misunderstanding is yet another barrier to the introduction of effective measures to tackle Britain's growing income and opportunity gaps.

Footnotes
1 S Lansley, *Life in the Middle, The Untold Story of Britain's Average Earners*, TUC Touchstone Pamphlet, June 2009
2 See eg, R Pahl et al, *Inequality and Quiescence: A Continuing Conundrum*, ISER Working Paper, 2007
3 Bamfield & Horton op cit p 14
4 Pahl op cit
5 P Toynbee and D Walker, *Unjust Rewards*, Granta, 2008, p 25
6 *Daily Telegraph*, 29 January, 2008
7 *Daily Mail*, 9 February, 2008
8 Lansley op cit, p 9-10
9 Pahl op cit p 1

Is Equality Fair?

3. HOW WE TREAT THE RICH AND POOR

Kate Green

The research found that people treat the rich and poor differently. The public's attitudes towards those on low incomes were often more negative and punitive than their attitudes towards the rich.

For anti-poverty campaigners, the story is self-evidently simple. Inequality and child poverty are wrongs to be righted. It is both morally just and economically sensible to pursue policies that prevent and eradicate poverty and narrow the inequality gap. Indeed, campaigners point to the existence of a flawed economic model (which rewarded a privileged elite with excessive and unfettered wealth while leaving millions of children growing up in poverty) as underpinning the near-collapse of our financial system last September and the subsequent severe recession. Such an analysis leads compellingly to the conclusion that responsible stewardship of the economy goes hand-in-hand with eradicating poverty, requiring that rewards and resources are more equitably shared.

Yet this Fabian research makes clear that this is not necessarily the widely shared perception of a public increasingly anxious about their personal financial prospects, alarmed by high levels of public debt, uninformed but resentful about perceived levels of benefits for those seen as undeserving, and unlikely to contribute to society.[1] As Polly Toynbee and David Walker have pointed out, moreover, the richest in our society are unaware of the true extent of inequality and income disparity in the UK – or of the progress that has been made in reducing child poverty over the past ten years.[2]

So policy-makers and campaigners alike must become smarter about telling their story if the redistributive policy solutions which reduce inequality and end child poverty are to be sustained by popular support. At one time, it seemed that ministers understood this. Although showing a certain timidity in the run-up to and immediately after the 1997 general election (where they wooed rather than led public opinion, as Ruth Lister has put it), New Labour promoted a highly coherent political narrative, made manifest in its public policy programme. 'Progressive universalism', 'rights and responsibilities', 'work for those who can, support for those who can't' – these mantras underpinned a set of policy initiatives (such as new tax credits, the New Deals, rights for parents at work, investment in childcare and early years provision, and the national minimum wage) that helped to reduce child poverty and increase parental employment levels.[3] However, it has to be acknowledged that the effect on income inequality was considerably less marked.

Yet more recently politicians of all parties have begun to muddy the waters as they pursue increasingly contradictory policy approaches. High profile policy initiatives that both stigmatise and regulate the behaviour of the poorest groups, in contrast to a less regulated approach to those at the top end of the income scale, have compounded inequalities and done little to build public understanding and sympathy for those living in poverty. So today, a bold cross-party commitment to the ambition to eradicate child poverty is accompanied by a failure to increase the level of the financial safety net to the minimum standard needed to secure an adequate income for every family. This is coupled – again with high levels of cross-party agreement – with an increasingly coercive model of so-called 'welfare reform' which will likely see more families financially penalised for failure to seek paid employment in increasingly difficult economic conditions.

This is perverse in a recession. Half of all poor children currently grow up in households where at least one adult is working, but calls for pay restraint, not least in the public sector (which employs a quarter of all low-paid workers), are matched by a failure to take the same strong line when it comes to regulating and curbing excessive City bonuses.[4,5] To be sure, politicians have expressed their wish to see top salaries capped at a more realistic level, but it was the chief of the Financial Services Authority, no less, who floated the notion of fiscal measures with real bite to control the risk-taking behaviour of City institutions while politicians backed away.[6] And while even normally-sympathetic commentators proclaim the need for more means testing in the social security system, Labour's hesitant approach to a more progressive system of taxation (despite recent welcome announcements in the budget in spring 2009), and a reluctance even to acknowledge the problem among Conservatives, go widely uncriticised.[7] Meanwhile, ministers continue their attacks on benefits fraudsters which fail to acknowledge either the damage this does to take-up, or the fact that benefit fraud is at its lowest level ever.

Unsurprisingly, as a result, public understanding both of the moral and the economic case for progressive policy-making is increasingly being lost. Instead of using the recession and a mounting sense of injustice to embed arguments for the economic benefits of redistribution in the public's mind, policy-makers have allowed the opposite to happen. As people feel, understandably, fearful of the economic consequences of recession, popular support is growing for reining in public borrowing – with a real danger of swingeing cuts in spending which will harm the poorest the most.

Yet if only policy makers could be bold enough, this could be a time of opportunity. Today's exceptional economic circumstances could be used to build positive support for a programme of policy solutions in which redressing inequality and eradicating poverty take centre stage. Selecting policies that increase the incomes of the poorest, taking fiscal measures which protect families from the worst effects of recession, is not just right, it would contribute to a swifter economic recovery and underpin long-term economic stability by reducing the risk of damaging patterns of economic 'boom and bust' and reducing costly cycles of intergenerational poverty and exclusion. But the political space to do that requires politicians to take the lead in selecting, designing and articulating policies which respond to the concerns and challenges faced today by ordinary families, their anxieties about the future, and the attitudes and values that the Fabian research has revealed.

The findings suggest that in functional societies, reciprocity is important, and yet those in receipt of benefits are not trusted to offer it. But politicians have a unique opportunity to develop and describe policies that challenge those perceptions and concerns. And looking at the reality of family lives, this shouldn't be as difficult as it might seem. Today, the preoccupations of middle Britain's families will include job security, personal finances and debt. They worry about their children's education, prospects and life chances, about how to provide care for family members who need it, and about provision for old age. Policies which meet these concerns should shape and underpin the design of a modern, 21st century, welfare state, serve to improve equality and reduce poverty, and create a sustainable economic future, while providing an appealing, effective and indisputably relevant response to the life courses, experiences and needs of families today.

Rooting policy-making in the reality of families' lived experience offers progressives the best chance to remake radical policies which can command popular support. Families need adequate financial support to help them keep their heads above water when jobs are at risk; those who are out of work or struggling on poverty-level pay need training and re-skilling to compensate them for the shortcomings of their educational experiences and help them advance in an unequal labour market. Meanwhile, investing in 'new industries' where good quality new jobs can be created while ensuring access to the best possible education for all children will ensure everybody's future ability to participate and contribute. It doesn't need to be spelt out in a recession that policies to get people into or to return to work, to provide for their children, to earn and pay taxes, rest on decent protection for and investment in families now. Nor does it need to be spelt out that the hardship and risks families face today are scarcely of their own making. Never has it been more apposite to point to external factors which place families under pressure - or to highlight our reliance on a universal system of social support which all can access at time of need.

Rooting policy-making in the reality of families' lived experience offers progressives the best chance to remake radical policies which can command popular support.

And here perhaps is the opportunity that policy-makers have missed. Although some signs of visionary politics can be found in the rhetoric of both left- and right-wing politicians, too often in attacking the so-called 'dependency culture', our political leaders sound defensive – even grudging – about our system of social protection and social support. Instead they should seize the opportunity to promote sustained investment in a welfare state that provides mutual support, celebrates the public institutions that bind our society together, and advances an economic model that will share the proceeds of growth and prosperity, risks and rewards more fairly. As recent public outrage at attacks on the NHS have shown, it is the boldest, the most inclusive, and the most visionary policy solutions which command and retain the strongest popular support. Policy-makers concerned to secure greater economic justice have something to learn from that.

Footnotes

1 T Horton and L Bamfield Understanding attitudes to inequality, Joseph Rowntree Foundation 2009. Also see the research carried out by Ipsos Mori for the JRF (Castell and Thompson Understanding attitudes to poverty in the UK: getting the public's attention, Joseph Rowntree Foundation 2007)

2 P Toynbee and D Walker Unjust rewards Granta 2008

3 R Lister, 'New Labour: a study in ambiguity from a position of ambivalence', Critical Social Policy, 21(4), 2001

4 Department for Work and Pensions Households below average income: an analysis of the income distribution 1994/95-2006/07, National Statistics 2008 Table 4.3

5 New Policy Institute www.poverty.org.uk

6 See http://www.dailymail.co.uk/news/article-1209359/Head-FSA-backs-tax-transactions-combat-swollen-city-bonuses.html

7 See http://www.guardian.co.uk/politics/2009/jul/24/gordon-brown-budget-cuts-whitehall

Ben Page

The research identified four fairly equal clusters of opinions: the 'traditional egalitarians'; the 'traditional free marketeers'; the 'angry middle'and the 'post-ideological liberals'. This pattern of attitudes offers some challenges, but also some good news, for anybody seeking broader support for egalitarian strategies.

The Fabian research helps explain exactly why Britain is as unequal as it is – and also the challenges for politicians of doing anything other than something stealthy to address it.

The research confirms Ipsos MORI's own work showing that anyone worried about this issue must recognise just how unconcerned Britain as a whole (and middle Britain in particular) is about equality – and that if anything there is less concern now than ten years ago. This is clearly the reason for a debate, but it is worth emphasising. When we ask what people see as the most important issues facing Britain – which we do every month – inequality doesn't register compared with big issues like crime, health, immigration and the economy in general. If anything it has declined as a concern over recent years.

It is true that over 80 per cent think the gap between high and low incomes is too large – which is fairly consistent across social classes, and middle England is certainly no less likely to agree. But we're among the least likely in Europe to say the Government should intervene on inequality – in fact we're third from bottom out of over 20 countries. And the Fabian research confirms that a large proportion of people think that by and large an unequal society can be 'fair', in that both at the bottom and the top, incomes are mostly deserved. Now of course there are a lot of riders on this, including widespread misunderstanding about how many people really are on high incomes, but there is a broad acceptance of the status quo, which this new research examines in depth.

There is even some evidence that public opinion is getting more sceptical on this – we're certainly more likely to say that people are taking advantage of the benefits system than ten years ago – and less likely to say the Government should do more to reduce inequality. These, again, are trends that are seen at least as much in middle Britain – the electoral battle ground for 2010. And the Great Crash of 2008 has not seen any real shifts in attitudes. Although the Fabian research points to support for curbs on excessive corporate pay, we have seen no shift in underlying attitudes towards individualism or collectivism, or indeed towards policies designed to reduce income differences. In 2006 46 per cent supported a society which allowed people to be as rich as they could, rather than preferring similar incomes for all. After the crash, this figure fell by only two points to 44 per cent (not a statistically significant difference): it is true that half of us like the idea of similar incomes and rewards for everyone – but nearly as many do not.

Indeed a recent paper by John Bartle and colleagues at Essex University used a number of attitudinal questions – including on whether people feel some other people don't deserve benefits, whether we should redistribute wealth, and questions on equal opportunities for women – to create an index that identifies where the political centre of the population is. And they conclude it has moved to the right in recent years. Their quite literal measure suggests it is only getting

A new sober age?

Q: People have different views about the ideal society. For each of these statements, please tell me which one comes closest to your ideal.

A society which emphasises the social and collective provision of welfare

A society where individuals are encouraged to look after themselves

A society which allows people to make and keep as much money as it can

A society which emphasises similar incomes and rewards for everyone

Source: Ipsos MORI Political Monitor. Base: c. 1000 British adults 18+ each month.

harder to convince the public about the need for greater equality, looking at changes in attitudes over time.

However we should not be pessimistic about the future. I agree with the authors that part of any change on this issue would involve appealing to key British values. People's acceptance of 'fair inequality' relates strongly to the value we attach to 'fairness' generally. Fairness in governance and the provision of public services is a key British value, seen in our national obsession with 'postcode lotteries'. When we ask whether people would prefer public services to provide just minimum standards across the country but then allow local variation to meet local needs or whether they want services to be completely the same – the vast majority always choose completely uniform services across the board, regardless of the service. This is driven by the sense of fairness that says everyone has to get the same opportunities, even where areas have greater or different needs.

So a debate about the unfairness of extreme inequality would have traction. This is a key basis for appealing to people, particularly middle Britain, by raising awareness of just how unfair the barriers to opportunity faced by many groups in society still are. Ipsos MORI's work on communicating equality and poverty shows it is the term 'fairness' that chimes most with people, especially images around life being a game where the rules are unfair for some and the sense that the dice are loaded against some people.

This presents us with a number of challenges. Firstly we need to make inequality 'real' through real life case studies of people who want to get on and contribute but are not being given a fair opportunity. It is worth noting that in terms of communicating the idea, there are no positive images of people suffering inequality in popular discourse, but plenty of negative ones – scrounging 'chavs' playing the system, or bogus asylum seekers. There are few images of people who want to contribute but are at mercy of events. Campaigners need to get that story across to people better.

As the Fabian work suggests, one would also need to address common misperceptions. The use of surprising facts – such as the proportion of children who go without a warm winter coat because their parents can't afford it – has real impact. People are shocked and moved by that type of information when we test it in focus groups.

As well as appealing to emotional reactions, there is also a rational element to the most successful communications. Britons do see that there are risks to themselves from greater inequality in incomes, through a loss of social cohesion, greater crime and antisocial behaviour. Evidence that links lower levels of disorder with greater equality, maybe using international comparisons from more equal societies, could help.

Any communications need to start from people's existing values. Segmenting people into whether they are broadly liberal or sceptical on inequality, as the Fabians have done, is important. In our work we use the metaphor of 'big tent' people (who have an open and inclusive view of the welfare state) and 'small club' (which is more contingent on people contributing or qualifying for help). And the evidence suggests there are roughly equal proportions of each in country as a whole – but middle Britain tend to be more in the small club/sceptical group.

A debate about the unfairness of extreme inequality would have traction. This is a key basis for appealing to people, particularly middle Britain, by raising awareness of just how unfair the barriers to opportunity faced by many groups in society still are.

Finally what Fabian work reveals is that people are more inconsistent and contradictory on equality than on some issues. We call it 'cognitive polyphasia' – people's ability to hold contradictory opinions on the same subject at the same time, without feeling any cognitive dissonance. For example far more people think the income gap is too large than actually support any measure of redistribution. Similarly, 15 per cent of those who say that the Government should not redistribute incomes also say that the Government is doing too little to redistribute income – which seems like a clear contradiction.

This can be explained just by two key characteristics of human beings. Firstly, when it really comes down to it, most of us do not really want to give up too many opportunities for the good of others. Ipsos MORI have a huge amount of qualitative evidence that when one delves deeper, it is easy for people to agree in principle to more equality, but much harder when we talk to them about the sacrifices they might make. This is particularly the case when they have an image of an undeserving group getting help (and the research confirms we are more negative about the poor than the rich in terms of just deserts), or if people feel enough has already been done.

Reaching a new societal consensus on this issue then, will need not only to deal with very common misperceptions at all levels in society, and build on shared values to shift perceptions about how 'fair' major inequality in incomes really is: it will also have to convince a pretty sceptical public that the Government is actually capable of doing something 'fair' about it. A pretty tall order, but still worth trying.

6. EQUALITY OF LIFE

Zoe Williams

The research found people really rally around the concept of improving quality of life for every citizen, and many of our participants found claims about the possible negative social consequences of income inequality intuitively convincing.

So, there is plenty of good news: we instinctively support redistribution, we support progressive ideas in the taxation system, and we instinctively react against people having more than they need or could possibly spend. How, then, did we ever get into the situation we're in today, where even the mention of tax is a political fart in a lift, and the mention of deliberately raising it – openly robbing the rich to give to the poor – would be monstrous?

This, unfortunately, is what a country looks like after 12 years of a meritocracy. (Goddammit, wasn't there a fifties satire that warned us this would happen?) In a world of infinite possibility, people who don't achieve have only themselves to blame. People who do achieve can, conceivably, be emulated. Since we aspire to be them, we certainly don't want to see them penalised for their wealth, so we both strive to protect it from the taxman, and, to justify all this, invent qualities and expertise for them that they don't possess (meanwhile, for symmetry, inventing deficiencies for the very poor that they don't possess either). We might believe in progressive taxation measures when confronted with their fiscal reality, but while we despise the poor and desperately suck up to the rich, these progressive ideas are somewhat strangled. There is so much internal contradiction in the position, that any attempt to move in any direction will be painful; better to just stick to the mantra, "no raising of taxes" and move on.

To get out of this political half-Nelson, we should recap in the broadest possible terms how we got into it. Everybody blames Tony Blair for the rise of the meritocracy. He would blame himself; he would be proud to. What he did, incredibly, was to find a way to be in the Labour Party that didn't involve hating the rich. You can say what you like about his underlying commitment to socialist ideals, but you cannot deny that, in the end, he was right about toff-hating rhetoric: people didn't like those attack-dog politics. They didn't fit with optimism or opportunity, they were not modern, they weren't feel-good. In the sunny, newly-Americanised culture of the early nineties, any of us might have become very rich. Their pips might be our pips: if you squeeze us, do we not also squeak?

And that pip-speak was the only language anyone had ever found to discuss redistributive taxation; it was never updated to appeal to the post-New Labour voter, the person who might think to become JK Rowling one day, but didn't necessarily want to bathe in gold or to trash society once they got there. But this person isn't an oddball, it's an everyman. We all over-identify with the super-rich, and we all search to make life better for them, on the off chance that we might become them. This is a natural optimism, no more or less idiotic than buying a skirt that might one day fit. I don't think this optimism should be trampled, mindless or not. I don't think anybody would emerge from that feeling very good. And I certainly don't see a place for any opportunistic tub-thumping about bankers' salaries, on the crest of the credit crunch. People might be angry now, but that emotion is not a very long-lasting or creative motivator; you don't want to be the person still doing the angry dance when the music stops.

Likewise, I would feel reluctant to try and tackle negative views of the very poor. One of the many interesting things to emerge from this research is the way that people overestimate the cost to us all of benefit cheats, and underestimate the cost of tax evasion. It's interesting because it appears irrational and yet makes perfect sense. We all think of our own behaviour as being possibly cheeky but essentially benign; we think of harm as something that is caused by others. And everybody pays tax, while only some people qualify for benefits. So naturally, most survey respondents would identify more with taxpayers than benefit recipients, and would identify more sympathetically, by extension, with tax avoiders than benefit cheats. We will always, instinctively, give ourselves and people like us the benefit of the doubt, while judging very harshly the people we deem unlike us. It's a waste of time, in other words, trying to redraw the 'other' more sympathetically. If we're going to have a revolution of perception, it needs to go in the other direction.

Besides, to return to the underclass: this picture, the lazy sponger who costs the state a fortune, who has children willy nilly for the child benefit, who spends the child benefit on fags and uses plastic bags instead of nappies – this is the creation of the tabloid media. No doubt you could find an individual of this sort if you scoured the country, but they are no more representative than the media creation of the eighties. (This was the teenage mother who got pregnant on purpose so she could get a council flat. I believe she was the catalyst for the Thatcherite brainwave of flogging off all council flats, which was some going, considering there were only about six of her.) I simply don't believe politicians should waste their time refuting this picture, you could turn yourself blue trying to get tabloid newspaper journalists to represent their fellow citizens in a fair and reasonable way. The inadequacies of the underclass are a redtop mire, lent credence by the odd academic (Phillip Blond, essentially), unarguable in any meaningful way because you're fighting the spectre of someone else's imagination. Instead, we should do what Tony Blair was always so good at. Don't get into that debate. Change the debate.

The Cassandras have plenty to work with: we can, en masse, be very judgmental, we can play cognitive tricks on ourselves; we can stay wedded to the status quo however abusive it is. But we also have very clear instincts of fairness, evinced pretty strongly, I believe, by the fact that we support progressive taxation even having bought the propaganda about how undeserving are most of the people it benefits.

We should start a new conversation, in which it doesn't matter what the poor are like, and whether they deserve more money or less money, and what they should do to prove their just deserts. And it doesn't matter what the rich are like, or what counts as rich and what counts as superrich, or whether they deserve their riches, or whether they can possibly spend them, or whether curbing their riches will destroy our status among market economies.

The real question is what we're like. We need a return to Bennite rhetoric: do we want to be net recipients and net contributors, or do we want to be brothers and sisters? Do we want to earn with morbid intensity, then spend half of our riches guarding the other half from people who earn less? Or would we rather share it? What kind of person do

I want to be? Do I think of myself as a fair person? How much of my sense of identity rests on that? How much does the belief I have in society rest on notions of fellowship and on the idea that humans are inherently sociable?

Because the fact is that sociability is at the centre of all meaningful pleasure, and that it relies, not just on fairness but on taking an active delight in being fair.

Is Equality Fair?

Fabian Review

www.fabians.org.uk

Winter 2008/09

NOW or NEVER

NOW MORE THAN EVER
...FAIRNESS IN A RECESSION

INTERVIEW
Roger Liddle
interviews Vince
Cable

JOHN McFALL
We must not stand
idly by

CITY BONUSES
New data on what
the public thinks
about the rich

The quarterly magazine of the Fabian Society Volume 120 no 4 £4.95

Fabian Review

www.fabians.org.uk

Spring 2009

THE FAMILY SPECIAL

FAMILY VALUES

The left's winning ticket?

The Royals... the left... schools... work... the Tories... marriage... parents...

The quarterly magazine of the Fabian Society   Volume 121 no 1   £4.95

Fabian Review

www.fabians.org.uk

Summer 2009

THE NEXT LEFT ISSUE

RED SHOOTS

In search of ideas
for the next left

The quarterly magazine of the Fabian Society   Volume 121 no 2   £4.95

Fabian Review

www.fabians.org.uk

Autumn 2009

CONFERENCE SPECIAL ISSUE

200

DAYS OF POWER
(and how Labour should use it)

Peter Kellner, Yvette Cooper, Oona King,
Douglas Alexander, Patricia Hewitt, Phillip Blond,
Sunder Katwala, Richard Reeves, David Blunkett
Mary Riddell, Roger Liddle, James Macintyre

The quarterly magazine of the Fabian Society   Volume 121 no 3   £4.95

British Muslims and the politics of fairness

In 'Fairness not Favours', Sadiq Khan MP argues that an effective agenda to provide opportunity and tackle extremism across all communities must go beyond a narrow approach to security, and sets out new proposals for a progressive agenda on inequality and life chances, public engagement in foreign policy, an inclusive Britishness, and rethinking the role of faith in public life.

The pamphlet puts the case for an effective agenda to provide opportunity and tackle extremism across all communities must go beyond a narrow approach to security, and sets out new proposals for a progressive agenda on inequality and life chances, public engagement in foreign policy, an inclusive Britishness, and rethinking the role of faith in public life.

FABIAN SOCIETY

Narrowing the Gap
The Fabian Commission on Life Chances
and Child Poverty

How can we make poverty history at home?

One in five children still grows up in poverty in Britain. Yet all the political parties now claim to care about 'social justice'. This report sets a litmus test by which Brown, Cameron and Campbell must be judged.

'Narrowing the Gap' is the final report of the Fabian Commission on Life Chances and Child Poverty, chaired by Lord Victor Adebowale. The Fabian Society is the only think tank with members. Join us and help us put poverty and equality at the centre of the political agenda.

> 'The Fabians ask the most difficult questions, pushing Labour to make a bold, progressive case on taxation and the abolition of child poverty.'
>
> – Polly Toynbee

How to defend inheritance tax

Inheritance tax is under attack, and not just from the political right. The critics of this tax have dominated the debate over recent years but, as the authors of 'How to Defend Inheritance Tax' argue, this tax is one of the best tools we have for tackling inequality and kick starting Britain's stalled social mobility.

Defending inheritance tax is not just the responsibility of politicians – there must be a citizen-led campaign too. In this Fabian Ideas pamphlet, **Rajiv Prabhakar, Karen Rowlingson and Stuart White** provide progressives with the tools they need to win this argument.

They set out the evidence on inheritance and inequality, tackle the common objections to the tax, and demonstrate the moral and pragmatic arguments for an inheritance tax.

JOIN THE FABIANS TODAY
Join us and receive two Fabian Reviews, plus our award-winning equality report, 'Narrowing the Gap'.

I'd like to become a Fabian for just £9.95

I understand that should at any time during my six-month introductory membership period I wish to cancel, I will receive a refund and keep all publications received without obligation. After six months I understand my membership will revert to the annual rate as published in *Fabian Review*, currently £31 (ordinary) or £14 (unwaged).

Name	Date of birth
Address	
	Postcode
Email	
Telephone	

Instruction to Bank   Originator's ID: 971666

Bank/building society name	
Address	**DIRECT Debit**
	Postcode
Acct holder(s)	
Acct no.	Sort code

I instruct you to pay direct debits from my account at the request of the Fabian Society. The instruction is subject to the safeguards of the Direct Debit Guarantee.

Signature	Date

Return to:
Fabian Society Membership
FREEPOST SW 1570
11 Dartmouth Street
London
SW1H 9BN

Secret

Secrets, lies…and seduction!

Three passionate novels!

In July 2007 Mills & Boon bring back
two of their classic collections, each
featuring three favourite romances
by our bestselling authors…

SECRET PASSIONS

The Greek's Secret Passion
by Sharon Kendrick
A Shocking Passion
by Amanda Browning
Passion in Secret by Catherine Spencer

MARRIED TO A MILLIONAIRE

The Millionaire's Marriage Demand
by Sandra Field
At the Millionaire's Bidding
by Lee Wilkinson
Surrender to the Millionaire
by Margaret Mayo

Secret Passions

THE GREEK'S SECRET PASSION
by
Sharon Kendrick

A SHOCKING PASSION
by
Amanda Browning

PASSION IN SECRET
by
Catherine Spencer

MILLS & BOON®

*MILLS & BOON and MILLS & BOON with the Rose Device
are registered trademarks of the publisher.
Harlequin Mills & Boon Limited,
Eton House, 18-24 Paradise Road, Richmond, Surrey, TW9 1SR*

SECRET PASSIONS
© by Harlequin Enterprises II B.V./S.à.r.l. 2007

The Greek's Secret Passion, A Shocking Passion and *Passion in
Secret* were first published in Great Britain by Harlequin Mills &
Boon Limited in separate, single volumes.

The Greek's Secret Passion © Sharon Kendrick 2003
A Shocking Passion © Amanda Browning 2002
Passion in Secret © Kathy Garner 2003

ISBN: 978 0 263 85519 7

05-0707

*Printed and bound in Spain
by Litografía Rosés S.A., Barcelona*

THE GREEK'S
SECRET PASSION

by

Sharon Kendrick

Sharon Kendrick started story-telling at the age of eleven and has never really stopped. She likes to write fast-paced, feel-good romances with heroes who are so sexy they'll make your toes curl!

Born in west London, she now lives in the beautiful city of Winchester – where she can see the cathedral from her window (but only if she stands on tip-toe). She has two children, Celia and Patrick, and her passions include music, books, cooking and eating – and drifting off into wonderful daydreams while she works out new plots!

CHAPTER ONE

A MAN'S voice flowed over the air like warm, sweet honey and something about its lazy caress had Molly putting her pen down and staring blankly at the open window.

'Nato, Zoe,' said the voice again. 'Maressi!'

A Greek voice. Unmistakably. Soft and sexy and deep.

Little sizzles of awareness pricked at her skin until Molly deliberately sent them packing. Having a Greek lover a lifetime ago didn't mean you had to have an attack of the vapours every time you heard one of his compatriots speak, surely? The pang she felt was instinctive but only momentary, and she picked up her pen again.

Then she heard the voice again, only this time it was laughing and this time she froze.

For a laugh was something unique, wasn't it? Voices changed and some voices mimicked others you had heard—but a laugh. Oh, no. A laugh was different and this one took her right back to a place which was out of bounds.

She walked over to the window with a heart which was beating far too fast for the sight of something which would surely mock her and tell her that she was being a sentimental fool.

But the rich ebony hair of the man who hoisted a case out of the car with such ease did little to reassure her that her thoughts had been of the mad, ridiculous variety. Yet what had she been expecting—that the owner of the voice would be blond? Because if the man was Greek—as he surely was—then, of course he would have coal dark hair and olive skin and the kind of strength which few men she encountered these days seemed to have.

He slammed the car door shut, and, almost as if he sensed he was being watched, he began to lift his head towards the house and Molly hastily withdrew from the window. What kind of impression would *that* create? A stereotype of the nosy neighbour busy twitching behind a curtain to see just what kind of family the latest house-let would yield.

But a vague sense of disquiet kept her heart racing as she heard the front door of the adjoining house close, and when she went to pick up her pen again she noticed that her fingers were trembling.

Forget it, she told herself. Or put your mind at rest.

Later, she decided as she began to make notes— she would do just that.

Dimitri put the bag down in the hall as his daughter began exclaiming about the high ceilings, the huge windows and the view from the back onto a dream of an English garden. He smiled. 'It is a good house, yes?'

'Oh, it's a *wonderful* house, Papa!'

'You want to go and choose your room?'

Zoe pulled a mock-shocked face. 'Any room I like?'

Dimitri flashed her an indulgent smile, which briefly softened the hard, stark lines of his dark face. 'Any room you like,' he agreed equably, glancing idly through a pile of mail which had been left stacked on the table in the hall. Mostly bills and circulars—and one large and expensive white envelope addressed, 'To the New Residents!'

His lips curved and he put the whole stack down, unopened, then spent an hour unpacking—shifting silk and linen into various cupboards and drawers with the kind of automatic efficiency which evolved after frequent trips abroad. He had just set up his computer on a desk in the room he intended to use as an office, when the front door bell rang, and he frowned.

None of his business contacts would come here. He had a couple of friends in the city, but he had planned to give them a call once he was settled. Which left, he guessed, a neighbour—for who else could it be, other than someone from one of the adjoining houses, who must have seen them arrive?

He sincerely hoped that this was not the first in a long deputation of well-wishers—though maybe that was wishful thinking on his part. Nothing came without a cost and he had deliberately chosen the house in a residential area, mainly for Zoe's sake. Neighbours promised an element of security and safety and normality which you didn't get in hotels—

but the downside to neighbours was a tendency to intrude, to try to get close.

And Dimitri Nicharos didn't allow anyone to get close.

He went downstairs and opened the door with a cool smile, preparing to say hello and goodbye in quick succession. But the smile died on his lips and something unknown and forgotten stirred into life as he stared at the tall blonde woman who was standing on his doorstep, a bottle of wine held in her hand and an incredulous expression on her face which made her look as if she had seen some terrible ghost.

It took a moment or two for it to dawn on him just exactly what—or who—it was he was seeing and, when it did, he felt the same kind of incredulity which had made the woman's luscious lips part into a disbelieving 'O', but he kept his own face calm and impassive. He needed time to think, to assimilate the facts, and he would not be seen to react. He had learned that. He never let anyone know what he was thinking, for knowledge was power, and he liked to hold the balance to favour him.

He stared at her. 'Hello,' he said softly, as if he was talking to a complete stranger. But she was, wasn't she? And maybe she always had been.

Molly stared back, her breathing rapid and shallow. It was like suddenly finding yourself on the top of a mountain, without realising that you had been climbing. She felt faint. From shock. From disbelief. And just from the sheer overriding awareness that, yes, this was Dimitri. Her fantasy on hearing the rich, deep laugh had not been fantasy at all. A man from the past—*the* man from her past—was here, and exuding that same lethal brand of sexual charisma which had once so ensnared her. It was ensnaring her now, for all she could do was to greedily drink in the sight of him, like a woman who had been starved of men all her life.

His skin was glowing and golden, with eyes dark as olives, framed by lashes thick as pine forests. He had filled out, of course—but not in the way that so many men in their mid-thirties had. There was no paunch hanging over the edge of his belt, nor any fleshy folds of skin around his chin denoting an indolent lifestyle with not enough attention paid to exercise. No, Dimitri was sheer, honed muscle, the pale linen trousers and cool silk shirt emphasising every hard sinew of his body.

True, the black hair was less unruly than before and there was a touch of silver at the temples, but the mouth was exactly as she remembered it—and, boy, did she remember it—a cushioned, sensual mouth which looked as though it had been designed purely for a woman's pleasure.

But the eyes. Oh, the eyes. There was the difference, the one big, tell-tale difference. Once they had shone at her with, not love, no—though she had prayed for that—but with a fierce, possessive affection.

Today these eyes were as coldly glittering as jet. They gave nothing away, and expected nothing in return.

She drew a deep breath from dry lungs which felt as though they had been scorched from within. 'Dimitri?' she managed. 'Is it really you?'

Dimitri raised his eyebrows in question, enjoying her discomfiture, almost as much as he was enjoying looking at her. But then he always had. Women like Molly Garcia were rare. Physical perfection—or as close to it as you would find in one lifetime. An irresistible combination of hair that was moon-pale and streaked with sunshine—and eyes so icy-blue that they should have been cold, yet he had seen them hotter than hot and on fire with need and desire.

Deliberately taking his time to answer a question which was as unnecessary as it was pointless, he let his eyes drift slowly over her body. And what a body. Still. Even though that body had inevitably changed during the journey from teenager to woman. Back then she had been as slender as a young lemon sapling, so slender that sometimes he had feared she might break when he made love to her—but now she bore the firm curves of a fruit-bearing tree. Her hips were still slender, but her breasts were rich and ripe and lush and Dimitri had to work hard at appearing impassive, only just succeeding in keeping the studied look of indifference on his face. His body he had less control over.

'Perhaps I have acquired an identical twin brother?' he mocked. 'What do you think?'

Part of her had been hoping that it was all some kind of mistake, even while the other part had prayed for it not to be so, but any lingering doubt fled just as soon as he began to speak, with that heady mixture of deep, honeyed emphasis she remembered all too well.

She could do one of two things. She could stand there, gaping at him like a fish which had suddenly been starved of water, or she could be herself—the bright, successful and independent woman she had become.

She smiled, even though her mouth felt as though she were stretching a coat-hanger through a jar of glue. 'Good heavens!' she exclaimed, with just the right amount of amused surprise. 'I can't believe it!'

'I can hardly believe it myself,' he murmured, thinking that this was fevered fantasy brought to life. His eyes strayed to her fingers. No wedding band. Did that mean that she was free? *Available?* 'It's been a long time.'

Too long, and yet not long enough—for surely time should have gone some way towards protecting her from his sensual impact. So why had time failed her? Why did she find herself feeling overwhelmed with weakness when confronted with the sight of her former Greek lover? She sucked in a dry breath as memories of him pressing her naked body against the soft sand washed over her.

'What on earth are you doing here?' she demanded.

'I am staying here.'

'Why?'

But before he could reply, she heard the sound of a voice speaking in Greek. A woman's voice. And reality shot home. Of course he had a woman with him. Probably children, too. Large houses in this part of London were let to families, and he had doubtless brought his with him.

It was no more than she had expected, so why did it hurt so much?

And then she stared in a kind of disbelieving daze as the most beautiful creature she had ever seen came loping down the stairs towards them.

Glossy black hair cascaded down over high, pert breasts—her jeans and T-shirt showing off a slim, boyish figure and emphasising legs which seemed to go on and on forever. Her face was a perfect opal, with deep-set black eyes which dominated it and a luscious, smiling mouth.

And Molly's determination not to appear fazed almost failed her as the woman grew closer—why, she looked almost young enough to be... Her forced smile faded from her lips. Had he become one of those men who paraded a female on his arm who was young enough to be his daughter?

'Papa?'

She *was* his daughter.

Molly found herself doing rapid sums inside her head while Dimitri answered the girl in Greek. She looked seventeen—maybe eighteen—but that would mean...that would mean... She shook her head. She didn't understand. For that would mean that Dimitri had had a daughter when he had known *her*. And surely that was not possible? Or had she been so wrong about so many things?

Suddenly, she felt faint, wishing that she could just disappear, but how could she? Instead she stood there like some dumb fool with a bottle of wine in her hand, the last of her youthful dreams shattering as the teenager approached them.

Rather reluctantly, Dimitri spoke. He had been rather enjoying the play of emotions across her lovely face, which Molly had desperately been trying to hide. This was indeed a unique situation, and the novelty factor of that for a man like Dimitri was almost as enjoyable as the sight of Molly Garcia looking so helpless.

'Zoe!' He smiled. 'We have a visitor.' And the black eyes were turned to Molly in mocking question. Over to you, the look seemed to say, unhelpfully.

Speaking was proving even more difficult than it had been before. 'I live next door,' said Molly quickly. 'I, er—I saw you arrive, and I thought I would bring you this…to welcome you. Welcome,' she finished. She held up the bottle with a grimace, but the girl smiled widely and took it from Molly, casting an admonishing little look at her father.

'How very kind of you,' she said, in softly accented English. 'Please—you will come in?'

Like hell she would! 'No, no, honestly—'

'Oh, do. Please,' said Dimitri, in a silky voice. 'I insist.'

She met his eyes and saw the mischief and mockery there. How dared he? Didn't he have a single ounce of perception? Didn't he realise that she might actually find it difficult to meet his wife? Though why should he, when she stopped to think about it? Maybe this unusual situation was not so unusual for a man like Dimitri. How many other women were there like her, dotted around the place—never quite able to forget his sweet, sensual skills?

And she noticed that he hadn't introduced her. Did that mean he had *forgotten her name*? Nor had he told his daughter that they had once known each other—though maybe that wasn't so surprising, either. For what would he say?

Molly and I were lovers.

Put like that, it sounded nothing, but it *had* been something—it *had*. Or had she just been fooling herself all these years that her first love had been special and had just ended badly? And just how old *was* his daughter? Even if she was younger than she looked that still meant that he must have fathered her just after Molly had left the tiny island....

She couldn't think straight.

And maybe that was why she felt as if setting foot inside the door would be on a par with entering the lion's den. Some memories were best left untouched. Parts of the past were cherished, and maybe they only stayed that way if you didn't let the present intrude on them.

She shook her head, mocking him back with a meaningless smile of her own. 'It is very kind of you, but I'm afraid that I have work to do.'

He glanced at the expensive gold timepiece on his

hair-roughened wrist. 'At four o'clock?' he questioned mildly. 'You work shifts?'

Did he still think she was a waitress, then? 'I work from home,' she explained, then wished she hadn't, for a dark gleam of interest lightened the black eyes and suddenly she felt vulnerable.

'Please,' said the girl, and held her hand out. 'You must think us very rude. I am Zoe Nicharos—and this is my father, Dimitri.'

'Molly,' she said back, for what choice did she have? 'Molly Garcia.' She shook Zoe's hand and let it go, but then Dimitri reached out and, with an odd kind of smile, took her fingers and clasped them inside the palm of his hand.

Outwardly, it was nothing more than a casual handshake but she could feel the latent strength in him and her skin stirred with a kind of startled recognition, as if this was what a man's touch *should* be like.

'Hello, *Molly*,' he murmured. 'I'm Dimitri.'

Just the way he said it made her stomach melt, despite him, despite everything and she wondered if he could feel the sudden acceleration of her heart. She tried to prise her fingers away, but he wouldn't let her, not until she had met his amused black gaze full-on, and she realised that she was the one who was affected by all this—and that Dimitri was simply taking some kind of faintly amused pleasure in it all. As if it were some kind of new spectator sport. As if it didn't matter—and why should it? She should be flattered that he remembered her at all.

Her smile felt more practised now; she was getting quite good at this. 'Well, like I said—this was just a brief call to welcome you. I hope you'll all be very happy here,' she said.

He heard the assumption in the word 'all', but he let it go. This was going to be interesting, he thought. *Very* interesting. 'I'm sure we will,' he answered, with a smooth, practised smile of his own. His eyes lingered briefly on the swell of her breasts, outlined like two soft peaches by a pale blue silk shirt which matched her eyes. 'It's a very beautiful place.'

It had been a long time since a man had looked at her that way and she felt the slow, heavy pulsing of awareness—as if her body had been in a deep, deep sleep and just one glittering black stare had managed to stir it into life again. She had to get away before he realised that, unless, of course, he already had.

'I really must go,' she said.

'Thank you for the wine,' he said softly. 'Maybe some time…when you're not so busy *working*…you might come round and have a drink with us?'

'Maybe,' she said brightly, but they both knew that she was lying.

CHAPTER TWO

MOLLY let herself into her house, trying to tell herself not to overreact. It was something that was nothing—just something which occurred time and time again. And that the only reason this had never happened before was because they lived in different worlds.

She had come face to face with a man she'd once been in love with, that was all—though a more cynical person might simply describe it as teenager lust and infatuation. Her Greek-island lover had materialised with his family in the house next door to hers, and it was nothing more than an incredible coincidence.

And not so terrible, surely?

But the thought of just going upstairs and carrying on with her research notes was about as attractive as the idea of putting on a bikini to sunbathe in the back garden, wondering if everything she did now would be visible to Dimitri's eyes. And telling herself that, even if it was, she shouldn't care. These things happened in a grown-up world and she was going to have to face it.

Just as she was going to have to face his wife—and though the thought of that had no earthly right to hurt her, it did.

She went through the motions of normality. She met a friend for a drink and then went to see a film. And spent a night waking over and over, to find that the bright red numbers on her digital clock had only moved on by a few minutes.

She showered and dressed and made coffee, and when the doorbell rang she bit her lip, telling herself that it was only the postman, but she knew it was not the postman. Call it sixth sense or call it feminine intuition, but she knew exactly who would be standing on her doorstep.

And he was.

She opened the door and stared into the black, enigmatic eyes.

'Dimitri,' she offered warily.

'Molly,' he mimicked, mocking her wary tone. 'I am disturbing you?'

He couldn't do anything but disturb her, but she shook her head. 'Not really.'

'You aren't working?' He raised his eyebrows.

'Not at the moment, no.' She answered the question in his eyes. 'I write,' she explained.

'Novels?'

She shook her head. 'Travel books, and articles, actually, but that's really beside the point. Look, Dimitri—I don't know what it is you want—I'm just a little surprised to see you here.'

His eyes mocked her. 'But you knew I would come.'

Yes. She had known that. 'Was there something particular you wanted?'

'Don't you think we need to talk?'

'To say what?'

'Oh, come on, Molly,' he chided softly. 'There's more than a little unfinished business between us, *ne*? Do you think we can just ignore the past, as though it never happened? Pass each other by in the street, like polite strangers?'

'Why not?'

'Because life doesn't work like that.'

'No.' She wondered if his wife knew he was here, but that was his business, not hers. And he was right—there *was* unfinished business. Things that had never been said that maybe should be, especially if she was going to be bumping into him all over the place. 'I guess you'd better come in, then.' Her voice sounded cool as she said it, but inside she felt anything but.

'Thank you,' he murmured.

He hadn't expected it to be so easy, though maybe he should have done if he had stopped to think about it. For hadn't it always been too deliciously easy with her? Such a seamless seduction it had been with Molly, and hadn't there been some perverse, chauvinistic streak in him which wished she had put up more of a fight?

He observed the polite, glacial smile—thinking that there was a coolness about her now, which might suggest something else. That she didn't give a damn whether she spoke to him or not. Or that there was another man in her life—for surely someone as beautiful as Molly would not be alone?

Another man whom she adored as once she had said she adored him.

He stepped inside, and the pert, high thrust of her buttocks hit some powerful button in his memory. He felt a pulse begin to throb deep and strong within his groin and his body felt as though it had betrayed him. She moved with a confident assurance, and something about this new, older Molly set his loins melting in a way which both frustrated and infuriated him.

He had known her one long, hot summer on Pondiki—a summer of thoughtless passion. She had driven him and every other hot-blooded man on the island insane with desire that summer. Those tiny little cotton dresses she had worn when she had been working. Or outrageous scraps of material only just covering her body on the beach. Or naked as could be, with just the darkened circles of her nipples and the faint fuzz of hair at her thighs—the only things breaking up the smoothness of that bare, pale flesh.

He had triumphed in the joy of knowing that only *he* had seen her undressed and uninhibited like that, but in that he had been wrong. And he had been a fool, he thought bitterly. Even now, the memory still had the power to anger him—but then it had been the first and the last time he had been betrayed by a woman.

She turned to face him, determined to present the image of the slick, urban professional, even if inside she felt like the impressionable teenager she had once been. Yesterday, she had reacted gauchely, but yesterday she had had a reason to do so. Yesterday his appearance had been like a bolt out of the blue. Today there was no excuse. 'I was just having some coffee—would you like some?'

He smiled. How times had changed. She used to practically rip the clothes from his body when she saw him. Who would have thought that one day she would be offering him coffee in a chilly, distant way he would never have associated with Molly? 'Why not?'

She felt like a stranger in her own home as he followed her into the kitchen and sat down on one of the high stools at the breakfast bar, but then Dimitri dominated his surroundings like some blazing star. He always had.

'Do you still take it black?'

He gave a careless smile. 'Ah. You remember?'

Molly's hand was shaking slightly as she poured their coffee, automatically handing him a cup of the strong brew, unsugared and untouched by milk, and he took it from her, a mocking look in his black eyes.

Oh, yes, she remembered all right. Strange that you could learn your tables and French verbs by heart for years at school and some of them would stubbornly refuse to reappear and yet you could remember almost everything about a man with whom you had enjoyed a brief, passionate affair. So was the memory selective—or just cruel?

'Don't read too much into it, Dimitri! Everyone in Greece takes their coffee that way!' she countered as she reached for a mug.

But he wondered what else she remembered. The feel of his flesh enfolding hers, the sheer power as he had driven into her, over and over again? Was she remembering that now? As he was. She had left him dazed—in a way that no woman before nor since had ever quite done—and where once he had revelled in that fact, it had afterwards come to haunt him.

She pushed the coffee towards him, hating herself for thinking that his silken skin was close enough to touch. For a long time she had yearned to have him this close again, and now that he was she felt... Briefly, Molly closed her eyes. She was *scared*, and she wasn't quite sure why. 'Here.'

'Thanks.' But he ignored the coffee and instead let his gaze drift over her.

She wore a short denim skirt and a white T-shirt which had flowers splashed across the breasts. Her feet were bare and her toenails painted a shiny cherry-pink, and he felt his mouth dry with automatic desire. Some women knew how to press a man's buttons just by existing—and Molly Garcia was one of them.

'You're staring,' she said quietly.

'Yes. I imagine that most men do.'

'Not in quite such a blatant way.'

'Ah.' He smiled. 'But I am Greek, and we are not ashamed to show our appreciation of beautiful things.'

She remembered *that*, too, and how much it had appealed to her at the time. And it wasn't just where women were concerned—it was the same with good food, a cooing baby, or a spectacular sunset—Greek men were open about showing their pleasure in the good things in life.

With an effort, he tore his eyes away from the diversions of her body, forcing his attention on the high-ceilinged room instead. 'And this is a beautiful house.'

'Yes, it is.' She forced herself to concentrate. 'But you aren't here to talk about my house.' And neither was he here to stare at her in a way that reminded her all too vividly of how close they had once been.

'No.' He was scanning the room for signs of male habitation, but there was none. None that he could see. 'You're married?'

'I was. Not any more. I'm divorced.'

'Ah.' A jerk of triumph knifed its way through him. 'There is a lot of it about.'

The way he said it made her feel guilty—or had that been his intention? She knew his views on divorce. The break-up of families. He had condemned the easy-come, easy-go way of life which had been so alien to his own. She knew what his next question would be before he asked it.

'Children?'

'No.' Molly stirred her coffee unnecessarily, then lifted her eyes to his. So far he had been the one asking all the questions, but she had a few of her own. 'Do you have any more—apart from Zoe?'

He shook his head. 'Just Zoe.'

'And your wife? Won't she think it a little strange

that you've come here this morning? Are you planning to tell her about us?'

'What "us" was that, Molly?' he retorted softly. 'What is there to tell? That we were lovers, until someone better came along?'

Someone *better*? As if anyone could be better than Dimitri!

'Someone else to lose yourself in and to vent that remarkable, newly discovered sexual hunger on?' he continued, quietly yet remorselessly. He remembered the sight of the man's bare chest. Of Molly's unbuttoned dress. Of the way that the man's hand had rested with possession over the swell of her hip, and the image had the blinding power to take him right back. To recall how he had wanted to smash his fist into something. 'Was he a good lover, Molly? As good as me?'

Even now, the sense of injustice was powerful enough to hurt her. To be wrongly judged struck at the very heart of her. And stung as she was by the need to defend herself, everything else dissolved into insignificance—for wasn't he now giving her the opportunity to tell him what he had refused to hear at the time? The truth?

'You don't really, honestly think that I had sex with James that night?'

'*James,*' he mimicked cruelly. 'Ah! I did not know his name. James.' The black eyes glittered. 'It was, of course, simply a little craziness on my part, was it not, *agape mou*—that when I find my girlfriend in bed with another man, to assume that they had been having sex? Whatever could have given me that idea? Don't forget, Molly—I knew what you were like. I knew how much you *loved* it—I have never known a woman who fell so completely and utterly in love with sex the way you did.'

What use would it serve now to qualify his accusation with the plaintive little cry that it had been *him* she had loved? And *that* had been what had made it so mind-blowingly and uniquely special. Sex with Dimitri had seemed as easy and as necessary as breathing. She could no more have been intimate with another man at that time than she could have grown wings and flown

'Had you tired of me?' he demanded. 'Was that why you took the American into your arms and into your bed? Had you taken your fill of me, Molly— eager to try out your newly acquired skills with someone different?'

But she was still filled with the burning need to separate truth from falsehood. 'I never touched him, Dimitri,' she whispered. 'Nor he me—not in the way you are thinking.'

He remembered the abandoned posture of her sprawled, bare legs. It had been the first time in his life that he had experienced real jealousy, and its potency had unsettled him. 'What way am I supposed to think? He was asleep on the bed next to you!'

'It wasn't like that!'

'*Ochi?*' He gave a slow, cruel smile. 'Then how was it? I am so interested to hear.'

'He was comforting me.'

'Comforting you?' He laughed. 'Lucky man indeed—to offer comfort in such a way! I must begin to offer comfort to beautiful women—how very noble it will make me feel!'

And suddenly Molly had had enough. He was in *her* house and this was *her* territory and yet she was allowing him to dominate in the way that came so naturally to him. Throwing accusations at her and here she was, weakly trying to defend herself—when didn't she have a few accusations of her own?

'Actually, yes, he was comforting me,' she said. She looked him straight in the face. 'Because I had just found out about Malantha, you see.'

He stilled then, became so still that an outside observer might have wondered if he breathed at all. Only the ebony glitter from the narrowed eyes showed that he did.

'What about Malantha?' he questioned softly.

'That she was the girl you were promised to! I discovered that I had been nothing but a light, summer diversion, one in just a long line of willing lovers! I saw you both together, you see, Dimitri. I discovered that night what everyone else on the island knew—that Malantha was always the girl you were intended to marry—and, yes, I was upset. Very upset,' she finished, though the word sounded tame when she said it now.

Upset? At the time it had felt as though her heart had been torn from her body and ripped apart, with the edges left raw and jagged and gaping. First love and first heartbreak—and didn't they say that the cut of first love was the deepest cut of all?

Everyone had told her that the pain would fade and eventually heal, and heal it had. It had just left a faint but indelible scar along the way.

She lifted her head and stared at him, her eyes bright and searching. 'What happened to Malantha, by the way?' she asked.

There was a pause, a pause that seemed to go on for ever and ever.

'I married her.'

The world shifted out of focus, and when it shifted back in again it looked different. It was what she had half known and half expected and yet not what she wanted to hear. For hadn't there been a foolish part of her that longed for him to tell her that she had been mistaken? That he had not been promised to Malantha at all? Or that he had, but had changed his mind along the way?

In a way it made things worse, and yet in a funny kind of way it made things better. So she had not been wrong. Those nights when she had lain awake wondering if she had ruined everything by jumping to a stupid conclusion had been wasted nights. Her instincts had been right all along.

She sucked in a dry, painful breath. 'Then hadn't you better be getting back to her?' she questioned coldly. 'In the circumstances, I doubt whether she would approve of you sitting in my kitchen, drinking my coffee—do you, Dimitri?'

'My wife is dead,' he said baldly.

There was a moment of terrible, stunned silence and Molly was rocked by emotions so basic and conflicting that for several long seconds she could not speak.

Dead? She looked at him blankly, seeking and finding the sombre affirmation in his eyes. 'I'm so sorry,' she whispered. 'W…when?' she asked ineffectually.

'When Zoe was a baby.'

'Oh, God, Dimitri—that's awful.'

He shook his head. He didn't want her sympathy. It was mistimed and irrelevant now. He wanted *her*, he realised. He always had and he still did. To lose himself in the soft white folds of her body. To feel that tumble of blonde hair swaying like silk against his chest. Desire could strike at any time, and this could not be a more inappropriate one, but that didn't stop him feeling its slow, stealthy course through his veins, like some unstoppable drug.

'It was a long time ago. It is past.'

For a moment, all that could be heard was the ticking of the clock.

'How old is Zoe now?' she asked suddenly.

The black eyes narrowed. 'Fifteen.'

This time the sums were easier. 'So you married Malantha soon after I had left?' But she didn't need an answer to that. 'Of course you did.' She looked him straight in the eye. 'Just tell me one thing, Dimitri—were you sleeping with her at the same time you were sleeping with me?'

His eyes iced over and his mouth curved with distaste. If anything could demonstrate their fundamental differences, then that one question had managed it with blinding simplicity. 'Of course not. Malantha was brought up to be a virgin on her wedding night.'

It was meant to wound, and it did—but it was the truth, and who was she to argue with that?

She wanted to tell him to drink his coffee and go, and yet wasn't there some irrational side of her that wanted the very opposite? To take him into her arms as if the intervening years simply hadn't happened— and, in the process, to exorcise him and his sensual influence once and for all.

'So now what?' she questioned, amazed at how steady her voice sounded. 'You haven't even told me why you're here, or how long you're staying. Or even how you ended up living so close?'

Her eyes were questioning and he gave a soft laugh. 'You think I tracked you down? Found where you were living and moved into the house next door?'

As he said it she realised how preposterous the idea was. 'So it's just a terrible coincidence?'

Terrible? Right at that moment, it didn't seem so terrible. The woman who had always been able to take him straight to heaven and back was living in the house next door. Thoughtfully, Dimitri stroked the pad of his thumb against the warm circumference of the coffee-cup. If fate had provided such a breath-taking opportunity for a taste of former pleasures, then who was he to refuse such an opportunity?

He stared at her, wondering if there really was such a thing as coincidence? Now that he came to think about it, hadn't she once described Hampstead to him, telling him how beautiful it was and painting a picture of the heath and all its glories? Had that description planted a seed in his subconscious mind, so that, when he had been choosing where to stay in London, he had instinctively plumped for the leafy green area which seemed so far from the centre of a city it was so close to? Had he subconsciously willed fate to step in—and had it not done just that?

'I am here for a few weeks,' he said slowly. 'Zoe is going to an English summer school and I wanted to accompany her.'

Her mind ticked over; she was getting quite good at mental arithmetic. A few weeks. It wasn't a lifetime. Surely it wouldn't take too much planning for both of them to be able to keep out of the other's way for that long. As long as they were agreed.

'So what are we going to do?'

'Do? What do you suggest?' More as a diversionary tactic, he picked up his coffee and sipped it, black eyes challenging her through the thin cloud of steam which rose up like clouds. He wondered what she would say if he told her exactly what he would like to do at that precise moment, and how she would react. Would she open her mouth to his if he pulled her into his arms and began to kiss her? He saw the inky dilation of her pupils and once again he felt the powerful pull of desire. Because nothing was more seductive than mutual desire, particularly if one of the parties was doing their utmost to suppress it. 'We are neighbours, Molly,' he said softly. 'And we must behave as neighbours do.'

'You mean...' she swallowed '...avoid each other wherever possible?'

'Is that how English neighbours behave?' he mocked. He shook his head and smiled. 'On the contrary,' he said, and the gravel-deep voice sounded as sweet as honey as he rose to his feet, managing to make the high-ceilinged kitchen look like a doll's house with his tall, dominating figure. 'We will say good morning and talk about the weather whenever we meet!'

'Ha, ha, ha,' she said automatically.

He raised his eyebrows. 'But we are both grown up now, *ne*? I have been married and you have been married. What is it that you say—about a lot of water?'

'Has flowed under the bridge,' she filled in automatically, and remembering how she had helped him with his English was curiously more poignant than anything else. She slid her legs down off the stool and wished she hadn't. She was a tall woman, but Dimitri managed to make her feel like a tiny little thing; and her skirt was suddenly feeling as though it had shrunk in the wash.

'Gallons of the stuff!' she joked, thinking that soon this would be over. It had to be. He would see sense and realise that they couldn't possibly ever be friends, and they certainly couldn't be anything else, either. Not now.

He smiled then, but it was an odd, grown-up smile

that Molly didn't recognise and it threatened her more than a smile ever should.

'So I will come to your party,' he stated softly.

She stared at him. 'My p-party? What are you talking about?'

'You are having a party, Molly.'

Had he turned into a mind-reader? Were there balloons and boxes of champagne glasses lying around the place, giving him clues? Feeling half mad and disorientated, Molly looked round the kitchen. No. 'How the hell did you know *that*?'

She wasn't thinking straight, or clearly—and there was usually only one reason why a woman acted in such a distracted way, he noted with a warm sense of triumph. 'You sent me an invitation, remember? "To The New Residents!"' he quoted drily.

Of course she had. She had posted them all the way down the road; she always did. Her heart had begun to thunder and she wasn't such a self-deluding fool as to deny that part of the reason was excitement. But it would be madness if he came. Sheer and utter madness.

'I sent an invitation to all my neighbours,' she said wildly. 'Because it'll probably be noisy, and late.'

'Well, then.' He shrugged his broad shoulders. 'You want to pacify your neighbours, of which I am one? Then pacify *me*, Molly.'

'Dimitri,' she appealed, steeling herself against the sensual undercurrent in his tone, wondering if that had been deliberate or just part of the whole irresistible package he presented. 'You can't seriously want to come?'

'Oh, but I can,' he demurred. 'It will be good for me to mix a little while I'm here, don't you think? And besides—' he gave a slow, curving smile '—I like parties.'

She bet he liked them!

'Well, of course I can't *un*invite you now,' she observed slowly. She raised her face to his with a defiant tilt to her chin, in a gesture which told him quite clearly that she could cope with his presence. She certainly wasn't going to give him the pleasure of being barred! 'So if you insist on coming, then I guess I can't stop you.'

When she lifted her face like that, she was almost begging to be kissed and the desire to do so almost took his breath away. What *would* she do if he kissed her? he wondered. 'You could stop me if you wanted to,' he taunted softly. 'You just don't want to. Do you, Molly?'

Not if she was going to show him that she didn't really care one way or the other. 'Oh, it'll be interesting to see your predatory instincts at work with my friends,' she said sweetly. She made a great pantomime of looking at her watch. 'Now I really do have things to do—shall I show you out?'

Without waiting for an answer, she marched out of the kitchen towards the hall, and, reluctantly, Dimitri began to follow her. He was being dismissed! It was behaviour that he simply would not have tolerated from another woman and he felt the dull, hot ache of frustration as she opened the door. Then allowed himself to think of the tantalising inevitability of what was going to happen between them.

He glittered her a smile.

The kiss could wait.

CHAPTER THREE

BUT after Dimitri had gone, Molly did something she had not allowed herself to do for years. She ran upstairs, to the clutter of the junk room which lay at the very top of the house. Here there were books and documents and certificates: things you told yourself you might need one day, but rarely did—yet things you didn't dare throw away, just in case.

The old leather box was dusty, packed with shells, an old charm-bracelet, a lucky four-leaf clover sellotaped to a piece of card. In here was a sentimental record of the years, and, right at the bottom, a photograph.

She pulled it out and looked at it. Her and Dimitri, frozen in time, their arms tight around each other, carefree smiles on their young faces. The only photo she had.

Visual images had the power to drag you right back, to take you to a place which you had kept firmly out of bounds, and as Molly stared in Dimitri's heartbreakingly beautiful young face she stepped right back into the past.

A holiday job on the Greek island of Pondiki had seemed like heaven to an eighteen-year-old schoolgirl in the long vacation before she went to univer-

35

sity. One minute she was hurling her blazer across the room, the next she was stepping out onto the blistering tarmac of Pondiki's tiny runway on a high summer's day. Grown up and free—with a suitcase full of cotton dresses and bikinis and not a care in the world.

There were just three hotels on the island and at that time it was off the beaten tourist-track. Most people opted for the bigger, livelier Greek destinations, and only discerning travellers and students had discovered the unspoilt beauty of the mouse-shaped paradise, with its lemon groves and pine trees and the towering Mount Urlin which dominated it.

Molly was a waitress in one of the tavernas and she worked lunchtimes and evenings. Afternoons, she was free. The work was undemanding—though she developed strong arms from carrying trays of beer and wine—and she was given her own small, shuttered room which overlooked the main square, which at night was lit by rainbow-coloured lights. When she lay in bed, after the busy shift had ended, she could hear the sound of the waves lapping on the soft white sands and sometimes she thought she had died and gone to heaven.

She made friends with the daughter of the owner— a Greek girl named Elena who was as keen to learn English as Molly was to learn Greek.

It wasn't easy. Greek was a difficult language.

'You should get one of the boys to teach you,' ventured Elena shyly.

Molly wrinkled her nose. 'I'm not into boys,' she said.

It was true; she wasn't. She had no interest in the youths whose dark eyes followed her as she walked across the sunlit square in a cotton dress, with a straw sunhat to protect the blonde hair which seemed to fascinate them.

And then she met Dimitri and suddenly everything changed.

She and Elena had borrowed a scooter and ridden round to the opposite side of the island, where Pondiki's most exclusive hotel lay sheltered in splendid isolation, and they had just sputtered to a halt when they heard an angry shout, and as Molly had turned around her heart had turned over.

She fell in love with him right there and then, it was as simple as that. She didn't know why or how she knew it, she just did.

It wasn't just because he seemed like a man, and not a boy—though he was only a few months older than her. Nor because his dark good looks made him look like some kind of diabolical angel. Nor the fact that his hard brown torso was bare and he wore just faded denims which clung to the narrow jut of his hips and his long, muscular legs.

It was something in his eyes. Something indefinable in the look he directed at her. It was a look which her upbringing should have made her rebel against. A swift, assessing look. Almost judgemental. But it made her feel as if she had come home—as if she had spent all her life seeking just that look.

Except that, for now, it was a very angry look.

And it was only afterwards that she discovered he made every English girl who visited Pondiki feel the same way, but by then it was too late. If only someone had told her—yet if they had, would she have listened?

'Who *is* that?' she whispered.

'It is Dimitri,' whispered Elena, as if indeed it really *were* the devil himself.

'Dimitri who?'

But Elena shook her head, because he was striding towards them. He completely ignored Molly and let out a torrent of furious Greek which was directed solely at Elena.

Molly listened uncomprehendingly for a moment or two. 'What's the problem?'

Dimitri stopped speaking and turned to look at her, his heart beating fast, and it was more than his usual instinctive and hot-blooded reaction to a beautiful blonde. She was English. He had heard about her, of course, but he had been too busy helping his father to go looking for himself, and this was the first time he had seen her.

He was Greek through and through and he loved beautiful women. He took and enjoyed what was on offer, but it lasted only as long as his interest—which was never long.

Yet there was something indefinably different about this woman. A goddess of a woman, her icy-blue eyes almost on a level with his own, with a beauty he found almost overwhelming. But he saw the returning spark of interest in *her* eyes and this normal state of play was enough to allow his naturally arrogant masculine superiority to reassert itself.

'Are you crazy?' he hissed, in English, from between clenched white teeth.

As an opening gambit, she had heard better, but Molly didn't care. She had never seen anyone like this before—with his flashing black eyes and his perfect body and an air of strength and devil-may-careness that you simply didn't get with Englishmen.

'Sometimes.' She smiled at him, and cocked an eyebrow. 'Aren't you?' she said gravely. 'Crazy is good.'

He was expecting a tongue-tied and stumbling answer—not a cool retort in a voice as confident as his own.

There was a moment's pause—a heartbeat and a lifetime of a pause—before he began to laugh, and it sounded as delicious as the sprinkle of fresh water on sun-baked stone.

But then his eyes grew serious.

'You are not wearing helmets,' he growled. 'These roads are not like your English roads.'

'You can say that again,' murmured Molly. She thought of the fumes and the bad-tempered drivers back home, and compared them to Pondiki's clean and silent beauty.

He narrowed his eyes. 'You will both come with me,' he ordered abruptly. 'And you will wear helmets back.'

It was ironic that if anyone else had spoken to her

like that, then Molly would probably have refused, on principle. But now that she had found him, she didn't want to lose sight of him and, quite honestly, if he had told her that she was going to be put in handcuffs for the return journey, then she couldn't have seen herself uttering a word of objection.

He ordered coffee and they drank it on the terrace of his father's hotel, with its breathtaking views over the sea. Only Molly found it hard to concentrate on the view.

So did Dimitri. He shook himself slightly, as if trying to shake off the inexplicable spell she seemed to have cast over him.

Beautiful young women came to his island every summer and he was no innocent. Greek men lived very defined lives. Greek women were strictly out of bounds until marriage. If a man had trouble-free temptations of the flesh, then why not enjoy them while he could?

But this Molly was different, and he could not work out why. It was not just her pure, clean beauty, nor the sparkle of mischief which lit her ice-blue eyes. She had something which he wanted, something which made him ache unbearably.

He gave them helmets and saw them safely away, but just before Molly put hers on he lifted a hand to lightly brush a stray strand of hair away from her brow and their eyes met in a long, spine-tingling moment.

It felt like the most erotic thing which had ever happened to her, but then maybe it was—for what fumbled kisses could compare to the touch of a man like Dimitri?

'Can I take you for a drive some time?' he said, and felt her tremble.

She didn't hesitate. She wouldn't play games. Games were a waste of time when she only had six weeks on this island and she wasn't going to squander a single moment of them.

'Oh, yes, please,' she answered.

'Tomorrow?'

'Tomorrow,' she agreed.

And that was how it started.

She slept with him that very first day—she couldn't not have done—and afterwards she wept with sheer pleasure as he held her tightly, his expression fierce as he looked down at her, smoothing his palms over her damp skin, his eyes burning as brightly as lanterns.

'You were a virgin,' he stated, and his voice sounded strained.

'Not any more.' She touched her lips to his arm.

He closed his eyes, his feelings confused. He hadn't been expecting that, not from someone who looked like her. And he wondered if her virginity had been the indefinable something he had wanted. He had never slept with a virgin before, even though one day his wife would inevitably be one. And somehow it made it different. It shouldn't do, but it did. His kisses were tender on her eyelids and he pulled her closer against his bare skin.

'Sweet Molly,' he said softly.

'Sweet Dimitri,' she said drowsily.

She was slipping in deep and then deeper still, and maybe it showed because Elena tried to warn her. 'Molly, you know that Dimitri—'

'Yes, I know. Believe me, I know. He's Greek. I'm English.' She saw Elena's concerned face and smiled. 'I'm only here for the summer,' Molly said gently. 'Then I'm off to university. Don't worry, Elena—I'm not expecting to buy a white dress and have the people of Pondiki pin money onto it!'

Yet it was funny how you could know something on an intellectual level, but that didn't stop your foolish heart yearning for more. But she never showed it. Not to Dimitri, nor to Elena. She even tried to deny it to herself. And even though she sometimes wove little fantasies which involved her changing her university course to read Greek and returning here to help Dimitri run his hotel, she just tried to live each day for what it was. Paradise.

His parents, naturally enough, disliked her. She had never actually been introduced to them, but the couple of times she saw his mother at the weekday market in the square she was met with a stony-eyed look of hostility. But she understood that, too. They probably thought that she was some kind of loose-moralled tourist out for a summer of hot sex and there were enough of *those* on the island. She could hardly go up and explain that her son had captured her heart as well as her body, could she?

And there was a girl, too—a beautiful dark-eyed girl with a curtain of raven hair which fell to her slender waist. Molly saw her sometimes, and caught her looking at her with a sad, reproachful look.

'Who is that girl?' she asked Dimitri one afternoon.

He stared out to sea. 'Just a girl,' he said, and his voice sounded distant.

Something in his voice made her narrow her eyes, but she didn't ask another question; afterwards she suspected it was because she'd known what the answer would be.

Her time on Pondiki was slipping away like the soft white sand she trickled through her fingers, and, with only a couple of weeks until she had to return home, some American guys came to stay at the hotel.

One of them was gorgeous. Textbook perfect. James, with eyes as blue as her own and a lazy, outgoing manner. He liked her; he made that clear, and Molly thought how much simpler life would be if she liked him back.

But life was never that simple and she had eyes for only one man.

And then Dimitri rang, cancelling their date. It was her Sunday off and he had planned to take her climbing to the very top of Mount Urlin.

His voice sounded oddly strained. 'Molly, *agape mou*, I cannot make it. Not today.'

Molly bit her lip, trying not to feel disappointed, determined not to quiz him, but for once her resolution failed her.

'Oh, *why*, Dimitri?' she asked him plaintively. 'I've only got a couple more weeks and you've been promising to take me up there for ages!' Her voice softened. 'I've been so looking forward to it.'

And so had he. The summit of Mount Urlin was as stunning and as beautiful a spot as he had ever seen and he had planned to make love to her up there. The heat of desire warred briefly against the brick wall of duty. He sighed, then scowled at his reflection in the mirror. 'I know. And there will be another time—just not today. It's a family party.'

'Oh, I see.' And suddenly she did. Perfectly. Naturally, she would be excluded from anything which involved his family—his *real* life—for what did their time consist of other than deep, passionate kisses with their inevitable conclusion?

'Molly, I *have* to go.'

She said what was expected of her. 'Of course you do.'

She hung up, and then impulse sent her off to find Elena who was slicing up lemons in the bar. She looked up as Molly came in.

Molly poured herself a glass of fizzy water and perched on a high stool next to the counter. She twirled the lemon idly with her little finger and stared intently at the yellow circle bobbing around among the ice and the bubbles.

She glanced up. 'Dimitri's going to a family party tonight—do you know anything about it?'

Elena looked uncomfortable. 'Not really. It's just a party,' she said.

Molly would have needed to have been made of

stone not to have heard the evasion in her voice. 'At his home?' she questioned casually.

'At the hotel, I think.'

Molly bit her lip. She still had a night off. She still had use of the scooter. Why *shouldn't* she go and have a nose round, to find out what she could see? Because something wasn't right—she could feel it, deep down, and she could hear it too, in Elena's voice, see it in her reluctance to meet her eyes.

Her heart was pounding as she fetched her helmet and walked through the bar, where James was sitting, sipping from a glass of beer, wearing swimming trunks which were still damp from the sea. He crinkled his tanned face in an interested look as she stuffed her thick blonde hair up beneath the helmet.

'Off to see lover-boy?' he said ruefully.

Molly gave a forced smile. 'Not tonight. I just want to watch the sunset.'

'Like some company?'

She shook her head. 'No, thanks.'

'You take care, now—those roads are dangerous.'

'I will.'

But his words came back to haunt her. It wasn't just the roads which were dangerous—so were the emotions which drove her on to the bottom of the Urlin Road, towards Dimitri's hotel. She knew that what she was doing was wrong—like eavesdropping—yet she couldn't seem to stop herself.

She heard the sounds of a party well before she saw the twinkling of coloured lanterns, faint against the glorious sunset, and the mill of people clustering on the terrace. Laughter rang out over the water and Molly turned off her engine and parked the scooter in case someone heard her.

She felt like a jewel-thief as she silently approached the hotel, but she did not need to go far to recognise the two figures at the far end of the balcony, deep in conversation.

It was Dimitri and the beautiful raven-haired girl with the reproachful eyes. She saw the shadowy figure of his mother standing close by—with just the right amount of distance which spoke volumes of her role as chaperone.

Of course.

'Who is that girl?' Molly had asked him and he had replied, 'Just a girl.' And suddenly Molly understood. She was not "just a girl"—she was Dimitri's girl. Oh, not now, maybe not even next week, or month, or even next year. But one day he would marry the beauty from Pondiki. He could have fun while he could, indeed—with whoever was there to provide it—but it certainly wouldn't be a Greek girl.

And maybe that was why she had felt the unspoken hostility—because, for once, the fun had become a little too serious. Dimitri liked her, she knew that— *really* liked her—he'd told her that and maybe his family had seen that, too. For once, it was not just some English girl who had been bedded and discarded after two nights.

Molly felt the taste of salt at the back of her throat as she willed the tears away. She had always known that there was a price to be paid for passion, and that she would break her heart when she left, but this changed everything and, instead, she felt the devastating and debilitating cocktail of anger and foolishness.

On autopilot she made her way back to her scooter and wheeled it a little way before starting it up, half fearing, half hoping that Dimitri would have somehow seen her, heard—and come after her to tell her that there was no other girl, no intended marriage and that she was the only one he wanted.

But life was not a fairy tale and Dimitri was a Greek pragmatist, not a romantic hero—even if he looked like one and acted like one most of the time.

By the time she got back she was shaking and James was still sitting in the bar, where she'd left him. He looked up when she walked in, and frowned.

'Looks like the sunset wasn't as good as you thought it would be,' he observed wryly. He indicated the chair. 'Have a drink?'

Molly hesitated for only a moment. She didn't want to be on her own, and what was the alternative to a drink with a kind, friendly face? Sit in her room and mope—worse, cry the unshed tears which were just dying to come out?

'I'd love one,' she said steadily.

'Ouzo?'

She shrugged, barely hearing him. 'Why not?'

She found the sickly-sweet taste of the aniseed drink vaguely comforting, and by the third her thoughts on the subject of Dimitri had become vehemently less charitable. But she kept them to herself. Better be a fool to yourself, than have the world know about it.

'Want to talk about it?' he asked.

'About what?'

'About what's made your eyes so sad?'

She shook her head with determination, but the movement made her feel slightly whoozy.

James narrowed his eyes. 'Have you eaten?'

She shook her head. 'Not hungry,' she mumbled.

'Say, Molly,' he said gently. 'Go easy on that stuff—it's dynamite.'

Maybe dynamite was just what she needed right now—something to blow away the crazy dreams she'd had about a man who had never promised anything more than a holiday romance.

'One for the road,' she said unsteadily, and waved her empty glass.

He looked uncertain, but he bought it for her. 'That's your last,' he warned.

'You can't stop me!' she said brightly.

But in the end he didn't need to. Molly went very hot and then very cold and her head began to swim.

'I don't feel so good,' she said indistinctly.

'You don't look so good,' he said. 'Maybe you need some food?'

Her face going very slightly green, Molly clapped her hand over her mouth.

James nodded. 'Food's out, then. Come on, Molly—you should go and sleep it off.'

Her legs felt like jelly and James had to put a restraining arm around her waist.

'For God's sake, Molly,' he said. 'Easy does it. Slow down, or everyone will think you're drunk.'

Molly gulped. 'Will you—will you see me up to my room please, James? I'm not sure my legs are going to carry me.'

A couple of dark heads swivelled in their direction as James led her out of the bar and up the narrow, rickety staircase at the back, but she barely noticed them. She stumbled into the room and collapsed on the narrow single bed, and shut her eyes.

'The room's going round and round,' she moaned.

'Open your eyes, then.'

'I *can't*.'

'Molly, turn onto your side,' he said urgently.

'Lemme sleep.'

'*No.*'

She felt sick and alone and frightened. Dimitri was somewhere else with the girl with raven hair and one day he would marry her. She stared up into the tanned face which kept shifting in and out of focus. 'Don't leave me, James.'

'I ain't going nowhere,' he said firmly. 'Here. You're hot.' He loosened two buttons on her sundress and her eyes flew open in alarm. His mouth twisted. 'Don't worry about a thing, Molly,' he said drily. 'I've never particularly been into women who are in love with someone else, and I've never had to stoop quite so low as to take advantage of someone who's drunk.'

She opened her mouth to deny the first part of his statement, but then shut it again, and a kind of stifled sob came out instead.

'It's okay,' soothed James as he fanned her with a magazine. 'You're going to be okay.'

And that was how Dimitri found them. Only by then it was later, much later—and James had fallen asleep on the bed beside her, still in his bathing trunks and a protective hand was possessively caught against her waist.

She discovered afterwards, from Elena, that someone had overheard her in the bar, asking James to take her upstairs, and had made it their responsibility to let Dimitri know. And soon after that he had burst into her room and she would never forget the expression on his face as her glued-up eyelids somehow opened. As if he couldn't believe it, and yet, oddly enough—as though he *wanted* to believe it.

And she didn't even have the opportunity to offer him an explanation, because he refused to see her again and she was too proud to beg—and, besides, Dimitri had his pride, too. The look of fury on his face told her that she had betrayed him, and in a way which meant that the rest of the island would know. And Pondiki was too small a place to tolerate such outrageous behaviour as a woman taking another man to her room, no matter what the reason.

'Why didn't you call for *me*?' Elena asked her sadly as Molly packed her clothes.

Molly shook her head. Didn't matter what she said. Not now.

'Is Dimitri going to marry Malantha?' she asked, her eyes clear and questioning. 'Tell me, honestly.'

Elena shrugged. 'Probably.' Her expression softened. 'That's the way things work, Molly.'

So that was that. Things would never be the same. They couldn't possibly be.

She left the following evening. Her employers understood without needing any explanation, which told Molly exactly how fast news travelled around Pondiki. And she had never felt quite so enveloped by a sense of shame—as though she had let everyone down, herself included—even though nothing had happened. But if she protested *that*, then who would believe her?

She looked around her in the tiny airport terminal—some last fairy-tale hope refusing to die as she imagined that he might suddenly run in, his dark eyes shining as he caught her into his strong arms, telling her that it had all been a terrible mistake. That he was liberated enough to understand her explanation.

But he didn't come.

Instead, she boarded the plane, and not until after the take-off—when the lights of Pondiki became as twinkingly distant as the stars above them—did she allow the first tears to slide from behind her tightly closed eyelids....

Molly blinked. The photo had become blurred and she realised to her surprise that there were tears in her eyes now. Quickly, she wiped them away and put the photo back in the box and snapped it shut.

There was nothing wrong with mourning the past, she decided, just so long as you weren't foolish enough to get it muddled up with the present.

If she could manage to have a civilised and friendly relationship with her ex-husband, then surely it wouldn't kill her to be polite to Dimitri for a few short weeks.

And, besides, he was coming to her party now. She really didn't have any choice in the matter.

CHAPTER FOUR

MOLLY drew in a deep breath as she surveyed the dazzle of gold which was reflected back from the mirror.

Was the dress too risqué?

The sales assistant had assured her not. 'For a party? Not at all! You have a wonderful figure, Madam,' she had purred. 'Why not show it off to advantage?'

Was that what she was doing? Was that why she had let herself be talked into buying it—fuelled by some belated desire to have Dimitri see what he had missed? That she was a different, grown-up Molly. A new person.

Because the old Molly would certainly never have worn a dress like *this*.

It was made of a dull, gleaming gold material and it fell in soft drapes to her knees and clung like melted butter to her body. At the back it was completely bare, leaving lots of skin on show, and she had rubbed moisturiser all over herself so that she gleamed as subtly as the dress.

She turned away from her reflection as the sound of the doorbell heralded the arrival of the first guests and she fixed a smile to her lips as she went into the hall to greet them.

But inside, she was on tenterhooks, starting every time the wretched doorbell rang and trying not to look disappointed when it was anyone—everyone—except Dimitri. She felt like a teenager again, with that horrible churned-up mixture of expectation and excitement and dread, and she felt angry with herself for wanting to see him so much. And angry with him for making her wait.

She had convinced herself that he had changed his mind and he wasn't coming after all, and telling herself that it was the best possible outcome for all concerned, when the doorbell sounded again, and she could see his tall, shadowy figure outlined through the stained glass.

Her heart began to speed erratically beneath her silk-covered breasts and her fingers were trembling as she opened the door and said, in a voice which didn't sound quite like her own, 'Dimitri! Hi! So glad you could make it—come in!' If it sounded rehearsed, then that was because it was—she had searched hard for just the right combination of casual greetings.

For a moment Dimitri didn't move, but that was because he didn't dare to. He scarcely recognised her—this shiny, beautiful, sexy blonde creature with her hair piled high up on her head. She looked a contradiction in terms—both so untouchable, and yet so eminently touchable.

He felt blood pounding at all his pulse-points. Temples. Wrists. Groin. His mouth twisted into an odd kind of smile.

'Molly,' he said unsteadily. 'You look...*oreos*.'

She knew the word beautiful from her time in Pondiki, but, even if she hadn't, she would have known that the word was a compliment. No, she amended silently. Compliment was the wrong word. When a man paid you a compliment, he shouldn't look as though the word were being torn reluctantly and sourly from his mouth, like a man having his teeth pulled. Nor should his eyes, black and hot and smouldering, rove over you in such a way that you felt desired and yet...resented.

'You might say it as though you meant it,' she commented breathlessly.

He raised his dark eyebrows in arrogant query, perversely angry at the sudden and overwhelming state of arousal in which he now found himself. He was a man used to dampening the hunger of the flesh when required, yet now his body was stubbornly refusing to obey his will.

'Surely you do not doubt that, *agape mou*?' he queried softly. 'Every man in the room will be wondering what—if anything—you are wearing beneath that outrageous gown.' Black eyes glittered an intense, hungry fire. 'And wondering if they will be lucky enough to be the one to remove it at the end of the evening.'

Molly's heart clenched as she imagined him doing just that, but she shook her head in an expression of amused outrage. 'I should ask you to leave for saying something like that!'

'But it is the truth. A dress like that is sending out

a very definite message.' He shrugged. 'I imagine that is why you wore it.'

What could she say? That she had wanted to look her most impressive best? And that his mocking assessment made her wish that she had covered herself up from head to toe?

She pulled herself together. 'Are you going to stand here all night insulting me, or would you like a drink?'

He allowed himself the brief and frustrating fantasy of refusing. Of pulling her outside, instead. Of taking her into his arms and kissing her until she was in such a fevered state of need that she would ignore all her party guests and take him upstairs and spend the rest of the night letting him make love to her.

And wondered why he had consented to endure a noisy party filled with people who would no doubt be vying for her attention all night.

But this was called playing the game and he could not have her. Not here and not now and not yet. His eyes gleamed. 'A drink would be wonderful.'

She pointed with a finger which was not quite steady, though her voice thankfully was. 'Everyone's in here.'

Molly was aware of the momentary lull in the buzz of party chatter as they walked into the main reception room. She grabbed a glass from a circulating waiter and handed it to him. 'Champagne okay?'

'Champagne is always perfect.' He took the flute and studied the fizzing bubbles for a moment, then raised his head and lifted his glass to her, his eyes

never leaving her face as he took a sip of champagne,
and Molly thought that if any other man had done
that she would have found it unspeakably corny. Yet
when Dimitri did it…she found herself gazing back,
tempted to lose herself in the black blaze from his
eyes.

She smiled instead. 'You must let me introduce
you to some people who will be dying to meet you.'

She thought that there would certainly be no short-
age of takers. He put every other man in the shade—
quite literally—with his towering height and the
hard-packed muscular body. Dark, tailored trousers
and a white silk shirt of breathtaking simplicity
showed off his muscular physique to perfection and,
judging by the covert glances cast in their direction,
Molly wasn't the only woman in the room who
thought so.

His rugged face was darkened by the hint of five
o'clock shadow and yet she suspected that it couldn't
have been too long since he had shaved. And maybe
women just homed in automatically on that, the way
they had been programmed to do—the shadowed jaw
sending out the subliminal signal that here was a man
at his most glorious and virile peak.

Her palms felt clammy and surreptitiously she
smoothed them down over her shiny gold hips.
'Now, let me see—who would you like to meet?'
But it was an academic question—she didn't even
have to go in search of someone, because a stunning
redhead had appeared, her question directed at
Molly, but her attention fixed on Dimitri.

'Hello! Just who is *this*, Molly?' she demanded, with a delighted little smile. 'And where have you been hiding him away?'

Molly smiled. 'Hello, Alison,' she said, slightly amused by her friend's reaction. No prizes for subtlety *there*—she was eyeing him with unashamed interest—though maybe Dimitri liked that. She stole a glance at him. Difficult to tell, with that dark, shadowed face giving nothing away. It never had—even when he had been making love to her, his eyes had been shuttered, his thoughts a complete mystery. 'This is Dimitri Nicharos. Dimitri—I'd like you to meet Alison Dempster.'

'Hello, Alison,' he said softly, and smiled, and Molly saw Alison almost dissolve beneath the sensual impact of that voice, that face, that body, that smile.

'You're Greek?' enquired Alison breathlessly.

'Indeed I am. But as you will see, I come bearing no gifts—so there is no need for you to beware!'

'Are you sure?' laughed Alison.

Dimitri looked at Molly, thinking how edgy she looked. 'How do you two know each other?'

'Oh, I've known Alison and Will for years,' Molly answered. 'He's over there.' She pointed at an owlish lawyer who stood laughing with a small group of men.

Alison raised her eyebrows in surprise, as if to say, Why the hell did you have to tell him *that*? And Molly wondered herself. She knew that married women liked to flirt at parties—it was all part of the sophisticated urbane game of life they played. So was it a ploy to tell Dimitri that Alison was definitely not available—even though she had no right to be possessive about him?

Dimitri sipped his champagne. What a mine field of emotions a party always threw up! He was beginning to enjoy himself. 'You've known each other for a long time?'

It was clearly Alison's turn to get her own back.

'We met through Molly's ex-husband,' she said chattily. 'He came to my husband for advice, when he was setting up his business.' She turned a pair of innocent green eyes up to him. 'Have you met Hugo yet?'

'Unfortunately, no.' Black eyes glittered in Molly's direction. 'Not yet.'

Molly was beginning to wish that she were anywhere other than here, but there was a whole evening to get through, and she was the hostess. And she was not going to spend it keeping tabs on *him*. 'Can I get you another drink, Dimitri?'

He shook his head. 'I'm fine. Go and see to your guests—don't feel you have to look after me.'

She felt her cheeks burn, feeling like an unwelcome fly which had just been swatted away. Saw Alison's curious glance. 'Right. Well, I'll leave you to it,' she said, rather weakly.

She moved away to flit between groups of people, introducing those who didn't know each other and drawing in would-be outsiders with a skill she had learned through years of attending corporate events with Hugo.

Waitresses offered plates of expensive delicacies which satisfied the taste buds but not the appetite, but Molly hadn't wanted the fuss of a full meal. They refilled glasses as music played softly in the background and people began to relax and let their guard down.

To an outsider, it must have seemed like a good party—but to Molly it was an endurance test from beginning to end. Because it was as if no one else in the room existed, save him. He dominated his surroundings, simply by being. She still wanted him, she realised.

She let her gaze drift across to him. He was surrounded by a small group of men, and he was making them laugh and that somehow surprised her. Had she thought that he would be commandeered by women all evening? And yet he was mixing like a seasoned party expert, fitting easily into her circle of friends. He seemed as cosmopolitan and sophisticated as the rest of them, and she wondered whether he socialised much on Pondiki.

She glanced across the room and he looked up, his black eyes glittering, as if he had sensed that she was watching him and she quickly turned away, half afraid that he might be able to guess at her thoughts.

But Alison had seen her and came to stand next to her.

'We're about to leave. Will has got a big case in the morning,' she said. 'Thanks for a lovely party.'

Molly smiled. 'My pleasure.'

There was a moment's silence. 'He's quite some-thing,' Alison remarked.

'Who?'

'The man in the moon, of course!' Alison giggled. '*Who!* Molly, I'm one of your oldest friends, you can't fool me—the Gorgeous Greek, of course. Who is he?'

'Someone I knew years ago.'

'And he's back in your life?'

Molly shook her head. 'Oh, no, he's just…passing through.'

'Well, I've never seen someone exert so much magnetism over women. Myself included,' Alison added ruefully. 'There isn't a woman in the room who hasn't been eyeing him like a hungry tiger all night!'

Molly's shoulders felt bare and exposed in the flirty golden gown and her skin suddenly felt chilled. She knew what Alison meant. Despite his air of so-phistication and the immaculate clothes he wore, nothing could disguise the fact that Dimitri was the kind of man which cities did not breed. There wasn't another man in the room who looked as though he could catch a fish with his bare hands, or climb a tree as effortlessly as she had seen him do. 'That's because he likes women—but then, Greek men do and women home in on that.'

'Aren't you in danger of being a touch stereotyp-ical?'

'Not really, no. They're different from English

men.' Molly successfully suppressed an erotic shiver of memory. So different.

'How?' Alison's face was interested.

'Oh, they think about women differently, treat them differently. A woman was put on this earth to love,' she recited from memory, without even realising that she was doing so. 'Women are soft but men are hard and the two complement each other.' Her cheeks went pink as she recognised just how much she had given away.

'So he was your lover?' guessed Alison slowly.

'I'm surprised it took you so long to ask.'

'I'm surprised you didn't tell me.'

Had she really hoped that by inviting him she would be able to keep it secret? Molly supposed that it was inevitable that Alison might have guessed— even if she hadn't given her such glaring great signposts along the way. She nodded. 'Yes. He was. A long time ago.'

'And he hurt you?'

'Oh, you know—it was just the normal teenage heartbreak. A youthful affair that ended naturally, that's all.' It was nothing but the truth—but it was funny how bare and inadequate the truth could sometimes sound.

There was silence for a moment. 'But you still want him?'

Molly shook her head. 'Not any more. I'm not interested in him. Not now.'

'I think you are,' contradicted Alison. 'You may not want to be, but you are—it's written all over you.

You might as well have a huge sign stuck to your forehead, saying "Make love to me, Dimitri!"'

Molly's eyes widened. 'Oh, God,' she breathed. 'Is it that obvious?'

'Maybe only to me—but that's because I know you.' She smiled. 'There's no need to look so tragic, Molly! Lots of women want men they know are trouble—I'm afraid that some of the qualities which make them trouble are the same qualities which make them irresistible. But you don't have to submit to him, you know! Oh-oh, he's coming over! I'll be a good friend—time I was going, I think.'

Molly looked after Alison helplessly as she began to weave her way through the room in search of her husband. Part of her wanted to say, *Don't go! Please don't leave me with this man who exudes the kind of danger and excitement I can do without!* But then Dimitri was there, towering beside her, the raw male scent of him so evocatively familiar, and all she could think was, *He's here—he's here at last—and I have him all to myself!*

Dimitri looked down at her and saw the brief tremble of her lips. Her gold-covered breasts rose and fell as she breathed, and not for the first time desire and frustration combined to make him wonder just for whose benefit she had worn such an outrageously sexy garment. A tight, hot fist of predatory jealousy hit him somewhere in the solar plexus. 'This is quite some party, Molly,' he observed coolly.

'You sound surprised.'

'Do I? I suppose I am a little.' He fixed her with a steady black stare. 'So who pays for it?'

She stared back, aware of the undercurrent of hostility. 'I'm not quite sure I understand what you mean.'

'Don't you?' He looked around the room. 'You live in a big house. You serve champagne to your guests. So either your travel books earn you a huge income, or your divorce settlement was exceptionally generous. Or...' He paused deliberately.

'Or what?'

He shrugged. 'Maybe you have a lover who likes to lavish things on you.' He glanced around the room. 'Someone here tonight, perhaps—a secret lover?'

'A kept woman, you mean?' she demanded. 'Somebody's mistress? One of my friend's husbands, perhaps?'

'Why not?'

'You really think that's the way I live my life?'

'How should I know, *agape mou*? Women do.'

'Not this woman,' she said furiously. 'If you must know, then, yes, my writing pays enough to support me. I'm lucky enough not to have a mortgage because, yes, my divorce settlement *was* generous—but it was nothing more than fair, since I helped my husband set up and run his business! Does that answer your insulting question, Dimitri?'

He allowed himself the slow expulsion of a breath he had not even realised he was holding. So there wasn't someone. He looked down into her furious face, where the cat-shaped eyes sparked blue fire at him, and he smiled, wishing that they were alone and that he could subdue her temper with a kiss. 'Then I must congratulate you on your independence.'

Molly's furious expression didn't waver. 'Is that all you've got to say?'

'Why are you so offended, Molly?' he mused. 'It's the way of the world. Rich men support beautiful women—it's been going on since the beginning of time. Simply a trade of commodities, that's all.'

He was unbelievable! He hadn't even had the grace to apologise! Well, she was not going to have a stand-up fight with him in front of her friends. 'I'd better go and see my guests out,' she said icily. 'If you want to leave, then please don't let me keep you, Dimitri.'

But he didn't bite. Instead, he wandered across the room and began talking to Molly's accountant, much to her annoyance. And then, just when she was wondering whether he was intending to be the last to leave, and her heart had begun to thunder at the prospect of *that*, he came to say goodbye.

'Thank you for coming,' she said stiffly. But her anger seemed to have fled, dissolved by the potent power of his proximity and stupidly, illogically—she wanted him to stay.

'Thank you for having me,' he said softly. 'It was a good party.'

That wasn't what it felt like to her. She closed the door behind him, and briefly laid her hot forehead on a cool pane of glass, feeling weary and deflated. Well, she had done her neighbourly duty. With a little bit of planning and foresight, their paths need never cross again.

CHAPTER FIVE

MOLLY woke the next morning with a splitting headache, which she thought was slightly unfair as she
had drunk nothing more than a couple of glasses of
champagne. Maybe it had more to do with an unsettled night, and dreams invaded by a man she had
never thought she would see again.

She showered and dressed, tied her hair back and
went downstairs, preparing herself for the aftermath
of the party, and it was as bad as she had thought.
True, her friends were well behaved and fairly grown
up in their outlook—there were no cigarettes stubbed
out on the rugs, nor spillages of wine or beer over
the furniture. But she still found a number of half-
full glasses concealed behind the curtains and there
were stacks of glasses to unload from the dishwasher
before the next lot could be put in.

She ate a bowl of cherries and set to work, mop-
ping the kitchen floor and wiping down all the sur-
faces and throwing all the leftover bits of party food
into the bin. The place was just starting to look like
home again when the doorbell rang and she went to
answer it, her footsteps slowing as her heart-rate
soared when she saw it was Dimitri.

She could always ignore his summons, of course.

Deliberately not answer the door and then he might get the message.

But what message would that be? That she didn't want to see him? Because then the message would be a lie. Or, at least, a very mixed-up message— nearly as mixed-up as she felt inside. She *did* want to see him, that was the trouble.

She opened the door. 'What do you want?' she asked, but the words faded away into nothing when she saw that he was carrying an enormous bunch of pink and yellow roses, big as fists. The clashing colours shouldn't have worked, but somehow they did; they looked wild and exotic—and so did he. 'For me?' she said stupidly as he held them out to her.

'Who else?' He thought how much more beautiful she looked this morning, with her pale, bare face and the faint blue smudges beneath her eyes. Last night, the too-glamourous gown had made her look like someone out of a magazine. Unreal and unknown. This Molly looked like a living and breathing woman and he wanted to touch her.

'Oh, they're gorgeous! You didn't have to do that,' she said instinctively, burying her nose in their petals, partly to inhale the glorious scent but partly because her cheeks had flushed pink with pleasure and inwardly she cursed herself. Acting as if she had never received a bouquet before!

'Yes, I did,' he contradicted softly. 'You very sweetly invited me into your home and I did nothing but insult you.'

She looked up then. 'Yes, you did,' she agreed.

'All that ridiculous stuff about me being a kept woman! As if!'

He bit back a smile. She had answered him back the very first time he had met her, and she was still doing it. 'So do you forgive me, Molly?'

She looked into the face she knew so well, and yet scarcely knew at all, and knew that she was in danger of forgiving him almost anything. 'Only if you promise never to make any assumptions about me again. And that includes your assumption that I was intimate with James. I was not. Understand?'

Reluctantly, he nodded. '*Ne*, Molly,' he sighed. 'I understand.' The black eyes gleamed. 'Now are you going to invite me in?'

'Is that why you bought me the flowers?'

'The flowers were to say sorry.'

'But coffee would be a bonus, right?'

'Coffee would be a good start,' he agreed steadily.

But a start to what? There was a split-second where logic warred with the heady danger of the unknown, but the soft gleam from his eyes made logic fall by the wayside. 'I won't have time to sit down and chat,' she warned as she opened the door wider. 'I'm clearing up after the party.'

'Then let me help.'

'You!' Molly couldn't resist it. 'Doing ''women's'' work?' She raised her eyebrows at him challengingly. 'Whatever next?'

'Do you mend your own car?'

'I send it to the garage.'

'Where, no doubt, the place is overrun by female mechanics?'

She opened her mouth and shut it again. 'None you'd notice.' Molly sighed. 'Okay, you win.'

But there was no victory for Dimitri. Not yet. He knew the prize he wanted, but he must tread carefully, for Molly was no longer an eighteen-year-old lulled and seduced by the hot beat of the sun and the power of her sexual awakening.

The kitchen was bathed in sunlight, and as she walked into it, her arms full of the fragrant flowers, Molly thought that she had never really seen it before. The scent of coffee which wafted from the pot smelt so *intensely* of coffee, just as the newly washed glasses gleamed brighter than diamonds. Outside she could hear the birds chirruping in the garden and they had never seemed to sing so loud as they did then. Her senses were raw, she realised, and he was the cause of it, and yet the sensations were too persuasive for her to want to do anything to stop him. And she wasn't doing anything wrong, was she? She was only making him a cup of coffee, for heaven's sake.

'I'd better put these in water,' she said, and even her voice sounded different, low and clear, like a bell.

He watched in silence as she pulled a huge vase from beneath the sink and turned the tap on full, so that it splashed all over her, and slopped over the sides of the vase.

'You're making a mess,' he observed softly.

'Yes.'

She didn't look round. She could feel her neck growing warm and contrasting with the splash which had plastered her little vest-top to her breasts like an icy skin. And suddenly she didn't know what to do, afraid to move or to say anything for fear that he would read the terrible hunger in her eyes. Her fingers were trembling as she began to spear the roses into the vase. She could hear him moving behind her, could feel his body heat, though he wasn't touching her.

'So what are we going to do about it?'

'What?' she questioned weakly, for his breath was warm against her neck.

'This.' His hand moved round to cup her soaking breast, and he closed his eyes as he felt it peak against the palm of his hand. 'You're so wet,' he murmured.

Her knees sagged, and she gripped the forgotten flower, hard. 'Ow!'

He turned her round. 'What have you done?'

She was staring at her hand, hazily aware of the scarlet contrast of blood against her pale skin. 'Pricked myself. On the thorn.'

'Let me see.'

She lifted her eyes to his as he took her hand and studied the injured finger. And then, very deliberately, he raised it to his mouth and began to suck on the blood, his eyes never leaving her face, and it felt almost indecently erotic.

'Dimitri,' she whispered.

'*Ne?*' His voice sounded muffled against her skin.

'Stop it.'

'The bleeding? That is what I am trying to do, *agape mou*.'

He was wilfully misunderstanding her, but she didn't care. It felt like heaven to have him touch her again—the aching familiarity mixed with the delight of the new and unknown. And yet she despaired. One touch and she was jelly. Marshmallow. Everything that was soft and sweet and subtly overpowering. And hadn't it always been like this?

He took the finger from his mouth and leaned forward and kissed her instead. She could taste the saltiness of her blood on his lips and she closed her eyes, swayed, gripped his shoulders, pressing her fingers hard into the silken sinews of his flesh, feeling him shudder and glad of it, sensing a barely restrained abandon which matched her own.

He took his mouth away from hers and looked down at her, his eyes black and glittering with both danger and promise. 'Take this off,' he ordered, his fingers inching beneath the soaking vest-top to feel the cool skin beneath.

But Molly was about as much use as a statue, frozen to the spot with desire, and he gave a little click, and then a slow smile as he shook his head in mock reprimand.

'It seems like I will have to do it myself,' he murmured. He peeled the top over her head and tossed it with arrogant disregard onto the floor and then he stared down at her lace-covered breasts, as if he had just unwrapped the most delicious present. And some of his habitual control slipped away. 'Oh, Molly,' he moaned softly. 'Molly.'

She knew that his groaned delight was for her breasts, and the prospect of what was to come and she wished it was more than that—of course she did. She wanted to know that the pleasure was because it was *her*, and her and only her. But that was a woman thing—wanting more than a man was prepared to offer.

'Oh, God!' Her head jerked back as his lips began to tease the tip of her breast through the bra, so that the lace felt like barbed wire on the sensitised flesh. She gripped his dark head between her hands as he opened his mouth and began to suckle her. 'Dimitri, don't!'

He ignored her, drifting his hand down over the flat of her stomach, snapping open the poppers of the little denim skirt she wore, so that it fell uselessly to her feet. Had she worn the tiny little garment knowing the ease with which it could be removed? he wondered. His finger skimmed aside the tiny panel of her panties and slid into the honeyed slickness of her flesh. Did she always make herself so delightfully accessible?

Again, the hot shaft of jealousy shot through him, fuelling a hunger which was already near-combustible and he moved his hand away, heard her squeaked protest, and lifted her up into his arms instead.

Dazedly, she looked up at him. It was like something out of a dream and yet nothing could be more real than the way she felt. Every nerve ending felt sizzling, sensitised, clamouring for him.

'What are you doing?'

The strain of trying to think straight made his voice harden. 'What do you think I'm doing?' he ground out. 'You want that I should take you here, in the kitchen, among the roses and the pots and pans?'

Any minute now and she was going to explode. 'Just take me somewhere; anywhere,' she begged. 'Upstairs.'

Despite the heated flames of his building desire, there remained in him a coolly questioning part which wondered if the journey upstairs would give her time to change her mind. But then he noted the rosy flush which outlined her high cheekbones, the fevered glittering of her eyes and he knew that she was as hell-bent on this as he was.

And her eagerness disconcerted him almost as much as it satisfied him. For equal desire meant that there would be no mastery. If her longing matched his, then they were going to be on an equal playing field. And he was a man who usually delighted in a sense of mastery.

He thought of going upstairs. To the bedroom she had shared with her husband? Or perhaps to the spare room, where she usually took her lovers? A shiver of distaste ran through him.

He shook his head, and he dipped his head, kissed her lips and felt her tremble. 'No. Not upstairs.'

'W-where?' she questioned dazedly, as if it were his house and not hers.

He carried her from the kitchen, straight into the sitting room and she looked around her. 'Dimitri?' she questioned, in a kind of befuddled daze, but by then he had reached the huge sofa, and had put her down and was turning to draw the heavy velvet curtains so that the room was dimmed with the surreal glow of blocked-out daylight. 'H-here?'

He turned back and began to walk towards her, kicking off his shoes and unbuttoning his shirt as he did so. 'Why not?' He saw her eyes widen as the shirt fluttered to the ground like a white flag of surrender, and the irony of that did not escape him. For hadn't he once told himself that, if she were the last woman on earth, he would not make love to her again? No matter if she fell to her knees before him and begged him to. But he had been young then, hotheaded and impetuous. He unzipped his trousers and stepped out of them and it satisfied his male ego to hear her gasp when she saw just how aroused he was.

But he honestly could not remember ever feeling as aroused as this. As if it were the first time and the last time and all the times in between.

He saw her bite her lip as he moved over her. He shifted away from her a fraction. 'Molly?'

She shook her head. It would be sheer folly and weakness to say that the sight of his body was unbearably poignant—for what conclusion would he draw from that? That there had been no other to compare with him? And there hadn't been, had there? Never.

She wrapped her arms tightly around his naked back and kissed him back, and there was something so evocative about that kiss that she had to will back a little sob.

He moved his lips to her neck, her breasts, and it felt like drowning in slick, sweet and honeyed waters from which there could be no escape—but who was trying? Not Molly. It had been too long. Much, much too long. She felt as though her body had been as dry and as arid as a desert, and Dimitri's lips were bringing her flooding back to life, her blood beating out a remorseless, drenching heat in her veins once more.

'Dimitri,' she breathed, and her hands came up to lock themselves around his head, imprisoning *him*, just in case *he* dared try to escape.

'I'm here,' he groaned, though he felt as if he had shifted onto another planet.

Oh, God, she wanted him so badly—but was she just asking for trouble and heartbreak? Resurrecting something which had hurt her so much. And hadn't the pain healed now? By letting him make love to her again, wasn't she in danger of reopening the wound and making it raw and livid all over again?

She pulled her lips away from his. 'I feel that I ought to stop you,' she said indistinctly.

'But you will not stop me.'

No. She could not. Not now. Not when he was sliding her panties down over her knees like that.

'Oh, God! Dimitri!'

'You like that?'

'Oh!' His fingertips were playing with her heated flesh, like a virtuoso playing some exquisite solo on the violin. Oh, sweet heaven—she would *die* if he made her wait much longer.

She writhed hard against him and heard him utter a curse, and she let her eyelids flutter open to see the dark helplessness on his face.

'What are you trying to do to me, *agape mou*?' he demanded, in a voice of dangerous silk which made her pulses race even faster.

She writhed again, driven by instinct and desire, unable to stop herself. 'What do you think I'm trying to do, Dimitri?' she murmured distractedly.

He caught a rope of her silken hair in his hand and possessively wound it round his fingers, drawing her face closer to his. 'I cannot believe that you know so little of men not to realise that if you continue to do that, then this will all be over very quickly.'

The inference was clear—that she had an encyclo-paedic knowledge of the opposite sex, but at that moment his fingers untangled themselves from her hair and he reached out to trace the outline of her lips with a fingertip touch which was so gentle that it disarmed.

'Take it slowly, *ne*?'

'I don't know that I can,' she said, a slight note of desperation touching her voice.

He tilted her chin with his finger, frowned as he looked into her face and felt the tremble of excitement in her body. 'You want me very much, Molly,' he observed, a note of surprise in his voice.

She heard the disapproval, too. Did he think she was like this with other men? Doubt shivered over her once more, but then he had begun to kiss her— soft, searching kisses which became harder, more frantic, seeking kisses with a power to dissolve every last lingering inhibition. She had this, and she was going to savour every moment of it.

'Make love to me, Dimitri,' she urged. 'Now. Please.'

He entered her with one slow, powerful thrust, impaling her, making her his and she felt it pierce her almost to her heart as he began to move inside her, almost passing out with pleasure as he began a slow rhythm, touching his lips to hers as he did so. It seemed so familiar and yet so poignantly different— and, oh, how could she have forgotten just how wonderful it felt, to be made love to by a man?

This man.

She wrapped her legs possessively around his back and heard him groan in response.

He lost himself in her dark, warm heat—giving himself up to sensation, but not completely—watching Molly, revelling in her own uninhibited pleasure, nearly going out of his mind as she moved in perfect synchrony with him. Her eyes were closed and her lips were parted. And only when did she gasp, once, his name, and her eyes snap open in a kind of startled recognition—did he allow himself to let go, and it went on and on and on. Unknown words were wrenched from his mouth as the sound of her small, gasping cries rang in his ears.

There was a time—how long, she couldn't have said—when they just lay there, gathering their breath, half-shuddering bodies still joined and slick with sweat, his head bent upon her shoulder, his lips pressed against her skin.

Molly stared at the ceiling. Now what?

Fighting sleep, she stirred a little beneath the weight of his inert body and realised that he had fallen asleep. She shook him, gently, her fingertips kneading into the oiled silk of his skin. 'Dimitri.'

From the depths of some heavenly dream, Dimitri made a little moan of protest. From some dreams you never wanted to waken.

'Dimitri!'

He felt himself stir inside her sweet, wet warmth. He was still asleep! He moved his body luxuriously against the soft, giving flesh which enfolded his.

'Will you wake up?'

Okay, he was awake, but the reality was even better than the dream. He smiled against her neck, realising that he was still inside her, and he began to grow hard once more, instinctively beginning to move.

She fought desire. Fought her greedy wish to have him do it to her one more time, but, oh, it wasn't easy. 'Dimitri!' she said, as sternly as an irate schoolmistress.

His eyes opened, taking in his surroundings with

a sense of disbelief. Here. On Molly's sofa. In Molly's sitting room. In Molly.

He groaned as he withdrew, and looked down at her face, all rosy and glowing, the icy-blue eyes slitted by lids which were heavy and drowsy.

She met his impassive gaze and in that moment she felt a million miles away from him—but then, she had to face it, she was. Just because they still had that whatever-it-was which made them dynamite together sexually—well, it was nothing more than that. Chemistry. Attraction—call it what you wanted.

'Molly,' he said softly.

She was not going to be an emotional limpet. She was going to think like a man, even if inside she felt as vulnerable as any woman. 'Mmm?'

'That was…amazing.'

A tinge of hysteria nearly surfaced. She felt like asking him for marks out of ten, but she didn't, just kept the dreamy smile of fulfilment pinned to her lips, which wasn't exactly difficult. 'Yes, it was,' she agreed calmly.

He levered himself up onto one elbow, and idly lifted a stray strand of damp hair from her forehead and that one gesture almost broke her resolve. For that was how it had started, wasn't it? All those years ago. The same thoughtful, almost gentle action which seemed so at odds with the strong, powerful Greek with the ruggedly handsome face.

'So now what do we do?' he questioned.

'You mean, as of—right now?'

That had not been what he had meant, at all, and

she knew it. Left to him there was only one thing he would like to have done after making love to her and that was to make love to her all over again.

But he had to be sure of what Molly wanted or expected—and she had to know what his own agenda was. If she was one of those women who had started thinking hearts and flowers and happy-ever-after just because he had given her a spectacular orgasm, then this would—unfortunately—be the first and last time, however difficult he might find it.

Usually, his demands were met because he stated them openly and honestly, but this was going to be more difficult. In truth, it felt different from usual, but maybe that was because they had history between them. Molly had known him at the height of passionate and impressionable youth. He had told her things he had never told another woman, not even his wife—and Molly had to be certain in her mind that the man who had said those things no longer existed. How could he, after everything that had happened? Time took from you, as well as giving—and his idealistic dreams had long ago given way to the constraints of life in an adult world.

He bent his head to kiss the tip of her nose and saw her quickly shut her eyes.

'Molly?'

She opened them only when she had had time to compose herself. Whatever he said next she would deal with. She had no choice. She rubbed the tip of her finger along the outline of his mouth. 'What?'

'Shall we be lovers?'

Her heart lurched beneath her breast. 'I thought we just had.'

'I mean again.'

She knew that it would be uncool to ask for a timescale, but she needed to get things straight in her mind. 'You mean while you're in England?'

Dimitri narrowed his eyes. 'But of course.'

Well, that told her one thing—he certainly wasn't thinking long-term. He was here for weeks, no longer. The only question was whether she wanted to be his lover, although it was a pretty academic question. Of *course* she wanted to be his lover, but could she do it and survive with her heart intact?

She gave him a considering stare. 'You're saying that you want an affair?'

'Why not?'

She could think of plenty of reasons, but none that a man would understand, and especially a man like Dimitri. 'With no strings?' she asked.

His eyes narrowed in a swift look of surprise. 'That is supposed to be *my* line, Molly,' he murmured.

She knew it was, but she had deliberately taken the initiative away from him. If she let him lay down all the guidelines that would give him a position of power and she was only going to allow this to happen if power were shared. As equals.

'That's not an answer,' she pointed out.

He gave a soft, low laugh. 'Strings are the very last thing I want, or need. I am here for a little over a month—no more and no less. After that, I return to Pondiki.'

With his appetite presumably satisfied, and with her left feeling…what? Regret?

But wasn't life too short for that? After all, she was a mature woman now, and she was divorced. Maybe an affair with Dimitri was perfect for her at this stage in her life. Wasn't that the kind of decision that grown-up women made?

She wasn't looking for love—and if she was, she certainly wouldn't go looking for it with *him*. Neither did she want commitment—a man living with her, a one-on-one relationship with all the heavy demands that brought with it. She had already tried that and it hadn't worked.

And, yes, he had reacted badly all those years ago. He had accused her of things she had not done, even though he hadn't bothered to tell her that he was intended to another woman, but that should not have surprised her either. Because the man she had fallen for was precisely the kind of man who would be insanely jealous, who would live life on *his* terms without considering whether she should also live by those terms. He was, at heart, rather old-fashioned and that was part of his charm. It was not, she realised now, what she would want for a partner if she were looking for a partner—which she *wasn't*. But that didn't disqualify him from having the perfect qualities for a lover, did it?

'What about Zoe?' she asked.

His face grew shuttered. 'What about her?'

'Won't she mind?'

'She won't know, Molly.' There was a silence. 'This is just between you and me.'

Well, what had she expected? That he take her next door by the hand and introduce her to his daughter as his latest girlfriend? Giving their 'no strings' affair a veneer of respectability. 'So you're talking about a secret, clandestine affair?'

'There is no point in Zoe meeting you, surely you can understand that?'

'Oh, perfectly.'

He could hear the tremble of hurt in her voice. 'Look, I know it isn't ideal—'

'No, it isn't ideal!' she agreed, wondering if her objections would be enough to scare the hell out of him, to make him go away and find someone less demanding. And perhaps that would be best for them all—certainly for *her*. 'Dimitri—'

He shushed her by putting his finger on her lips and she answered by nibbling at it. He winced, but the slight discomfort turned him on. Unbearably. He remembered the scratch-marks she had once left on his back because, she'd told him, he had treated her like a second-class citizen in front of his friends. Maybe he had done, maybe he had been showing off—unwilling for his friends to see the macho Dimitri Nicharos doing the bidding of the blue-eyed Englishwoman who, by rights, should not have lasted beyond a few days. He had had to cover up with a T-shirt for a whole week and he had accused her of branding him and she had smiled a witchy kind of smile and kissed the weals she had made.

'Molly,' he soothed.

'You think I want to be hidden away, as if I'm something to be ashamed of!' She very nearly said that at least on Pondiki he had been open about it. But wasn't that because back then he'd had no responsibilities? But he had, a cynical voice in her head reminded her. He had had Malantha waiting patiently in the wings. Who knew what was going on in his current life—with all its secrets and its different compartments? 'Maybe you should find someone else.'

'But I don't want anyone else,' he said patiently. 'You are all the lover that any man could want, *agape*.'

'I sense there's a "but" coming.'

He nodded. 'But I have a daughter.'

'And you usually keep your lovers secret from her, do you?'

He shook his head. 'Usually there is no need because usually I travel solo,' he said. 'This is the first time that Zoe has been abroad with me.'

Molly was silent for a minute. Even his honesty about his 'usual' lovers hurt, when it had no right to hurt. What had she expected him to say? That she was the first lover he had taken since his wife had died? And wasn't that what she would have liked, deep down? She was doing exactly what she had vowed not to—giving him a hard time. Making demands that could not be met. Entertaining hopes which would not be met. Either she took what was on offer, or she turned her back on the proposal without another thought.

'I am a good lover, Molly,' he murmured.

'Oh, the arrogance, Dimitri! The conceit!' she mocked back. And the total lack of comprehension that women didn't choose lovers because they were dynamite in bed. Women chose men with their hearts, not their bodies—that was the difference between the sexes and that was where the danger lay.

But the flip side to danger was excitement, and excitement was what Dimitri was offering her. Yes, there was a risk that she would be hurt again, but what was life without risk? A life lived safely to safeguard against possible hurt was surely no life at all.

His thumb began to stroke at the cool flesh of her inner thigh and Molly felt herself squirm.

'That isn't fair,' she said weakly, feeling him stir in response, hard and pushed against the soft cushion of her belly.

'What isn't?'

She licked the finger that she had bitten. 'Using depraved methods to get me to agree to what you want.'

'Depraved? You think *that* is depraved? Molly, you haven't seen anything yet.' With a smooth movement, he pulled her to lie on top of him and entered her when she wasn't expecting it, and she sucked in an instinctive breath of protested pleasure.

'Dimitri!'

He began to move. 'Mmm?'

'I haven't given you my answer yet.'

He moved again, and he was taken aback by how good it felt, as good as before. No. He groaned. Better. Much better. With an effort, he opened his eyes, looking up at her to see her caught up in the rapture herself, her neck and breasts still rose-smudged from the time before. 'Then what is your answer to be, Molly?'

She touched his eyelids with her fingertip. Then his nose and his lips, as if rediscovering his beautiful face, even while their bodies were joined so intimately, and she was filled with warmth and an unbearable longing. 'It's yes,' she choked. 'You know it's yes!'

For how could it ever be anything else?

CHAPTER SIX

'WHAT time is it, *agape mou*?'

Molly peered over at the clock on the bedside table. 'Nearly twelve,' she yawned.

They were lying in bed. The sun was streaming in through the cracks in the blinds, which meant that they had precisely an hour before Dimitri would shower and dress and arrive home in time for Zoe to return. His arrivals and departures were like clockwork—and even the intervening hours had developed a pattern. They made love. She made coffee. They talked and then they made love again.

And then one of them would notice the time and Dimitri would sigh and shrug, and she would pretend not to care as he sauntered naked across the bedroom into the shower.

Sometimes Molly wondered whether his daughter found it odd that his hair was always damp at lunchtime, but she didn't ask. The last thing she wanted to do was to waste time checking up on the mechanics of how he was managing to keep the whole thing a secret.

She rolled over to face him, the sheet swathed around her body. 'Want some coffee?'

He propped himself up on one elbow. 'No.'

'You don't?'

'Not if it means you leaving this bed.'

'Then you'll have to go without, I'm afraid—I'm a little bit short of servants!'

He turned onto his back and stared at the ceiling, wondering what was troubling him. This should have been a dream scenario, and in a way it was. In bed with the most passionate woman he had ever known, with no questions asked and no demands made. The perfect no-strings affair and perfectly suited to Dimitri and his lifestyle.

He thought of the way her mouth had moved over his body only minutes earlier and some dark demon reared its head. He wondered how many conversations like this had taken place, with men like him. And when he was gone, how long would it take for her to replace him with another? A black wave of jealousy rose up to envelop him.

'Do you always bring your lovers here?' he asked.

Molly stilled. 'I'm sorry?'

He gave a faint, cynical smile. 'Prevaricating, Molly? You won't offend me, I can assure you. I simply asked whether you always brought your lovers here.'

She could only see his profile, stony and unyielding. 'What kind of a question is that?' she asked, in bewilderment.

He turned his head to look at her. 'You don't want to answer?'

'I don't think it's any of your business. I don't ask you about any of *your* lovers, do I?'

He shrugged. 'Ask away. What do you want to know?'

'That's the whole point—I don't want to know anything!'

'I don't believe you. Women are always curious.'

Maybe the women he usually slept with *were*, but maybe they were more used to playing this no-strings affair game than Molly was. Better equipped to deal with the inevitable outcome of such affairs. And besides, the questions she would liked to have asked him weren't 'Who?' or 'When?' or 'Where?' or 'How?' but the way they made him feel. And no answer he could give would ever satisfy her. 'Not this one,' she said stubbornly.

'Well, *I* am curious,' he murmured.

'Tough!' she said crossly. 'Is that how you get your kicks, then? Discussing who came before, and how much better you are at it than them?'

He smiled. 'Molly! You pay me a great compliment!'

'Oh, do shut up!'

He watched as she sat up and angrily tossed her head, the pale tumble of hair spilling down all over her shoulders. It was a gesture he had known so well and forgotten until this precise moment and he was disconcerted by it. 'You look like a goddess,' he whispered.

But she steeled her heart against his words. 'I bet you say that to all the girls!'

He frowned. 'Molly, you are very flippant.'

Well, of course she was—because what was the

alternative? Let a murmured compliment like that go to her head? Have her sighing and cooing and imagining it meant more than the fact that all he wanted was to make love to her again? Well, he could want in vain—she wasn't there to do his every bidding. She was an independent woman, and she was going to behave like one.

She threw the sheet aside and stepped out of bed.

'Where are you going?'

'To make some coffee. Would you like some?'

No, he would not like some, but he recognised the light of determination in her eyes. And besides, it was an entrancing spectacle to have a bristling, indignant Molly walking naked across the room. He lay back on the pillows and watched her. She moved like a dream, with her long, long legs and that high, firm bottom and rose-tipped breasts which were so lush.

'I can't think of anything I would prefer,' he said sardonically. She looked at him, and burst out laughing and he held his arms open. 'Molly,' he murmured. 'Come back to bed.'

'No!'

'Come on.'

It was terrible, but she did. Climbed back in and let him take her into his arms to feel the warm yielding of her flesh and the inevitable rush of heat.

He kissed her neck. 'You know you don't want coffee, *epikindhinos* Molly,' he whispered against her ear.

She closed her eyes. 'What's *epikindhinos*?'

'Look it up.'

'Tell me!'

'Dangerous,' he said slowly.

'Oh.' She quite liked that. He was dangerous, too.

He nibbled at her ear. 'Tell me about your books, then, if you don't want to tell me about your lovers.'

'Books?' She didn't want to talk about *anything*. She wanted him to make love to her again, and obliterate all the doubts and insecurities from her mind. 'What books?'

'What books?' He laughed. 'The books you write! Had you forgotten them?'

'Oh, those.'

'Yes,' he teased. 'Those.'

She had to frown to concentrate—almost as though she *had* forgotten, but then maybe she had. Her other life—her real life—seemed like a distant dream, a misty memory. As if the only life she had was the one here, in this bedroom, telescoped into the few short hours she saw him every day. Really saw him.

She didn't count the snatched glimpses, when she caught sight of him through the window, when he was returning having taken Zoe out somewhere. Then she would duck out of sight, afraid that he would think she had been watching out for him. Hiding back in the shadows of the curtain, like an obsessed woman with a guilty secret—which was crazy. She wasn't doing anything that she should be ashamed of, and neither was he—not really.

And if he had a somewhat over-developed and

protective attitude towards his daughter, then who was she to criticise? She couldn't really blame him for wanting to keep Zoe in the dark about their affair. Greek fathers ruled by example—and if he was seen to be having a casual affair with their next-door neighbour, then what kind of message would that send out to her? Especially as he was never going to see Molly again.

'I write books about different cities,' she said slowly. 'Especially for women. A woman's-eye view on a place, if you like. The kind of places they can go without getting harassed. The best hotels for women on their own, the places to visit and the places definitely *not* to visit, that kind of thing. I've done Rome and London and New York and San Francisco. Next month, I'm doing Paris.'

'But not Athens?' he mused.

She shook her head. 'No. Athens doesn't really have a big enough appeal. Most people just use it as a stepping-stone to get somewhere else—like the islands.'

'So why don't you write about Pondiki?'

'Because I won't write about anywhere that isn't already a tourist trap,' she said vehemently. 'Pondiki would be ruined if people discovered just how beautiful and unspoilt it was.'

He ran a fingertip across the tip of her breast and she shivered. 'You loved my island, didn't you, Molly?'

'Of course.' She stared at him as though it was a given, but her memories of it were all interwoven with her love for him. 'It is probably the most beautiful place I have ever visited in my life.' She closed her eyes, and could see it all quite clearly in her mind's eye. 'That blue, blue sea and all that soft white sand. Deserted beaches—'

'Not quite so deserted these days,' he put in. 'The tourists have discovered Pondiki's beauty for themselves. There are more people than you will remember.'

Molly opened her eyes and grimaced. 'You don't mean it's become *commercialised*, do you?'

He smiled at the expression of outrage on her face, then frowned. 'Fortunately, no. We saw mistakes being made elsewhere in the Aegean, and were determined not to follow them.'

'And how did you manage to do that?'

'A couple of us got together—and tied up most of the available land.'

'Your hotel must be doing well, then.'

There was a pause. 'Yes.'

'And who is running it while you're over here? At the very height of the season, too!' she teased.

Again, he hesitated, and Molly thought how uncharacteristic that was.

'My sisters' husbands are in charge,' he said. 'And two of my nephews.'

'Gosh, quite the little empire!'

He shot her a quick look. 'It's still a family-run business, Molly, the way it always was.'

'Don't frown,' she said lightly, and rubbed her finger against his brow.

He smiled as he stretched luxuriously, and flipped over onto his stomach. 'Make me relax, then.'

'You want me to massage your back?'

'And the rest.'

'You'll have to turn onto your back if you want *that*!'

He turned over again, and looked at her through narrowed eyes. She was so generous, so giving of her body. She gave with as much pleasure as she received. He groaned as she began to tiptoe her fingers up his leg, and beyond.

'Molly, where the hell did you learn how to do that?'

'No questions, Dimitri. Remember?'

'Yes,' he groaned. 'I remember.'

There was silence for a while, until he moaned softly as her mouth worked its sweet magic, and then he pinned her back onto the bed and kissed her where she was moist and soft and warm, until she bucked and called his name out loud, in a cry that went on and on. He sent a wry look towards the open window and Molly saw it, pushing her hair back from her flushed face.

'I made a lot of noise.'

He smiled. 'A little.'

'It's a good thing Zoe isn't there.'

'Yes. Speaking of which…I'd better get going.'

'Better had,' she agreed lightly. 'She'll be back soon.'

He glanced at her. 'You think I'm an over-protective father?'

'I think you're a very *Greek* father.'

'Which doesn't answer my question.'

'How can I possibly say what you are or what you aren't, Dimitri? I've never been a parent, so I haven't got an earthly clue.'

'So why not?' he asked suddenly. 'Why not a parent?'

She stilled. 'Oh, you know…things.'

'What things?' He lifted her fingertips to his lips and began to tease them with his teeth. 'I don't know unless you tell me.'

'Is it relevant?'

'Mmm?' The nip became a kiss. 'To what?'

'To us. To what we have.' Oh, Lord—did that sound as though she was building it into something it wasn't? 'I mean, do you really need to know?'

'On a need-to-know basis,' he reflected thoughtfully, 'no. I don't. But I would like to know. Is that not natural? You cannot compartmentalise an affair to the extent that it's just no-holds barred sex and off limits for everything else.'

But wasn't that exactly what he usually did? Didn't he normally steer clear of any line of questioning which might throw up emotion? And didn't the fact that he was breaking one of his own rules spell out the word he had used to her earlier? *Epikindhinos.*

She shook her head. She felt vulnerable and exposed and not just because she was lying naked in bed next to him. She hadn't expected him to ask questions like that, and certainly not now. How could you talk about the non-fulfilment of your dreams in a few snatched moments? 'We haven't got time for this discussion,' she said, looking pointedly at the clock. 'You've got to go.'

It was rather ironic that because she was virtually ordering him to leave, he wanted to do the exact opposite. How contrary was human nature? he wondered wryly. He was more accustomed to the scenario of women begging him to stay. Elusiveness could be very provocative indeed—but ultimately, he reminded himself, it was all just a game played between the sexes.

He went into the shower, using the soap and shampoo he had installed in there, telling Molly that it might arouse suspicions if he went home smelling of lavender!

Yet it was crazy, it was as if he were leaving something of himself here. Some kind of territorial marking. His soap. His shampoo. Bizarre, or just expedient? Because this wasn't an affair like any other he'd had, was it? The normal rules did not apply, which was maybe why he seemed to be breaking them. She lived next door, and his daughter was with him.

And he knew her.

Or did he?

Did the past have more powerful tentacles than you gave it credit for? Playing tricks with your memory and with time itself—so that it seemed easy to shrug off today, and to lose yourself in part of yesterday?

How much of the eighteen-year-old Molly remained in her today, any more than the eighteen-year-old Dimitri did in him? How much of character was formed then, and how much evolved by the trials and the hurdles you had to leap over in life? He had had an explosive sexual compatibility with Molly then, and that much had not changed. She had always been able to make him laugh, and that much had not changed either.

But she had always been able to infuriate him, too—and to drive him wild with a jealousy which raged like a black demon inside him. He had always put that down to the difference in their respective upbringings, but maybe it was something more fundamental than that.

Just to look at her was to want to possess her, and that kind of possession constrained and tied you in a way in which he did not want to be tied. A way which was incompatible with life as he liked to live it.

'Have you drowned in there?' she called from the bedroom.

'Yeah—come and give me mouth-to-mouth resuscitation!'

He walked back into the room, tiny droplets of water still drying on his naked body, rubbing a towel at the wet ebony hair, and his mouth hardened when he saw her.

She had put on some oversized towelling robe. A man's? It made her look a beguiling mix of innocence and sensuality, and she had made a tray of coffee which was scenting the air with its bitter, pungent aroma.

It was a scene which mocked a domesticity they would never have, the kind of cosy scene which should have sent him running straight out of the door.

He pulled on his boxer shorts and Molly thought how incredibly beautiful he was, how graceful for such a big, strong man.

He looked up to find her watching him and something he read in her eyes made his mouth dry, until he remembered. 'It's the weekend,' he stated flatly.

She looked up from the steaming cafetière. 'So it is,' she said lightly.

'And I won't be able to see you until Monday.'

'No. That's right.' She had been practising for just this moment. 'Planning to do anything special?'

He frowned. She was rewriting the script, and he didn't like it. She might have had the finesse to look even a *little* bit disappointed.

'You're frowning again,' she teased.

He ignored that. 'Are *you*?' he questioned. 'Planning to do something special?'

Well, what did he expect? That she would be sitting around the place mooning over him? Hoping to catch a brief, furtive glimpse of him over the garden wall—their eyes sending silent, frustrated messages? Gazing with longing as he took Zoe off somewhere?

'I'm going to a gallery tomorrow afternoon, and then out to dinner with some friends in the evening.'

'Oh. Which gallery is that?'

'Tate Britain. They've got a huge exhibition of Rembrandt—it's supposed to be quite something.'

'Maybe Zoe might like to go along. She likes art.'

Molly raised her eyebrows at him. 'And accidentally bump into each other, you mean?'

'Why not?'

'Because it's dishonest, that's why,' she found herself saying. 'It's pretending to be something it's not. A casual meeting—which isn't casual at all! And maybe she might pick up on the fact that we're...' Lord, but it was a struggle to find socially acceptable words for a no-strings relationship! 'More friendly than neighbours usually are.'

He gave a faint smile. 'What a delightful way to describe it.'

'Perhaps you could come up with a better description?' she questioned sweetly.

He looked at her with frustrated admiration. Had he thought that this would be easy? With *Molly*? The getting her into bed had been a piece of cake, but she was somehow managing the impossible—of being more intimate than he felt entirely comfortable with, while managing to hold him at arm's length!

'Look, maybe we could have lunch on Monday?' he suggested.

'Where, here?'

'No, not here!' he exploded. Anywhere but here! Nowhere within a fifty-metre radius of a bed! 'There must be a restaurant, locally.'

'Of course there is.'

'Well, then.'

'What about Zoe? What will you tell her?'

'Oh, Zoe has made friends with another Greek girl. She can go back with her after school, she'd like that. We'll have lunch on Monday—how's that?'

How *was* that? Well, considering he had simply asked her out for a meal, her heart was pounding with the kind of excitement she couldn't remember feeling in a long, long time. Was he finding the trysts in her spare room claustrophobic? she wondered. Already?

'I'll book it, shall I?'

He began to button up his shirt and nodded. 'Book it,' he agreed.

'And you'll come round here first?'

He saw the fire of sensual hunger which lit her eyes from within, and smiled. He knew what she meant, come round and go to bed with her first.

'No. I'll pick you up just before one,' he said coolly.

CHAPTER SEVEN

THE small Italian restaurant was noisy and crowded and the waiter greeted Molly with a beaming look of surprise. *'Signora!'* he exclaimed. 'It is too long! Where have you been?'

Molly smiled back. 'Oh, I've been around,' she said. 'Just busy, that's all.'

'My sister—I send her your book all about Roma!'

'But she lives there, Marco,' said Molly seriously as she took her seat. 'Why would she want a guide-book?'

'Because my sister, she not like my mother! She and her friends—they like to go places without men, and your book tell her where.'

'Your English is improving,' said Molly diplomatically.

He shrugged. 'My girlfriend is Italian. We don't speak English.'

Dimitri took the menu he had been offered with a thin smile. Perhaps she should invite the waiter to draw up a chair!

Molly leaned forward. 'What would you like to drink, Dimitri? This meal is on me.'

He went as still as if she had suddenly leapt up on the table and started dancing on it. 'You are not paying,' he said flatly.

'Oh, yes, I am,' she contradicted and saw the glower on his face. 'For heaven's sake! Think of all the meals you bought me on Pondiki!'

'You had little money—you were a student.'

'And now I do, and I'm not a student any more. People often go Dutch, these days.'

'I have never been bought lunch by a woman,' he said darkly.

'Then why not try it?' Her eyes glittered. 'You could be in for a treat.' She shook her head as she saw his expression. 'I thought you might have moved a bit more with the times.'

It was difficult to shrug off an attitude which had been ingrained in him. 'I will buy lunch today,' he stated unequivocally. 'To repay you for your party. Next time, you can do it.'

She opened her mouth to object and shut it again, seeing from the resolute look in his dark eyes that to object would be pointless. And wasn't there a stupid side of her which loved the mastery which spilled over into all other aspects of his life? You didn't get to be such a consummate lover as Dimitri without some of the arrogant assurance he was demonstrating right now.

'Champagne?' he questioned.

'Are we celebrating something?'

'I thought you liked champagne.'

'Yes, I do. Thank you.'

Marco brought over the bottle, poured them two glasses and stood waiting for their order for food, though for once Molly lacked her usual enthusiastic appetite for the delicious Italian food she could smell.

'Know what you want?' asked Dimitri, with a quick look at the menu.

'The same as you,' she said.

He raised his eyebrows only fractionally and then proceeded to give their order in fluent and seamless Italian and, after Marco had gone, Molly leaned back in her chair, cradling her cold champagne and looking at him ruefully.

'I'd forgotten you spoke Italian.'

'And Spanish,' he reminded her arrogantly.

'Must be handy for lovers, being able to converse in their tongue!'

'I prefer to converse with *my* tongue,' he said wickedly, touching his glass to hers and enjoying her furious blush.

'That was completely uncalled for!'

'You started it,' he pointed out. 'Are we going to argue our entire way through lunch?'

'No.'

'Then stop sulking.'

'I'm not.'

'Yes, you are—do you mind telling me why?'

It would be completely outrageous to tell him the truth, surely? 'You didn't even kiss me when you picked me up.'

'Ah.' He removed the glass from between her fingers and put it on the table and placed his own next to it, then enfolded her hand between both of his instead. 'You know why?'

'No, I don't.'

'Because when I kiss you, it drives me crazy. It makes me want to take all your clothes off and to make long, slow and passionate love to you.' His eyes glittered. 'Or hard, fast passionate love to you!'

Her fingernails bit into the palm of his hand. 'Dimitri, stop it,' she urged desperately.

'Am I making you want me?' he teased.

'You know you are.'

He let go of her hand and put the champagne back. 'Drink this instead.'

'I'll be as high as a kite!'

'On one glass?'

She didn't like to tell him that she felt high already, before she had taken even a single sip. But that was the effect he had on her, and maybe she didn't have to tell him. Maybe he knew.

And besides, his physical effect on her wasn't what was in question, was it? So what was? Their compatibility outside the bedroom? No. Lovers didn't need to be compatible—they just needed to be able to get through the occasional restaurant meal, for propriety's sake, without falling straight into bed.

'Look, here comes our starter!' she said.

'Oh, good,' he said drily.

She pushed a bit of Parma ham around on her plate. 'Look,' she said conversationally. 'It's so thinly sliced that you can see the plate through it.'

'Are we going to make small talk?' he asked.

She looked up, the unwanted ham forgotten. 'So

that's no arguing and no small talk. Could be a bit limiting, Dimitri. What do you want to talk about?'

He glowered at the piece of melon on his fork, comparing it to its infinitely sweeter and more succulent Pondiki equivalent. What did he want? Why, perversely, when he avoided in-depth conversation like the plague—did he find himself wanting one with Molly?

Because the past made them comfortable together, and he wanted to catch up. And Molly was sensible and liberated enough not to read anything into it— why, it had been *her* who had suggested the 'no strings', hadn't it? And taken the wind right out of his sails into the bargain.

'Tell me about your marriage,' he said suddenly.

'My *marriage*?' She blinked at him. 'Why would you want to know about that?' Had she thought— hoped—that he would be jealous of Hugo?

'I am interested to hear about the man who won your heart.'

It seemed a curious way for him to describe it— an overly romantic description which seemed a world away from the cynical man who sat in front of her. Maybe that was true for him and Malantha—but it was certainly not true for her.

'Don't you know that you can never get an objective opinion on someone from their ex-spouse?'

'Do you hate him, then?'

She shook her head. 'Oh, no, I don't hate him. It makes it all seem so pointless if I do that—anyway, there's nothing to hate.' And that had been part of the problem. She had felt all the *right* things about Hugo—all the things she had thought you were supposed to feel about the man with whom you wanted to spend the rest of your life. Respect, liking, admiration. All those worthy qualities which turned out not to be worth anything when they weren't laced together with a healthy dose of passion.

But Molly had been frightened of passion. She had seen the stormy extremes it could provoke in her. And men might initially be attracted to a passionate woman, but in the end they chose the quieter, calmer, safer option for a lifetime commitment. Look at Dimitri and Malantha.

So she had quelled her passion, though that had been easy with Hugo. It had been her mind he had fallen in love with, or so he had said. And although at the time she had been immensely flattered by that, it had not been a strong enough glue to cement an honest relationship between a man and a woman.

'We were complete opposites, really,' she said slowly. 'He kept my feet on the ground and I guess I helped him let his hair down a bit. I admired his steadiness, and he liked my get-up-and-go.'

'So what was he like?'

It was tempting to say that he was as unlike Dimitri as possible, but she didn't. What would that say about why they were sitting here together today?

'Quiet. Bookish. Clever,' she said slowly.

'He doesn't sound your type.'

'Thanks.' She pursed her lips together in a wry

smile. 'Which bit? The clever? The quiet? Or maybe even the bookish?'

'I did not mean that. It is not a very flattering way for a man to be described,' he observed.

'What would that be, then?' she challenged. 'Rampant stud?'

His eyes grew steely and cold. 'Is that how you see me, then, *agape mou*?' he questioned silkily.

'Well, partly,' she said truthfully. 'But you're clever, too. But I didn't come out for lunch to compare you to my ex-husband.'

'No.' He sat back while Marco took their plates away. 'Did he want children?'

She bit her lip. 'Dimitri, that's an incredibly personal question!'

He leaned forward and took her hand again, rubbing it softly with the pad of his thumb. 'You don't think that what the two of us have been doing together entitles us to ask questions like that?'

She shrugged. Wasn't he in danger of confusing sexual intimacy with *real* intimacy? But when she thought about it—why shouldn't she tell him? Her desires would not affect him, and anyway—he had a daughter of his own and she was very nearly grown up.

'We talked about having children, of course—in that vague, hopeful way that you do when you get married. And of course, we always put it off for various reasons—you know, we wanted a bigger house, and then we had to remortgage the house to start the business. Then we worked all hours to get the business up and running, and when we could finally afford to have them we looked around and realised that we didn't love one another any more.'

'Just like that?' he echoed sardonically.

'Well, no, of course not. We tried going to counselling, but that didn't work, and I think we were about to call it a day when Hugo fell in love with someone else and that, in a funny kind of way, seemed to make it easier.'

'And he married her?'

'No, but they live together. Both of them think that marriage is an overrated and outdated institution and neither of them want children.'

'And do you…?' He paused for a moment and nodded his thanks to Marco who had removed their starters and replaced them with two steaming plates of chicken and pasta which he suspected that neither of them would touch. 'And do you think it an outdated institution, Molly?'

'Of course,' she said lightly. 'Unless you have children, of course—then it's different.' He was topping her glass up; she hadn't even realised that she had finished the first, and maybe that was what gave her the courage to ask her next question, even though he had been quite open about quizzing her about *her* marriage. But then, *her* marriage wouldn't give him any pain, would it? And that was where the imbalance lay.

'What was your marriage like, Dimitri?'

He had known that this was coming, and she had been honest enough with him, but it was still difficult to talk about. 'I guess it was over almost before it began—we barely had any time together,' he said quietly. 'It seems such a long time ago now.' He was quiet for a moment. 'It was. A very long time. There was so much adjustment, to life as man and wife—and then to becoming parents.'

'It must have been…hard. Not to have had much time together as a couple.'

'Yes.' His expression was one of acceptance. 'But it was the way things were.'

'And Malantha?'

He smiled. 'Malantha was sweet and sound and she adored me.'

Somehow she got the words out, telling herself that she had no right to be jealous, no right at all. 'And you adored her too, presumably?'

'Yes, I did,' he said simply. 'She was easy. Comfortable. No stress. No worries.'

She wanted to say to him, Then *why me*? Why, if you adored each other so much, did you make love to me and take my heart and then break it up into tiny little pieces? But she did not say it. Now she understood that passion could be separated from the common goal that he and Malantha had shared. And maybe he guessed at her unasked question, for he seemed to answer it with his next words.

'We had grown up together,' he explained. 'We shared the same experiences, the same hopes, the same dreams. We wanted a big family—lots of children running around, brought up with the same values that we had known.'

It was so different from the world she had been brought up in, and for the first time Molly was able to see that what had happened had perhaps happened for a reason. For what would have been the alternative?

Just say, just say that Dimitri had loved her as deeply as she was sure she had loved him. Thinking it through—did she really think it would have worked if the fairy-tale scenario had come true? Her as his young bride, her studies abandoned. Living in a starkly different culture with people who were hostile towards everything she stood for?

The scales fell from her eyes and the realisation brought with it a sadness—for seeing youthful dreams for what they were was always sad—but also a regenerating kind of freedom.

'Go on,' she said softly.

'But what we both wanted was not to be. Fate had other plans for us.'

She wanted to stroke his hand, to tell him that she was so terribly, terribly sorry, but she knew that it would be the most inappropriate thing of all, so instead she said nothing. His deep, silken voice sounded very distant.

'And unlike you, there were no reasons to put off having children. We think that Malantha became pregnant on our honeymoon....'

He seemed reluctant to continue, but something made her prompt him; she didn't know what, because the honeymoon bit had hurt like hell and there was doubtless worse to follow. But not for her. For him. 'Go on,' she said, again.

Her words barely registered. 'It was a…difficult pregnancy. Malantha needed a Caesarian and they had to send a helicopter to Crete. She…she took a long time to come round after the operation—the anaesthetic had affected her badly. They said that might have been a contributing factor.'

There was a pause and Molly scarcely breathed. Suddenly the hubbub and jollity of the lively restaurant faded into nothing. All she could see and hear was the man with the pain etched on his face and in his voice.

'She suffered a pulmonary embolism,' he said finally. 'And when Zoe was just three days old, she died.'

This time she did take his hand. She didn't care what he thought. Sometimes human beings needed comfort, proper physical, tactile comfort. She squeezed his fingers and he looked at her, his eyes clearing, like someone who was coming out of a bad place.

'I've never told that to anyone before,' he said simply. 'Not since it happened.'

She could imagine. He had needed to be strong. For the new baby. For his family and, presumably, for Malantha's family too, who must have been heartbroken. And who could the strong, capable Dimitri Nicharos possibly confide in? Who would he dare confide in, for fear of appearing weak, and less of a man? His tears must have been shed in private, his grief borne alone.

And suddenly his behaviour became understandable. Who could blame him if since then he had avoided commitment? If he compartmentalised his pleasure so that it would not intrude on the close and loving unit he had built up with his daughter?

Her own worries and fears became puny and insignificant in comparison. She lifted his hand to her mouth and kissed it, very, very gently.

'Malantha would be so proud and so pleased if she could see Zoe now,' she said softly. 'I mean, I've only spoken to her once, but she seems polite and sensible. And she is just so very beautiful.'

He smiled. 'Yes. And she's pretty bright, too. She wants to become a doctor.'

'That's a long, hard training,' she observed.

'I know. But she's had her heart set on it since she was a little girl.'

Suddenly she badly wanted to be on her own with him. 'Dimitri, shall we go?'

He withdrew his hand. Picked up his glass of champagne and drained it in one. Then glanced at his watch. 'No pudding?'

'I'm not hungry.'

'No.' Their eyes met. 'Me neither.'

'You can…pay the bill if you really want to,' she said.

'Is that a climb-down?' he questioned.

'Of sorts.'

His eyes smiled. 'Or split it?'

'Okay,' she said breathlessly. 'We'll split it.'

It felt like a victory of sorts, and when they walked out into the bright summer day he caught her in his arms, so tightly that she had to struggle to breathe.

His expression was fierce when he looked down at her. 'Do you know what I'm going to do now, Molly Garcia?'

She shook her head, even though she had a pretty good idea. But she wanted to be told.

He put his mouth to her ear. 'I am going to take you home and undress you and make you undress me and then I will spend the rest of the afternoon making love to you until you beg me to stop.'

'And what if I don't?'

'Then I won't stop.'

She shivered with excitement and an almost unbearable sense of expectation and she had the courage to link her arm through his. Until they turned the corner into the street and she removed it like a person snatching their hand from a fire.

'Oh, Lord,' she moaned.

For there, walking towards them from the opposite direction, was Zoe.

CHAPTER EIGHT

DIMITRI said something very softly in Greek.

'What shall we do?' hissed Molly.

And something in her frantic tone told him that this was all in danger of getting out of hand. 'We're neighbours, remember? Neighbours can go out and eat lunch together,' he said. 'Act normally.'

What was normal at a time like this?

She smiled rather helplessly at Zoe, who didn't seem at all fazed to see her walking side by side with her father.

'Papa!' She smiled her blindingly beautiful smile. 'Hello, Molly!'

Dimitri looked at his daughter and frowned. 'I thought I was due to collect you later this evening, from Cara's house?'

'I changed my mind.' Zoe shrugged. 'Cara had a boy round.'

'A *boy*?' exploded Dimitri. 'What boy?'

Zoe sighed. 'Just a friend of Cara's, Papa.'

'Where is he now?'

Zoe began to look alarmed. 'Papa, it's nothing. Really.' She shot Molly an agonised look as if to say, Help me!

'Don't you think you're overreacting a little, Dimitri?' said Molly mildly. 'She *is* getting on for

115

sixteen.' He shot her a furious look and she realised that she had said too much. A neighbour would never have started dishing out advice to a man like Dimitri unless they knew one another very well. She just hoped that Zoe wouldn't guess how well.

'Where have *you* been, Papa?' Zoe asked.

'Don't change the subject!' he thundered. 'How did you get home?'

'On the bus.'

'The *bus*!'

'Papa, *everyone* takes the bus.'

'Not my daughter! You should have taken a taxi!'

They drew up outside Molly's house and she let out a small sigh of relief. 'Well, time I was going,' she said. 'Nice to see you again, Zoe. Call round any time you like, you're very welcome.'

'Thank you,' said Zoe.

'Bye, Dimitri,' said Molly casually. She lifted her face to his, wondering if he would send a silent see-you-tomorrow message with his eyes, but his eyes were as coolly distant as if they had just been introduced for the first time. No, cooler than that—positively icy. So was he angry with *her*? For being caught with her in the first place? Or was he thinking that she had interfered by trying to intervene when he was arguing with Zoe?

Well, damn you, she thought as she let herself into the house. She thought about all the sad things he had told her and the way he had coped but that didn't change a thing. He could not and should not get off with behaviour like that. Just because you had had to cope with terrible tragedy in your life, it didn't give you carte blanche to treat people as though they had no feelings to hurt.

She wondered did he think he would just stroll round tomorrow and she let him, and that they would go straight upstairs and undress and make mad, passionate love and then off he would go, his face a study of innocence.

Then he was wrong.

What had she been thinking of? To imagine that she could tolerate such a 'relationship' with a man to whom she had once been so close. Accepting whatever scraps he saw fit to throw at her. To settle for so little from someone who had once meant the world to her.

Deliberately, Molly set her alarm clock early, showering and dressing to be out of the house by eight, when she knew that Dimitri and Zoe would be at breakfast.

She walked up to Hampstead village where she went shopping for clothes she neither wanted nor needed. Forcing herself to go through the mechanics of trying on skirts and T-shirts and dresses. Sifting through the sale racks with a lacklustre hand until she came away from them empty-handed.

She went to a pavement café and sat outside drinking a cappuccino, but the world seemed full of lovers that morning. Real lovers, mocking her with their open displays of affection—not lovers hiding away, as if they were doing something wrong and shameful.

She browsed in a bookshop and bought a couple

of paperbacks she had been meaning to read for ages and ate a Caesar salad for lunch in the adjoining restaurant. And only at two o'clock, when she was certain that Zoe would be home and that Dimitri wouldn't dare come round—God forbid!—did she wend her way home.

But she was just putting her key into the front door lock when she heard a silky dark voice behind her.

'Hello, Molly.'

She didn't look round. 'Careful, Dimitri,' she said sarcastically. 'We could be seen! Even now, there could be paparazzi lurking in the bushes waiting to capture us for all eternity.' She opened the door and turned to face him, but he pushed her inside and closed the door shut behind them.

'What the hell do you think you're doing?'

He steadied his breathing, tempted to kiss her, but he did not want to seduce her into rational thinking. If she couldn't think straight without being in his arms, then what was the point? For an uncomplicated 'no strings' affair, things certainly didn't seem to be going according to plan!

'Where were you this morning?'

'That's none of your business.'

'I thought we had an arrangement.'

'Oh, did you? You mean another surreptitious assignation? I'm surprised you were afraid to risk it after nearly being caught out yesterday!'

'Molly…Zoe knows.'

Her eyes flashed. 'Knows what…exactly?'

'She saw us coming down the road together and

she came to the conclusion that we were in some way…involved.'

Clever Zoe. 'But she doesn't know that we were…lovers…all those years ago?'

He shook his head. 'No. On a need-to-know basis, I didn't think that was necessary.'

'And was she shocked? Horrified?'

'No.' In fact, his daughter's reaction had surprised him. He had a couple of male friends—one American and one English—who had told him that their off-spring had made their lives a living hell when they had become involved with other women. Though maybe it was different for divorcees, than for wid-owers, he reflected.

Far from being angry, or jealous, or appalled at the thought of her 'Papa' seeing a woman, Zoe had given him a lecture on how it was about time and that he was only thirty-four and should not behave like a hermit. That you only had one life to live and that she thought it was a good idea he had started to go out with women, and that she gave him her bless-ing.

Her blessing!

He had sat there, bemused, listening to the oddly mature speech from his daughter and wondering when she had started to grow up so much, and how had he come to miss it along the way?

He shrugged, and suddenly he looked about eigh-teen again and all the fight went out of Molly and she put her arms around him, put her cheek next to his.

'I'm sorry,' she whispered.

'No, I'm the one who should be sorry.'

'Shall we toss for it? Whoever wins is the sorriest?'

He started laughing and he put his arms tight around her waist. 'Ah, Molly,' he sighed and kissed the tip of her nose. 'Tell me what is it that you want from me?'

She didn't answer for a moment. He would expect, and he would receive, a calm, considered response, not some emotional outpouring of impossible desire from a woman old enough and experienced enough to know better.

She took a deep breath. 'There's nothing wrong with what we have. An affair suits me fine.'

'It does?'

'Sure. Why not? It's just all this secrecy stuff I don't like.'

'Well, there is no need for secrecy; not now. Zoe knows.'

'I know she does—but that doesn't really change anything. I mean, you can't just come round and disappear inside and the blinds come down and two hours later—hey, presto!—you're back again! Can you? Where is she now, by the way?'

'She and Cara have gone to the cinema.'

Her heart leapt, and she cursed it. 'She may be mature, but she's still your daughter—and daughters are notoriously bad at recognising that their fathers are entitled to some kind of sex-life.'

He winced slightly at the baldness of her statement. Sex-life. But what she said was true, wasn't it? Did that sum up what they had? All they had?

'And quite rightly so.' Molly shuddered as she continued. 'I could never bear to think of my own mother and father doing it—I mean, who can?'

His smile was indulgent as he ran the flat of his hand down over the pale, blonde sheet of hair which tumbled down past her shoulders.

'Molly, Molly, Molly. You want that we should do other things? More exciting things?'

She widened her eyes deliberately. 'Just what *are* you suggesting, Dimitri? Swinging from the chandeliers? Bondage?'

'Molly!' he protested. 'Be serious!'

But she didn't dare. Keeping it light and flippant meant that she could keep the whole thing in perspective. He might feel bad about the furtiveness and the secrecy, but that didn't mean that he was suddenly pulling another, more committed option out, did it—like a magician pulling out a rabbit from a hat?

'I'd just like to do some other stuff,' she said. 'Apart from the bed bit.'

'What kind of stuff?'

She moved her shoulders restlessly. 'Oh, you know—normal stuff. Walks in the park, that kind of thing. Taking a boat down the river. Everyday things which are so much fun.' She saw an odd kind of expression on his face. 'What is it?'

'You don't want to go shopping?' he said drily.

'You don't want jewels, or designer clothes and meals in fancy hotels?'

She understood the implication immediately, but she wasn't tempted or seduced by it. She had always been happy with the simple things in life—especially with him. 'Is that what women usually want from you, then?'

'They try. Women are fond of symbols, and status.'

'Well, I hope you don't give in to them,' she said crossly, any jealousy of the other women in his life momentarily eclipsed by indignation that her own sex could behave in such an outrageously mercenary way. 'You may have a share in a gorgeous hotel on a Greek island, but that doesn't make you Rockefeller!'

He gave a comfortable, lazy smile. 'I never give what is asked for; gifts should only ever be given freely. Come, Molly.' He kissed the tips of her fingers. 'It is a beautiful day. Let us go and find your park.'

But she shook her head. 'No, not today,' she whispered and she coiled her fingers into the rich, ebony silk of his hair, pulling him towards her so that she could feel the hard, sinewy jut of his hips. 'Today I want you to take me to bed.'

He groaned. 'But you just said…'

'I know I did. But I'm a woman, Dimitri and I'm entitled to change my mind. If you'd tried to take me to bed, I'd have wanted to go to the park.'

'There's only one way to shut you up, Molly Garcia,' he murmured.

'And what's that?' she questioned innocently, but she knew what the answer was even before he began to kiss her.

'That?' he murmured into her mouth.

'That,' she agreed.

He pulled his mouth away and smiled and she looked up at him, feeling oddly shy, as if all her defences had somehow been stripped away, leaving her vulnerable and open. He planted a kiss on each eyelid. Small, sweet kisses which ensnared her more than the deep demonstration of passion might have done. Left her shaking inside.

'You want to take me upstairs?' he questioned.

'I—I guess.'

He followed her upstairs and they removed their clothes swiftly, almost clinically, as if they couldn't wait to be rid of them, then they lay on the bed and he felt her soft sigh as their warm flesh met, and he ran a reflective finger around her mouth.

'Wouldn't it be great to spend a night together?' she blurted out, then saw his face close and wished she could unsay it.

'And maybe we will,' he said idly. But he never spent a night with a woman. If you slept with a woman it put things on a different footing—a too-intimate footing. The little things like brushing teeth and taking a bath together—somehow those things spelt danger. Took things onto a different sphere.

'Oh, I'm not fussed,' she said convincingly. 'You probably snore!'

He smiled at this and then bent his head to kiss her. And kiss her and kiss her and kiss her.

'Dimitri,' she gasped, against his mouth.

'Ne?' But his tongue flicked sensuously inside her mouth.

'Dimitri,' she said again, indistinctly.

'What is it, *agape mou*?'

'Oh, Dimitri,' she half sobbed. 'Dimitri!'

Now she was squirming against him, her body inviting him into hers in unspoken plea and he made a little imprecation against her mouth, slipping his hand between her thighs, feeling her hot and slick and ready. This was not how he had planned it. He had planned to take for ever, but it seemed that for ever would now never come. He was powerless, he realised helplessly, as with a small moan he entered her.

Afterwards, they lay in silence for a while, and Molly was sure that Dimitri had fallen asleep, when he spoke.

'So maybe you might like to come round to my house?'

She sat up in bed, frowning, looking down at his face to properly understand what he meant. 'You mean, to go to bed there?'

'No. Very definitely not to go to bed there. But as Zoe knows we are…friends—'

'Interesting choice of word, Dimitri,' she commented drily.

'There seems no reason why you shouldn't meet socially.'

It sounded like the opposite to taking someone home to meet their parents, thought Molly, slightly hysterically.

'And she should mix with more English people,' he added.

Well, that very definitely let her know where she stood! When she wasn't making love to the father, she could engage in polite conversation with his daughter!

'Sounds good to me,' she said steadily.

'Why don't you come round for tea, next Saturday?' he suggested casually.

'I'd…I'd love to.'

Which was how Molly found herself next door sipping Earl Grey tea the following Saturday, with Dimitri and his daughter, in the sunny sitting room which mirrored her own.

Zoe *was* very bright—almost precociously so, thought Molly—but she seemed eager to talk about all the kinds of things which girls of that age invariably did. Fashion, mainly. She was going to be a very elegant doctor, thought Molly ruefully as she eyed her linen crop-trousers and a matching little top which showed off a perfectly flat midriff.

Molly was just telling her about the latest outrageously expensive designer shop in Notting Hill, where all the season's must-have clothes were, when the telephone rang and Dimitri threw them both a questioning look. 'Seems like I'm pretty superfluous to requirements,' he commented with a smile. 'That's a call I've been expecting—mind if I deal with it?'

'Oh, no, Papa,' said Zoe quickly. 'Take as long as you like.'

'I think I can just about take a hint as big as that one,' he said drily.

But the fashion-fest dried up just as soon as he had left the room, and Zoe put her cup down.

'Molly?'

Molly smiled. 'Zoe?'

'You are close to my father, yes?'

Tricky. 'Well, we have become friends.' And that was the truth. 'Why?'

Zoe sighed, her beautiful full mouth expressively turning down at the corners. 'He thinks I am going to be a doctor.'

'Well, that's because you *are* going to be a doctor. Aren't you?'

Zoe shook her head, the thick black hair which hung almost to her waist swaying like a pair of satin curtains around her oval face, and for one brief moment Molly saw Malantha sitting there. 'I don't want to. Not any more.'

'That's okay,' said Molly easily. 'Lots of girls change their minds about their career choices. What did you have in mind instead?'

There was a pause. 'I want to be a model.'

And then Molly understood. Or rather, she saw it how Dimitri would see it. 'Oh, Zoe—are you sure? It's such a competitive world. I mean, I think you're very, very beautiful—well, you are—and I'm sure you've got what it takes. But there are hundreds of girls out there who want to be models.'

Zoe nodded. 'I know this. But an agent in America has given me a card.'

'Do you *know* him?' asked Molly worriedly.

'Her,' corrected Zoe with a smile. 'The agent was a woman. I am not stupid. I checked the agency out and her credentials. It is one of the top agencies in the world. I can earn a lot of money, Molly. And see the world.'

'Are you quite sure you've changed your mind about medicine?'

'Yes.' Zoe nodded her head with firm resolution. 'Once, I cherished that dream, but no more. I don't want to do it any more, and I have to make Papa understand that. He is so...*old-fashioned*...with me. He hates me wearing make-up and he hates me seeing boys, even as friends.'

'Maybe he's just trying to protect you,' suggested Molly gently.

'But I would never do anything to lose my father's respect,' declared Zoe. 'He has to realise I'm growing up, and I must be free to choose how I live my own life.' There was a pause. 'And you can help me, Molly.'

Molly shook her head. 'Oh, no. No. Definitely, no. I have absolutely no influence over your father. Why would he listen to me?'

'Because you have talked to me. Tell him that I have thought it through—that it is not just some mad idea of a young woman. I can be a successful model,

I know that.' She struck her hand over her heart. 'In here.'

Molly smiled. Youthful passion—how clear and yet how blind it could be! 'Can't you tell him that yourself?'

'He will not listen to me. Our roles are too clearly defined, Molly—surely you can see that?'

'What about someone back home? Another woman who knows you both well? Someone you can confide in?'

Zoe shook her head. 'There is no one. Papa's sisters would think the same as him. They all treat me as a child. And sometimes it is better if an outsider steps in, you know? What is it that you say? They have no axe to grind.'

She really *was* a clever girl, thought Molly. Her assessment was accurate and true, if painful. The outsider. Yes.

But she sighed, unable to steel her heart against the look of appeal in the huge black eyes. Hard to believe that she had only been a few years older than her when she had first met Dimitri. Then she had thought she had known everything, just as Zoe did now.

'I'm not promising anything,' she said.

'Just promise you'll speak to him,' begged Zoe. 'That's all.'

All? Did she have no comprehension of the formidable will of her father? It was at that moment that Molly realised just how young Zoe was. 'Okay,' she said reluctantly. 'I promise.'

CHAPTER NINE

MOLLY'S face was thoughtful as she brushed her hair, clouds of newly washed blonde hair surrounding her face like a halo.

Dimitri watched her reflection in the mirror. 'Deep thoughts?' he asked.

Of course. All good things came to an end. There was a season for everything. He was going tomorrow and although she had resolutely tried not to think about it, sometimes her resolution failed her.

'Just thinking,' she said.

'About tomorrow?'

'No, about my tax return!'

He laughed, but it was a laugh edged with regret. Things changed. People changed. You could never predict the outcome of anything, he knew that. All he *did* know was that tomorrow he would be heading back to *his* world and leaving Molly in hers.

'It has been wonderful, Molly,' he began slowly, but she shook her head, so that the blonde hair flailed from her head, like the rays of the sun.

'No!' she said quietly. 'I don't want to go there. I don't want to spend our last few hours talking about what's happened, in the past tense. It *has* been lovely, yes. It was what it was, so let's just leave it at that, shall we?'

He pulled a shirt on. If this was one of those unspoken ultimatums, then she had better understand that he would not be forced in a corner. 'Sure.'

But Molly's nerves had been on edge this morning for another reason, too. She had made a promise to Zoe and she could not put it off any longer.

'Dimitri, I don't quite know how to say this.'

He stilled, his senses on alert. Here it came: the ultimatum. 'Say what, *agape*?' he queried, his eyes warning her not to say anything which she would regret.

Molly read the message and took heed of it, even though she was filled with a sense of sadness. Don't worry, Dimitri, she thought—I'm not about to tell you that I love you and that my heart will be broken the day you take your flight out of Heathrow. Even if she was beginning to suspect that it was true.

'It's about Zoe.'

His body language remained just as forbidding. This was not her territory and she had no right straying into it. 'What *about* Zoe?' he questioned repressively.

'Dimitri, she still thinks that you treat her like a child!' she blurted out. 'And I'm afraid that I agree with her.'

'Molly,' he said warningly.

She ignored the warning. And the flashing look of displeasure in his black eyes. 'I think you've got to understand that she's growing up. Fast.'

'I do not intend having this conversation—'

'Well, you're going to have it!' she retorted,

blanking the thunderous expression on his face, as if he couldn't believe that someone had just spoken to him like that. Maybe people didn't—and that couldn't be good, surely? 'She says that she isn't allowed enough say in matters, or enough freedom—'

'Freedom?' he echoed tightly.

'Yes, freedom! It's what teenagers crave—it's the loosening of the bonds which tie them—the thing which puts them on the road to independence!'

'The freedom for her to paint her face?' he roared. 'To behave like a tramp? To indulge in under-age sex...' He saw her face and stopped. 'Molly, I didn't mean—'

'Oh, please don't try to backtrack now!' she snapped and rose to her feet, her voice trembling with rage. 'You know exactly what you meant! And for your information, Dimitri—I was *not* under age when we first had sex! I was eighteen years old, young, yes—but it was legal! I hadn't planned it that way, but it's hardly a capital crime.' And she had loved him—but from the look on his face he didn't want to be reminded of *that*.

'Are you advocating free love for my daughter?' he questioned.

'Of course I'm not! She's only fifteen!'

'Exactly!' he thundered.

They glared at one another and Molly steadied herself. She wasn't exactly being much help to Zoe if she continued with a slanging match and started bringing her *own* feelings into it.

'Dimitri,' she said quietly. 'You know that the world has changed since we were young. Even on Pondiki.'

Yes, he knew that. 'I am not guilty of living in the Dark Ages, Molly—I simply want to protect my daughter.'

'Of course you do—but you can't wrap her up in cotton wool. You can just guide her and teach her your values and hope that she wants to emulate them.'

'You think that my values are worth teaching, then?'

There was a pause. 'Only you can answer that. But Zoe finds life on such a small island constricting. Surely you can see that.' She took a deep breath. 'She wants to be a model, you know.'

He shook his head as if she were mad. 'She wants to be a doctor,' he contradicted.

'Not any more. An agent who was on holiday on the island gave her a card and told her to call. A top New York agency. She thinks that she has what it takes, and Zoe wants to do it. Badly,' she finished.

He felt as though he had been slapped in the face. 'Who told you this?'

'She did, of course!'

'She has never once mentioned it to me!'

'No, of course she hasn't. She's scared to. She thinks that you will be upset because she no longer wants to do medicine.'

'I never said that!'

'Well, have you discussed the future with her? Lately?'

'She's too young to know what she really wants. If she no longer wants to be a doctor, then that is fine—but not modelling. No, not that.'

'She is *not* too young, Dimitri! She's going on sixteen, for heaven's sake! She's really very mature for her age—and that's hardly surprising considering the knocks she's had in her life!'

It occurred to him that this was really none of Molly's business, but she seemed to know more about his daughter's wants and needs than he did. Had he been guilty of wrapping her in cotton wool, as Molly had said?

Molly's courage was growing by the minute. She had nothing to lose—Dimitri would soon be gone from her life—and she owed this to Zoe. Maybe in a funny kind of way she owed it to Malantha, too.

'She loves you very much,' she said carefully. 'But feels she can't really talk to you—'

'The way she can with you, you mean?' he interjected silkily.

The silence which followed seemed to go on for an eternity. 'And just what is that supposed to mean?'

Dimitri's black eyes were like some hard, cold metal. 'It hasn't ever worked before, and it won't work this time,' he said obliquely.

'You're speaking in riddles, Dimitri,' she said, in a low voice. But she knew exactly what he was getting at. She just wanted him to say it aloud, knowing that when he did it would shatter everything they had ever shared, even the past. And perhaps that was best.

'Trying to inveigle your way into my life by whatever means it takes. Making yourself my daughter's confidante—and an invaluable one. I am not looking for another wife, Molly, and she is not looking for a substitute mother.'

She stood up to face him. 'And I'm not looking for another husband and even if I were…' she paused deliberately for effect, injecting the words with the meaning she really felt at that moment, as strongly as if it were tatooed onto her skin '…even if I were, it would not be you! A man stuck in the Dark Ages! A man who picks women up and then puts them down again as he would a cup of coffee!' She headed towards the door.

'Where do you think you are you going?' he demanded.

'Where do you think? To buy my trousseau?' she spat out sarcastically. 'I'm going downstairs while you finish dressing! And then you can get out!'

'Don't go!'

'Oh, no!' She shook her head. 'You can't talk to me like that and you can't stop me, either! I am not your possession, Dimitri, and neither is Zoe. Children are only loaned to you, you know—you have to learn to let them go!'

He took a deep, steadying breath. 'Have you quite finished?'

'No, I have not! Because I'll tell you something

else, Dimitri Nicharos! I *agreed* to become your lover, and I must have needed my head examining! You're just as bloody hotheaded and narrow-minded as you ever were! You still see the world according to *you*, and your prejudices—without bothering to look at the whole picture!' She moved towards the door.

'Do not walk out of here!'

She laughed, hearing the slight tinge of hysteria in her voice. 'Why? Has no woman ever walked out on you before?'

'No,' he said, without thinking.

Something inside her snapped. It wasn't just his arrogance, though that was bad enough—it was his tacit acknowledgement of the women who had gone before her. Up until now she had accepted the knowledge of those women very calmly—she had had no choice—but in the light of everything which had been said, it just became too much to bear. Well, they were welcome to him!

'Don't go,' he said again.

'Just watch me!'

She wrenched open the door but he had moved across the room before she could make her escape and she shook her head, her eyes wild and frightened—not of him, and what he would do. She knew exactly what he would do—try to kiss her into submission, the way he knew he could. No, she was frightened of her own reaction, of her body responding to him while her heart and her mind told her that it was wrong. Disastrous.

'Don't you dare to lay a *finger* on me!'

'Molly, you are angry—'

'Damned *right* I'm angry!'

'And you have every right to be,' he said unexpectedly.

Molly blinked. 'I do?'

'Yes. You do.' There was a pause. 'I am sorry for the things I said, for the things I accused you of. Truly, truly sorry.'

She blinked. Dimitri sounding so *contrite*? It took the wind completely out of her sails.

'Do not leave, Molly,' he said again, very softly. 'Please.'

And a plea from Dimitri was about as subtly powerful as it was possible to be.

She leaned against the door and closed her eyes, composing herself before she opened them again.

'I was only trying to help,' she said.

He nodded. 'I know you were.' And he was a man unused to accepting help—from anyone. He had shouldered life and its burdens completely on his own, but now he recognised that Molly had no hidden agenda, other than telling him something which his daughter had felt unable to tell him herself. 'I know you were,' he said softly, and put his arms around her.

'Please, don't—'

'You don't mean that,' he murmured.

No, she didn't. Molly closed her eyes against his shoulder. This felt close, closer almost than any other time she had been with him. Safe and warm and secure in his arms. She relaxed into his big, strong body for a moment, and then pulled away. Because the haven he represented was just an illusion.

'We'd better go, hadn't we? Zoe will be home soon.'

'We have a little while yet.' He ran a reflective fingertip down the side of her face. 'And I don't want to go. Not yet.'

How could such a simple action have such a profound effect? Just a whisper of a touch could have her trembling. 'Dimitri—'

'What?' His lips followed the path of his fingertip and Molly shuddered. 'What is it?'

She wanted to say that making love wouldn't solve anything—but then, Dimitri probably didn't think that there was anything to solve. She wanted to say that they had only just made love and that every time they did it brought her closer and closer to him in a way which she knew in her heart spelt danger.

His mouth reached her lips and she didn't resist—couldn't, and didn't want to resist, if the truth be known. And she wound her arms around his neck, the gesture telling him tacitly that, yes, she wanted him, too. This might be the last time. She bit her lip. There was to be a farewell lunch tomorrow, with Zoe too, and then he was flying home. And that would be that. She would probably never see him again.

Is this the last time? she wondered desperately.

He led her back to the bed and his expression was almost tender as he began to unbutton her dress once more, his lips anointing kisses onto her aching flesh and driving all rational thought away.

Except for one. That this was a little like a savings account—like putting money away for a rainy day. Each time that Dimitri made love to her it would be something to remember him by.

After he'd gone.

Rather fittingly, there was a grey and relentless drizzle as Zoe clambered into the back of the taxi with the suitcases, which just left Molly and Dimitri standing on the pavement. The lunch had been fine, if a little on the superficial side. Nothing had been said about medicine, or modelling, for which Molly was inordinately grateful. She didn't want to spoil the day or her memories with an atmosphere—and she was grateful for Zoe's presence, too. Having her there meant that things were kept light and breezy. Lots of things were said, but nothing of any significance.

Molly took a deep breath. 'So.'

'So.' Dimitri smiled. 'It has been wonderful, Molly.'

'Yes.'

They looked at each other and he felt a frustrated sense of longing that he could not kiss her as he really wanted to kiss her. His daughter might like Molly, might know about their affair on some subconscious level, but knowing that something was happening in theory was a little bit different from actually seeing it acted out in front of you.

So he contented himself with a swift kiss. Or rather, the swift kiss left him feeling distinctly *dis*-contented.

Next time he came to England—and maybe it would be sooner than he had originally planned—then he would come alone. Though of course, by then Molly might have someone else…but that was a risk he would just have to take.

His eyes imprisoned her in a glittering ebony blaze.

'Goodbye, Molly,' he murmured. 'I'll ring you.' He hesitated, knowing that his next choice of word was important. If he said 'some time' it would mean never and if he said 'tomorrow' it would commit him to something he was not sure he wanted to commit to. 'Soon,' he added. 'Okay?'

'Okay.' She wasn't going to count on it, but she nodded anyway, and gave him a bright, grown-up smile. 'Goodbye, Dimitri,' she managed. 'Safe journey.'

She watched the tail-lights of the taxi retreating, and Zoe waving through the back window, and Dimitri beside her, his handsome face thrown into shadowed relief, so that it was impossible to read his expression.

Funny. They said that sorry was the hardest word to say, but saying goodbye to someone you loved had to come a close second.

CHAPTER TEN

MOLLY waited for Dimitri to ring, telling herself that she wasn't waiting at all. That she needed to be around the house—and then she found a good reason to be, because she started decorating the sitting room in dramatic shades of blue and grey. As if she wanted to change the externals in her life, to match the changes which had taken place inside, although she took care not to analyse *those* too much. Close scrutiny of her feelings might bring her to the conclusion that the love she had felt for Dimitri had been reborn in a new and rather terrifying form.

She spoke to her editor on the phone and agreed that she would fly out to Paris at the end of the month to start her new book. And she told herself that if he hadn't rung after three days, then he wouldn't ring at all, and even if he did she would be as cool as a cucumber.

So that every time the phone rang she deliberately counted to seven before she answered it. Until…

'Molly Garcia.'

'Mol-ly?'

A few days could seem like an eternity when you were waiting, and she seemed to have been waiting for so long to hear the rich, deep voice that now she finally had, it threw her. 'H-hello?'

140

'It's Dimitri.'

'Dimitri.' Deep breath. Take it easy. Don't show him how much this means. 'How are you?'

He thought of the long, aching nights. 'I miss you.'

She swallowed. 'You *do*?'

'Don't you miss me?'

Did she miss him? Oh, yes—she missed him all right. How was it possible to miss a man so much—when, up until a few short weeks ago she had consigned him firmly to memory?

'A little,' she murmured, and that *wasn't* being hypocritical—it was simply protecting herself.

'Only a little?'

'Mmm. I've been busy.'

'Oh.'

She thought he sounded—if not disappointed, then a little surprised. 'Think I've been crying into my pillow every night, do you, Dimitri?' she teased.

'Well, if you haven't been crying, what else have you been doing at night, Molly?' he purred. 'Shall I tell you what I've been doing?'

She blushed, even though he was thousands of miles away. 'Stop it.'

'Last night I dreamt that I was running my hands all over your body, Molly, and when I awoke…'

His voice had tailed off to a silky and suggestive whisper, and Molly knew exactly what he was doing. Or trying to do.

'I'm not having phone-sex with you, if that's what you're thinking!' she said crisply.

Her schoolmistressy tone was like having a bucket

of cold water tipped all over him, and as the ache subsided Dimitri gave a low laugh of pleasure. Did he really imagine that Molly would settle for dirty talk over the telephone?

He rubbed the back of his neck and yawned. 'So tell me what you have been so busy doing?'

'Oh, I've been painting the sitting room.'

'Mmm? Anything else?'

'And making travel plans for the next book.'

'In Paris?'

'That's right.'

'So when do you go to Paris?'

'At the end of the month.'

He did a hasty calculation in his head. 'And will you be too busy to see me?'

Her heart leapt with excitement and she cursed it. Some things you had no control over—like your body's reaction—but some things you did. Like your voice, and now she kept hers calm. 'I didn't think that was an option.'

'There is always an option,' he returned. 'How about if I meet you there?'

'Where? In Paris?'

'Why not?'

Her heart raced. 'Just like that? You can take another holiday when you've only just got back?'

'Not a holiday,' he answered quickly. 'You will be working and therefore I will be working, too.'

'But won't they mind you being away from the hotel again, so soon?'

'Do not concern yourself with that. Think instead of Paris…and all the fun we can have together.'

'Okay,' she said lightly, as if it didn't matter to her one way or the other. 'I'll meet you in Paris.'

'I'll book us a hotel.'

The thought of spending a night with him—a whole night—made her dizzy with desire, but… 'No, Dimitri,' she said softly. '*I'll* book the hotel.'

'Is this a replay of the restaurant bill?' he questioned wryly. 'An attempt to show me how independent you are?'

'Not at all. This is strictly business, not personal—and hotels are my business.'

'They're mine as well,' he pointed out, in an amused voice.

'But the whole point of me going to France is to research places for women to stay, whereas I assume you aren't planning to uproot a hotel and have it flown wholesale back to Pondiki?'

He laughed. 'So you're going to subject me to a place all pink and frilly?' he suggested sardonically.

'That may be *your* perception of what women like,' she laughed. 'But if it is, then I'm afraid you're way off the mark. Women these days want comfort and value for money.'

'And what else do women want, Molly?' he questioned softly.

She felt more confident now. 'I'll show you,' she promised.

'I can hardly wait.'

Neither could she. Never had a business trip held

more allure for her. He was there waiting for her at Charles de Gaulle, tall and striking, his black hair gleaming ebony beneath the airport lights, his narrowed eyes glittering with anticipation as she walked towards him, only just stopping herself from running and hurling herself into his arms.

But she was a woman in her thirties, she reminded herself as she had done again and again, and that was not how women her age should behave. She had told him that she would make her own way to the hotel, but he had insisted on meeting her—and wasn't there a stupid, feminine part of her that had *liked* him insisting, for all her protestations? Maybe, deep down, there was a part of every woman who liked a strong, dominant man, for all their hard-earned independence.

He watched her approach, thinking how the years had changed her. All the passion and the exuberance which had been so much part of her had now been contained and channelled into this coolly beautiful creature with her pale blonde hair and her icy blue eyes which matched her sun-dress. Oh, she still had passion—that much was not in doubt—but she only displayed it when he was making love to her.

Which should have made things perfect. Dimitri did not like overt and possessive displays of affection from his women, particularly in public. So why was he left wanting to shatter that calm demeanour of hers? Was it simply a case of wanting what he hadn't got? He was used to women who idolised him and put him on a pedestal and once Molly had been among their number, but then, he too had felt the same way about her.

But putting people on a pedestal was dangerous. It was such a lonely place to be and who could blame them if they fell?

'Hello,' she said, and wishing that this awful, inexplicable *shyness* would leave her. 'You didn't have to meet me, you know.'

'So you told me,' he said drily, and smiled. 'But here I am, and here you are—so let us waste no more time talking about it. Shall we go?'

No kiss, then.

'Let's.'

In the taxi, she turned to him. 'How's Zoe.'

'She is well.'

She didn't ask and therefore he felt free to tell her. 'The ongoing discussions about her future continue.'

She gave him a coolly curious look. 'And?'

He shrugged. 'She seems to be wearing me down.'

Molly hid a smile. It seemed that Dimitri was learning that he would never be truly happy unless his daughter followed her own dreams.

'You seem to have given her the courage to stand up for what she wants,' he commented ruefully.

'Good!'

'Fighting words, Molly,' he murmured, and ran a reflective finger over the outline of her lips, feeling the instinctive tremble his touch provoked. 'Will you fight me later, *agape mou*?'

'I…I hope I won't need to,' she said shakily. If there was any fighting to be done, it was with herself—telling herself to accept this for what it was, and not for what she wanted it to be. And if she were being practical, she knew in her heart that it could never be any more than this. There had been very good reasons why it had not worked before—even if you discounted their age—and nothing had fundamentally changed.

Their lives were still too different. And, yes, the relationship was now running over his original time-scale, but she would be mad to think he would ever marry her.

She turned her face to blindly look out of the window, appalled at the direction of her thoughts. A weekend in Paris and she was thinking *marriage*? How appalled would *he* be?

'We're here,' he said quietly, wondering what had caused her to move away from him like that.

In the suite they stood facing each other.

'What is it?' he asked, frowning.

'I'm supposed to be making notes on everything,' she said.

'You want to?'

'No,' she said, rather desperately.

He smiled. 'What do you want to do, then?'

'This.' She walked over to him, put her arms around his neck and kissed him, with a kiss that was deep and sweet and right.

He lifted his head, dazed by the power of it. 'Molly,' he said simply.

He undressed her. Slowly, almost tenderly, and then undressed himself and when they were both naked, on a bed and in a room which Molly had barely registered, he began to kiss her. To kiss her as if he never wanted to stop kissing her.

She opened her mouth to him as her eyes fluttered to a close, pulled his warm, hard body against hers and, moments later, into hers. And with each exquisite thrust, she gave a helpless little cry which soon— almost too soon—became a sound which was a mixture of sobbed fulfilment and an aching kind of regret.

He moaned her name, felt the world recede, and when his senses began their stealthy pulse back to something which resembled normality he felt the slick sheen of her tears against his shoulder and lifted her head, staring at her wet eyes with a frown.

'Tears, Molly?' he questioned sombrely.

If she wasn't careful she would blow everything with an over-the-top display of emotion.

She gave a smile and dropped a kiss on his parted lips. 'Sorry.'

'Why are you crying?'

She wiped them away. Don't go there, Dimitri. 'Oh, it's just a woman thing.'

'Tell me.'

She shook her head. 'Sorry—no can do!' She gave him a mock-stern look. 'We are creatures of mystery, didn't you know? Men don't understand us, that's what makes us so alluring.' She moved away from him, sat up and gazed round the room. 'Nice room,' she remarked.

'Mmm.' But he wasn't looking at the room. 'What do you want to do now?'

She would have liked to have spent the rest of the evening in bed with him and made love with him over and over again until they were both spent and fell into an exhausted and sated sleep. In fact, she wouldn't have given a damn if they didn't set foot outside the suite for the duration of their stay—but that wasn't why she was here. And that kind of behaviour was not only non-productive—it was extremely dangerous, too. She had a job and a living to earn. A life to lead, of which Dimitri was only a tiny, tiny part.

'I have a list of bars we should visit,' she said. 'And a restaurant I'd like to give a whirl. How does that sound to you?'

It sounded hell, if the truth be known. 'Fine,' he said flatly.

They put their clothes back on in silence, and Molly thought sometimes the act of getting dressed could be more intimate than getting undressed. Once the fires of passion had burnt out, there remained nothing but cold, harsh reality—and this reality suddenly felt very cold indeed. And it was intimate only in so much as the fact that she was putting on her underwear in front of him—a false intimacy, in fact—for there were no shared looks, or giggles or jokes or any of the accompanying things which would have occurred if they truly *were* a couple.

She pulled her sleek black jersey dress over her head, brushed out her hair and slid on a pair of high-heeled shoes which wouldn't normally have been her number one choice for sightseeing, but hell—surely this was work *and* pleasure?

Dimitri finished fastening his cuff-links and glanced up at her, his eyes as shuttered as his brief smile.

'Ready?'

'Sure.'

But Paris somehow managed to weave its subtle magic, despite the fact that she dragged him to four different bars where he moodily drank mineral water in each. Because only when they were seated face to face in a restaurant close to the Champs-Elysées and had been handed menus the size of large atlases did Dimitri allow his lips to break into a slow smile.

'You have exhausted me, *agape*,' he murmured.

She looked up from behind the menu, raising her eyebrows. 'After only once? Shame on you, Dimitri!' she teased. 'Why, in the old days you wouldn't have let me out of your arms.'

'That's because in the old days you wouldn't have wanted to!'

'No, well.' The French words danced unintelligibly on the page before her. 'Things change.'

'Do you wish they didn't?' he asked suddenly.

She put her menu down. This was deep, coming from him, and the expression in his eyes cautioned her not to be flippant. There was a time for flippancy, and it was definitely not now.

'Well, of course I do! Sometimes.' She drew a deep breath and let the words tumble out. 'There's a silly, romantic side to every woman who wishes that her first love could have worked out and that they had lived together, happily ever after.'

'But you think that's impossible?' he guessed.

She nodded. 'In ninety-nine point nine of all cases, yes—and very definitely in ours.'

He put his menu down. He had eaten little, but the food held no interest for him.

'And now?' he questioned softly.

It was one of those key questions—give the wrong answer and everything would be lost. She suspected that he was testing the ground, to find out just how serious she was and that if she came over as serious, then he would run as fast as he could in the opposite direction.

'I've learned not to look ahead,' she said slowly. 'Or to look back—there's no point, is there?'

He smiled. 'You mean live for today.'

She nodded, and, although it hurt her to say it, she knew that she must. Before he did. 'Yes. Because today is all we have, Dimitri.' All they would ever have. And after this weekend was over, they would each go back to their very different lives. She would have to learn to compartmentalise, just as he did, as all men did—otherwise she would be one of those women who yearned for the impossible, and the relationship—if you could call it that—simply would not survive.

'Shall we order?' she asked brightly.

'You order for me.'

'Me?' she squeaked.

'Sure. You're the one who has been studying the menu.'

Or giving the appearance of it. 'What do you fancy?'

He leaned forward, and beckoned her towards him, planted a kiss that lingered on her lips for far longer than it should have done, considering that they were in the window table of a restaurant, completely exposed to passers-by and other diners. But this *was* Paris—and Paris never frowned on lovers.

She closed her eyes briefly and drew away from the sensual invitation of his mouth. 'You— you…taste of sex,' she said weakly.

'I know. So do you. What was it that you asked me, *agape*?'

'I asked what you wanted to eat.'

'You,' he answered simply, and smiled at her look of shock and delight. 'Don't you know that in Greece we eat the women and the chicken with our fingers?'

'Dimitri.' She swallowed. 'I'm supposed to be reviewing this restaurant, and you're making it very difficult for me.'

'I know.' He pushed his menu away. 'Shall we go?'

'But we haven't eaten anything!'

'So?'

She put up one last, half-hearted fight. 'You'll be hungry later,' she warned.

'There's always room service.' His eyes flashed a stark black challenge. 'Come on, let's get your coat.'

She pushed her chair back. 'You're too used to

getting your own way,' she accused, and he laughed in response.

'Yes,' he agreed silkily. 'But we both know that what I want is what you want, too. You just wanted me to show you how much.'

She couldn't think of an answer, but then any rational thought was proving very difficult indeed. Other than the one glorious realisation that they were going back to the hotel for the night. *For the night.*

'You do realise that this is the very first time we've ever slept together?' she asked.

His face looked almost sad. 'Don't you know that I've thought of nothing else all evening?'

And then the taxi came.

CHAPTER ELEVEN

THE moon hung low over the sea, like a giant silver disc suspended in the dark sky by an invisible thread, and the reflection on the calm water was almost as bright as the moon itself.

Molly sighed. 'It's so beautiful, isn't it?'

But Dimitri didn't answer. She turned to him, seeing his profile as unmoving as if it had been carved from one of the rocks on which they sat, having just had dinner in a glorious open-air terrace restaurant just behind them.

The sounds of diners drifted out towards them, as did the faint burst of accordion music somewhere in the distance. She had thought that it had been a perfect evening, but Dimitri had seemed...distracted, almost. Not like him at all, though then she was forced to ask herself—how much or how well did she know him? Or he her?

Their relationship had continued—despite her fears that it would not—for just over a year since he and Zoe had left London. An exciting relationship—certainly as far as her friends were concerned. As Alison had said, what could be more perfect than meeting a man like Dimitri for wild weekends of uninhibited sex in some of the most beautiful cities in the world?

'You've got all the best parts of a relationship with a man, without all the dreary everyday things,' she had remarked. 'I tell you, if I never had to wash another shirt again or go hunting for that elusive stray sock, then I would be a very happy woman indeed.'

And Molly had laughed, and agreed.

But nothing in life was that simple, was it? She saw the best bits of Dimitri, true—so was it just something perverse and contrary in the female psyche which made her long for the other, normal, everyday bits, too? Not that she would ever be enamoured of hunting for his socks, of course. For a start, she knew he never wore any when he was on Pondiki, but as going there was never likely to be an option, then she wasn't likely to get the opportunity.

But she sometimes found herself longing wistfully to rub the strain away from his temples when he had had a long, hard day and then she found herself wondering whether that was just a sublimated maternal instinct.

Because, of course, there was the subject of children, too. Not with Dimitri—he already had his family, in Zoe, and she couldn't really see him wanting another one, not with his daughter going on seventeen and soon to fly the nest. But Molly's biological clock was ticking away relentlessly. If she wanted children she couldn't wait for ever.

And Dimitri had shown no sign of wanting to commit; she had never expected him to—but the fact remained that if she wanted children, then she was going to have to find a man to father them. Which meant falling in love with someone, and that was never likely to happen while she stayed with Dimitri.

Yet she couldn't bear the thought of letting him go. Catch-22, or what?

Sometimes she thought about it, telling herself that she was wasting her time with him—but could the intense pleasure she experienced in his company ever be described as time-wasting? If she tried broaching the subject with him, of suggesting that they both might like the freedom to look elsewhere—him for a suitable wife who could live with him on Pondiki and her for a potential father to a child she might one day have—then wouldn't that have the air of the ultimatum about it? And didn't he just loathe those? She had seen his reaction when she had brought up the subject of Zoe—he had imagined that she was pushing him into a corner, and his instinct had been to flee.

No, all things considered, she was content enough with what she had.

'Dimitri?'

He stirred himself from his thoughts, lapsing automatically into Greek, as he sometimes did when he was distracted. *'Ne?'*

She never knew what he was thinking, but then, when did she ever ask—and risk getting answers she did not want? No, it was easier this way. Light and loving—in the way that loving could be if it was never declared. Though she was only sure of her own feelings, not his, because Dimitri had never told her that he loved her—not in a year of meeting and travelling together. Of being, to all intents and purposes—a couple. She told herself that she was glad. Glad that he wasn't saying things he didn't mean, just to please her, but maybe that was because he was a sensible and pragmatic man.

Once you said those three words which shouldn't mean as much as they always did, well, then—things changed. Inevitably.

People started getting ideas and expectations. Declared love seemed to involve some kind of commitment to the future and that didn't fit in with either of their lives. Well, it certainly didn't fit in with Dimitri's—he had told her that, a long time ago— and what had happened to make him change his mind?

A couple could go on for years having just the kind of relationship as theirs—until, she supposed, one of them tired of it. Or until someone else came along... The shirt-washing and sock-hunting scenario often destroyed a romance—and romance was what they had. People put a high price on romance, they chased it and yearned for it. Now that she had it—she mustn't knock it.

'What did you say?' he questioned.

It was the kind of question which sounded inane when you repeated it. 'I just said that it was beautiful. It is, isn't it?'

'Very,' he said flatly.

She felt the first intimations of unease. He had definitely been in a preoccupied mood, now she thought about it—ever since she had met him at the airport. Now that Zoe was older, he was able to make their meetings more frequent, and yet over the past couple of months she'd suspected that something was driving a wedge between them.

Was he worried about leaving his hotel so much?

'And it was a lovely dinner,' she added, inconsequentially, as people did when they wanted to say something, but couldn't really think what to say.

'Lovely,' he agreed, still with that odd, flat note in his voice. 'Lovely dinner, lovely hotel, lovely view.'

The dark profile was still gazing out to sea.

'What's the matter?' she asked suddenly, and as soon as she asked it she knew that she had placed herself in a vulnerable position. An open question like that might mean he might tell her. Tell her what? That their affair had also been 'lovely' but now it was over?

He turned then and his eyes were glittering as brightly as the moon, but their message as enigmatic as the moon itself. 'Shall we go for a walk, *agape*?' he questioned softly.

It sounded like more than a simple invitation to do just that. It sounded…not exactly threatening, but filling her with a faint sense of foreboding. Molly looked down at the strappy silver shoes she wore, expensive designer shoes which matched the silver dress. Her heart was beating very fast. The palms of her hands were clammy, and it wasn't just the hot, balmy Mediterranean air. No, there was some unknown and steely quality to Dimitri tonight and suddenly she knew that whatever he had to tell her might be easier heard if they were walking side by side by a seashore.

'Sure,' she agreed, kicked off her shoes and picked them up. They were not as equal as she had thought they were, she realised. If they had been then she would have fixed him with a direct stare and asked him what he wanted to say. And she would have shruggingly accepted it whatever it was. So what had happened to the cool, calm woman who had decided that this was a grown-up affair and that she would regard it as that, nothing more and nothing less?

She had fallen in love and left her by the wayside, she realised. And like all women in love with a man who did not reciprocate the emotion, she walked on eggshells, even if she weren't aware that she were doing so.

Until now.

She watched silently as Dimitri took off his own shoes and socks and rolled up his trousers, leaving those luscious dark-skinned ankles bare. Then he jumped down onto the sand and held his arms up to catch her, but she shook her head and jumped down. Independently.

It might just be a good idea to remember what that felt like.

Because she also realised that although, to all intents and purposes, her life *was* independent—emotionally she had come to rely on him a great deal. No, more than that. To fulfil all her emotional needs—and most of that fulfilment was purely fantasy. Because a man couldn't fill all your emotional needs if you only saw him once a month, could he? Even if that time together *was* pretty close to perfect; of course, it was going to be perfect—fantasy always was.

'Are you happy like this?' he demanded suddenly, as they came across a secluded, half-hidden stretch of sand.

Here it came. 'What, you mean right now?' she prevaricated.

'Mol-ly,' he growled and came to a halt, catching her into his arms and staring down at her, his face as stern as she had ever seen it. 'Why do you always play such flippant games with me?'

Because the alternative to playing games was the truth game, and Molly had never been quite so frightened of the truth as she was right then. 'Was I?'

He gave a grim kind of smile. 'You know damned well you were,' he said softly. 'I asked were you happy?'

'Of course.'

'You are?'

'Well, aren't you?'

Dimitri sighed. 'I thought that this would be perfect,' he said.

'What?'

What kind of a relationship did he want with Molly? he asked himself. An honest one, surely?

'This.' He shrugged. 'Us.'

'So it's not?' Fear ran in cool skitters over her

skin. 'That means you aren't happy,' she rushed on. 'Well, if you aren't, then it's best you tell me, best we finish it now, before one of us gets hurt.'

He raised his eyebrows. 'You want to finish it?'

For a moment she felt like a schoolgirl again, remembering the way she had ended an innocent relationship with a boy in her year because she had known, deep down, that it had been on its last legs and she had wanted to get in first. To salvage her pride.

But what she had with Dimitri went deeper than that, even if it was about to end. And she could not and would not lie about something as important as this, simply to salvage her pride.

'I've been thinking about it,' she said truthfully.

'Ah! And you want it to end?'

'Of course I don't!'

'Why not?'

'Well...well, because I like you.'

He nodded. He noted her careful use of the word. She really *had* been thinking. And so had he. 'And this—this life we have been living—it is enough for you?'

She thought of his sweet fluency with English and yet at that moment, he sounded very Greek. Looked very Greek, too, she thought with a little shiver of longing, but she suppressed it. Longing could get in the way of things sometimes. And hadn't she been suppressing other stuff, too? Like her feelings?

'It isn't proper living, is it?' she ventured.

'Tell me,' he urged softly.

Why her? What if she just poured out how she felt, and found that it was different for him?

'Why don't you?'

He shrugged. 'It is true, I am a little tired of it.'

'Tired of it?' So he *did* want to finish it!

'Aren't you?' he questioned seriously.

Again, she felt the icy chill of fear. 'I don't know whether ''tired'' is the word I would have used to describe it,' she said faintly.

'Perhaps it was a poor choice of word,' he continued thoughtfully. 'Maybe discontented.'

'With me?'

'No, not with you—with the way things are. Always the hotel rooms! Always the fancy restaurants!'

'What's wrong with them?'

He shook his head. His thoughts were spinning and, for once in his life, his words could not seem to keep up with them. 'They are not real. Are they?' he questioned, and she dropped her eyes to stare at the white sand which ridged up between her bare toes.

'No. They're not,' she whispered, and looked up at him. 'That's exactly what I was thinking.'

'It is as if we had sat down for a meal together and never got past the first course,' he mused. He stared at her. 'Do you want to come back to Pondiki with me?'

Her heart pounded. She must be very careful not to leap in with both feet. 'You mean for a holiday?'

'Of course. I'm not about to get you your old job back in the taverna!'

Which hadn't been what she had meant at all.

'Would you like that?' he asked.

A holiday, that was all he was offering her, but even so, it was a change, a step…she just wasn't sure in which direction. 'You don't think that it will incite…comment?'

'I would be astonished if it did not, wouldn't you?' he answered drily.

'And memories?'

But he shook his head. 'Not so many memories now, Molly. Time fades them away.' He looked down at the shoreline. 'Just like the waves washing away the sand.'

Molly wasn't so sure. 'Don't people have long memories?'

'Some, I guess—though many of the older generation are dead now, of course.'

She heard the sadness in his voice. His mother had died last year. Another chapter closed. Things never remained the same. They couldn't. Life moved on.

'But where would we stay?' she questioned. 'In the hotel? Or maybe,' she put in quickly, 'maybe I wouldn't stay with you at all?'

He burst out laughing at this. 'This is supposed to be an enjoyable interlude,' he murmured. 'Not an endurance test!'

An interlude—well, *that* was an interesting word, too. 'Well, where then?'

He hesitated. 'On Petros. You remember Petros?'

Briefly, she closed her eyes. How could he even ask her a question like that? Of course she remembered Petros—the tiny sister island to Pondiki, which lay like a sleeping cat just to the west. On some days, it looked as though you could swim to it in a couple of minutes—though she knew that it was five miles away. And sometimes, when the rains came, it disappeared altogether—as if it had been a figment of the imagination all along. Like so many things...

Sometimes, when they had lain together beneath the sheltering rocks on the beach, their bodies warm and sandy and spent, they had stared across at the uninhabited mound.

'One day I will build a house there,' Dimitri had vowed, and Molly had rested her cheek against the faint stubble of his, and thought that it was just a pipedream.

'Of course I remember it. Why, is there a hotel there now?'

He shook his dark head. 'Not a hotel, no—I have a house there.'

Her eyes widened. 'You said you'd build one!'

'Ah! You *do* remember! Well, I did build one. It is very private and no one goes there but me and Zoe—though she finds it too quiet, now, of course. But that is as it should be,' he mused and looked at her. 'I have accepted, you see, that my daughter loves the bright lights of the city.'

'Doesn't mean that Petros won't always be her home—even if she doesn't actually live there.'

He smiled. 'Feminine logic! But, yes, I take your point.'

'And she's still set on modelling?'

'Hell-bent.'

'You don't mind?'

He gave a quick grimace. 'It would not have been my first choice of career for her, but if her heart is set on it, then who am I to oppose it? Better she does it with my blessing, for to alienate her would achieve nothing. At least this way she can turn to me for help if things do not turn out as planned. Come on—let's sit down.'

They sat side by side in the soft, cool sand and Dimitri glanced at her rucked up silver dress with amusement mixed in with a little lust. 'You're going to ruin that dress,' he remarked.

'It's only a dress—and if a dress can't withstand moonlit sand, then it doesn't deserve to be worn.'

'It doesn't deserve to be worn now,' he murmured.

'Shall I take it off?'

'In a minute. You'll distract me.'

'You're distracted already. You have been all evening.'

'I know. So when will you come?'

And suddenly she was afraid. Afraid of why he really wanted her to go. Was it some kind of test? To see if they were truly compatible? Two weeks on a deserted island would certainly tell you if that were the case.

'Zoe is visiting London with one of her aunts,' he

said slowly. 'She isn't back until next week. You could come now, if you like.'

She stared at him. 'When?'

He smiled as he slipped the bodice of her dress down, to discover that her breasts were completely bare beneath. 'Tomorrow. Fly back with me.'

'I don't have enough clothes for a holiday.'

'But you won't need many. Not on Petros.'

Now he was distracting *her*, with his fingers splaying possessively over her, heating and arousing her air-cooled flesh. 'O-okay,' she agreed shakily, and pulled him down onto the sand. 'I will.'

The tarmac was as hot and as blistering as she remembered, as was the heady mixture of lemon and pine which scented the air when Molly alighted from the plane. The warm wind from the engines whipped up her hair and she had to hang onto her straw hat.

Dimitri glanced at her. 'How does it feel?'

'Hot.' She glanced back at him. 'It feels strange,' she admitted. 'And beautiful,' she added, looking around.

It was as breathtaking as ever, this tiny Greek paradise. Mount Urlin still rose in the distance, mighty and magnificent—and further still she could see a sea so darkly blue that it looked almost black.

So much of what she remembered was the same, but there were differences, too. The airport terminal had been completely modernised and it now looked sparkling and spanking new and deliciously air-conditioned.

And she noticed that people stood up straighter as she and Dimitri were waved through customs and that people turned to look at him, a bit like the way women did at parties, only more so, and it was men, too.

'Why is everyone looking at you?' she asked.

'Because I'm so good-looking?'

'No, seriously.'

'Oh, I'm such an important man, Molly,' he murmured.

She wasn't sure whether or not he was joking. His family's hotel had been the best on the island—but she could not remember quite the same amount of deference all those years ago. Though maybe she hadn't noticed that kind of thing then. Teenagers weren't into status much, were they?

'There are more cars,' she observed wryly as she slid onto the seat of the smart silver car which was waiting outside for them.

'I know.' He shrugged. 'Such is the price of progress. But there are no cars on Petros,' he promised. 'I won't allow it.'

'You can't stop it, can you?'

He didn't answer, just spoke in rapid Greek to the driver as the car moved away. They drove slowly around the island, through Urlin Square, where the lemon trees were still draped with rainbow lanterns which would be lit when night-time fell. And past the taverna where Molly had once worked, and a little cry of nostalgia escaped from her lips.

'I wonder what Elena is doing now,' she said.

'I can tell you exactly what she is doing—she is living right there.' He pointed to a white house opposite. 'She helps her husband run the taverna, when she's not too busy with her four children.'

'Four!' commented Molly faintly.

'That's right. We can go and have lunch with her one day, if you'd like that,' he mentioned casually.

She turned to him. 'Oh, Dimitri, can we? I'd love that!' She frowned. 'But only if you think she'd like to see me?'

'I think she would like that just as much as you would,' he answered. 'Elena was very fond of you and she thought that I had behaved very badly towards you, as she told me at great length, after you'd gone.'

'Did she?'

'She did.'

'That must have taken a lot of courage on her part,' said Molly. 'She always seemed a little bit in awe of you.'

'Maybe it's that female bonding thing you all seem to have,' he said drily.

She turned to him as the car moved towards the Urlin Road, remembering the night she had travelled out on her scooter to spy on him. Then the way had seemed never-ending and all she had been able to focus on were the potholes to be avoided and the pine cones scattered in her path. But today she just saw the incredible loveliness of the place. The peace and the quiet. The sense of completion and continuity.

She could understand Zoe's take on the place as restricting. She could see that someone her age might view the island as a bit of a prison. But Elena had stayed, and so had Dimitri. They had seen its beauty and seen it grounded in generations, repeating the same cycle of a life which fundamentally never changed. But then human nature never did.

She let out a little gasp when she saw his hotel, for it had grown. Not upwards, but outwards—with clusters of small, white bougainvillea-clad buildings nestling in the green hillside.

'Wow!' she murmured. 'Expansion!'

He sent her a frowning look of query. 'But it works, *ne*? It is not an ugly development?'

She shook her head. 'Not at all. It all looks as though it was meant to be there. Who designed it?'

'I did.'

Somehow she had known this. 'So you're an architect now?'

'An architect of my own destiny,' he responded, with a smile.

'And do your sisters know I'm coming?'

'Of course.' There was a pause. 'I thought we might have dinner with them one night. When Zoe's back.'

She turned to him. 'They won't mind?'

'They wouldn't dare,' he commented drily.

The car moved through lemon groves, acid-bright mixed with lush green and he opened the window so that she could catch their fragrance and she breathed it in.

'This isn't the quickest way to Petros, is it, Dimitri?'

He shook his head as the car drove down a steep road to where the sapphire-blue sweep of a bay awaited them, with a little boat bobbing there, and in the distance, Petros—clear and close enough to touch today. 'No, I brought you by the longer, more scenic route. Do you mind? Are you tired?'

'No. No, I'm not tired.'

On the contrary, she felt as though she had suddenly been brought to life. She stepped out of the car, welcoming the heat of the sun on her face. The air smelt so clean and so fresh, so sweet with natural scents. Only the drowsy, mechanical hum of the cicadas could be heard and the lapping of the waves against the sand.

She looked at the boat, gleaming cobalt and white in the crystal water. 'Is that how we're getting out there?'

'It's the only way out there.'

It looked a bit small. 'Sure it won't sink?'

He laughed. 'Not with just us two.' He gestured to the car. 'The cases will follow later.'

The motor roared into life and they sped over to the island. The house he had built was fashioned into the side of a rock, so that the back half was deliciously cool and shaded, while the vast sea-staring windows at the front meant that it was almost like being outside.

It was simply and sparsely furnished, more like a monastery than a house, she thought, but the simplicity did it justice—the view over the sea was decoration enough.

'Shall we go and have a drink on the terrace?' he asked.

'Sounds like heaven.'

'I hope so.'

It *was* heaven—almost too much so—for how was she ever going to be able to go back to her old life when she had tasted these simple, stunning pleasures with the man she loved?

Each morning they woke early and swam naked as the sun rose over the sea, gilding it with rose and gold, tingling their skin with its first soft rays, though the water was as warm as fresh milk.

They explored every inch of the small island and Dimitri pointed out all the plants and the tiny insects; he seemed to know everything there was to know about the place, almost as if it was part of him—which, of course, it was.

He caught her fish, and they drizzled it with oil and lemon and cooked it over a fire on the beach, drinking rich red wine and watching the stars come out and listening to the faint sound of the holiday-makers' merriment over on Pondiki.

One day he took her back across the water to lunch at Elena's house and the two of them fell into each other's arms, unashamedly nostalgic, while four brown-eyed children peeped out shyly from behind a flowered cotton curtain and gradually crept out.

'How long you are staying?' Elena asked, when Dimitri had gone to the kitchen to find a corkscrew.

Molly shrugged. 'Only a couple of weeks.'

There was a pause. 'And you still love him?'

'Elena!'

'You do.'

'Of course I do.'

'So?'

'So nothing.'

'But he has brought you here, Molly. Why?'

She didn't know, she didn't dare ask, for fear that questions would shatter the magic which clung to her skin like insubstantial stardust.

They would read and sleep and make love and the hours flowed like honey into one another. Sometimes Molly felt as if she had fallen into a dream, never to wake again, but she didn't want to wake—she wanted to go on living this dream for ever.

And then Zoe phoned. She was flying into Pondiki with her aunt.

'Good.' Dimitri nodded. 'She will be pleased to see you.'

She shot him a slightly worried look. 'Dimitri, does Zoe *know*? That I'm staying here with you?'

'I no longer have secrets, Molly,' he said slowly.

'And—' she drew a deep breath '—does she know that you and I were once lovers?'

He shook his head. 'I haven't told her,' he said. 'Not that. And I doubt that anyone else will. There are some things it is not necessary that she knows, but if she asks I will tell her the truth.'

'She will hate me.'

'Her mother did not hate you, so why should she?'

She stared at him. 'You mean, you discussed me? With Malantha?'

'Of course I did,' he answered gently. 'She understood,' he said, nodding slightly as if to reaffirm that to himself. 'She had always known about the other girls. She knew that was the way it was, but she also knew that one day I would return to her.'

His honesty was reassuring, but it gave her an insight into the fact that his marriage really had been a marriage, no matter how short, and that he had loved and confided in his wife. And Molly was glad.

'So was I...was I just another body to you, Dimitri?' she asked painfully.

'You insult me by asking that,' he answered quietly. 'You know you weren't.'

But he had stopped short of saying that he loved her then, just as he had never indicated that he loved her now. And maybe he didn't, even though sometimes he acted as if he did. But he was a man who kept his feelings locked away—look at his reaction when Malantha had died: he had kept all his grief bottled up. It all came down to that old thing whether it was important to hear someone say, 'I love you,' or whether you were prepared to accept what you had.

'She knew that you were different,' he added softly.

'And she accepted that, too?'

'It wasn't easy for her, and perhaps in my youthful arrogance I asked too much of her, but, yes, she accepted it.'

They sat in silence for a while, letting the past retreat again to its proper place.

'Do you want to come to the airport when I collect Zoe?' he asked eventually.

Molly shook her head. 'No. I've had you all to myself—you go to your daughter.' She smiled. 'She must be dying to see you.'

He gave her a brief, hard kiss. 'Thank you.'

In a year Zoe had changed almost out of all recognition. The adolescent had gone and she had become a woman, a head-turning woman—even more beautiful than Molly remembered.

She was fizzing over with excitement and the sight of Molly sitting in her father's house didn't seem to faze her in the slightest, she was too full of her own plans and dreams to bother about theirs.

'You see, Papa,' she was saying, once he had brought them chilled lemon juice out onto the terrace, 'I've changed my mind about modelling in New York!'

'You have?' he questioned casually.

Molly thought how much he had changed. How softer and more accepting of life he had become.

'Because London is where it is happening! And that's where I want to be! And Molly lives in London, doesn't she? Molly can keep her eye on me!' She beamed a huge smile. 'Papa arranged for me to see someone at an agency in London, and they were just so *sweet*!' Her big dark eyes were trained anxiously on Molly. 'You can be my chaperone if I come and live in London, can't you, Molly?'

Dimitri gave a slow smile. 'Ah! I was kind of hoping you might come to that conclusion yourself. It seems the ideal solution.' His eyes caught her in their soft black blaze. 'What do you say, Molly?'

And Molly suddenly felt sick.

He had planned the whole thing! Like some grandmaster moving the chess pieces around, only in this case the pieces were people! Arranging for Zoe to 'see' someone in London—because, of course, London was a safer bet than New York. London was nearer and *she* was in London, and he was confident that she would do anything for him. Molly who would walk to the ends of the earth if he asked her to. Stupid Molly.

Here she had been, thinking that Dimitri had brought her here with some kind of idea in mind for the future—*their* future. To see if they could be compatible for more than spaced-out weekends spent in fancy hotels. And they had been, or so she had thought.

But all the time she had been agonising over their future, and fretting about her body-clock and wondering about having children…well, Dimitri had obviously just been testing her out. To see whether she was a fit kind of person to keep her eye on his daughter!

So now what did she say? If she turned Zoe down, it would look as though she was holding out for something more—and there was no way she wanted anything more. What had Dimitri once said? That things should be given freely. Well, there was no way she was going to ask anything of *him*. And she liked Zoe. She couldn't, in her heart, turn her down—but at what cost to her *own* feelings?

'I'd have to discuss it with your father, Zoe,' she said slowly. 'But I can't see that there would be a problem with that.'

'Honestly?'

'Honestly,' she echoed faintly, and pushed her chair back. 'Well, I expect you've got lots to talk about so I think I'll go and take a shower before supper. Will you both excuse me?'

Dimitri stood up, frowning. Her face had gone as pale as the moon. 'Molly?' he questioned. 'Are you okay?'

She gave him a bright, brittle smile. 'Of course I am. I'll see you in a while.'

She only just made it to the shower room. At least in there she could lock the door. At least in there, her tears could be mingled with the streaming jets of water.

CHAPTER TWELVE

'MOLLY?'

She ignored it. The jets of water were so loud that she could quite reasonably say she hadn't heard him, couldn't she?

'Molly. Either you open this damned door or I will take it off at the hinges!'

She turned the water off. She believed him. There was something in the tone of his voice which left her in no doubt whatsoever that he meant it. She slicked her wet hair away from her face and wrapped herself in a towel, then went to open the door, registering the look of dark fury on his face.

His eyes flicked over her. 'Put something on,' he snapped, and turned his back to gaze out at the sea, as if he couldn't bear to watch.

She thought of defying him, but what would be the point? She was trapped. Trapped on a paradise island which had become a prison, with a man who didn't love her.

She pulled a cotton dress over her still-damp naked body. 'You can turn round now.' But when he did, she recoiled from the cold, hard look in his eyes.

'What was that all about?' he demanded.

Was he so dense he couldn't see? 'I wanted a shower.'

'You wanted to let me know in no uncertain terms that the idea of including my daughter in your life obviously appalls you!'

'Mightn't it be easier all round if you employed a *professional* chaperone!' she bit back. 'Or are you planning to put me on the payroll?'

And suddenly he understood. She was confused, just the way he had been. Frightened, too—just as he had been. And the tumult of coming to terms with the way he really felt came out in a simple statement. 'I was planning to make you my wife, actually. But chaperone seems a better word than stepmother, don't you think? That makes you sound like a wicked witch. Which sometimes, *agape mou*, you really are.'

Molly sat down on the bed. Had they blown it? Had *she* blown it? 'Was?' she questioned faintly and then pulled herself together. 'You don't have to marry me, Dimitri,' she said tonelessly. 'I'm happy to do what I can for your daughter.'

He sat down on the bed next to her and took her face between his hands. 'Molly,' he said simply. 'If I told you that I love you, would that make a difference?'

Her heart lurched. Her hands shook and so did her head. 'Not if you're just saying it to make me feel better.'

'You think I would say something as big as that if I didn't mean it?'

She stared at him suspiciously. No, she didn't, but she had to know. 'Just like that?'

He shook his head. 'No, not just like that.'

'Then why now? Why, today?'

He sighed. Maybe his timing hadn't been perfect, but timing had always seemed set to work against him, especially where Molly was concerned.

'I've loved you for a long time, Molly,' he said. 'But I needed to be sure. I needed to know that it wasn't just some kind of overpowering physical attraction between us—something which had been cut off in its prime and which we both just needed to work out of our system. Loving someone is always a risk, but it doesn't have to be an impetuous risk.'

She nodded. Willing to just listen, but then he had never really spoken like this before, had he? From his heart.

'I tried to tell myself that it would wear itself out. That what we had would fade with time. But it hasn't. It's just got stronger. And then I thought about what it would be like if we finished.' He shrugged and for the very first time she saw his vulnerability. 'I couldn't bear it. I knew, deep down, that if I met you again, that this thing we have between us would always be there. Overpowering. Neverending. Fate brought us back together, sweet, *agape mou*—and who are we to argue with fate?'

'But the differences still remain.' She forced herself to see reason. If risk this was, then it must be a considered one. For both of them. 'You still have your life here in Greece, while mine is London.'

'I know. But time has merged those differences. You can be happy on Petros—I have seen that—and

I can be happy in London. We can move between both places.'

'But your life is *here*, Dimitri! And Zoe is to be in London—how are you going to fix that?'

'But I can work from London, too.' He saw her uncomprehending look, and smiled. 'I am, you see, Molly, a very wealthy man.'

She nearly said, *Maybe by Greek standards*, but she stopped herself and he was smiling.

'Yes, by Greek standards,' he said softly. 'And by international standards, too.'

She gasped. 'Can you read my mind?'

'I don't need to.' He touched her cheek. 'It's all written in your face. You wear your emotions in your eyes, Molly, didn't you know that?'

'D-do I?' So much for hiding the way she felt about him!

'You do. That was the main reason why I refused to see you after I found you with the American. I knew that if I looked at you I would know whether or not you had been unfaithful to me, and I didn't want to know that. It was easier all round to think that you had. Otherwise I would never have been able to let you go.' At the time it had come as a blessed relief to him—to find a legitimate reason to stop something which had been hurtling way out of his control.

And suddenly she understood. At eighteen, the risk had been too great. To devastate his life and his plans on the strength of a summer romance with a foreign teenager who was just starting out, the way he had been—well, it would have been madness.

If Zoe came to them in a year or two and told them that she was going to throw everything in to live an unknown life with an unknown man in an unknown place, then wouldn't they do everything in their power to stop her?

She noticed how easy it was to think in terms of 'we'. 'Will you kiss me now?' she begged.

He shook his head. 'Not yet. Not until you're wearing my ring on your finger.'

'You mean I have to wait until we're married?'

'I was thinking more of engagement. A *short* engagement,' he added with a smile when he saw her aghast look. He stood up and went to the pocket of his jacket and took out a tiny box, extracting a ring from it which, even from across the room, glittered as brightly as any of the clear stars which hung over the island, and Molly blinked at it in disbelieving joy.

He sat down again and slid it on her finger.

'Oh, it fits,' she gulped. 'Perfectly.'

'Of course it does. I knew it would. I know every centimetre of you, Molly. I knew exactly how wide your finger.' He lifted it to his lips and nibbled it. 'How soft. And how very sweet. Now come here and kiss your fiancé properly.'

But, reluctantly, she drew away after a minute. Zoe was somewhere in the house, and there were still a couple of questions which needed to be answered.

'What would you say if I told you I wanted children?'

'I would say that I wanted them, too.'

'You *do*?'

'But of course. If we are blessed.'

'You're sure?'

'I am Greek,' he said simply. 'How many would you like, Molly? Three, four, five?'

'Oh, Dimitri,' she sighed.

He kissed her again, until she thought of something else.

'When you say *rich*.' The mammoth diamond sparkling on her finger bore testament to his claim, though Molly wouldn't have cared if he had sealed their union with a curtain ring. 'How come? I mean…I don't understand. I know you have the hotel and everything, but…?'

He touched the cold diamond thoughtfully, then looked at her. 'When Zoe was a baby I knew that I was going to have to change something in my life—that unless I was less hands-on in the running of the hotel, I would never see her. I realised that Pondiki had a lot of resources which had not been tapped. I have an American friend, and he helped me get started. We began to manufacture the olives into oil—and then to export it.

'Pondiki oil is pretty special,' he said, unable to keep the pride from his voice. 'Prized among chefs all over the world. Next, our lemons were distilled, to make a rather potent liqueur.' He pulled a face. 'Not exactly to *my* taste, but it's very popular now, particularly in Germany.'

'Gosh,' said Molly faintly. 'Did you earn buckets?'

'Buckets,' he echoed, with a smile. 'It's another of the reasons I was, shall we say…*suspicious* of women. Avarice is a real turn-off and there are a lot of women out there who are drawn to men with big bank balances.'

'Oh, yeah?' she mocked. 'Nothing to do with your outrageous good looks, of course—or the fact that you're dynamite in bed?'

'Why, *agape mou*,' he murmured. 'You do say the sweetest things.'

But the thought of other women hurt. It had no right to, but it did.

He saw that, too. 'The other women are forgotten,' he said gently. 'There is only you. I don't let myself think of the other men in *your* life, Molly.'

'Well, you'd need a pretty fertile imagination to do that,' she said drily. 'Because there haven't been many, and no one since my husband. But you can wipe that look of smug satisfaction off your face and tell me about your semi-riches to real-riches story!'

He laughed. 'I ploughed the money back into the tourist industry. I bought up land—which meant that I could have control over what building went on. I wanted the island to retain its character,' he said. 'That was very important to me. Not to become crass and commercialised as so many places have done.'

'So you're King of Pondiki?' she teased.

'Mmm. But a benevolent one.' His eyes glittered. 'And I need a queen very badly.'

'Even an English one?'

'English, Greek, American—it wouldn't matter.' His mouth softened and so did his voice. 'Just so long as her name was Molly Garcia.'

EPILOGUE

'SHE looks beautiful, doesn't she?'

Dimitri flicked a glance at the glossy magazine and scowled. 'She looks all right.'

'Dimitri, she looks *beautiful*!' Molly thrust the magazine under his nose. 'Doesn't she?'

He stared down at the eight-page spread. Hard to believe that his little daughter—his baby—was cavorting across the Barbadian sand wearing a succession of what looked like torn sheets. And being paid an obscene amount of money to do it.

He nodded and a smile curved his mouth. 'Yes. She looks very beautiful,' he agreed softly. 'She is a very smart and successful young lady.'

Molly stretched. 'She rang last night when you were at the hotel. She wants to have a twenty-first party.'

'In New York?' he questioned wryly, since, despite all his machinations, his daughter had ended up living there anyway. Quite safely and sensibly, too, as it had turned out. In a stunning if over-priced loft apartment.

'No, here.' She stood up and went to massage the back of his neck. 'On Pondiki.'

He gave an almost imperceptible nod of approval,

but Molly saw it. 'What do you think?' she asked innocently.

'I'm happy to do it for her.' He wriggled a little as her fingers kneaded the stiff knot of muscle at the side of his neck. 'Mmm. That's good, Molly. Do it some more.'

'Shall I start to plan it with her, then?'

'Whatever you want, *agape*.' He sighed, but it was a blissful, happy sigh. 'You usually seem to get it, no matter what I say. Come here.' He pulled her round to sit on his lap.

'I thought you were enjoying that massage!' she protested.

'I was.' He gave the wicked, captivating smile which never failed to ensnare her. 'But it got me thinking of different, better ways to relax.'

'Oh?' She let him kiss her neck.

'Well, the boys are asleep.'

'And we don't know how long for,' she agreed.

'We could go and look in on them first,' he suggested. 'Just to check they're okay.'

'Any excuse!' she teased, but she loved him for his fierce devotion to *all* his children. She had given birth to the twins—twin boys which had driven the whole island into utter ecstasy and completely removed any lingering traces of resentment that anyone might still have felt for her. And Dimitri had more time this time around.

One day, she and Zoe had been watching him play in the water with them, patiently teaching the boisterous two-year-olds to swim.

Zoe had been paying one of her brief but frequent visits to the island, bringing in her wake hordes of paparazzi, which in turn had attracted the glitterati. Pondiki was in danger of becoming fashionable. Thank heavens that Dimitri had the control and the power not to let things get out of hand; not to lose the simple essence of the island, Molly had thought.

'Do you mind that your papa has more time to spend with them than he did with you?' she asked.

Zoe shook her long raven hair. 'Never. I'm so grateful for what he did for me. He changed his life to make mine better.'

'Yes.'

She had had the boys in London. Dimitri had suggested it and she had agreed to it readily, knowing the unspoken reason why. He did not want another wife airlifted by helicopter. In fact, he had been determinedly calm throughout her pregnancy, but she had seen the fear in his face sometimes, when he'd thought she hadn't been watching. And that was why she would not have any more children. They had enough. Their family and their happiness was perfect and complete.

After the birth, she had sold her big house in Hampstead, and bought a smaller one. She wanted to keep a base in London, for Zoe to use, and the boys when they were older, and for her and Dimitri. But she doubted she would ever live there again. She loved her Greek life too much, particularly now that she was halfway fluent in the language.

'Come on,' said Dimitri, and lifted her from his lap.

The two of them tiptoed along the corridor to the boys' room where their two black-haired boys were snuggled in adjoining cots, both sleeping the angelic sleep of the loved and the innocent.

Dimitri stared down at them, silent for a moment. 'It's hard to tell them apart when they're sleeping,' he admitted.

'But not when they're awake.'

'No.' Alexander was the bold adventurer—Lysander the quieter, more thoughtful of the two.

She watched while he smoothed down their glossy black curls, and Alexander stirred a little, while Lysander just slept on.

Dimitri said something in Greek.

'Goodnight, my sons,' whispered Molly and he turned to her and smiled.

Then he said something else, something soft and murmured which took much longer. 'Do you know what that means, Molly?'

She did.

He had just told her that she was his love, his life, his world. But she didn't need to understand Greek to know that. For as their love had grown, so had Dimitri learned to show it.

And these days she could read it in his eyes.

A SHOCKING PASSION

by

Amanda Browning

Amanda Browning still lives in the Essex house where she was born. The third of four children – her sister being her twin – she enjoyed the rough and tumble of life with two brothers as much as she did reading books. Writing came naturally as an outlet for a fertile imagination. The love of books led her to a career in libraries, and being single allowed her to take the leap into writing for a living. Success is still something of a wonder, but allows her to indulge in hobbies as varied as embroidery and bird-watching.

Don't miss Amanda Browning's exciting new novel *The Millionaire's Marriage Revenge,* out in October 2007 from Mills & Boon® Modern™

CHAPTER ONE

ELLIE Frazier was content to wait. High overhead the sky was a dazzling cloudless blue, before her stretched the sparkling azure of the sea, and the sun was warm on her bare arms and outstretched legs. Whilst the Marina Piccola, with its bristling array of yachts, bustled about her, she was happy to do nothing except soak up the atmosphere and wait for Paul to arrive.

She noted, but did not respond to, the appreciative male looks coming her way, for she was not in the market for even a mild flirtation right now, and had no wish to be approached with lines she had heard often in her twenty-six years. Without vanity she accepted that her shoulder-length blonde hair, right now hidden under a large floppy sun hat, huge grey eyes with their rim of long lashes and a generous smiling mouth drew men like moths to a flame. As did a willowy figure, with its very feminine curves, and the fact that she moved with unconscious grace. Yet it was all a matter of pure happenstance, due to her Scandinavian forebears, and she never traded on it.

There were even times when Ellie felt Mother Nature had done her a dubious favour by making her beautiful. Such as when she discovered the man she had always thought she wanted had turned out to have no heart at all. He had never loved her. Even for the short time they had been together, fidelity had been an unknown concept to him. So, after some serious soul-searching, when she

5

realised she didn't like him anymore, let alone love him, she had ended the one-sided relationship. Which was the reason she had initially decided to boycott the family gathering at the villa on Capri this year. She had no wish to spend several weeks in his company. Now, though, she had no option. Luke had got engaged to be married, and her presence was expected.

Luke Thornton, of course, was the man she had expended so much wasted time and emotion on. He had been her idol all the time she was growing up, and now she wondered how she could have been so blind. Certain people had tried to tell her, but she had put him on a pedestal and only bitter experience had toppled him back down to the ground where he had always belonged.

He was, in fact, her stepbrother, the middle of three, Paul being the youngest at thirty, and Jack the eldest at thirty-six. Her mother had married their father when Ellie was ten. As a child, she had hero-worshipped Luke, but that had changed in her early teens to a monumental crush. She had even gone to the lengths of taking a modelling course because he was a photographer. Her adolescent heart had ached for him. She had loved him then, unquestioningly, but no longer. Thankfully her heart had only been slightly bruised, a reflection of how little she had actually loved him, but her pride had taken a knock. She had learned a hard, yet valuable lesson.

They had only been lovers for a few months, and it had been a closely guarded secret, hidden from the family. At first she had thought it was because he hadn't wanted to share her, and rather liked the spice it added to the affair. Later she realised he had a darker motive. He enjoyed doing things he knew the family would disapprove of, and they would definitely disapprove of his toying with her. Though it galled her to let him get away with it, she had no intention of revealing their affair at this late stage, for she didn't want anyone to know how stupid she had been.

It was painful to remember her foolishness. She was amazed how long a crush could last without any encouragement. Luke had never shown any sign of even noticing her, but undaunted she had stubbornly continued to love him. Going to college had opened her eyes to a whole world of young men and, though she had embraced it with youthful enthusiasm, dating and flirting and eventually having two love affairs, secretly she had been waiting for Luke, who had been off enjoying the fruits of his glittering career.

Whilst never giving up the belief that one day they would be together, Ellie had concentrated on using her talent for needlework to become a restorer, a specialist job that she took great pride in. Luke barely visited his family above twice a year, but it had been enough to keep her going. Then just before last Christmas their paths had crossed at a fund-raising in London, and her dream had finally come true.

She had looked at him and known he was seeing her at last. When he turned on the charm, she had fallen for it hook, line and sinker. They had become lovers. Luke told her then that he had always intended they should be, he had simply bided his time until she was all grown-up and away from the family. She had thought she was in seventh heaven. As she realised later, he had planned his campaign carefully, and knew how to choose the right moment.

Disillusionment had set in all too soon, but it had taken two months, and several infidelities, for her to admit he was just using her. He didn't love her. She was simply available whenever he was between other women.

That was when Ellie finally admitted to herself she didn't love him, and never had. It had been quite a revelation to realise she had been in love with love, not Luke, the man. Her pride had taken a knock, and her self-respect demanded that she put an end to the affair. She was no longer the teenager crippled by the enormity of her feelings. She was a woman who finally had the rose-tinted spectacles whipped from her eyes.

When she told Luke it was over, he had laughed and said she would be back, because she was his and they both knew it. That had shown her how he really thought of her, and it brought forth her fighting spirit. She was no man's sure thing and told him so. He had been furious. It appeared women did not drop Luke Thornton— he did the dropping. Despising him more than she thought possible, she had walked away and never looked back. Six months later, she didn't regret it. Leaving Luke was the sanest thing she had ever done.

Her hand rose to the cabochon emerald hanging from the chain around her neck, rubbing the stone like a talisman. She never went anywhere without it. It had been her grandmother's and was supposed to bring the wearer happiness in love, but it had failed her so far. She was seriously beginning to doubt there was any real magic in it.

When the news of Luke's engagement had reached her, she had been surprised. She had come to know that Luke valued his freedom too much to tie himself down to any one woman. Yet strange things did happen. Perhaps he had actually fallen in love. Whatever the reason for his engagement, she had altered her plans because she knew how Luke's mind worked. He would take her absence as affirmation that she was still tied to him, added to which the family would want to know why she wasn't at such an important family occasion. So last night she had telephoned the villa, hoping to speak to her mother.

As it happened only Paul had been home, which was a relief because she would not have wanted to talk to Jack, her *bête noir*, who had teased and taunted her and refused to take her adolescent feelings for his brother seriously. If only she had listened to him! Hindsight could be a painful thing. Anyway, Paul had been delighted to hear that she was coming to join them, and had faithfully promised to pick her up. Her watch told her he was a little late, but that didn't surprise her. Paul was a vulcanologist. No doubt he was on the computer, logging information, and had forgotten all about her. Her lips curved into a wry smile at the thought, but it didn't upset her. When he remembered, he would come for her.

Ellie shifted into a more comfortable position and allowed her gaze to lazily scan the harbour, in no particular hurry to move. She had always loved this place. School holidays had been idyllic. Endless days of sun and sea. Later she thought it the perfect place for falling in love. Unfortunately, it couldn't guarantee that the man would be worth loving.

Her head jerked round as a muffled roar disturbed the peace. An instant later a black Ferrari suddenly appeared from one of the narrow streets and slipped like an arrow into a parking spot across the bay. Ellie's eyes widened as she watched the dark-haired driver climb out, removing his sunglasses as he did so and tossing them carelessly on the dash. It was the kind of self-possession that expressed wealth and supreme confidence, which many men strove for and failed to achieve. This was natural, and undeniably alluring. Curious, she sat forward to see him better but the distance was too great to see well, especially in the glare of the sun and the heat haze coming off the ground.

Yet there was something about the way he stood, hands on hips, scanning the harbour, that instantly tightened the muscles of her stomach. Perhaps it was the way his white chinos fitted his long legs, emphasising their powerful muscles, or the way his blue silk shirt, sleeves rolled up, collar open, clung to his broad-shouldered torso. Who could tell. All she knew was that everything which was female inside her recognised a perfect male animal with a purely primal shiver.

'Wow!' Ellie exclaimed under her breath. Whoever he was, the man had that indefinable thing called machismo, and he had it in spades. More importantly he was the first man since Luke who had roused a spark of interest in her. She had begun to think herself incapable of responding but, like one of Paul's volcanoes, it appeared her sensuality was dormant, not dead. All at once she felt as if a dark cloud was lifted from her and she could breathe freely again.

Unaware of her regard, the man turned away as someone called to him, then strode over to a nearby building and disappeared inside. At which point Ellie sat back with a bemused smile tugging at the corners of her mouth. Strange how she had to come all this way to react to a man again. Of course he had to have a particularly potent brand of masculinity, in order to set her heart racing at a distance. Whatever, there couldn't be a better time to be having a sexual response to another man, for it proved once and for all that Luke no longer meant anything to her. Boy, did that feel good. Her response had been instant, and her body still tingled with sensual awareness.

Ellie couldn't recall having responded to any other man quite so strongly before, not even Luke. She shook her head in wonder. One glance at that man had switched her on with a vengeance, her senses leaping to attention, as receptive as the next woman to a pull as old as time.

Right then the cause of her increased pulse rate emerged from the building and, with a wave and laugh to whoever had been inside, began walking her way. Fascinated and curious, she gave in to the moment and allowed herself the luxury of watching him. Not that she could have ignored him for long anyway. He drew her eyes irresistibly with his easy way of moving. It was a walk that could only be described as catlike. Big catlike. Pantherish. With an economy of effort and yet more than hinting at leashed power. She had never seen anyone to compare with him for sheer magnetism. Definitely not Luke.

Who was this man who had the power to turn her into a seething mass of ultra-sensitive senses?

One thing was plain, she was soon going to find out. The closer he got to her, the clearer she could see him, and that was when a dawning sense of disbelief began to fill her, for she knew that face as well as she knew her own. Handsome somehow couldn't quite capture the reality of him. There was strength in the set of his chin, humour in the tiny lines at the corners of his eyes and lips. Yet there had been nothing but mockery in them for her over the years. He had been the bane of her existence. No wonder she was stunned, for it was Jack of all people she had been responding to so powerfully.

Jack Thornton?

No way! Fate couldn't be so unkind. Surely she would wake up soon and find it had all been a terrible dream. Dream or not, her shocked gaze remained riveted until somewhere out of sight a motorcycle backfired, causing her to start and finally breaking the spell. Yet, when she blinked and refocused, nothing changed. It was still Jack walking towards her. It had been no dream.

Safe in the shadow of her hat, Ellie hastily dropped her gaze. Her thoughts were whirling chaotically. This couldn't be happening to her, it just couldn't. The last time she had seen Jack she hadn't experienced any of this. It had been last Christmas when she was still in the throes of her imagined love for Luke, and they had fought as usual. So what made the difference?

Whatever the cause, the result was dreadful. Thank goodness for her hat which shaded her face for she had virtually eaten him with her eyes, for heaven's sake! If he had seen that, she would never have lived it down. The only thing that mattered now was that her momentary aberration would be her secret. He infuriated her, like an itch she couldn't scratch, and the response she'd had to him couldn't be more unwelcome. Well, it was not about to happen again. The quicker she got her wayward senses under control the better.

Glancing through her lashes, she noted with a lurch of her heart that Jack had stopped a short distance away. Ready or not, she had to face him. Schooling her features into a cool mask, she raised her head, looking up at him with disdain.

'Oh, it's you,' she declared in her slightly husky

voice, making no effort to mask her dislike, and found herself looking into a pair of the bluest of blue eyes that were dancing merrily. They were, without doubt, nice eyes, and it irked her that she had to admit it. They were the sort of eyes that invited you to dive into their halcyon depths. Something she had never been tempted to do before, but now she could understand why women did. More fool them.

'It's always a pleasure to see you, too, Angel,' Jack Thornton drawled mockingly, at the same time allowing his gaze to rove over her in a leisurely male fashion. Something she had never been aware of him doing before and, to her dismay, she could only liken it to a lick of flame. As a consequence her heart knocked against her ribs in alarm. 'Why so glum? Were you expecting someone else? Sorry to disappoint you, but Luke's too busy with his fiancée to chase about after you.'

That stung, but not for the reason it was meant to do. Luke was actually the last person she wanted to see. But at least they were back on familiar ground and Ellie glared at him, thankful to be momentarily distracted from the unexpected way she was feeling. 'I wasn't expecting Luke at all. Paul said he would pick me up,' she countered frostily. 'So why are you here? Where is Paul?'

Clearly pleased with the result of his hit, Jack grinned down at her. 'He's waiting for an important message to come through, so he asked me to collect you. As I had nothing better to do, I said I would.'

She was not going to rise to the bait. She absolutely was not! 'It took you long enough to get here,' she complained, wondering how three brothers could be so unalike. Luke was the charmer—if totally insincere, Paul was endearing, whilst this man… Suffice it to say, he came from a different mould.

Those irritatingly fascinating blue eyes took on a provocative glint. 'Don't get on your high horse with me, Eleanora. I'm not impressed by tantrums. They never did work with me when you were a child, and they aren't going to work now.'

Ellie ground her teeth together in frustration. She had been named Eleanora after her grandmother, and Jack knew how much she hated it. He only said it to get her goat. She took a steadying breath and held on to her annoyance by a very slender thread. 'I don't throw tantrums, no matter what the provocation,' she responded shortly.

He laughed. 'Hmm, what a selective memory you have, Angel. A truly female trait. I could give you chapter and verse about all the tantrums you've thrown down the years.'

She just bet he could. He seemed to delight in remembering every horrible thing about her and throwing it back in her face.

'We're wandering from the point. The fact remains I've been waiting here for over an hour,' she pointed out, conveniently forgetting the fact that until a moment ago she was quite happy to sit and while away the time.

'Unfortunately Paul didn't remember to tell us you were coming until twenty minutes ago. I broke the speed limit all the way here in case you were getting anxious. Instead I arrived to find you draped seductively over the dock, wearing next to nothing, to the enjoyment of the local male population.'

O-oh. She only had to be in his company five minutes to recall why she disliked him so much. 'I happen to be wearing more than some of the women around here!' she snapped, for, whilst none of the women were actually topless, the scantiness of their bikinis meant they might as well be. She on the other hand was wearing respectable shorts and a vest-top. Modest by any standards.

Those blue eyes ran up and down the length of her, and the small smile which curled his lips was the epitome of irony. 'I thought perhaps it was for Luke. You've tried everything else, so it was only a matter of time before you got to sex,' he drawled softly and, though she tried to prevent it, hot colour stormed into her cheeks.

'I would never do that!' Ellie protested faintly, uncomfortable with the fact that Jack still believed she was angling for Luke. But she only had herself to blame for that, and for the fact that she couldn't tell him their affair was long over. So far as anyone knew, it had never happened. He wouldn't like it if he found out the truth, so she would have to make sure he never did.

Those blue eyes softened a little but still held hers steadily. 'Wouldn't you?'

'No!' she insisted, outraged at the idea, though in the back of her mind she knew as a teenager she had thought of it. At the time she just hadn't had the nerve to try it. If it came to that, she still wouldn't have the nerve. It simply wasn't in her nature. Something she felt Jack ought to know.

Jack was shaking his head disbelievingly. 'I'm pleased to hear it, even if I don't quite believe it. So, you have some other plan up your sleeve, do you?'

This visit, she realised, was not going to be as easy as she thought. Keeping up the pretence of an unfulfilled longing, was going to call for a lot of nifty footwork on a very tangled web. Somehow she must find a way to make it known she no longer wanted Luke, but without having to explain the how or why. Not an easy task. Until then she had to keep up the fiction that they had never had a relationship. So her eyes shot daggers at him, albeit not very sharp ones. 'I don't know what you're talking about. I have no plans.'

'You mean you didn't hotfoot it out here the second you heard Luke had got engaged, intent on somehow breaking them up?' Jack demanded with an icy edge to his voice that was quite unpleasant. The more so because she didn't want his brother anymore. All she wanted was to hide her own stupidity in ever falling for Luke in the first place.

'I wouldn't do that,' she denied, as forcefully as she was able, and he snorted.

'You mean you would if you could, but you're afraid you can't!' he countered scathingly, and quite without warning it brought her close to tears.

'Why are you being so horrible to me?' she charged, in a choked voice, and saw him sigh.

'Because you're a fool, Ellie, hankering for what can never be yours,' he said, with unexpected gentleness, making her throat close over.

At that moment a tiny gust of wind blew up out of nowhere and caught at her hat, whipping it from her head before she had a chance to stop it.

'Oh no!' she wailed, making a wild grab for it before it ended up in the sea. She failed, but a long arm reached for it, plucking it from the edge of the dock and an inevitable watery grave.

Jack examined his catch without amusement. 'This is

why you're a fool, Ellie. You should have let it go,' he said sternly, holding the hat out towards her.

'Why? It's a perfectly good hat,' she insisted. Retrieving her hat, she decided to hold it against further attacks from the wind.

'It's also the hat Luke gave to you,' he enlarged drily.

That sent a shudder through Ellie, because she had actually forgotten. Once it had been a precious object, now it was simply the most comfortable hat she possessed, despite the fact that it was going home. She tipped her chin up at him, aggravated that he had such a long memory. 'So what if it is?'

Jack looked her squarely in the eye. 'It's time to put away childish things, Angel. Give it up. Luke doesn't want you. He never did.'

He had no idea how right he was, Luke hadn't wanted her in any permanent sense. All he wanted from her was a willing partner in his bed. To know it was one thing. To hear it stated as bluntly as that drained the colour out of her, leaving her grey eyes looming huge in her pale face. 'You're hateful!' she gasped tightly, reacting to the remembered humiliation of admitting the truth to herself. 'You know what I think? I think you enjoy hurting me.'

There was no humour in his glance, only a steely purpose. 'Angel, the truth only hurts because it is the truth. Open your eyes and look around you. Luke may not want you, but other men will.'

Maybe they would, but the wound was too fresh. She wasn't going to tread that path again any time soon. 'I don't happen to want anyone else!' she retorted pugnaciously, aware that the statement was open to misinterpretation, but not caring. Let him think what he liked. He would anyway. Jack shook his head.

'Then you're condemning yourself to a lonely, bitter life.'

Ellie drew her legs up, wrapping her arms around them protectively. 'Maybe, maybe not. Whatever happens, it's my life, not yours. Stop telling me what to do.'

A rueful laugh burst from him. 'God, but you're stubborn!'

She shot him a scathing look. 'And you're obnoxious!' she returned smartly, causing him to grin broadly. A funny feeling settled in her chest, and she fidgeted uneasily. It was probably nervous indigestion due to their latest confrontation. He made her so mad she could spit. He ought to learn to keep his unwelcome thoughts to himself. She had enough of her own to keep her going for years to come.

With another wry shake of his head, Jack held out his hand towards her. 'Come on, let's get you back to the villa. You're tired and hungry. A rest and some good food will hopefully sweeten your disposition.'

'There you go again!' Ellie protested irritably, but nevertheless she reached for his hand and allowed him to pull her to her feet.

Unfortunately in the process she stumbled over a rope and would have fallen except for Jack's quick thinking. He gathered her into his chest, and Ellie found her cheek pressed against firm male flesh. In response to which the whole of her nervous system leapt as if she had received an electric shock, then sent tingles rippling outwards. She became vitally aware of the strength, breadth and scent of him assailing her senses. Her body seemed to go into a state of flux and, when it solidified again, nothing was the same. It was as if every atom of her being was attuned to his presence.

'Hey, are you OK down there?' Jack queried in amused concern and, still in a state of bemusement, she tipped her head up searching his face for clues to what had just happened, for she had never experienced anything quite like it.

Whatever he saw in her eyes made him go still, his own widening before turning thoughtful. For Ellie the noisy harbour seemed to fade away, leaving the two of them alone in a frozen tableau. It was the weirdest moment, and the only way she could later describe it was as if something elemental occurred leaving her feeling supercharged. She had no name for it, but it was pretty darn powerful.

'Comfortable?'

The gently ironic query brought her back to reality with a bump, to find Jack looking down at her with a decidedly rakish gleam in his eye. Immediately upon that she discovered she was still locked fast against him, and seemingly content to stay there. Shock raced through her, galvanising her into action.

'What in the world are you doing?' she gasped in a strangled voice, struggling to push him away, but they seemed all tangled up somehow. Finally, however, she was free, and stood watching him warily, breathing hard.

'Preventing you from taking an early bath,' he responded lightly, slipping his hands into the pockets of his chinos and watching her carefully.

Ellie brushed her hair from her eyes and made a meal out of straightening her clothing. Anything to give her time to get her equilibrium back. 'Thanks, but there was no need to hold on to me so long.' What was she thinking of? She could imagine just what sort of signals she had been sending out, and groaned inwardly. She had just come out of a dead-end relationship with his brother, and it was not the time to get entangled with another Thornton, no matter how he affected her.

Jack rocked back on his heels, studying her in amusement. 'Actually, I was as much held as holding,' he corrected softly, bringing her eyes back to his in a rush.

'I was not holding you, Jack,' she denied hotly, determined to deny everything, but he merely smiled.

'Sure felt like it to me.'

She found she couldn't hold his eyes and glanced away. 'Well, you were mistaken.' She hold him? She would sooner suffer the death of a thousand cuts! Good Lord, they had been at daggers drawn for years! She mustn't forget that he didn't like her.

'Hmm, I wonder if you know how revealing your reaction is?'

Oh Lord, how like Jack to make a federal issue out of it! Crossing her arms, she tapped her foot irritably. 'If it revealed how much I dislike you, then it was entirely accurate,' she returned, shooting him an icy look, daring him to continue.

Jack combed back his hair with his fingers and took her on. 'Interestingly enough, that was the one thing you didn't show.'

That was the trouble! 'Oh, well, next time I'll do a better job. Can we go now?'

'Don't you want to know what it did reveal?' he taunted softly, and she knew that whatever it was, she wasn't going to like it.

'I'm not the remotest bit interested,' Ellie asserted, bending and beginning to pick up her luggage. With any luck he would take the hint.

Jack being Jack, didn't. 'You felt it too. I saw it in your eyes.'

The simple statement sent a tremor through her system, and her throat closed over. She didn't want to talk about it, but she couldn't allow that to pass unchallenged. 'I felt nothing.'

'Liar,' came the softly goading reply and she was compelled to look at him then. 'You felt the connection, Ellie. It was like having a million tiny sparks crackling over your skin. Like it or not, it felt good to be in my arms, didn't it?'

The claim made her go hot all over, because it had felt good. Not that she would ever dare admit it. For she didn't want to feel this way about him. Their past was a battlefield. Any personal involvement was sure to be a disaster too. Knowing it, she faced him with a laugh. 'You've said some crazy things in your life, Jack, but that has to be the most ridiculous.'

He smiled with the kind of male arrogance which made her want to hit him. 'We'll see.'

Ellie's back went up at the confident reply. 'No, we won't see.'

'There's no need to be scared.'

She sent him a basilisk stare. 'The day I'm scared of you will be never.'

'I was thinking more along the lines of you being scared of your own feelings,' came his startling response, and her lips parted on a gasp.

'What do you mean?'

'That there's nothing wrong in wanting someone other than Luke.'

Gracious of him! 'I'm glad you approve,' she retorted sarcastically.

'I couldn't do otherwise when it's me you want,' he grinned at her and she blew her stack.

Of all the arrogant...! 'O-oh, that's it! Just leave it right there! You've said more than enough. I don't have to stand here and listen to it!' With gritted teeth Ellie clamped her hat on her head, adjusted her hold on her luggage, and headed off down the dock away from him. It would serve him right if she pushed him off the edge!

'Where do you think you're going?' Jack asked, easily falling into step beside her.

Ellie kept her gaze fixed firmly ahead. 'I'm going to look for a taxi.'

He laughed. 'Good luck. This is the tourist season. If you can find an empty one, I'll eat your hat.'

'Go away,' she insisted hardily, though she knew he was right. At this time of year taxis were as hard to come by as hen's teeth.

'You know, running away isn't going to change anything,' Jack said next, and Ellie came to an abrupt halt, dumping her bags down angrily before squaring up to him.

'I am not running away. There is nothing I have to run away from.' She couldn't make it any clearer that she wasn't interested. Why wasn't he taking the hint?

'Prove it. Have dinner with me tonight,' Jack invited, taking her completely by surprise by the change of tack.

'And risk terminal indigestion? I don't think so,' she refused point blank. It would be crazy spending any time alone with him until she had got her disconcerting reaction to him under proper control. Which, she told herself, was just a matter of time.

'In case you're wondering, Luke and Andrea are dining out tonight,' Jack advised her, and she knew he would be surprised if he knew how glad she was to hear it. The longer she put off seeing Luke the better.

Ellie shrugged. 'That will give me more time with Mum and Dad.'

'Sorry to rain on your parade,' Jack interrupted without any sign of remorse. 'It's bridge night.'

Ellie glowered at him in exasperation. 'You're enjoying this, aren't you?'

His laughter admitted as much. 'You always were entertaining. So, what's it to be? Dinner with me, or an evening spent discussing the finer points of vulcanology with Paul?'

She closed her eyes momentarily. There was no contest and he knew it. Paul was a darling but... To put it kindly, sometimes his mind was a little one track.

'OK, I'll go,' she accepted grudgingly. By dinner she would have strengthened her defences anyway. She would not be giving out the wrong signals again.

Jack stooped and picked up her luggage and shepherded her towards his car. 'Gracious to the last, eh Angel.'

Ellie collapsed into the passenger seat whilst he stowed her bags in the boot. 'I know you too well to get all twittery over a dinner invitation.'

'Do you, Ellie?' Jack queried as he joined her and wasted no time starting the engine and getting them moving. 'You'd be amazed at what you don't know about me.'

She glanced at him sideways, but his attention was fully on the road. To give him his due, he was one of the safest drivers she knew.

'We've all got secrets.' Hers would send shock waves

through the family. All the more reason to keep them to herself.

'You're not interested in finding out what mine are?'

Ellie sighed and gazed out over the vista which was opening up as they climbed into the hills. 'There would be no point. It wouldn't change the fact that we don't like each other.'

'Don't we?' he challenged softly, and she glanced at him sharply.

'Are you saying you do like me?' she charged and saw him smile though he didn't take his eyes off the road.

'There's a lot to like about you, Angel.'

'There is?' she blinked, then realised how dim that sounded. 'I mean, this is such a surprise. I don't know what to say.'

His grimace told her she was overdoing it. 'Of course, it's all spoiled by this ridiculous crush you have on my brother, but you'll grow out of it.'

She inhaled sharply, thrown back into the murky waters of deception without any warning. 'There's nothing ridiculous about what I feel for Luke.' She knew how Jack would take that and he didn't fail her.

'There wouldn't be if you were ten years younger.'

Ellie turned in her seat. 'Age has got nothing to do with it. Look at you. You're, what, thirty-six now, and you're not married. Isn't that a little old to still be playing the field?'

Jack grinned as he pulled out to pass a slower vehicle. 'Not when you've found the real thing, and know you can't have it, Angel.'

His meaning took a while to penetrate, but when it

did it left her a little stunned. 'Real thing? You mean there was someone and you lost her?'

'I mean there were obstacles to our getting together. I decided, eventually, to cut my losses and look elsewhere. I'm still looking,' he explained evenly, surprising her yet again.

'Didn't that hurt?' Ellie winced sympathetically, knowing how it would have torn her apart to give up on Luke—before she realised how unworthy he was, that is.

'Thanks for assuming I could be hurt. And, yes, it did. But I wasn't going to waste my life away pining for someone I couldn't have,' he explained simply and she bit her lip.

'Like me, you mean,' she sighed, wishing his version of events was true instead of the actual reality she had lived. She had wasted so much time. Time that could never be reclaimed no matter how hard she wished.

'Don't be too downhearted. You'll see sense like I did. Then a whole world of possibilities will open up.'

Ellie shook her head vehemently. 'It's too late for that.' She had learned the lesson the hard way.

Jack steered the car into the sloping roadway that would eventually bring them to the villa. 'I'll make a bet with you that by summer's end you'll have forgotten all about Luke.'

She would never forget Luke, but not for the reasons he supposed. 'And what do I win when you lose?' she demanded confidently, as he would expect, making him laugh as he brought the car to a halt before a sprawling white stucco villa with those terracotta rooves that can only be truly found in the Mediterranean.

'Angel, if you win, you can name any prize you like.

But if I win, what will you give me?' he charged softly, but with a decided glint in his eye.

She could hardly be less generous. 'Something you want, of course.'

Reaching across, he trailed a gentle finger down her cheek to the decided point of her chin. 'I'll hold you to that, Angel,' he said with a grin before climbing lithely out of the car. 'Oh, there is one thing you should know,' he added as he opened the boot.

Ellie, who was fingering a cheek that still tingled from his brief touch, snatched her hand away and climbed out after him.

'What is it?' she asked, not quite liking the way his eyes were dancing.

'Well, when you said you weren't coming, Mum gave Andrea your room. So I'm afraid you're just going to have to use the guest room next to mine.'

He didn't hang around to check her response, for he would have known it anyway. Ellie ground her teeth together and shot daggers at his departing back. That really crowned the day. First she had found herself inexplicably attracted to the man who had been the bane of her life. Now she discovered that Luke's fiancée had been given her room. Everything was just peachy!

CHAPTER TWO

CLAD ONLY in the minuscule set of black lace underwear she had donned after her shower, Ellie padded back and forth across the cool tile floor of the guest room, brushing her hair as she went. She was feeling more than a little depressed. Her mother had barely had time for a brief chat in passing before rushing off to get ready for her bridge night, but the short time they had spent together had been worse than her meeting with Jack.

Lord, how she hated having to deceive people. Luke had never seemed to have any trouble, but she realised now that that was because he had no conscience. She had suffered agonies in the past from all the lies, and those minutes with her mother tonight had been equally painful. Ellie could still picture the scene.

Having first satisfied herself that her daughter was well, Mary Thornton had gone on in her usual cheerful vein.

'So,' she had begun, squeezing Ellie's hand encouragingly. 'How do you feel about Luke and Andrea's engagement?'

Strangely enough, Ellie hadn't anticipated that question, and her mind had floundered around for an acceptable reply before she realised that the same thing applied to her mother and Tom as it did to Jack. She needed them to know she was over Luke, without having to go into the whys and wherefores.

'Well, I was surprised, naturally, because Luke has never been a one-woman man, but to be honest, his choosing someone else didn't bother me in the least. I didn't feel even the slightest twinge of jealousy. Isn't it amazing? Whatever I felt for Luke for so long has simply disappeared. So I have no trouble at all in hoping they'll both be very happy,' she finally managed to say, and her mother had been delighted.

'That's so good to hear, darling. You know, we're glad you decided to come after all. Tom and I knew you'd see how silly you were, clinging to that thing you had for Luke. I'm so relieved it's in the past now, for your sake. You needed to move on. I had this awful feeling that you'd miss Mister Right because you were fixated on Mister Wrong. Not that Luke is really Mister Wrong, just wrong for you. Anyway, as I say, that's all past now.'

She smiled so happily, that Ellie had been unable to do more than smile back wanly. She felt more like crying. Everyone had been able to see what she had not— that Luke was the wrong man for her. Pigheadedly she had had to go her own way, and now had to suffer the consequences. It would have been wonderful to cry on her mother's shoulder, but the deception had gone on too long, and she was stuck with it. Forcing herself to be upbeat, they chatted for a while longer, then Mary rushed off, leaving Ellie to flop down miserably on her bed, her throat aching with unshed tears.

'At least I've made my mother happy,' she sighed wistfully now, fighting with a tangle that had magically appeared. 'She believes Luke is in the past, and he is. Just too late to be of any real comfort,' she added wryly.

Just then two sharp knocks sounded on her door.

'Are you decent?' Jack called out a split second before he pushed the door open and blithely stepped inside.

Shocked, Ellie stood frozen like a rabbit caught in the

headlights of a car. Jack was similarly transfixed, but only for a second. Their next actions had all the makings of a Whitehall farce. With a startled yelp Ellie remembered her state of undress and dropped the brush, grabbing up her silk robe from the bed and holding it defensively before her. Jack, meanwhile, had turned his back on her in one swift movement.

'Hey! You've got a nerve!' she charged angrily, struggling to get the robe the right way up so she could put it on.

Jack glanced over his shoulder, saw that she was in difficulties and turned back. 'Several actually,' he quipped, advancing towards her. 'All registering how good you look in black. Let me help you with that,' he offered but she slapped his hand away.

'Don't you lay a finger on me!' Ellie ordered, then blinked as he stepped back, folded his arms and closed his eyes. 'Now what are you doing?' she demanded irritably. This was so like him! He was always mixing her up, doing unexpected things.

'Closing my eyes so you can put your robe on and retain your modesty. Not that it will change anything. I've already got a perfect mental picture of you, and it's doing my libido a power of good,' he teased, making her want to hit him, though she chose to use the time more constructively and slip into the robe.

Tying the belt with hands that carried a faint tremor, Ellie walked away from him round the other side of the bed. It seemed advisable to have some distance between them. 'Do you always walk into people's bedrooms uninvited?' she charged, and Jack opened his eyes again.

'I asked if you were decent.'

'Then barged right in. You're the absolute giddy limit Jack Thornton. I could hit you!' Ellie smouldered.

'Don't worry, your revenge will come when I can't sleep tonight. Do you have any idea what the thought of you in those scraps of nothing can do to a man?' he flirted outrageously.

Actually, she had a pretty good idea. It was probably close to what having his eyes on her had just made her feel. She also knew that, now she had had time to notice, he looked incredibly sexy in his dinner suit. Scrubbed and brushed, he was more than presentable. He oozed the kind of male sensuality that scored a direct hit on a woman's senses. Hers were jangling merrily, and a wave of warmth suffused her skin. Even her breathing was a little awry.

Why hadn't she noticed this charisma before? Probably because she had never looked at him as a man before, only a pain in the neck. She was certainly seeing him now though, and the sensation it provoked was as exhilarating as it was unwelcome. She didn't want to respond to him in any way. He was the wrong man at the right time. A Thornton male, and her experience of them was not calculated to make her jump for joy.

Deciding that ignoring Jack's provocative question was the best course, Ellie folded her arms in a gesture that was half protective, half aggressive.

'OK, now that you are here, what do you want?' She got to the point and had no trouble seeing the gleam deepen in his eyes.

'You can ask that when I know under your robe is a delectably exquisite body clad only in black lace? Any hot-blooded male could tell you what I want,' he returned in a silky undertone that turned her knees to jelly and set her pulse racing.

Ellie's eyes widened at the flirtatious response. He had never spoken to her this way before, though she was used to it from other men and, whilst she was surprised, her body was registering the message on quite another level. To be blunt, it liked it.

'Be serious!' she commanded, just a tad breathlessly, hoping he wouldn't notice, but little escaped Jack.

'What makes you think I'm not?' he countered, quirking an eyebrow challengingly.

Ellie heartily wished she hadn't started this conversation, but there was no way she could back out now. 'Because you don't think of me that way.'

His lips curved. 'Don't I?'

She drew in a deep shaky breath. 'Then you shouldn't.'

'Why not?'

'Because we… That is, you and I are…' Faltering to a halt, she stared at him in perplexity.

Jack smiled, and there was no mockery in it. 'We're nothing…yet, but we will be,' he promised confidently.

Her heart lurched against her chest. 'Th-that's rubbish,' she denied, stumbling over her words, all her poise deserting her in the face of what he was suggesting.

He looked at her quizzically. 'If it's rubbish, why are you getting so nervous?'

A good question. Why was she so edgy all of a sudden? Jack had seen her in the same amount of clothes on the beach any number of times over the years. The answer was simple. Because she was now vitally aware of him as a man, and it was unsettling her, heightening her femininity. Truth to tell, she'd never been quite so aware of herself as a woman until now. There was something about the way he looked at her, so different from Luke, that was incredibly arousing. She was doing her best to ignore it, with little success. It was scary to have no control over her reactions, just when she needed to remain level-headed.

None of which she could possibly reveal to him, so she took a steadying breath and prevaricated. 'If I'm nervous, it's because you're behaving out of character.'

Both his brows rose at that. 'Is that so? Tell me something, Ellie. When did you look at me long enough to know what my character was?' he asked softly, yet with a surgeon's precision. 'No man has ever really existed for you except Luke. You've dated, probably had the odd affair, but it's all been clinical, hasn't it?'

Guilt was an uncomfortable companion, but what he said was true. The men before Luke, had simply been time fillers. She'd had no real interest in them. Until six months ago, Luke had been everything. She knew now how wrong she had been, how unfair to them. They had deserved better, and so did she.

Admitting it, though, was out of the question. Ellie tipped up her chin and fell back on the increasingly distasteful shield of her unfulfilled crush. 'I've never wanted anyone else,' she declared, and knew the instant she said it that she was asking for trouble. As expected, Jack shook his head and tutted reprovingly.

'That might have been true yesterday, Angel, but not today. Like it or not, I exist for you now.'

Her throat closed over and, shifting her weight from foot to foot, Ellie fiddled with the knot of her belt. 'You've always existed.'

Jack's smile appeared and, in a manner fast becoming familiar, her heart kicked. 'Precisely. The difference being you've seen me. There's no way back. You're aware of me, and somewhere inside you're beginning to realise you do actually want me.'

She almost laughed. If only he knew, 'realising' she

wanted him wasn't the issue. If he had been anyone else… But he wasn't, so all the more reason to deny it. 'I don't want you.'

He was less than impressed by the rebuttal. 'Because you want Luke? But he's not available, Angel. I on the other hand, would be more than willing to take his place.'

No way. Never. Absolutely not. One Thornton was more than enough for a lifetime. 'In your dreams!' she returned scoffingly but, to her aggravation, all he did was grin.

'Been there, done that.'

Ellie's jaw dropped. 'You haven't!'

The grin got broader. 'Admit it, Angel, the idea gives you a buzz.'

She stiffened in instant rejection, though in truth the thought was more than a little intoxicating. 'Not in this lifetime!'

Jack tipped his head to one side thoughtfully. 'Now what, I wonder, does that mean? That you didn't get at buzz…or that you'll never admit you did?'

Goaded, because the damn man was right…again, she shot him a snooty look down her nose. 'That's for you to decide, isn't it?'

'I wouldn't tip that perfect little nose up any higher, Angel, or you'll get frostbite,' Jack retorted laughingly, and she lowered her head with a narrow-eyed glare.

'Have you quite finished?'

He couldn't have been more amused if she had been doing pratfalls around the room. 'I wasn't aware I'd started.'

Ellie jabbed an accusing finger in his direction. 'You started the instant you walked in, you…you…' She flung up her hands in despair of finding a suitably nasty word

for him. 'Ooo-ooh, damn you Jack, you are so aggravating! If you've achieved whatever it was you set out
to achieve when you came here, you might as well go!'

'You know, if you weren't so predictable, I wouldn't
tease you. But you rise to the bait so readily, I can't help
myself,' Jack confessed in the next breath and she stared
at him in something perilously close to disappointment.

'You mean this was all an elaborate ploy to get me
angry? None of it was true?' A cold lump settled in her
stomach at the possibility. Which was crazy, because she
didn't want him to want her—did she?

'Oh, I meant every word I said,' he corrected
smoothly, strolling towards her and reaching out to brush
an errant strand of hair from her cheek. 'It's also trite
but true that you're beautiful when you get spitting mad.'

Ellie experienced a telling burst of relief, and for a
moment could do nothing but blink up at him in considerable confusion. Finally she shook her head. 'You don't
think it's dangerous to get me mad at you?'

'I can handle anything you throw at me.'

Her brows rose. 'Even a knife?'

'Even that, unless your aim has improved out of all
recognition. You never could throw a ball,' he agreed
chuckling and, though she hadn't meant to, her lips
twitched.

'I remember you tried very hard to teach me one summer,' she mused, her thoughts drifting back to a time
when life had been much more simple.

'You were lousy at it. I encouraged myself with the
thought that you'd be a whiz at something else. After
all, throwing a ball will only get you so far,' Jack remarked wryly.

'I'm good at my job.'

Jack nodded, his mood sobering. 'That you are. I just wish you'd been that positive about the rest of your life.'

'What do you mean?' Ellie charged, frowning heavily.

'Angel, almost all your life choices have been because of one man. Nothing you've done has been because you wanted it for yourself. You've let Luke be your guiding star, but he's bound on a course you can't follow. Trim your sail, Ellie, and look around you. You might be surprised at what you see.'

He sounded so earnest, as if he truly cared about her, that she found she couldn't hold his gaze. She was sorely tempted to tell him he was right, that she'd seen sense at last, but that could lead to questions she wasn't prepared to answer. She was left only with more lies, and it was becoming an increasingly distasteful method of self-protection. Her lashes dropped to conceal her expression as she turned away. 'Why should I give up my dreams?'

Catching her by the shoulders, Jack turned her around to face him. 'Because that's all they are, Ellie, dreams. We have to have them, but we aren't always meant to see them come true. We have to change them, adapt them, and then one day what we want and what we have turn out to be the same thing.'

It was too late for that. Her dream had already come true, and it had failed her. Pride was all she had left, and it coloured her response. 'What if I can't change? What if I don't want to?' she countered as stubbornly as he probably expected and, with a flash of emotion that was hastily concealed, Jack let her go.

'Then you're a fool, Ellie. A blind, wilful fool.'

A wistful smile curved her lips. 'You'd better give up on me then, hadn't you,' she suggested, and it was balm to her wounds when Jack shook his head.

'Maybe, but not yet. Not until I've tried every possible means of saving you from yourself.'

Ellie stared at him curiously, knowing she didn't understand him at all. 'Why are you even bothering? I'm a hopeless case, you said so yourself.'

'That's for you to figure out, Ellie. If you ever do, come tell me,' he told her, then took a quick glance at his watch. 'Listen, Angel, I came to tell you I have some important phone calls to make. They shouldn't take long. I've booked the table for eight-thirty, so meet me downstairs in half an hour. That will give us time for a drink before dinner.'

He was gone as abruptly as he had arrived, leaving Ellie as unsettled as she had ever felt. If that was his intention, he was doing a grand job. She turned away from the door and, as she did so, caught sight of herself in the dressing table mirror. What she saw reflected there gave her pause for thought. There were high flags of colour in her cheeks, but she was honest enough to admit it was not brought about by anger. Neither was the sparkle in her eyes. She looked alive in a way she couldn't ever remember seeing—or feeling—before.

The why of it was vastly unsettling, and the who was nearly as bad. Jack. Annoying, aggravating Jack. She was used to him giving her a headache, but not of being so aware of him her teeth ached! He was right, he existed for her now in a way she never would have expected. Had he really dreamed about her, she wondered? Instantly she told herself not to be so foolish. It didn't matter what he had done, she was not going to get involved with him. Nothing was going to change her mind about that!

The clock in the hall chimed, startling her into the realisation that she was wasting time. Jack, no doubt, would put her lateness down to her brooding about him, which, adding insult to injury, was exactly what she had been doing. She really had to pull herself together.

Shifting into gear, she rushed around like a mini-tornado, and finished dressing and fixing her make-up in half the normal time. The half an hour was almost up as she snatched hold of her evening purse and hurried from the room. Slowing her pace as she reached the top of the stairs, she took a deep breath and made her way haughtily downwards, intent on making an impression of coolness. If she appeared remote and in control, then hopefully he would get the message that she wasn't interested. Unfortunately, when she reached the ground, Jack was noticeable in his absence, and her effort was entirely wasted.

Deflated, and secretly not a little disappointed, she folded her arms crossly. The least he could have done was be there for her grand entrance, especially as she had put so much effort into her appearance. Her make-up was perfect, there wasn't a hair out of place, and her blue dress with its tiny straps and silky fabric, which shimmered as she moved, fitted her like a dream. She had hoped to take his breath away, but instead she was left cooling her heels. How like him to demand her presence, then be late himself.

The object of her growing irritation suddenly appeared at the top of the stairs.

'Sorry I'm late,' Jack apologised with a winning smile as he descended.

Ellie was the one left looking up in awe as he jogged down the stairs with all the panache and élan of a latter-day Fred Astaire. When he reached ground level, he allowed his twinkling gaze to rove over her in lazy appreciation.

'You look good enough to eat in that dress. I'll be the envy of the whole male population.' He took her by the arm and turned her so they were reflected in a nearby mirror. 'We make a good-looking couple.'

Ellie had been thinking much the same thing. They looked sort of—natural together. A strange concept, but these were strange days. Out of the corner of her eye she caught him looking at her expectantly, and she sighed.

'OK, I'll probably have to fight off the women who want to claw my eyes out, too,' she declared grudgingly and Jack grinned.

'So you won't be ashamed to be seen with me?' he asked with a jaunty quirk of an eyebrow that made her want to grin, which was all wrong.

'Stop fishing for compliments. It's most unattractive,' she countered, not wishing to answer that. The truth was, it made her feel buoyed up inside to have him at her side. Not that she would tell him, for he had a big enough head already.

'If it's such an unattractive habit, why do women do it all the time?'

'Insecurity probably,' Ellie responded seriously, knowing it to be true in her case. 'Some women are convinced they only exist through a man's eyes.' That aspect hadn't been her problem. With Luke the fishing had been done in a last-ditch effort to hold his attention. Which was an uncomfortable line of thought, and she hastily changed it. 'Of course, there are also a lot of men who have to be coaxed into saying something nice.' At which point she couldn't resist shooting him a cheeky grin. 'They don't all have your style.'

Laughing he took her arm and urged her towards the front door. 'I learned at an early age that flattery will get me a long way. As I matured, I discovered it helps to mean what you say.'

'It got you further, you mean?' she charged drily, allowing him to help her into the passenger seat of his car.

Having taken his place beside her, Jack shot her a reproving look. 'I mean I felt more comfortable with myself.'

Ellie looked at him curiously as he set the car in motion. 'Sounds to me like you've got a bad case of integrity. Didn't it hamper your style?'

'Uh-uh. I also learned that the quality of the success far outweighed the quantity.'

Her brows rose. 'A sort of "less is more" philosophy,' she quipped, tongue-in-cheek.

His teeth flashed whitely as he grinned. 'Precisely. It's far better to like and respect the women I take out, than to see them merely as scalps on a belt.'

She couldn't help but respect him for that. Another first. His brother ought to be taking lessons from him. 'It's comforting to know you don't see me as a scalp. Do you like and respect me, too?'

'We've already established I like you,' Jack returned smoothly, taking time out to send her a smoky look.

Her heart kicked and lodged uncomfortably in her chest as she registered the deliberate omission. 'But you don't respect me?' That hurt. Far more than she would ever have expected.

'Of course I respect you, Angel. But I'd respect you more if you removed those blinkers you insist on wearing.'

So, they were back to that again, were they? Ellie thought tiredly, tensing automatically. He was like a dog with a bone, unable to let it go for an instant. 'I think we should change the subject, unless you want to be fighting all through dinner.'

'You're right. I'd rather be flirting with you than flirting with indigestion,' Jack quipped back, the remark sending a tiny frisson along her nerves.

Ellie wished she didn't find the sound of it quite so inviting. It shouldn't be. Nothing to do with Jack should affect her in any way...and yet it did. Even here in the car he was a tantalising presence. The warmth emanating from him was actually setting her flesh tingling, whilst the scent of his cologne had an allure that made her want to close her eyes and savour it slowly. It was a sensory bombardment she should be resisting, but her defences weren't co-operating. It had been a day for discovering startling things about herself, and it wasn't over yet. She didn't dare think about what the evening held in store.

Jack drove them to a popular restaurant perched on a hillside overlooking the waters of the Bay of Naples, where the food was excellent and the diners were encouraged to linger over their dinner and dance if they so desired. Ellie had never been there before, but Jack was clearly well known to the *maître d'*. They were shown to a table tucked into the corner of the terrace where gentle breezes cooled the balmy night air.

Sipping at a glass of chilled white wine, Ellie glanced around her with interest. She recognised one or two people, and exchanged smiling greetings with them, before her gaze moved on. One figure caught her eye, and she did a double take then froze, her heart lurching anxiously. Across the room, seated at a romantically secluded table was Luke. She tensed immediately, waiting for some reaction to set in. This was the first time she had seen him since their break up, and she had no idea how she would feel. Her hand shook a little, and she set her glass down with a tiny thump.

Jack's hand covering hers was almost as much of a shock as seeing Luke. 'Take it easy. Relax.'

Ellie blinked at him in amazement. Relax? He had to be joking. 'Luke's over there,' she hissed by way of explanation, attempting to ease her hand free, but he applied just enough pressure to keep her where she was.

'I see him,' he returned calmly.

'Well, I wasn't expecting to,' she responded testily. This was a meeting she wasn't prepared for. Frankly, she had been hoping to delay the moment as long as possible.

'I thought you'd remember this is Luke's favourite place, Ellie,' he reminded her with gentle firmness. 'Where else would he bring Andrea?' he added, and she glanced round quickly.

A young woman had appeared at the table, and now she and Luke were locked in rapt conversation. So intent were they in each other, they were oblivious of everyone else in the crowded restaurant. Jack was right, Luke loved this restaurant. She had forgotten, but naturally Jack hadn't. Ellie caught her breath as the implications of what he had said struck home. No wonder Jack had not been the least bit surprised to see his brother. Twisting round, she looked at him accusingly.

'You knew they were here.'

'I decided it was the best way for you to see them together,' Jack said by way of confirmation. 'This way you can get the first meeting over away from family scrutiny.'

Ellie groaned silently, for she knew he was right. It *would* be easier to have the first meeting out of the glare of the family spotlight. It didn't stop her wanting to hit him for his audacity. He had no business organising her life for her.

'Don't tell me, you mean you were only thinking of me, right?' she deliberately laid on the sarcasm with a trowel. Lord, he made her so mad!

'Yes, and Andrea too, of course. Your face might have given you away, and she doesn't need to know you hate her for existing,' Jack added mockingly, making Ellie grind her teeth in exasperation. Of all the nerve!

'I don't hate her,' she denied swiftly. She felt sorry for the woman, for she doubted Luke would be any more faithful married than free. 'I don't know her,' she went on, bringing a faint smile to his lips, though not, had she looked harder, to his eyes.

'Precisely.'

Ellie allowed her gaze to stray back to the other woman. She had fashionably cut short dark hair, framing a classically beautiful face. Her eyes were stunning, large and brown, whilst her mouth was a perfect curve. She was wearing a dress that simply shrieked haute couture.

'She's very beautiful. Elegant too,' Ellie was compelled to be honest. Would looks be enough though? That was the question.

'Don't be fooled by the sugar coating. Andrea D'Abo is independent and strong-willed, not Luke's usual type of woman at all. She isn't going to put up with any of his nonsense. If he wants to keep her, he's going to have to toe the line. It's going to be interesting watching the relationship unfold,' Jack responded with amusement, drawing Ellie's eyes back to him.

She had never been able to make Luke toe the line, and Jack was implying that he expected it would be so. 'You don't think I could do that?' she just had to ask.

Jack took a sip of the manhattan he had asked for. 'Andrea is in a league of her own. You're as different as chalk and cheese. You'll never be cold-blooded enough to do what has to be done to bring Luke to heel, Angel. You're far too passionate for that. Which is fortunate, because I never have cared for insipid women.'

The implied criticism of Luke's fiancée surprised her. 'Is that how you think of Andrea? Don't you like her?'

He smiled grimly. 'Frankly it's impossible to like her. She's only interested in what will make her look good. She knows what Luke is, and yet she's determined to have him because he's the flavour of the month. Luke wants her because she moves in glamorous circles. He's willing to suffer a woman who will stand up to him and rein him in, for the kudos of rubbing shoulders with the great and good. They make a perfect couple. They're both so shallow they will probably be blissfully happy. But to answer your other question, he never needed someone who would let him use her emotions against her.'

Ellie's chin dropped, her eyes widening at the accurate description of both herself and his brother. 'Are you saying I'd do that?' She couldn't believe he saw her so clearly. It was painful to think she had been such an open book. A book he had read so very easily.

This time the smile glittered in Jack's eyes, along with something else that smouldered away in the background. 'You're far too passionate for your own good. You'd give your heart completely, and a man like Luke would break it.'

It was as if he had been there and seen it. 'How can you know that? You can't know that!' she exclaimed faintly.

'I can, because I know my brother and I know you,

Angel. You have untapped fires inside, fires Luke isn't interested in. I, on the other hand, would like nothing more than to be engulfed by those fires. Going up in flames with you would be a hell of an experience.'

Ellie felt herself growing hotter by the second as Jack elaborated on his theme. He was so right. Luke's use for passion was as a source of immediate sexual gratification. Jack, on the other hand, seemed to be saying that passion was something to be explored and shared. Something to be developed so that it would satisfy the soul as well as the body. He wouldn't leave a woman feeling used and incomplete. He had too much respect for them. More to the point, this was what he was saying he wanted to share with her! His openness was as shocking as it was arousing and, cheeks flaming, she glanced around to check if anyone had heard him.

'It's OK,' Jack reassured her coolly. 'Nobody can hear us. The restaurant it planned so that people can have intimate conversations.'

Ellie took a much needed sip of her own drink. 'That may be, but I didn't come here with the intention of having an intimate conversation with you, Jack Thornton,' she pointed out in a forceful undertone. She felt as if the whole situation was rapidly getting out of hand. She needed to bring it within bounds she could control as quickly as possible.

He laughed softly. 'Intentions have a habit of re-arranging themselves to suit the situation. For instance, you intended to make a serious play for Luke, but now you won't.'

She bridled at the unfounded charge, but at least it had the desired effect of slowing her pulse down. On this subject she knew where she stood. It might be shaky ground, but she was familiar with it. 'Even if what you say is true, and I'm admitting nothing, how can you know I won't?'

Blue eyes looked steadily into hers. 'Because you've seen them now with your own eyes.'

The statement forced her to drop her eyes. Oh, hell. He was crediting her with integrity, and under the circumstances she wasn't sure she warranted it. Had the situation been what he thought it was, that she still hankered after Luke, she wasn't sure what she would have done. Still, it made her feel better to know he thought she had goodness of spirit. Through Luke she had lost sight of what good qualities she possessed. Perhaps Jack was right, and she wasn't such a bad person for being such a fool.

She sensed him waiting for her response and sighed. 'You know, I'm fast coming to the conclusion that love stinks!' she declared gloomily, taking another larger sip of wine.

'Only the unrequited kind,' Jack corrected softly.

That brought a crease to her forehead. 'How would you…' She broke off as she remembered. 'Oh, yes. The mysterious love of your life. Was she beautiful?'

'She's not dead,' Jack pointed out with a quirk of the lips. 'She's as beautiful as ever.'

Ellie blinked in surprise as she read between the lines. 'You still see her?'

His smile was wry. 'Occasionally.'

'How do you stand it?' If she had still loved Luke, seeing him and Andrea together would have torn her apart, so she could easily imagine his feelings.

Jack's answer was surprisingly matter-of-fact. 'It isn't as if I have an option, Ellie. Neither do you. You have to deal with it and move on.'

'Be adult about it, you mean,' she grimaced, knowing she had been far from that in the past.

'If you have any pride and self-respect, you'll never let them see how much it hurts. If you're willing to grin and bear it, I'll help you,' he offered, causing her to frown.

'Help how?' she asked suspiciously.

'Well, now, the easiest way to show the world you aren't interested in Luke, is to show an interest in somebody else,' he enlarged, with just the merest hint of a gleam in his eyes.

Her heart took a crazy leap in her chest as she had no trouble at all following his line of thought. 'You're volunteering to be that someone, I take it?'

His smile broadened. 'It would be no hardship. We're already attracted to each other.'

'I do wish you'd stop saying that!' Ellie complained, not needing to hear again what she knew all too well, and got a wry shake of the head for her pains.

'You might not wish to hear it, but wishing won't change the facts, Angel.'

'That doesn't alter the fact that it's a preposterous idea,' Ellie declared roundly. 'Besides, you're no substitute for Luke,' she added for good measure. She had to put an end to this now.

Something flashed in and out of Jack's eyes and was gone before she could pin it down. 'I don't intend to be anybody's substitute. The situation calls for some defensive action, and I'm offering my services. Don't refuse the offer out of hand. Think about it.'

'I don't have to think about it, Jack. I'm not interested. There's an old saying about frying pans and fires, you know.' If Luke was a dyed in the wool rat, what did that make Jack? No, she wasn't about to make the same mistake twice.

Blue eyes danced as he watched her disgruntled display. 'Except you were never in the frying pan. Fires, on the other hand, can be cleansing and bring new life.'

Ellie's lips twisted. On the contrary, she could tell him things about frying pans he had never imagined! As for fires... 'They can also destroy. I'd rather not risk it.'

'Even if I promise not to let anything bad happen to you?' Jack wheedled with a look that sent a shiver along her spine despite her best efforts to remain immune.

'I've a feeling your definition of bad and mine differ greatly,' she returned drily, and he laughed.

'The offer remains open, nevertheless,' he said as he handed over a copy of the menu. 'Come on, it's been a long exhausting day, and you need time to regroup. Get some food inside you, and give your brain a rest for a while.'

Ellie thought of refusing, but it *had* been a long day and, despite everything, she was hungry. So she would do as he suggested, but nothing was going to make her take up his other suggestion. She might be an idiot, but she wasn't a fool. Getting entangled with Jack for whatever reason would be a big mistake. Because she was attracted and, in her vulnerable state, she might do something she would live to regret.

Besides, she wasn't in the market for another man, no matter how attractive he was. She might have broken with Luke, but that didn't mean she had to accept the first consolation prize that came along. Even if that prize brought her senses alive in a way they never had been before.

No, she was going to get through this without Jack's help.

CHAPTER THREE

ELLIE sighed appreciatively and drained the last of the coffee from her cup. She felt much more relaxed now. Jack had been a surprisingly easy dinner companion, keeping the conversation flowing with consummate ease. It was surprising how similar their likes and dislikes were. She had never noticed before. He had a wicked sense of humour, too, and had made her sides ache from laughing several times. Quite unexpectedly, she had enjoyed herself. Life was full of surprises.

Now she came to think about it, she hadn't looked at Luke and his fiancée once during dinner. Truth to tell, she had actually forgotten they were there. An unexpected but very welcome result.

She glanced their way now and felt nothing. She still despised Luke, but none of the emotions she had thought she might experience were present. Surprised, she stared at him hard, probing old wounds, trying to rouse some emotion, but nothing came. It occurred to her that, for the first time in as long as she could remember, she was totally free of him, and it felt wonderful.

'It gets easier,' Jack remarked conversationally from across the table, and she jumped, coming out of her mood of introspection.

'I'm sorry, what did you say?'

'I said it gets easier,' Jack obligingly repeated, and she realised he had mistaken her absorption for some deeper emotion.

48

As well he might, for how many times in the past had she insisted she would love Luke for ever? Believing she still felt that way, he would expect her to declare herself heartbroken. It was so far from the truth, she felt more than a little guilty for misleading him. Unfortunately, she recognised she was now in a hole too deep to get out of with any dignity. There again, dignity be damned. She should make an effort to put some of the record straight. There were too many lies. At the very least she should attempt to make him understand she no longer wanted Luke. That he could stop worrying about her.

'Listen, Jack...' she began to say, but got no further.

'I know it's small consolation right now, but you're doing the right thing,' he told her approvingly, and she wished he would stop being so nice because it was making her feel more and more guilty.

Which in turn made her snappy. 'Will you please stop going on about it!' she pleaded in desperation. 'I've accepted the situation, and there's an end to it!'

Those expressively mobile brows rose in mocking arcs above his eyes. Then he was pushing back his chair and holding out a hand to her. 'You're still getting used to the idea right now. Come dance with me and take your mind off it,' he suggested, yet managed to make it sound more like a command.

Ellie bridled and stayed where she was. 'I don't feel like dancing right now,' she refused, but that only made him walk behind her and start to pull her chair out. She had two choices: go with him, or suffer the indignity of landing on her behind in a public place. 'All right, all right, I'll dance,' she conceded, rising quickly.

Jack tucked her hand into the crook of his arm. 'Sensible of you to change your mind.'

'You wouldn't care if I was suffering the torments of the damned, would you?' she accused him, whilst keeping a smile plastered to her face for the benefit of anyone who might be watching.

'You can sob into your pillow all night, Angel, but right now you have things to do,' Jack informed her ominously, and she glanced up at him quickly.

'Things? What things?' she demanded to know, and had her answer when Jack halted beside Luke's table. Ellie ground her teeth in annoyance, realising she should have known Jack wouldn't let the matter rest until he felt satisfied.

The couple glanced up. Luke didn't see her at first because she was standing slightly behind his brother. A smile broke across his face as he rose to his feet. 'Jack, what are you doing here?'

'I took Ellie to dinner as it was her first night here,' Jack informed him, moving just enough for his brother to see her. Luke turned her way, the smile freezing on his lips. He looked about as pleased to see Ellie right now as she was to see him.

Like the charmer he was, though, in a flash his smile became as warmly welcoming and impersonal as ever. 'Hey, Funny Face, how are you?'

The old nickname was a pointed reminder to remember her place in the scheme of things. It angered her, but she was not about to let the cat out of the bag for her own reasons. So she hid her dislike behind a polite smile. 'I'm fine, thanks, Luke. In fact, I couldn't be better.' It wouldn't hurt to let him know she was well and truly over him.

Luke's eyes narrowed for a moment before he grinned. 'Glad to hear it. You haven't met Andrea yet, have you?' Without waiting for a reply he turned to his fiancée. 'Darling, this is my little stepsister Ellie. You remember, I told you all about her.'

I bet you didn't tell her about us, Ellie thought waspishly. Honesty was not Luke's long suit. 'No, I haven't,' she agreed, with a polite smile, and didn't miss the assessing look the other woman gave her.

Nevertheless, Andrea held out her hand, albeit with a put-upon smile. 'Don't worry, he didn't tell me anything bad. I'm pleased to meet you at last, Ellie,' she greeted politely as the two women shook hands. It wasn't lost on Ellie that Andrea broke the contact swiftly.

'Luke always did know how to keep a secret,' Ellie responded slyly, and felt rather than saw both men look at her sharply. She could understand Luke's sudden anxiety, but hadn't intended to arouse Jack's suspicion. 'Congratulations on your engagement. I came as soon as I heard.' She included the pair of them in her blandest smile.

'Jack said you would,' Luke rejoined with a laugh, and Ellie caught the glitter of annoyance in his glance. She ignored it, for the time was long gone when Luke's disapproval could tie her stomach in knots. Instead she shot Jack a dry look.

'Well, we all know Jack's never wrong,' she said with heavy sarcasm.

'It's my most endearing quality,' he returned smartly, and she couldn't help but laugh.

'That doesn't say much for the others, does it?'

'You'll be sorry you said that later,' Jack countered

with a decided gleam in his eye that made her nerves skip about.

'Won't you join us?' Andrea invited, although Ellie could tell it was merely a polite gesture, she didn't really want them there. They didn't fit into her scheme of things. At the earliest opportunity she would probably insist on Luke going to the States with her and, from Ellie's point of view, that wouldn't be a bad thing.

Jack shook his head. 'We wouldn't dream of intruding. Besides, we have plans of our own for tonight. We're about to hit the dance floor. Ellie expressed a wish to dance, and who am I to deny her,' he declared seductively, and Ellie caught her breath at the message he was deliberately sending the other couple. He was pairing them up when it was far from true. To underline the words, he slipped his arm about her waist possessively.

Luke noted the manoeuvre, and sent her a speculative look which she returned boldly. Though he said nothing, she could tell he was not amused. It pleased her to annoy him. 'Ellie always could wind us around her little finger,' he finally said with a scowl.

'If that's true, why are you marrying Andrea and not me?' she teased him immediately. She felt Jack tense beside her, but it wasn't *his* reaction she was interested in, only Luke's.

'Because I love her,' Luke declared, staring down into Andrea's eyes, believing as he did so that he struck Ellie's pride a cutting blow.

Had she still believed herself in love with him, the confession would have been crippling. As it was, it still had the power to make her wince. One thing was very clear. He was still angry with her for ending the affair.

Luke was a bad loser, and she would do well to remember it.

Even so Ellie knew she couldn't let it pass unanswered. 'Perhaps we can get together whilst we're both at the villa, Andrea. I can let you in on a few things you ought to know about him,' she suggested provocatively. 'I could tell you things that would make your hair curl.'

'How sweet, but I'll pass, thanks,' Andrea said with a laugh definitely lacking in humour. 'I'm not all that interested in Luke's past,' she added and Ellie discovered that Jack was right, it was hard to like her, even on so short an acquaintance.

Fortunately they parted on that note, and Ellie allowed herself to be shepherded to the dance floor where they joined several other couples. Jack turned her into his arms and began to guide them around the floor.

'That was a downright sneaky thing to do,' Ellie complained, holding herself stiffly in an attempt to keep some necessary room between them. Not an easy thing to do when Jack held one of her hands against his chest, and his free hand sat in the small of her back. It was generating a disconcerting amount of heat which was slowly coiling its way along her veins, draining her of the energy needed to keep him at arm's length.

'I know, Angel, but unpleasant tasks should be done quickly,' Jack explained his actions logically, but Ellie wasn't to be so easily appeased.

'Hah! You mean you didn't trust me not to cause trouble!' she charged scornfully.

'Women who fancy themselves in love are apt to do ill-considered things.'

'I never fancied myself in love with Luke. I did love him,' she insisted. It wasn't love now, but she had be-

lieved it was before she had come to her senses. She had
thought she would love him for ever, but she saw now
he wasn't *the* one. She had been blinded by his glitter
of false gold, so that now she didn't know if she would
recognise the real thing if it did come along. Not that
she was looking.

'Whatever that is, it doesn't appear to have affected
your appetite,' Jack returned sardonically, and she shot
him a frosty look.

'I was hungry.'

Looking down into her angry face, his lips twitched.
'You don't think you shouldn't have been?' he teased
her, and she felt a childish urge to stamp her foot.

'I think...'

Whatever her thoughts were, they remained unspoken
for more couples had joined them on the small dance
floor, and someone bumped into her back, propelling her
into Jack's body. His arm closed around her instantly,
holding her tight as he deftly swung them out of the
way.

'You OK?' he checked as soon as they were in a less
populated area.

Ellie swallowed hard and nodded, very much aware
that the whole of her body was now pressed along the
whole of his, and that one powerful male thigh was
brushing between hers as they continued to dance. The
arm she had used to brace herself away from him had
somehow taken to clinging round his neck, bringing her
cheek into the curve of his shoulder. Speech was beyond
her as her senses were bombarded with highly charged
signals which set her pulse racing like crazy.

Lord, but it felt amazingly good, was the thought up-
permost in her mind. Which was why, instead of im-

mediately breaking free, she had a strong desire to press herself closer and prolong the moment. The softly sensual brush of their bodies as they danced was doing crazy things to her insides, starting up an ache deep within her. It was powerful and heady, and for one wild moment drove all other thought from her mind. Her fingers automatically tightened on the cloth of his jacket, and for one satisfying heartbeat she relaxed against him, drowning in the spell cast by her senses.

Until a gap in the dancers gave her a fleeting glimpse of Luke and Andrea, reminding her of where she was and who with. She stiffened up immediately. This was not supposed to be happening. She was not supposed to be turning to jelly in Jack's arms—and liking it!

'Jack!' His name snapped out in an imperative undertone as her attempt to pull away was countered by strong male arms.

'What is it, Angel?' he murmured, running his hand gently down her spine, in such a way as to make her want to purr not scratch.

'You can let me go now,' she insisted, fighting the lunacy of it.

'Now why would I want to do that, when I've actually got you where I want you?' he charged drolly, and she rolled her eyes helplessly. She was neatly trapped and they both knew it, for, apart from causing a scene which she was loath to do, there wasn't much she could do if he wouldn't let her go.

She fell back on an old defence. 'Do you know how much I loathe you?'

A soft laugh escaped him. 'Your message came through loud and clear. Unfortunately it's got a little mixed now. Was that you really, really hate me, or you really, really want me?'

Colour flooded her cheeks, and it was small relief that he couldn't see it. 'You are the lowest of the low.' So she had given in to temptation for a second; he hadn't had to mention it.

'I'm glad we got that cleared up,' he declared with a husky chuckle, raising her hand to his lips and pressing a lingering kiss to her palm.

A tiny shock wave ran through her, closely followed by a curling sensation that she all too easily recognised as pure sensual pleasure. 'What are you doing?' The challenge came out in a croaky hiss. Where was her vaunted control when she needed it so badly? She had to stop this right now, or... Or Lord knows what stupid thing she might do next.

'Just what do you think I'm doing, Angel?'

The muscles of her stomach clenched as a ripple of desire fanned out to touch every nerve in her body. 'Y-you'd b-better stop it,' she stumbled over the command, for the touch of his lips was threatening to buckle her knees.

'Anything to please a lady,' he acceded, and abandoned her palm only to draw one finger into his mouth and tease it with his tongue.

That curling warmth began to spread through her system at the delicacy of the caress. 'Cut it out, Jack!' she ordered, angry with herself that she sounded more breathless than determined. Yet how could she help it when he was devilishly good at what he was doing.

Raising her head the better to emphasise her point, she found herself caught in the beam of a pair of gleaming blue eyes.

'Coward,' Jack taunted, bringing her chin up.

'People are watching us,' she pointed out desperately, but it only deepened the gleam in his eyes.

'All the more reason to carry on. This is your opportunity to show the world you're footloose and fancy free.'

She wasn't falling for that. 'All you're doing is giving Luke the impression that I'm involved with you!'

'Wouldn't that be better than to let him worry that you're still not over him,' Jack remarked, and she frowned, caught unawares by the implication.

'What do you mean? Luke's never shown I existed,' Ellie countered quickly. She should know, she'd spent years trying to gain his attention. So far as the family were concerned, she never had. Or so she had always thought, until Jack shook his head.

'Just because he never showed it, didn't mean he didn't know. He simply didn't want to hurt your feelings by a blunt rejection.'

Ellie thought she must surely have misheard, and searched his eyes to check for mischief. There was none. A cold lump of anger lodged in her stomach. There was only one way for him to know that. 'Are you saying Luke talked to you about me?' she asked, each word enunciated with care.

'To all of us. It was some time ago. You remember, when we were all home for Christmas. He wanted our opinion on what he should do,' Jack acknowledged and, had it been anyone but Luke they were talking about, she would not have thought it odd.

'And what did you tell him?' she asked, keeping her voice as neutral as she could, whilst inside her stomach roiled. That Christmas he was talking about was when they had just begun their affair.

'I advised him to wait and see. He was hoping—as we all were—that you'd grow out of it.'

It was hard to proceed as if nothing was wrong, when she was so very angry inside. How Luke must have laughed in private. Whilst she had been covering their tracks, he had been discussing her with his brother, getting his sympathy—and all the time he had known the true nature of their relationship. How he must have delighted in the danger of it, all the while laughing up his sleeve. How could she have ever thought she loved him?

'I had no idea,' she mumbled in total honesty.

'Like I say, he didn't want you upset. The point is, Mum and Dad think you have grown out of it, but Luke isn't so sure. He hasn't seen you for a while, so he's hoping you could have come to your senses. It's up to you to convince him.'

Ellie glanced away quickly lest he see her reaction. Damn Luke and his manipulations. He didn't believe she was over him, but not in the sense his brother took it. He believed she would come running at the snap of his fingers—because she always had in the past. Well, he was very much mistaken. She had twenty-twenty vision where he was concerned. Convincing him wouldn't be easy, especially as she still wanted to keep their affair a secret. A shame, because it would do her the power of good to slap his face—hard.

'I thought I just had. I gave him my blessing just now,' she argued through a tight throat. 'What more should I have to do?'

'You know as well as I do, Angel. The only sure way to convince him that you see him only as a stepbrother, is to show a healthy interest in another man,' Jack reiterated.

'I doubt if I could be convincing,' Ellie muttered quietly. She had never felt less romantic. Murderous came closer to the mark.

'We'll work on it. It's a truism, but practise does makes perfect.' Jack quickly put in, and her lips twisted wryly.

'What makes you think I'd choose you for the task? There are other men around.'

'But I'm the only one here,' he pointed out, eyes dancing.

'You're forgetting Paul,' Ellie countered with a lift of her chin, but Jack laughed.

'It has to be believable, Angel. Nobody's going to think you've suddenly developed an interest in Paul.' He shot that down. 'Don't get me wrong, Paul's a nice guy, but the only passion in his life right now is his beloved volcanoes.'

Sadly true, she concurred silently. 'The same applies to you. Everyone knows I dislike you. We've fought like cat and dog for years,' she was quick to point out.

Jack ran his thumb over her bottom lip. 'Love and hate are two sides of the same coin. Nobody would bat an eyelid. My guess is, they're more likely to nod sagely and say they knew it all along.'

The soft caress sent a disproportionate amount of tingling through her system, and she pulled away, annoyed that she couldn't control it. 'They're never going to believe I've fallen in love with you just like that!' she argued triumphantly, but Jack wasn't put off.

'We're not talking love here, just attraction. A powerful sexual attraction that overrides past antagonisms. That they will believe, for one very good reason.'

Ellie's mouth went dry, for she knew the answer as well as he did. 'And that is?'

'There is a strong attraction between us, and if we act upon it, we would certainly be convincing.'

It would be pointless to deny it, and it would certainly put a dent in Luke's overwhelming ego, but... The snag was keeping control of the situation. How did she put up a convincing performance and not get caught up in the passion of the moment? She couldn't help feeling that in two seconds flat of them starting, the performance would become reality. However much she might enjoy it, and her senses were telling her she would, she didn't want to get involved with him.

'Hmm, I still think it would be better to find another way.'

'You can set the rules,' Jack put in temptingly, and she looked up at him with a wary frown.

'Meaning?'

'Meaning it will be up to you how far this attraction between us goes,' he enlarged, and her eyes narrowed again.

'Somehow I don't get the feeling you'll give up so easily,' she mused, and he grinned.

'I don't intend to. You set the boundaries, Angel, but I reserve the right to try and persuade you to change your mind.'

Now that sounded like Jack! 'I knew there had to be a catch! I don't trust you.'

Jack shook his head. 'It's yourself you don't trust. Say no and mean it. That's all you'll have to do.'

Easier said than done, if her responses so far were

anything to go by. Not a comfortable thought. It was all too much for a tired brain. 'Look, if you've achieved everything you set out to do, can we go now?' Ellie proposed, stifling a yawn that welled-up from nowhere. The exertions of the day were catching up with her—fast.

He took a glance at her tired grey eyes, and instantly stopped dancing. 'You're about out on your feet, aren't you? Come on, let's get you home.'

Jack made short work of paying the bill and collecting her purse, then they were heading out into the cooler air of the car park. It had the effect of clearing some of the cobwebs from her brain, but for reasons best left alone she didn't remove her hand from Jack's steadying arm. When they reached the car, she looked at the sporty shape quizzically.

'Isn't a Ferrari a bit ostentatious for a banker?' she asked goadingly, and he quirked an eyebrow at her. 'I mean. It has to make one wonder where the money came from, and that could open a whole nasty can of worms.'

'For your information, the car's rented,' he informed her repressively, but Ellie wasn't to be put off just yet.

'I suppose that's more your style,' she mused, 'but why a Ferrari?'

Jack released her and folded his arms. 'Perhaps it's got something to do with the fact this is Italy?' he suggested tolerantly yet warily.

'Ye-es, but why not choose a Fiat? No, I think you chose a Ferrari because it's part of a fantasy. It makes me wonder just what goes on in that head of yours,' Ellie mocked, eyes dancing with mischief.

His lips twitched. 'Stick around and you'll find out.'

Her eyes rounded. 'Am I in this fantasy too?'

'Wouldn't you like to know,' Jack teased back, then his gaze drifted past her, and what he saw brought a smile to his lips as he looked at her again. 'I thought you were tired,' he pointed out, and she sighed.

'The air woke me up.'

'Good,' Jack declared, reaching for her waist and pulling her up against him. 'I want you working on all cylinders right now. Kiss me,' he ordered, and brought his mouth down on hers.

Shock held Ellie where she was initially, but it was the sensory pleasure the touch of his lips created which kept her there, and set her hands lifting to his shoulders to cling on for dear life. Her eyelids fluttered down, and a soft sigh escaped her lips. The brush of his lips was magic, so soft she barely felt it and yet her whole body was caught in the spell. Every atom of her being wanted to know more, and the stroke of his tongue along her lips had her melting against him, her lips parting to allow him entrance.

What happened then was a slow ravishment of the senses. Sparks were ignited and coaxed into fires by each foray of his tongue. Ellie was helpless to do other than respond, joining him in a lazy, sensual dance which was all the more powerful for its restraint. She could never have imagined a kiss could be so enticing, and she gave herself up to the enjoyment of it. As her hands slipped about Jack's neck, her fingers tangling in the hair at his nape, his arms closed around her, pulling her close until not even a breath could pass between them. Passion flared, but it was slow and sultry, making their blood zing, never getting out of control whilst all the while threatening to.

Only the need for air made them draw apart, and Ellie

stared up at Jack in wonder, her heart still pounding. Jack held her gaze, and even in the darkness she could see the banked fires in his eyes.

Ellie gave her head a tiny shake. 'There must be something wrong with me.'

'You look OK from where I am.'

'I should be pushing you away.'

'Deep down inside you don't want to.'

She let that pass, and her silence was acceptance of the truth of what he said. 'Where did you learn to kiss like that?' she queried huskily, not caring that she sounded more than a little awestruck.

Jack laughed softly, running a finger gently across her tingling lips. 'Just natural talent. You were pretty awesome yourself.'

Her lips curved softly. 'I think I was inspired,' she confessed wryly.

'There was a lot of inspiration floating around tonight. I told you we'd make an explosive combination.'

Ellie might have enjoyed their kiss, but she hadn't totally lost her senses. 'Is this where I'm supposed to say, OK you've convinced me, we'll go with plan A?'

'Clearly not,' Jack grimaced, easing her away, not releasing her until she was steady on her feet. 'Believe it or not, that was light years from my mind when I kissed you. On the other hand...'

Lights illuminated the area around them as a car swept past and out onto the road.

'On the other hand, never look a gift-horse in the mouth,' Ellie finished for him, taking her eyes from the departing car and staring him out. 'That was Luke.'

Jack smiled wryly and rubbed a finger along the ridge of his nose in a gesture she knew well. It always meant he had been found out. 'They followed us out,' he admitted. 'It seemed too good an opportunity to miss.'

'How did you get to be so sneaky?' she demanded, though not as angrily as she should have. It was hard to appear affronted when she had enjoyed every second of what had just passed between them, no matter why it happened.

'I grew up with an expert at it,' Jack replied, bending to open the car door for her. Holding it, he glanced at her expectantly.

Ellie obediently climbed into the car, but she was frowning. 'What do you mean?'

'Luke always managed to get what he wanted one way or another,' Jack announced as he joined her and started the engine. 'He knew what to do and what to say, and most importantly, how to wait. As a consequence, he was rarely, if ever found out.'

Ellie stared at him silently as he reversed the car, then turned and headed home. That description fitted Luke to a tee. It was, after all, exactly what he had done in order to get her into his bed—and keep her there. Fortunately for her, she found him out, and it swept away the blinkers she had been wearing for years.

'To look at him you'd think butter wouldn't melt in his mouth,' she said distastefully, and Jack spared her a look.

'You don't sound surprised.'

'Actually, I'm not,' she confirmed, then sighed. She was tired of defending the indefensible. It was time to make another attempt to set the record straight. 'Listen Jack, I don't expect you to believe me, but I haven't been wearing those rose-tinted glasses for some time,' she added, feeling the need to prove that she wasn't a total fool where his brother was concerned.

'No? That wasn't the impression you were giving earlier,' he reminded her, and Ellie knew she would never have a better opportunity to tell him she was over her crush, and still keep her secret.

'I know, but you made me angry, so I decided to let you get on with it,' she told him sardonically.

'Let me get this straight. You're now saying you don't want Luke?' he charged doubtfully.

Ellie kept her eyes on the road ahead as she answered. 'I haven't for some while.'

'This is a very convenient change of heart,' he responded suspiciously, and Ellie shrugged.

'Come on, Jack, you're hardly the first person I'd tell. Look at today. The minute you saw me you were off again,' she reminded him caustically.

Jack was silent for about a minute or two, considering her comment. 'If it's true, then I'm glad to hear it. There might be hope for you yet, Angel.'

Trust him to keep doubting her, but at least she was making progress. 'Of course it's true. If you hadn't been so annoying, I'd have told you sooner.'

'As a matter of interest, just how long were you going to let me keep on thinking the way I was before letting me in on the secret?' he demanded to know, and she laughed.

'Hard to say, you were enjoying it so much.'

He harrumphed, but only said, 'Do the parents know?'

'Yes.'

'So now all we have to do is convince Luke.'

Ellie's nerves jumped. 'Surely that isn't necessary. He has Andrea now, and if I show no interest in him whatsoever, the effect will be the same,' she countered, knowing where his thoughts were heading.

'You can try it, if you think it will work, but my way will be better,' Jack pointed out softly.

Better for whom? Jack had another agenda, but she didn't intend to be part of it. 'Don't think this is getting you anywhere. Just because I don't want Luke, doesn't mean I'll turn to you instead!' she warned him off.

'But it doesn't mean you won't,' Jack responded with what sounded to her like satisfaction.

Ellie felt satisfied too, up to a point. At least Jack now knew how things stood. That was about as good as it was going to get. She might wish she could wipe the slate clean, but knew it was impossible. All she could really do was learn from her mistakes. Which meant not jumping straight into another one. Tempting as Jack was, she had to be sensible for once. Which was a shame, because that kiss… She sighed, knowing she was doomed to relive it many times in her dreams.

CHAPTER FOUR

NEXT morning Ellie was lounging in the doorway which led from the breakfast room onto the terrace, sipping at a delicious cup of coffee, when she heard footsteps behind her. Glancing round, she smiled as Luke's fiancée entered the room. She received a cool smile in return, and realised she was probably wasting her time. Andrea was elegantly dressed in white capri pants and a pure-silk red blouse, with not a hair out of place. Ellie herself had plumped for her favourite khaki shorts and a minimal vest top. When on holiday she simply wanted to relax, and fashion was the last thing on her mind. Andrea clearly had different standards. Nevertheless, she was prepared to be friendly towards her.

'Good morning,' she greeted the other woman cheerfully. 'I thought I was the last to come down.'

Andrea shot her a cool glance as she poured herself a cup of coffee from the pot on the table. 'You are. I've been up for hours, but I have a rigorous fitness programme that I follow, and I won't miss it even if I am on holiday.'

Ellie knew she was supposed to have been put in her place, but refused to go. She shuddered delicately. 'That's far too strenuous for me, though I jog when my work schedule allows.'

'I'm trying to get Luke to join me,' Andrea confided as she joined her, looking out at the view without any show of enthusiasm for the dramatic beauty of it.

Ellie almost choked on a mouthful of coffee, and took a gasping breath. 'Good luck!' she declared with heavy irony. To her knowledge Luke had never done one exercise in the whole of his life.

'Why do you say that?' Andrea charged sharply, frowning, and Ellie sent her a sympathetic look.

'Because Luke's indolence is legendary. Now if you want someone to work out with, Paul's your man.'

'Thanks, but I'm rather choosy about my exercise partners. I have to know they're on the same level as myself,' the other woman responded, and they fell silent for a moment, studying the view of sunlight on the distant sea. 'God, what do people do on this rock for entertainment?' Andrea asked after a while and Ellie shot her a puzzled look.

'Just about anything you can do anywhere else, and it's warmer too,' she joked.

'I'm sure that's fine for the tourist, but what about those of us who are used to a higher standard?' Andrea charged with a tiny shudder of distaste that set Ellie's hackles rising.

'Actually, most of us consider the standards are high here,' she returned just a tad frostily, and Andrea shrugged.

'Really? Oh well, I dare say a few days won't matter.'

Silence fell again and Ellie made no effort to break it. From her brief acquaintance with the other woman she knew they would never get along. Luke was more than welcome to her.

'That was some clinch you and Jack were in last night,' Andrea remarked a few minutes later, sending a tremendous jolt through Ellie, who had not expected it.

Ellie turned and stared at her, colour slowly rising into her cheeks. 'I…er…'

Andrea laughed, patently enjoying her confusion. 'Lord, you're embarrassed. How quaint. I only mentioned it because Jack always seemed a little reserved—until last night. I don't think either of you would have heard a bomb go off right beside you. Though perhaps next time you should choose a place a little less public for that kind of thing.'

Ellie found herself itching to slap the other woman—hard. Instead she smiled mockingly. 'We'll try, but when the urge strikes…you just have to give in to it, and things can get a little out of hand. You know how it is.'

Andrea's lips thinned. 'I'm glad to say I don't,' she denied with a delicate shudder. 'However, if you enjoy being manhandled, I wish you joy of it. I'll say no more. Except that Jack's…nice. You could do worse.'

Nice wasn't a word Ellie had ever used in connection with Jack, but considering it now, she realised that Andrea was right. For the most part, Jack was nice. He was kind, thoughtful and generous as a rule. Only in his dealings with her had he been nasty and scathing. It was something to think about, but not now, for someone else entered the room and both women turned.

It was Luke. Andrea looked inordinately relieved and went over to him. Ellie held back, choosing to watch him kiss his fiancée over the rim of her cup. He made quite a show, and Ellie couldn't help thinking that it was for her own benefit. To remind his ex-lover what she was missing. He missed the mark by a long way.

Unimpressed, she turned her back on them. Down below Paul climbed the path up from the pool and, catching sight of her, he waved a greeting. Ellie grinned and waved back. As he disappeared round the side of the villa, a hand came down on her shoulder. She jumped like a scalded cat and looked round hastily. Luke stood behind her, and they were alone in the room.

'Where's Andrea?'

Luke set his other hand on her other shoulder and smiled down at her. 'Gone to get ready. We're going into Anacapri to do some shopping. It's good to see you, Funny Face.' He lowered his head as if to kiss her, and Ellie jerked her head aside swiftly, shrugging out from his loose hold.

'You can't just kiss me whenever you feel like it, Luke,' she declared frostily, putting distance between them.

'Why not? As I recall, you used to like me kissing you,' he argued with a lecherous look that he fondly thought was alluring.

Ellie suppressed a shudder of distaste. 'Yes, well, that was before I grew more discerning.'

Luke advanced on her, smiling and shaking his head. 'You don't mean that. You still want me. You're mine, Funny Face. You've always been mine.'

She held up a restraining hand. 'You couldn't be more wrong. I'm not yours, and I don't want you.'

He laughed. 'Liar. You couldn't wait for me to touch you. You were insatiable. A real tigress. You'll be back.'

Ellie ground her teeth in impotent anger, stunned by his overweening ego. She didn't want him, and the more he said, the more she wondered how she ever could have. What did she have to do to make him understand it was over?

'Don't count on it,' she warned by way of a start.

A scornful look entered his eyes. 'Of course I'm

counting on it, because you love me, Ellie. Everyone knows it. Come back where you belong.'

Ellie set her empty cup down with a bang and squared up to him. 'Listen to me Luke, and try to understand. I do not belong with you and I do not love you. It's over.'

To her chagrin, he laughed again. 'You're saying that now because of Andrea, but you'll soon change your mind. You'll be back. I know you. All I'll have to do is snap my fingers.'

Ellie closed her eyes, choked with impotent anger. It was like talking to a block of wood. Nothing she said got through. But he was wrong. She was not his to command and, if words did not convince him, then that only left actions.

When she looked at him again, her expression was icy. 'You don't know me at all, Luke. You never took the trouble to find out, but I'm learning about you all the time, and I don't like what I see. Dream on if you must, but you'll never have me again.'

Luke was about to argue, but they both heard light footsteps echoing across the hall. Andrea was returning, and there was one thing both Ellie and Luke had in common. Neither wanted the other woman to know about their affair. Ellie made a play of refilling her cup, whilst Luke went to meet his fiancée.

'Ready, darling? Good. I know the perfect little restaurant where we can get the finest seafood for lunch. How does that sound?' he said caressingly as he slid an arm about her waist.

Andrea looked from one to the other as if she suspected something had been going on, but merely smiled. 'Sounds good.'

'See you later, Funny Face,' Luke called out as they

left, and her lips tightened into a grim line the second they were out of sight.

Not if I see you first, she thought ferociously. She abandoned the coffee she hadn't wanted anyway and braced her hands on the table, striving to regain her temper. What a slug! How had she ever let him touch her? She had to have been out of her mind. Thank goodness she'd recovered. Dealing with the fallout was proving more of a problem, though.

Of course, she had the answer to her problem—if she dared accept it. Jack. Not that she really had a choice. It was Jack or nothing, and nothing wouldn't work. So she would have to take him up on his offer, but make sure he understood it was not for real. It would at least raise her another notch in his estimation. She would, after all, be doing what he wanted, putting Luke's mind at rest. Boy, if he really knew what Luke was thinking, he would blow a gasket. But she would do just about anything to get Luke off her back. Desperate situations called for desperate measures. Now all she had to do was find him and set things in motion.

Which proved to be easier said than done. A search of the house failed to turn him up but fortunately she bumped into Paul on the landing and he sent her off to the pool. As she approached the pool area through its concealing barrier of shrubs, she caught sight of Jack's sleek tanned body, clad in only a brief pair of black trunks, cutting through the water with apparent ease.

She was smiling reminiscently as she walked round to where loungers had been set out. Jack was a natural in the water, and could churn out lengths tirelessly. He had taught her to swim, and she had felt totally safe in his hands. Strange, she had forgotten that once they had been far from antagonistic towards each other. She and Jack had been at loggerheads so long, it was like another lifetime.

However, as Ellie looked down at him, her smile slowly faded. Muscles rippled with each easy movement, and the water flowing over his back outlined every rise and fall of solid male flesh. She remembered that kiss they had shared last night, and the feel of his strong body pressed to hers. The same body which was within touching distance and had barely a stitch on. Her senses registered all this in an instant, and her mouth went dry. A frisson swept across her skin as she acknowledged that she wanted to touch him. Wanted to find out if his body was as smooth and silky as it appeared.

Desire, hot and powerful, ignited and pulsed through her system from its source deep within her. Ellie had never experienced a need so strong, had never been aroused by simply looking at a man. It was almost scary, and most definitely exciting, but not the reaction she wanted to be feeling if she expected to keep any form of control of the situation. Perhaps it would be better if she waited to speak to him when he had more clothes on.

Good idea, she thought, and turned to leave.

'Looking for me?'

Ellie looked round hastily. Jack had stopped swimming and was resting his arms on the edge of the pool. As she watched, he flicked back his wet hair in a casual gesture that should not have been sexy, but certainly was. In the next instant he was levering himself up out of the pool with consummate ease. As he walked towards her, she was presented with a perfect view of his bronzed figure, made all the more spectacular by the water trailing off him.

How come she had never noticed he had such a magnificent physique? Because, as Jack said, she hadn't ever seen him. She was seeing him now, all right, and scarcely knew where to look. She found his chest far too fascinating for her blood pressure, but dropping her eyes presented her with a far greater problem. Ellie decided that had she had a collar, she would definitely be hot under it. As it was, she was simmering.

'What did you want to see me about?' Jack enquired as he halted a scant few feet away, hands resting on his hips.

It proved incredibly hard to gather her scrambled thoughts together and, when she did, she had to clear her throat and lick her lips in order to speak. 'I...er...came to tell you plan A is on after all,' she croaked out, and Jack's brows rose questioningly.

'Really? What happened to change your mind?'

The truth being out of the question, Ellie quickly invented a logical reply.

'I've been thinking about what you said, and saw the sense of it. It would be better for all concerned that Luke has no doubts.'

Jack combed his fingers through his hair, and muscles rippled tantalisingly. 'Ah, the voice of sweet reason, hmm? I had no idea I was so persuasive. You seemed pretty adamant last night.'

She hadn't had that conversation with Luke, then. 'I was, but like I said, I've thought about it and I think you're right. Luke needs to know he doesn't have to worry about me. Pretending to be involved with you, will put his mind at rest.'

She didn't like perpetuating Luke's lie that he was concerned about her, but when the only way to disprove it was to confess the affair between them, she had little choice.

'And when do you want our little charade to start?' Jack queried, with a strange glint in his eye that set her nerves jangling the second she saw it. He was up to something. She would bet her bottom dollar on it.

'Luke and Andrea have gone shopping, so...'

'Then that's where we'll go,' he interrupted. 'The more they see us together, the more convinced he'll be.'

Ellie had been about to suggest waiting until later, but she could see his point. The sooner the better worked well for her too. She wanted Luke to get the message loud and clear.

'OK. I have to get a present for them anyway.'

'Sure you weren't subconsciously hoping you wouldn't have to buy one, Angel?' he taunted softly and she shot him an acid look.

'Actually, I wasn't intending to come here at all, so a present was the last thing on my mind,' she pointed out tartly but, as usual, Jack wasn't about to be won over that easily.

'Something changed your mind?'

Ellie sighed. 'I realised my non-appearance would look odd.' And send Luke entirely the wrong message.

Jack's lips twitched. 'So here you are, about to embark on a love affair with me.'

Her chin went up. 'A pretend love affair,' she corrected firmly. 'You said I could set the rules, remember?'

'Ah, but where does pretence end and reality take over?' he teased with a soft laugh, which sent a shiver through her system. 'Perhaps we should put it to the test, hmm?'

Had she moved quicker, she probably would have avoided him, but other factors were at work here. She was fighting an inner battle as to what would be best and what would be good. And, as everyone knows, she who hesitates is lost. Jack had no trouble capturing her and pulling her close. A hand in her hair angled her head for his kiss, and then his mouth took hers.

There was nothing languid about this kiss. From the first brush of lips, heat expanded outwards, consuming her, and her lips parted on a tiny gasp. That was all Jack needed to claim her mouth, his tongue demanding a response from hers which he got instantly. Ellie moaned as he ravished her senses, returning each stroking caress with mounting passion.

His mouth left hers, but only to plunder the sensitised skin below her ear. Ellie shivered in reaction to the scalding brand of his lips, and her head fell back, allowing him access to the sensitive chord of her throat which he was quick to accept. It was like drowning, and her hands clung on to his shoulders as the only stable thing in the turbulent waters of passion.

Then it was over, as quickly as it started. Jack groaned as he raised his head, at the same time pressing her head into his shoulder. Disorientated though she was, she felt his heart thudding as wildly as her own. For sheer eroticism, she had never known a few minutes like it. Had Jack not stopped, she doubted she would have. Above her, she could feel his cheek pressing against her hair, then he took a deep breath and eased her away from him.

There was no laughter in the eyes which held hers,

but an intensity she somehow couldn't look away from. Her heart lurched.

'Real or pretend, Ellie? You tell me.'

Oh, it was real. Very real. How could she pretend otherwise. This attraction between them was expanding out of all proportion. How could it get so hot so quickly? It was like a forest fire ignited from a single spark, which created a fire that consumed everything in its path.

'I'd like to say it was pretend, but I'm not that good an actress,' she finally admitted gruffly, for what was the point of lying? He knew.

Her answer brought a faint smile to his lips. 'Thanks for the honesty.'

Taking a deep breath, Ellie eased herself away from him. 'This changes nothing. I still won't get involved with you, Jack.'

'We already are involved, Angel. What we're doing now is sorting out the degree of involvement. I'm prepared to compromise—for now,' he told her blithely, and Ellie gritted her teeth.

'Maybe you are, but I'm not,' she argued, and he shook his head, laughing softly.

'It always was all or nothing with you, wasn't it, Angel?' Jack responded gently. 'Speaking as someone who has suffered the nothing, I'm looking forward to the all.'

Ellie shook her head helplessly. He made it sound as if an affair between them was a foregone conclusion. However, she knew how strong emotions can play you false, and she wasn't entering into another relationship in a hurry. 'You could be in for an awfully long wait.'

Far from being put off, he shrugged. 'No matter. I'm a patient man.'

Her chin rose a notch as that struck a nerve. 'Something you and Luke have in common!' she retorted swiftly, reminding him of what he had said last night.

Jack went still, and there was no amusement in his face now. 'When it comes to our dealings with you, Angel, Luke and I are not a bit alike. Remember that.'

Her eyes widened. 'You make it sound important.'

Reaching out, he ran a finger gently over her lips. 'Oh, it is. Very.'

Something in the way he said it made her heart skip a beat. It was almost as if he were telling her something, but she couldn't quite grasp the meaning. 'I don't understand you,' she confessed with a frown that he smoothed away with his thumb.

'Do you want to?'

Did she? Would it help to know what made him tick? Was it necessary to the fiction they were about to create? Certainly it was no to the latter, but for the rest...

'Yes, I do,' she replied honestly, for Jack was proving to be a mystery she wanted to solve.

'Then we're making progress.'

Ellie waited for more, but he remained silent and her brows raised. 'Is that all you're going to say?'

Jack grinned and turned her back the way she had come. 'For the moment,' he confirmed as he fell into step beside her and they began to walk back to the villa.

'O-oh, you are so aggravating! What do I have to do, ask questions?'

'Fire away. I promise to answer them as honestly as I can,' he invited, slipping an arm across her shoulders. 'Of course, to really understand a person, you have to spend time with them. Get to know them.'

'Unfortunately I don't have the odd twenty or so years

to spare,' Ellie retorted, very much aware that his close-
ness meant their thighs brushed with every step they
took. 'Would you mind removing your arm. Nobody can
see us.'

'I know, but this has nothing to do with anyone else.
I happen to like touching you. Your skin is as smooth
as silk, as soft as velvet.'

And his voice, Ellie added silently, was as seductive
as thick, dark chocolate. Sinfully sensuous—and not
necessarily good for you. The trouble was her senses
weren't as cautious as her brain, and they responded,
setting her pulse beating a little faster, and thickening
the flow of blood through her veins.

She groaned inwardly, doing her best to ignore the
curling sensation in her stomach. 'The idea was that this
was for Luke's benefit,' she argued staunchly, and could
sense the smile that spread across his face.

'True, but if we don't want the act to look stilted, then
surely we have to play the part all the time,' he coaxed
and she rolled her eyes. He had an answer for everything. Thank goodness they were back at the house and
they could go their separate ways.

As luck would have it, they met Paul coming out just
as they entered. He looked from one to the other, and
Jack's strategically placed arm, and a big grin split his
face.

'Hi, Jack. Ellie. Great to see you two have finally
stopped fighting. Must be catching, this love stuff!'
Laughing heartily, he jogged off to where he had parked
his Land Rover.

Ellie watched him go, appalled. 'Oh, great! Now look
what you've done!' she exclaimed, turning accusing
eyes on Jack, who looked highly amused.

'Me?' he gasped, placing a hand on his chest and trying to look aggrieved.

'You had to play the fool, and now Paul's got entirely the wrong impression!'

Jack took her by the shoulders and gave her a tiny shake. 'You're making a mountain out of a molehill, Ellie. He was joking with us.'

Ellie set her jaw. 'Well, I didn't find it funny.'

'Do you want him to think you're still mooning over Luke, too?'

'Of course not. I just don't want him to think that we're involved now.'

Jack gave her an old-fashioned look. 'He won't have any option soon. The whole family is going to believe it. Get used to the idea.'

He was right, darn it, Ellie conceded with a grimace as she preceded him indoors and made for the stairs. They couldn't go about switching their supposed romance on and off. It had to be on all the time. She understood the sense of it, but it didn't make her feel any less jittery. Tell herself though she might that it was all a sham, somehow she couldn't quite get convinced.

She might just have jumped from the frying-pan to the fire after all.

CHAPTER FIVE

THAT very evening Jack dropped the bombshell on the family—Ellie included. She had had no inkling of what he intended to do. They had gone into town as planned but by early afternoon hadn't encountered Luke and Andrea, though Ellie did manage to find an engagement gift for them. So it wasn't a total waste of time. Jack had been in a relaxed mood and they had actually spent the time quite happily searching the markets, stopping off at a small local restaurant for some lunch when energy levels began to flag.

They ate outside, watching the world go by.

'So, how are things in the investment banking business? Still making disgusting amounts of money?' she teased him over coffee.

'You might say we're living in interesting times,' Jack returned ironically.

Her brows rose at the description. 'You didn't buy into those technology thingummys did you?' she asked, shaking her head and tut-tutting reprovingly.

His smile widened. 'Not as heavily as some,' he admitted, not in the least fazed by her teasing.

'So there's no chance of you being out of a job?'

'You can sleep safely in your bed at night, secure in the knowledge that I will still be able to support you in the style you've become accustomed to,' Jack returned smoothly.

'Hey!' Ellie objected instantly. 'You won't support

81

me in any style, I make my own living.' Worked hard at it too.

'Sure you do, but I keep my eye on your trust fund.'

That was different. The fund he was referring to was the one she had inherited from her grandmother. She had come into it when she was twenty-one, but she had never touched it, preferring to make her own way in life. 'Oh, that. How's it doing? Should I still trust you with it?'

Another man might have taken offence, but Jack merely looked amused at her doubting his financial acumen. 'It's doing well. If you bothered to check you'd find it had increased quite considerably. However, if you think someone else could do better...'

Ellie wasn't really worried about the money, and knew of nobody else who would look after her interests so well. 'On consideration I'll stick with you,' she conceded grudgingly and he grinned at her.

'Big of you.'

'Well,' Ellie grinned back. 'I know that when it comes to money you're totally trustworthy.'

One brow curved up. 'Meaning I'm not trustworthy in other ways? I think you should elaborate.' Reaching across the small table he began toying with her fingers. 'In what ways don't you trust me, Angel?' he went on huskily, and Ellie suddenly found herself caught on the end of a gaze simply loaded with sensual mockery.

She drew her hand back but not without a shiver of awareness. 'I wish you would stop doing that,' she complained, though the quaver in her voice rather spoiled the effect.

'Just getting into the mood,' he taunted and she rolled her eyes.

'That's just my point. There is no mood to get into.

You don't have to touch me but you do. I can't trust you not to take advantage of the situation.'

Jack laughed unrepentantly. 'Angel, if you felt nothing, it wouldn't matter if I touched you or not. Your problem is you don't trust yourself. I'm the least of your worries. What are you going to do when you don't want to say no any longer?'

She had been wondering that herself but, as she had no answer, her chin rose a notch. 'What makes you think that will happen?'

He sat forward, closing the gap between them. 'Because you and I are a combustible combination. No matter how hard you tamp down the flames, they keep coming back.'

Which was true enough, but she wasn't about to say so. 'I'm a pretty good fire fighter. I'll cope.'

His smile took on that sexy curl which weakened her knees, so it was as well she was sitting down. 'Sometimes you have to set a fire to control another. Maybe we should get together and check it out,' Jack suggested silkily and Ellie uttered a groaning laugh.

'You have an answer for everything.'

'Not everything, Angel, or you and I would be somewhere a lot less public, doing something much more interesting than searching for my brother.'

Ellie shook her head, though her nerves did a high jump at his statement. 'There you go again, assuming I'd agree to be somewhere else with you. What an ego!'

Smiling, Jack rose smoothly to his feet and reached into his pocket for money to pay their bill. 'One day you're going to start being honest with yourself, and I intend to be around when you do. Come on, let's take another tour of the shops. In a town the size of this one, they have to be somewhere close.'

'I am being honest. It's you who has a lack of faith,' Ellie protested as she joined him. 'You don't believe anything I say.'

He laughed softly. 'That's because your lips say one thing and the rest of you another. You'll be incredible when you finally come to terms with yourself,' he told her, taking her hand in his and resisting all her attempts to pull away.

'Let me go,' she hissed through her teeth, very much aware that her undignified struggles were drawing a great deal of attention to herself, and not liking it.

'Behave yourself then,' he commanded continuing on his way to where the shops sold all sorts of things for the tourist trade. 'Be a good girl and I'll buy you a present.'

Abandoning her fruitless bid for freedom with a glare at his back, Ellie followed along like a grumpy dog on a leash, though in actual fact the way his hand held hers so securely, she was experiencing that strange bubbly feeling inside again.

'I don't want you to buy me a present,' she pouted.

'Tough,' came the short response. 'Ah, here we are.' He stopped at a display but didn't release her.

Glowering at his back, she poked her tongue out. 'I hate you.'

Jack shot her a grin over his shoulder. 'No you don't. You only think you do. Now, if I let you go, do you promise to behave and not run off.'

Ellie smiled at him sweetly. 'I'm going to hit you in a minute, Jack,' she threatened, but all he did was laugh—though he did finally release her.

All at once her hand felt strangely lost. It was amazing how such a simple touch had made her feel secure.

Which was sheer lunacy. She was going crazy. There was no other reason for it. Stark, staring...

'There you are,' Jack declared with satisfaction, plopping a hat down on her head. 'Now you can get rid of the other one.'

'You bought me a hat?' she exclaimed in surprise.

'I thought it was about time you had a new one.'

Automatically Ellie reached up and took it off to examine it. It was large and floppy, and the colour of sunflowers. You'd never lose me in a crowd, she thought wryly, and knew that she loved it. For no good reason her throat closed over.

'Thank you, it's lovely,' she said gruffly replacing it and setting it at a jaunty angle.

'You're welcome,' Jack responded softly and, when he took her hand again, she made no protest.

As luck would have it, they finally bumped into Luke and Andrea when they had decided to give the search up as a bad job and return to the villa. The couple were standing outside a boutique and appeared to be arguing.

'All does not seem to be well with the happy couple,' Ellie observed drily, vastly amused by the badgered expression on Luke's face.

'Hmm,' Jack agreed. 'There does seem to be a frosty nip to the air over there. Let's go see what's wrong.'

Jack hailed them as they strolled closer, and it was almost comical the way Luke and Andrea stopped fighting and plastered smiles on their faces. 'Hi there,' Jack greeted them when they met up. 'It looked like you could use a referee.'

Andrea immediately slipped her arm through Luke's and waved a dismissive hand. 'It was nothing.'

'A lovers' tiff? You should kiss and make up,' Ellie suggested jauntily, and the other woman smiled tightly.

'Not in public. I leave that kind of display to those less particular,' she shuddered delicately, and Ellie was left in no doubt Andrea was referring to the kiss she and Jack had shared last night.

Jack recognised it too, and laughed at her. 'You should try unbending a bit, Andrea, it can be fun.'

Andrea stiffened at the inference that she was too uptight, and sensing his fiancée's mood Luke cut in quickly. 'What brings you here?'

'Shopping,' Jack obligingly changed tack. 'I wanted to buy Ellie a new hat. The old one was long past its sell-by date,' he enlarged.

'Didn't I give you that hat?' Luke queried, eyes narrowing.

'That's right,' Ellie affirmed, staring him out. 'I thought it was great when I was fifteen, but it's dated now. This one is fantastic. I just love the colour,' she added brightly. 'What do you think Andrea?'

'It's a little garish for my taste, but it suits you, Ellie,' Andrea returned, and Ellie couldn't be certain whether she was being told yellow suited her, or she was a garish person. She rather thought it would be the latter.

'Oh, well, each to their own!' she said cheerfully, not about to be offended by an opinion that didn't matter to her. 'Are you going back to the villa now?'

'Not yet. There are a few shops Andrea hasn't been in yet,' Luke joked and got a frosty look for his pains.

'OK, we'll see you both at dinner, then,' Jack replied and, taking Ellie's hand once more, they turned away from the other couple and headed for where they had left the car. Ellie could feel two pairs of eyes on her back for a long time until the crowd swallowed them up.

'Andrea doesn't seem to like you,' Jack observed mockingly when they were safely out of earshot.

Ellie grinned up at him. 'I know. It's shattering.'

'So I see,' he grinned back.

'Isn't she awful!' Ellie exclaimed with a grimace. 'Can you imagine being married to her?'

Jack shuddered. 'I can, and I'm glad the lady is spoken for. I suppose I ought to feel sorry for Luke, but somehow I feel he's getting what he deserves.'

'I am so glad you're nothing like him,' Ellie went on earnestly, and he looked amused.

'I'm glad you're glad,' he responded and, as he smiled down into her eyes, Ellie experienced the strangest sensation. Something powerful passed between them. It was as if a bond had been forged, but quite what it meant she wasn't sure. All she did know was that it wasn't alarming. Far from it. She felt at ease with him, and it made her frown.

'Something wrong?' he asked, but Ellie shook her head.

'Not exactly. It's just…you're different from what I remember.'

One eyebrow quirked. 'I'm still me, but maybe you see me differently because you're different yourself. Have you thought of that?'

She hadn't, but she knew she had changed a lot these past six months, so he was probably right. 'Maybe,' she agreed.

Jack released her hand only to slip his arm about her shoulders. 'Don't worry about it. The past is another country. If we're wise, we won't go back there. You have to look ahead, see what you want and go for it.'

'Is that what you're doing?' she asked curiously.

'All the time, Angel. All the time. Come on, let's go

home. I could do with a shower and something cool to drink.'

Ellie didn't argue, for the prospect sounded wonderful. It had become stiflingly hot, and a shower sounded like bliss. Then, because she was still feeling the effect of the travelling from the day before, she intended to collapse onto her bed and sleep. And if she should dream about a certain person, she wouldn't be at all surprised.

There was a full house for dinner that evening and, as ever when the whole family was present, it was a lively occasion, with everyone having something to say and trying to say it louder than the rest. The family didn't gather together very often, which was why a tradition of meeting in the summer had grown over time. Everyone had to be brought up to date with what was happening, and it generally took the entire length of the meal to do it.

Afterwards, they all drifted out onto the terrace to drink coffee and soak up the scents and atmosphere of Capri. It was no wonder to Ellie that the Roman Emperors had chosen to have villas here, for it was perfect for relaxing and forgetting the stresses of everyday life. As the moon rose, she sighed in contentment. No matter where she went in the world, this place would always have a home in her heart.

'I've arranged a small party for you and Andrea, Luke,' Mary Thornton told her stepson some time later, when there was a brief lull in the conversation.

'You didn't have to do that, Mrs Thornton,' Andrea responded, before Luke could say a word, sounding just a tad aghast at the prospect to Ellie's sensitive ears. She had been quick to notice a coolness on the other woman's part to the other members of the family. It was as if they didn't quite meet her criteria for people to know, and Ellie found that offensive.

'Come now, you must call me Mary. Mrs Thornton is far too formal for us. And of course I had to do something. If you're to be married in America, then none of our friends will be able to attend the service. There are many people who've known Luke since he was small, and they will want to wish him well, so this is the best way all round,' Mary declared, smiling encouragingly at Luke's fiancée.

'I expect Andrea was just thinking of the amount of work it would be, Mary,' Jack put in casually, but the glance he shot his prospective sister-in-law spoke volumes, she would upset his stepmother at her peril.

Andrea tensed at the silent rebuke but wisely took the hint. 'Of course that's what I meant… Mary. Luke and I never expected you to go to so much trouble just for us,' she said with a tiny laugh.

'Don't worry, we'll all pitch in and help. Paul's a dab hand at putting things on sticks if you can drag him away from his computer,' Ellie put in teasingly, and he threatened to throw his coffee over her.

Everyone else laughed, but Andrea's chin visibly dropped. 'Things on sticks? You won't be using a caterer?'

Mary chose not to hear the dismay in her voice. 'Our housekeeper is a wonderful cook, and we enjoy doing the catering ourselves. It's half the fun. Not that I expect you to do anything, Andrea. You and Luke are the guests of honour, so you'll be allowed to make yourselves scarce.'

The relief on the pair of faces almost made Ellie laugh out loud. An imp of devilment took control and she composed her features into a serious look. 'Of course, those who don't help out front are left with the washing-up, but that's only fair,' she said solemnly, and had to bite down hard on her lip when Andrea paled. Then voices spoke up.

'Oh, Ellie!' her mother exclaimed with a laugh.

'Don't listen to her, darling, she's having you on!' Luke advised, shooting his stepsister a poisonous look.

Tom Thornton took pity on his soon to be daughter-in-law. 'You'll get used to Ellie's sense of humour, Andrea. Don't worry, we have a machine to do the washing, as she very well knows. Would you like me to freshen up your coffee, or would you prefer something stronger?'

Ellie watched as her stepfather went off to get the chardonnay Andrea had requested, and jumped when a hand closed on her thigh. She glanced round into a pair of dancing blue eyes.

'Take it easy,' Jack advised softly from his seat on the lounger next to hers.

'If she looks down her nose at my mother again, I might forget I'm a lady,' Ellie returned heatedly. Her mother was the friendliest of souls, and didn't deserve to have Andrea acting as if she had the plague.

'Mary knows how to deal with people like dear Andrea. Leave it to her to fight her own battle. You might be surprised.'

Ellie looked to where her mother was talking to the other woman and not looking in the least disturbed. 'You think she might sock her?' she asked hopefully, but Jack laughed.

'Her methods are far more subtle. Andrea will be given just so much rope, then Mary will utter a few quiet words and I'll guarantee that dear Andrea will be put well and truly in her place. So you can pull in your claws, tiger.'

Ellie sank back into her seat and sent him a knowing look. 'In which case you can take your hand off my thigh now,' she commanded him drily.

'Spoilsport,' he grumbled, but complied. Then made her jump again when he took her hand, lacing his fingers through hers.

'What are you doing?' she queried, and promptly gasped when he raised her hand to his lips and kissed the back of it. Heads turned, and Ellie laughed nervously as colour rose in her cheeks. 'Jack, cut it out!'

Instead of doing so he brought his lips close to her ear in what would look like a highly intimate moment between lovers. 'Too late for that. Just go with the flow, Angel,' he advised in a whisper that sent shivers down her spine.

Glancing round, Ellie saw her mother and stepfather exchange glances and could have died. Before she could do or say anything, though, Jack had risen to his feet and was pulling her to hers.

'Ellie and I are just going to take a little moonlight stroll. We may be some time,' he explained and she found herself being whisked away to the steps which led to the garden.

Ellie didn't know whether to laugh or stamp her foot at the way he had dropped this particular bombshell. Everyone would know they were an item now.

'Wow, that was subtle!' she exclaimed when there was little chance of them being overheard. 'You could have let me know what you intended to do!'

'I could have,' Jack replied, steering her down a path. 'But I didn't think your acting ability would be up to it.'

'You know what they're all going to think, don't you?' she grumbled.

'Naturally. They think we want to do some furtive fumbling in the dark,' Jack retorted, and she could tell from the tremor in his voice that he was finding the situation hilarious.

By contrast she felt murderous. 'I'll never be able to look my mother in the eye again.'

'Of course you will,' Jack pooh-poohed that. 'She was young once, too, you know.'

She shot a dagger look into his back. 'I didn't come down in the last shower of rain you know. So you'd better understand that there won't be any furtive fumbling going on,' she warned, then almost bumped into him when he stopped. Her chin went up and she dared him to do anything.

'Stop being a pain, Eleanora, and relax. I'm not about to do anything furtive,' Jack conceded, but she barely had time to feel a fleeting moment of relief before her pulled the rug out from under her. 'When I kiss you, it's going to be in full view of anyone watching.'

She was speechless, and he took advantage of it to slip his arm about her waist and urge her unresisting form along the path that bounded the hillside. A wall had been built to prevent accidents, and it was against this that he chose to lean, pulling her into the vee of his legs. His hands dropped to span her hips and Ellie knew that she couldn't pull away in case they were being observed.

'Still mad?' Jack asked, eyes twinkling in the moonlight, and the part of her that wasn't angry found them fascinating.

'By rights I ought to push you right over the edge,' she grumbled, knowing she was trapped.

'But you won't,' he said with such utter assurance she was instantly irritated.

'How can you be so sure?' she demanded and a slow smile spread across his lips.

'Because you want me to kiss you as much as I do,' he pronounced huskily and, if it hadn't been true before, it was certainly true now.

Being this close to him was pure temptation. She couldn't help but recall the kisses they had shared—and how they had made her feel. She had done her best to ignore it all day, but now, here with him like this, so close it would take little more than a breath to bring them together, she had to admit she wanted him to kiss her again. No, not merely wanted, needed.

'You're taking an unfair advantage because you know I can't fight you here. You've got a nerve!'

That brought a quirky grin to his lips and a sultry glow to his eyes. 'More than one, and they're all registering off the scale,' he growled sexily, and her own nerves began rippling like crazy.

Still she fought it. 'Stop flirting with me. I'm not going to let you get away with this. And I'm not going to kiss you!' she exclaimed, planting her hands firmly on his shoulders to keep the necessary distance between them.

He nodded past her. 'What, and dash everyone's expectations? They're all just waiting for the main event to start.'

Ellie had to curb the temptation to turn and find out for herself if they were being watched. Jack could be lying but, knowing her family, she knew that they would more than likely have an audience. Which was exactly what Jack had relied upon. He had manufactured the situation to put their relationship squarely on the map—as she had agreed—and she was caught.

'So,' he urged softly. 'What's it to be?'

Ellie licked her lips nervously, and felt her nerves jolt when his eyes followed the movement. 'I think I've made a pact with the devil,' she retorted gruffly.

'Why, because I'm tempting you?' Jack teased huskily.

Oh, he was tempting her all right. Her hands could feel the firmness of his shoulders and the heat of his body. His scent was an intoxication, and the press of his thighs on hers was setting her stomach quivering. She was fighting herself as much as him to keep the distance between them, because inside she just wanted to press closer and drown in his kiss as she had before. Her eyes dropped to his mouth, and it was a fatal error, because it only served to remind her of the magic it could create.

'Damn. Damn. Damn,' she whispered in a choked voice. 'I should be stronger than this,' she berated herself, even as her hands began to glide around his neck. 'What do you do to me?'

'Only what you do to me. Now, put us both out of our misery and kiss me,' he ordered tautly.

It was that desperate tone in his voice which did for her. The need it conveyed struck a chord deep within her, and she just had to kiss him. The distance closed and her lips touched his. The heat of them made her give a tiny gasp as his mouth opened over hers, then his tongue sought entry and all thought vanished. Passion caught fire at each stroke, reaching flash point in seconds.

Ellie moaned low in her throat as the throbbing ache of desire grew inside her. Just like that she wanted him and, from the hardness of his body, she was left in no doubt that he wanted her just as powerfully. She had never wanted anyone like this. Had never had her passions aroused to swiftly, nor ached so painfully for another human being. It was overwhelming and, in danger of losing all reason, she dragged her mouth away, drawing in deep gulps of air.

'Enough!' she cried in little more than a broken whisper.

Jack watched her from eyes blazing with barely contained passion. 'Hell, Angel, kissing is never going to be enough. You know it as well as I do. Stop fighting it, Ellie.'

'I have to,' she argued shakily.

'Why?'

Ellie groaned, resting her forehead on his. 'Because I don't want to want you, damn it.'

'What do you want me to do about it?' he asked wryly and she sighed because she knew there was nothing he could do.

'You don't happen to have a magic lamp tucked away somewhere, do you?'

Jack swore softly. 'Damn, I knew there was something I meant to pack!'

She laughed tiredly. 'Very funny.'

Reaching up, Jack framed her face with his hands and eased her away so he could see her. 'You're worrying too much.'

She frowned. 'Why aren't you worrying at all? Doesn't it bother you—the speed of this thing? I mean, why you? Why me? Why now?'

'Damned if I know. I only know this is a pretty powerful attraction, and I'm not about to walk away from it,' Jack answered simply.

Ellie swallowed to moisten a dry throat. 'What if it turns out to be a mistake?'

'Then we learn from it,' he said reasonably. 'Just understand this, Angel. It isn't going to go away. Something this powerful doesn't evaporate overnight. If you don't deal with it now, you'll only have to deal with it later.'

She knew he spoke nothing less than the truth, but it didn't make her feel any happier. This had all been too much, and she needed to be alone to think.

'Have we given them enough of a show for one night? Can we go now?'

'I should imagine the message has got across. But are you sure you don't want to sample a little more of the moonlight?' he teased her and, despite her worries, she laughed.

'I think I've experienced enough moon madness for one night. Heaven only knows what Mum and Dad are going to make of this.'

Jack eased her away as he stood up, and Ellie shivered slightly at the disappearance of his warmth. 'Take my word for it, they won't even mention it. This is between us.'

Ellie hoped he was right, for she didn't know what she would say if her mother did decide to ask questions. What she did know for certain was that there was no way out now. The relationship between herself and Jack had been established and they could only perpetuate it. The need for it hadn't changed, but it no longer seemed the bigger problem.

All Luke had to do was believe the relationship was real and she would be free of him. What troubled her was now just how real the relationship was becoming.

CHAPTER SIX

SHAM or not, a week later, it was clear to Ellie that the strategy was paying off. In the beginning they had had to take some ribbing about the turn of events, but, much to her surprise, in no time at all, she and Jack were an accepted couple. Nobody appeared to think it the least odd that they should have been at loggerheads one moment and supposedly inseparable the next. Nobody except Luke, that was. Though he was careful not to show it, her experience of him told her he was not impressed.

As each day passed, and he watched her with Jack, his mood grew angrier. At first Ellie couldn't resist checking for signs that the message was getting through, but increasingly she found herself forgetting about him altogether. Her concentration had quickly become centred solely on Jack. She had expected to be uncomfortable with her role, but that was proving far from the truth. As she had suspected it would, the line between reality and pretence had begun to blur.

Mainly because the attraction between them, always strong, was growing. It was there all the time, unspoken but oh so powerful. It wasn't long before Ellie discovered that the more she was with him, the more she wanted to be with him. So far she had been able to keep him at bay, but it was becoming harder. When he kissed her, and he did so often, she was finding it difficult to remember this was just an act. Somehow she had always managed to stop before things got too out of hand, but her defences were extremely shaky. Jack never complained or tried to take things further, but accepted her no—when she managed to say it. No matter how far things had gone, he was always self-controlled.

When she found herself wishing he would lose that impressive control for once, and override her objections, she knew she was in trouble. Her resistance had vanished somewhere along the line. Being honest with herself, she knew she no longer wanted to fight the attraction. All she really wanted to do was give in to it and let it take her where it would. It was only pride which kept her battling. Jack was certain she would surrender—so of course she couldn't.

She had been musing on her ability to keep doing that last night when Luke had sought her out in the laundry room, where she had been sorting out some washing. Absorbed in her thoughts, she hadn't heard him enter, and nearly jumped out of her skin when she turned and discovered him standing there. She almost dropped the basket of clean clothes, and hastily retrieved it before anything fell out onto the floor.

'Oh, God, you gave me a fright!' she exclaimed, pressing a hand to her racing heart.

'What's going on, Ellie?' Luke demanded curtly and, though she knew what he meant, she chose to misunderstand him.

'I'm sorting the washing. There are some things I want for tomorrow,' she explained obligingly, and was secretly pleased to see flags of colour in his cheeks.

'I meant what's going on with you and my brother?' he ground out tersely, and it did her morale a power of good to know she was getting to him at last.

'Come on, Luke. I'm sure I don't need to draw you

a picture,' she goaded him, turning back to the tumble-dryer. Setting the basket on top, she began putting the clothes in.

Luke caught her arm in an uncomfortably tight grip and tugged her round to face him. 'I see it, but I don't believe it. You've never wanted Jack. It was me you wanted.'

Ellie tried to prise his hand away but he merely tightened his grip. Hiding a wince, she smiled at him coldly. 'Did. Past tense. I don't want you now. I think I've made that more than clear.'

Luke's mouth twisted nastily. 'Using him against me isn't going to work. He's a pitiful substitute for me. Did you know he fell in love years ago with a mystery woman and still carries a torch for her. What a chump.'

To hear Luke talk so disparagingly of his brother made Ellie go cold with anger. He had no right to speak of Jack that way. No right at all. 'Jack's more of a man than you'll ever be!' she waded in with an explosion of fury. 'At least it proves he has a heart. Something you will never have. Jack will never be a substitute for anyone! He's the genuine article. Now let...me...go!' she gritted out and finally managed to break free of his iron grasp.

Clearly Luke didn't care for her opinion. 'I'd be careful what I said, if I were you.'

Ellie glared at him glacially. 'Is that a threat? Then here's one for you. Don't ever let me hear you talking about Jack like that again.'

Luke laughed, and it was an unpleasant sound. 'My God, he must be good in bed if he's got you defending him like a tigress with her young!'

He was so way off the mark it was laughable, but

Ellie wasn't laughing. 'What goes on between Jack and me is none of your business.'

Luke's eyes narrowed. 'I could make it my business. What do you think he would say if he knew about us?'

'What do you think Andrea would say if she knew you wanted to have her and me, and you not even married?' Ellie shot right back, and that had Luke backing off in a hurry.

'You won't say anything to her, do you hear me?' he ordered, jabbing a finger at her to emphasise the point.

Ellie stared him out. 'I hear you. Now you hear me. Leave Jack alone.'

This time Luke laughed aloud. 'My God, and you used to think of him as the devil incarnate.'

She smiled. 'I used to think you were wonderful, but I haven't thought that way for a very long time now.'

Luke's expression turned thoughtful. 'Are you in love with him?' he asked, and for some reason that made her heart lurch wildly. Yet she kept her expression stony.

'Won't Andrea be wondering where you are?'

To her relief he took the hint, but turned at the door. 'This isn't over,' he warned, and went out.

Ellie let out a ragged breath and sank back against the dryer. She was shaking, but it wasn't from fear. It was anger. His disparaging comments about Jack had stirred up a veritable hornets' nest inside her and she was still buzzing. She should have punched him on the nose when she had the chance, she thought. He deserved it, and more.

She began stuffing clothes into the dryer with more force than they deserved, and it wasn't until some time had passed that a thought struck her. *Why* was she so angry on Jack's behalf? He meant nothing to her. OK, so she was attracted, but that was purely physical. Yet she had flown to his defence like a wild thing.

It was probably because she hated injustice, she told herself, and Luke's remarks had been unjust. Her nerves stopped jangling. Yes, that had to be it. It wasn't right that Luke, a man with little integrity, should mock a man who had it in spades.

The rationalisation made her feel more comfortable with herself, and she finished off the washing in a more settled frame of mind.

That had been yesterday. Today, the four of them were on the beach. It had been Jack's suggestion that they make up a party, and he had hired a motor boat to take them to a secluded spot on a nearby island. Ellie had agreed, though she thought he was crazy. The idea of spending a whole day with the 'happy couple' had made her shudder. She and Andrea did not get along any better now than in the beginning. They were polite to each other, but nothing more—for it had been made clear to Ellie that she fell a long way short of Andrea's high standards. A fact she was inordinately grateful for, as it kept them apart for most of the time.

She wondered if Andrea's high standards would cause her to ignore Luke's infidelities—of which Ellie had no doubt there would be many, for Luke would not change. Had it been any other woman, she would have pitied her finding out, but Andrea was welcome to all that was coming.

'Penny for them,' Jack offered from beside her, and she glanced down to where he lay stretched out on the picnic blanket they shared.

She had avoided looking at him ever since they got here for, like her, he was dressed in skimpy swimming gear. His bronzed body had proved as tantalising as she remembered, and she had carefully kept her gaze averted. It hadn't stopped her from being vitally aware of him though, and the only way she had been able to resist the urge to touch him was to look anywhere but at him. From the glint in his eye now, he knew exactly what she was doing—and more importantly, why.

'I was just wondering if Andrea really knows what she's doing,' she said truthfully.

Jack came up on one elbow and followed Ellie's gaze to where Luke swam whilst Andrea hovered uncomfortably at the water's edge. 'I think she does. She wants him, warts and all.'

Ellie brought her knees up and wrapped her arms around them. 'How can she want him? He's never been faithful to anyone in his life.' She knew that from personal experience.

'You tell me,' Jack drawled mockingly. 'You wanted him yourself not so very long ago.'

She felt warmth flood her cheeks. 'Thank you for reminding me I showed distinct lack of judgement in my choice of men,' she responded wryly. 'But, like I told you the other day, I'm well and truly over him now,' she added, turning to look at Jack to make sure he believed her. She didn't want there to be any doubt.

Jack searched her eyes for an age before he nodded and lay back down again. 'Speaking as his brother, I never could see what you saw in him anyway,' he taunted softly, and she laughed—mostly at herself.

'Oh, Luke cuts a very romantic figure. He's handsome and dashing. A free spirit who loves to break the rules. A girl gets caught up in the romance of it all, but it's all show and no substance.'

'Something I tried to tell you more than once,' Jack returned drily, and she pulled a face at him.

'What teenager wants to listen to the voice of reason? We're all in love with the idea of being in love. Being sensible isn't on the agenda.'

'So had I left you alone, you would have seen the light sooner?' he charged her and her lips twisted into a wry smile.

'Probably not. At the time I was wrapped up it would have taken something more powerful to knock some sense into me,' she admitted.

'And what monumental act caused your vision to clear?'

Ellie knew she couldn't reveal the truth, but she kept as close to it as she was able. 'Actually, I saw him in London when he spent some time there. He was never with the same woman twice, and I looked at him and realised he wasn't the man I always thought he was. The scales fell away, and I knew I'd been in love with love, not Luke at all.'

Jack frowned. 'Luke never mentioned seeing you.'

Her nerves fluttered as she wondered if she had said too much, but she stared him out. 'Come on, Jack. You know Luke only tells people what he wants them to know. He's like an iceberg. Four-fifths of him are under water.'

He looked at her curiously. 'Suddenly you seem to know him very well.'

Ellie shrugged. To know him a little was to know him well when your eyes were open. 'I've known him a long time.'

'And for most of that time you were wearing blinkers.'

Ellie was rapidly beginning to wish she had never started the conversation. Without intending to she had aroused his curiosity, and that was the very last thing she wanted. 'I thought the idea was that I should see the light about Luke. Surely the swiftness of it is irrelevant?' she retorted irritably, and Jack sat up in one smooth movement.

'Believe me, it is. I guess it's hard to accept that I don't have to chafe you about him any longer.'

'Don't worry, you'll soon find something else to tease me about. *You* haven't changed,' she told him with a sardonic grin.

Jack smiled at her, and there was a sultry look in his eyes when he spoke. 'Trust me, Ellie. I can think of far more interesting things to do than tease you,' he promised and set her pulse quickening instantly.

Her mouth went dry, and she hastily licked her lips, very much aware that his eyes followed the action minutely. 'Is that so?' she challenged breathlessly.

'Uh-huh,' Jack confirmed, reaching out to run one finger gently along the curve of her arm.

Just like that the temperature on their particular part of the beach, rose quite significantly, making it difficult to breathe. Ellie was caught in the fire of his gaze like a moth, and to look into those blue depths was like drowning.

'This is crazy,' she whispered. 'You shouldn't be having this effect on me.' Not when she had sworn to steer clear of men, and this one in particular. But her instinct for self-preservation was fast disappearing. Saving herself wasn't even an option. All she wanted to do right then was plunge deeper.

His finger traced on down to her wrist, and she didn't

resist when he enfolded her wrist and tugged her hand free. 'What effect am I having?'

'You know,' she sighed, and Jack laughed softly.

'Be more specific,' he ordered, bending his head to kiss the tender skin of her wrist, then stopped abruptly. His head came up sharply. 'What's this?' he queried in a voice so far removed from seductive, it caused her to blink and look down.

There, a little way up her forearm, was a row of tiny bruises. The result of the force with which Luke had held her arm last night. Which, naturally, she could not tell him. 'It's nothing. I slipped in the bath and bumped it on the tap,' she invented. Rather neatly, she thought. Until Jack looked at her sceptically.

'A tap with four fingers and a thumb, apparently,' he jibed, and she flushed guiltily, which didn't help her cause at all.

'It's just a bruise, Jack,' she returned dismissively.

If she hoped to put him off, she was doomed to failure. His jaw became set and he held her gaze steadily. 'That's the size of a man's hand, and it must have hurt. Who did it, Ellie?'

'It wasn't intentional. I just bruise easily,' she rallied, trying to make light of it. 'Stop making such a fuss!'

'Being fussy is deciding which table napkins to put out. Someone wasn't gentle with you, and I want to know who it was,' Jack insisted doggedly.

'For what purpose?'

'So I can tell them in no uncertain terms, that they won't do it again. Nobody manhandles you and gets away with it.'

Ellie couldn't recall the last time anyone had come to her defence so insistently. Luke certainly never had. She stared at him in amazement, whilst a warm feeling began to swell in her chest. Irritating though it was to know he wouldn't let it go, it was incredibly heartening to discover he cared what happened to her.

She smiled at him, her expression half amazed, half amused. 'I didn't know you worried about me so much.'

'I told you there were a lot of things you didn't know about me,' he reminded her.

'You were right.'

Jack tipped his head to one side, observing her sardonically. 'You aren't going to tell me, are you?'

Ellie knew she wanted to but couldn't, and shook her head. 'No.'

He let out his breath in a long sigh. 'One day you're going to trust me enough to tell me the truth.'

Her gaze fell away, dropping to where he still cupped her wrist in his hand. Telling him the truth wasn't a matter of trust. The deception had gone on too long, and she and Luke had made fools of their family by that deception. They would be hurt by the truth, and she wouldn't blame them for being disappointed.

Looking at his hand, she realised again how different Jack was from what she had always believed. Having discovered that he didn't think so badly of her after all, she knew she didn't want to disappoint him now. In consequence, telling the truth was further out of the question. As for trusting him...

'I do trust you, Jack,' she said seriously, looking up, and knew as she said it that it was no less than the truth.

The confession brought a wry smile to his lips. 'With qualifications.'

She raised her shoulders helplessly. 'I'm sure there are things in your life you don't intend to tell anyone, and trust has nothing to do with the decision,' she pointed out reasonably, and he groaned.

'As always, you're right. So I'll say no more about the bruises—on one condition. If whoever did it bothers you again, you'll tell me. I don't intend to stand by and watch you get hurt if there's something I can do to prevent it,' Jack pronounced stoutly, and she couldn't help but smile.

'I never saw you as a white knight before. It suits you,' she teased, but Jack was not about to be diverted.

'Your word, Ellie, or I'll nag you ragged,' he threatened, and Ellie knew it was no empty threat.

'OK, I give you my word, but nothing is going to happen. I told you it was unintentional.'

Jack snorted in disbelief. 'If holding you that tight was the only way to save your life, that's unintentional. Anything else is deliberate. Most men are stronger than women. Not inflicting damage when harm can so easily be done, is something a man prides himself on.'

Ellie found her throat closing over as he spoke, for there was a nobility to Jack that she had been so ignorant of and, by that ignorance, she felt that she had somehow failed him. It was the weirdest feeling, and she had no idea where it came from or what it meant. She just knew she had to respond to it.

'She missed out on something special,' she declared with an edge of wistfulness, and Jack frowned.

'Who did?'

'The woman you're in love with.' He blinked, and she realised her line of thought had clearly taken him by surprise. 'I know you probably don't want to talk about it, but I just want to say, had things turned out differently, I know she would have been proud to be married to you.'

The oddest expression crossed his face, but it vanished in a flash and in the next second he was on his feet, pulling her up with him.

'You're right, I don't want to talk about it. Let's go for a swim instead,' he suggested, and without waiting for her to agree, he headed off down the beach, tugging her along behind him.

That he still cared deeply for the unknown woman, was made clear to her by his reaction, and she was caught by a stab of envy. Before she knew better, she had hoped that Luke would love her like that, but he didn't possess the capability to love selflessly. She, on the other hand, had a lot of love to give to the right man—if she was ever ready to risk her heart again.

Jack released her hand as they ran into the water, and she couldn't help smiling as she watched him dive into the next wave and disappear from view. He had always been at home in the water, and looked as if he still swam often from the tone of his muscles. Wading further in, she glanced around expectantly, waiting for him to pop up again, but the seconds passed and his dark head failed to appear.

A dart of alarm speared through her. Where was he? She knew Jack was a strong swimmer, but surely even he couldn't stay under water this long. She spun round, eyes furiously searching for sign of him, but he was nowhere to be seen. Her heart started to pound anxiously as she thought of all the possibilities. He could have got caught in something and be unable to surface!

'Jack!' Ellie called as she waded further out, though it was doubtful that he would have heard her.

Telling herself not to panic, because that wouldn't help him, she was just about to call again, when she felt herself being grabbed by the ankles and in the next instant her feet were being pulled out from under her. Ellie just had time to take in a gasp of air before she disappeared under the surface. She bobbed up again, coughing and spluttering, just as an arm came around her from behind and she was eased backwards onto the safety of a strong male body.

'I've got you. You're safe now,' Jack's laughing voice declared next to her right ear and, had she not been floating and had a hand free, she would have boxed his ears for the scare he had put her through.

'That wasn't funny, Jack!' she exclaimed angrily, and ground her teeth when he had the nerve to laugh. 'I was safe before!'

'Mmm, but you're safer here in my arms, where I can keep an eye on you,' he countered seductively, sending those inevitable tiny shivers through her system.

She wanted to stay angry, but his body was moving rhythmically beneath her as he kept them afloat, and it was creating a warmth all of its own. Ellie could feel herself softening, which wasn't at all what she wanted to be feeling—alluring as it was. She was angry with him, and intended to stay that way. He couldn't be allowed to charm her out of it that easily.

'Don't you dare try to seduce me! I'm furious with you, Jack. I thought you'd drowned, for heaven's sake!' she protested, struggling to be free of him. But he refused to release her.

'Would you have missed me if I had?' he taunted softly, and she just knew he was smiling.

Deflating him was paramount. 'Of course I would

have. I don't have that big a family that I can afford to lose a member!' she retorted smartly.

'But I'm not really family, am I? I mean, there's no blood tie between us.'

'Maybe not,' Ellie agreed as they lazily rode the swell, 'but I've always thought of you as a brother.'

'Ah, but right now your thoughts are no more sisterly than mine are brotherly.'

'Speak for yourself,' she advised, though it was all too lamentably true. Once more she tried to break away from him, and this time succeeded. Expecting to touch bottom, she didn't realise Jack had towed them further out. Almost going under, she was forced to make a grab for his shoulders to keep herself afloat. Treading water, she glared at him. 'You could at least have warned me I was out of my depth!'

'You're not out of your depth, Ellie, you're just finding your feet,' Jack responded silkily, and the gleam in his eye left her in little doubt that they weren't talking about swimming. 'Besides, I would never let you drown alone. It's much more fun together.'

Ellie closed her eyes helplessly as his charm wound invisible threads about her. There was something to that saying *soft words turneth away wrath*. How could she be angry with him when he said things like that! Sighing ruefully, she shook her head. 'You're incorrigible.'

Jack tutted. 'No, you've got that wrong, Angel. I'm encouragable. Extremely encouragable. In fact, right now you're encouraging me to do this…'

Before Ellie had a chance to anticipate what he was going to do, he had framed her head with his hands, and brought his mouth down on hers. Then his legs wrapped themselves around hers and they slid under the water.

The absence of sight and sound made the sense of touch all the greater. Ellie forgot about everything except the pleasure of returning the kiss. Letting her tongue engage in an erotic dance with his that heated up the blood and rekindled that ache of longing deep within her. Every throb of her pulse was a clamour for more.

Then it was over. Far too soon for her enthralled senses. Lost as she was, she wasn't aware that she needed air until a powerful thrust of Jack's legs brought them shooting to the surface, and she was able to take a deep gasping lungful of oxygen. Breathing hard and wiping the water from her eyes she was pleased to see Jack was taking deep breaths too, which meant he had been as caught up as she.

'How do you do it?' he asked as they trod water again.

Ellie licked lips bruised by the passion of his kiss. 'How do I do what?'

'Make me lose all sense of self-preservation. Drowning wasn't supposed to be on the agenda today. You're a dangerous woman,' he accused her, but there was a light in his eyes that set her errant nerves skipping.

Though a tiny part of her brain advised caution, she ignored it. 'Does this mean you aren't going to kiss me again?' she flirted with a tiny smile curving the corners of her mouth. His eyes followed it and it was as if she had been touched by flame.

'Hell, no. I'll just have to remember to keep my feet firmly on the ground in future.'

'But I thought you wanted to be swept away.'

'Swept away, yes. Drowned, no. Not unless it's in a sea of passion with you. The Mediterranean is fine for swimming, but for drowning you need a bed. Anywhere—with you in it,' he came back, turning her blood to liquid fire, and setting her stomach clenching with desire.

He was turning her on so fast, she felt more than a little dizzy. 'I think I need to get back to shore,' she said in a husky voice. 'Right now.'

'You're right,' Jack agreed. 'This isn't the time or place.'

It wasn't what she meant at all, but anything that got her away from temptation and back to the safety of the shore was acceptable. They swam back, Jack matching his stroke to hers so that they arrived together. There he surprised her yet again by sweeping her up into his arms as he strode up the beach to the blanket.

'I can walk,' Ellie protested, even as she slipped her arms about his neck.

'I know, Angel, but we're being watched. Smile and wave like a good girl now,' he directed sardonically.

Glancing round, she found they were indeed the centre of attention of the couple already seated on the blanket. Obediently she smiled and waved. Andrea raised a limp hand, but Luke remained impassive.

When Jack lowered her to the blanket, Ellie batted her eyelashes at him provocatively. 'My hero!' she gasped, grinning, and he made to swat her with the towel he'd begun running over his hair.

'You've put on weight since the last time I carried you,' Jack complained dropping down beside her and finger-combing his hair into order, leaving it looking rakishly charming to Ellie's biased gaze. This wouldn't do. She would have to stop finding everything about him so enticing before it was too late.

'Thanks!' she exclaimed in mock outrage. 'I was probably only about twelve at the time.'

'I never had to worry about my weight,' Andrea remarked with a note of self-satisfaction.

'She's improved a lot in certain necessary departments,' Jack agreed with a wolfish grin.

'True,' Ellie confirmed sadly. 'I was depressingly flat-chested for ages. It was the bane of my life.'

'I thought Jack was that,' Luke put in slyly, and Ellie decided that if that was the way he wanted it, she would follow his lead.

'Only because he used to tease me about this whopping crush I used to have on you Luke,' she told him with a smile, then turned to Andrea. 'You know how it is. I thought he was the bees knees, but thankfully that's all over. I discovered there were other fish in the sea, and haven't looked back.'

'Thank God I was spared that particular adolescent nightmare,' Andrea declared with another of her delicate shudders. 'My sister once had a crush—what an awful word—on our music teacher, and it was most unattractive. Thankfully when I told our parents they had him dismissed.'

'That was a bit drastic, wasn't it, considering we all grow out of it. I certainly did,' Ellie protested, and shot Luke an apologetic smile. 'Sorry, Luke, but then you never saw me that way anyway, did you? Which was why Jack told me you were so worried. You didn't want to hurt my feelings.'

That, she was pleased to note, came as quite a jolt to him. Obviously he hadn't expected his brother to say anything to her about the discussion they had had. He preferred to play both sides off against each other from a position of anonymity. His cover had been blown, and he was far from amused, but it only showed in the shadows of his eyes.

'You're family, Ellie. I couldn't bring myself to be blunt. I hoped everything would turn out as I wanted in time, and it did,' he shot back neatly, reminding her, unnecessarily, of their brief affair.

Ellie merely laughed. If he thought to strike a blow, he was way wide of the mark. 'Yes. I'm otherwise engaged, and you have Andrea. What could be better?' she added cheerily and reached for the picnic box. 'Who's for food. I don't know about you lot, but I'm starving.'

It was true too. The days were long gone when Luke could upset her appetite. Andrea helped her serve the food whilst Jack poured out glasses of chilled white wine he took from the cooler. For the next half-hour or so they chatted idly as they ate. When nobody could force down another bite, they packed everything away again.

Satisfyingly full, Ellie stifled a yawn behind her hand. 'Oh, excuse me, but I can hardly keep my eyes open. I'm going to have to have forty winks.'

'You go ahead, Ellie.' Andrea said as she climbed gracefully to her feet and tugged Luke up too. 'Come on, let's go for a walk. I need to burn off some of this food, or I'll be asleep too, and sleeping in the afternoon gives me a headache.' So saying she slipped her arm around his waist and dragged him off with her.

His reluctance made Ellie laugh. 'She's going to lead him a dog's life. It couldn't happen to a nicer guy.'

Jack had been laying on his back with his head resting on his arms. He opened one eye to look at her. 'Do I detect an undercurrent between you and Luke?'

Her thumbs pricked, sensing danger. 'A little. He was rather disparaging about you the other day, and I told him off,' she explained, as ever leaving out the main reason for their antagonism.

His other eye opened. 'Really? What did he say?'

'He called you a chump,' she enlarged, making herself comfortable on her front and shutting her eyes.

'Sounds mild enough to me.'

She stifled another yawn. 'Believe me, he deserved a black eye.'

'So you came rushing to my defence, did you?' Jack sought confirmation, sounding more than a little amused.

'I was the only one there. But even if I wasn't I'd do it again in a second,' she declared forcefully. She looked at him sleepily. 'You're not a chump.'

Jack smiled crookedly. 'Thank you.'

'You're welcome,' she sighed and, closing her eyes again, was asleep in seconds.

Jack stared down at her sleeping form for a long while, his expression sober and thoughtful. Finally he brushed a stray strand of hair away from her mouth then settled himself back down and closed his eyes.

CHAPTER SEVEN

ELLIE sighed and stirred, blinking her eyes carefully against the light. Idly she wondered how long she had been asleep but, from the lack of tightness or stinging on her back, she knew it couldn't have been too long. Nobody was in sight along the whole length of the beach, and only the seagulls disturbed the peace. Turning her head, she saw Jack was still stretched out beside her, and the last misty dregs of sleep vanished.

Careful not to wake him, she came up on her elbow, delighted to have this opportunity to study him unobserved. He was…beautiful. There was no other word for it that came close. How could she have been so blind as not to have seen it before? Was it any wonder she was finding him so very hard to resist.

Everything about him pleased her eye. He was toned and fit and the urge to touch him was as powerful as a magnet. She gave in to it because she really needed to know how he felt. If his skin was as silken as it looked. Very carefully, she reached out and lay her hand on his chest. Her eyes watched his face, seeking signs that he was aware of what she was doing, but there were none. He remained asleep, and she took courage from that and slowly ran her hand back and forth in a gentle caress.

Oh, yes, his skin was silky smooth and yet beneath she could feel the power of his muscles. It was extremely arousing touching him like this, and her teeth closed on her bottom lip as she concentrated on discovering more.

His stomach was flat, with not an ounce of spare flesh to be seen. She scanned its planes once more before her hand slowly progressed lower.

Quick as a flash a hand shot out and caught her wrist, and Ellie gasped, eyes shooting to Jack's face to find him watching her quizzically.

'Go any further and I won't answer for the consequences,' he warned thickly, and her heart lurched.

Ellie made no move to escape, for he wasn't holding her tightly. 'I was just...' She began to explain away her behaviour, but the heat in his gaze dried the words on her tongue.

'I know what you were just... Angel. Believe me, I want to do the same to you,' Jack declared huskily. 'However, making love to you on a public beach wasn't part of the plan.'

Her eyes widened and her throat closed over. 'We weren't making love,' she corrected, but he merely smiled.

'We would have been.'

The part of her that wanted him so badly, knew he was right, but to admit it was out of the question. 'You're taking too much for granted,' she accused him, and in the next instant found herself on her back with Jack looming over her as he rolled, taking her with him.

'I want you, Angel. You can feel that I do,' he told her, and she could feel the surge of his body against hers. 'My control will only get us so far. If you had kept touching me that way, the outcome was inevitable and you know it.'

'I thought you said you would stop if I told you to,' Ellie reminded him, though it was hard to concentrate when they were pressed so very close together and her need of him was a coil of heat inside her.

'I also said you had to mean it. Right now your lips are saying no, but every other inch of you is saying yes. I'm a man, not a saint. I only know you ache for me as much as I ache for you.'

Ellie stared up at him, knowing every word was true. 'This wasn't supposed to happen.'

'I was beginning to think it never would,' Jack breathed as he lowered his head to hers.

'What was that?' Ellie asked half-heartedly, concentrating on the lips so close to her own. If he didn't kiss her soon she might just explode. With a groan she abandoned all pretence of lack of interest. She wanted this—needed it. She would worry about the consequences later. Right now she just knew one thing—she was going out of her mind. 'Never mind. Kiss me, Jack. Please.'

'I'm yours to command,' he groaned back and kissed her.

Ellie sighed with pleasure as his body came to rest on hers and, as if coming home, her arms slipped around his neck, holding on as the kiss stoked the smouldering fires of their mutual passion. Soon, kisses, however passionately erotic, were not enough. Jack abandoned her lips to plunder her neck, and every brush of his lips was like a brand on her sensitised flesh. He forayed lower, seeking the shadowed valley of her breasts with their meagre covering, and Ellie felt her body responding. Her breasts felt tight, her nipples were turgid peaks that ached for his touch, and as if he knew it Jack sought a new target. Her body arched as he brushed the cloth aside and his mouth closed on her. His tongue flicked out, and her muscles clenched as a wave of desire swept through her.

'Jack!' she breathed achingly, needing more than words could say, and it was the sound of her voice that made him go still.

Groaning, Jack buried his face against her for a moment whilst he gathered his control, then he gently replaced the bikini top and looked up at her with eyes darkened by passion.

'You see what I mean? Next time I might not be able to stop,' he confessed, and Ellie licked lips still tender from his kisses.

'Do you know what the worst of it is? I don't think I'd want you to,' she admitted honestly, for there was no way back from here. No point in pretending. Their need was too powerful to be ignored. Only time and distance could cool it, and they had neither.

'What happened to vehement denial?' he asked, but his smile was free of any mockery.

'We just shot it full of holes,' she sighed, her eyes searching his face which had become strangely precious to her in such a short space of time. 'Some holiday this is turning out to be.'

She had come here to lay ghosts, not to find herself caught up in a powerful attraction for a man she thought she hated. Of course she didn't hate him. In fact her feelings for him had undergone a sea change, and become something deeper and warmer. It was all incredibly exciting and intensely alarming at the same time. She didn't mind admitting her intense attraction to him scared her.

'Aren't you having fun?' Jack teased, brushing salty

strands of hair from her forehead. 'That's a pity because I haven't enjoyed myself so much in years.'

'Fun isn't exactly how I would describe what's going on here,' she retorted drily and he smiled.

'What would you call it then?'

'A siege?' she suggested drolly, and Jack chuckled.

'Poor Angel, do you feel bombarded from all sides?'

Ellie scowled at him. 'You're doing your damnedest to undermine my defences right now.'

Blue eyes searched hers. 'Am I succeeding?'

Oh, yes, he was certainly doing that. Her defences were in such a parlous state they barely existed. However, knowing it and saying it were two different things. 'I'll never tell you. Do your worst, but I'm not about to surrender.'

Jack tipped his head on one side. 'You know it's only a matter of time. I will prevail.'

Her lips twitched as she enjoyed the exchange. 'No one could ever accuse you of lacking in confidence.'

'A faint heart never won anything worthwhile.'

She looked at him curiously. 'Am I worth winning?'

Jack shrugged, a smile quirking the corners of his mouth. 'Only time will tell, but I'm willing to take the risk. Come away with me and let's find out,' he suggested next, sending a jolt through her system.

'What? You can't be serious!' Ellie exclaimed attempting to sit up, but he was too heavy to move, so she was forced to lie there blinking at him.

'Never more so,' Jack confirmed. 'I'll hire a boat, then we'll sail down the coast for a couple of days and see what develops. How does that sound?'

She frowned doubtfully. 'It sounds as if you've had too much sun!'

'You think I'm crazy wanting to be alone with you? It sounds eminently sensible to me.'

'Going sailing with you would be too dangerous,' she pronounced huskily.

'You don't trust my sailing ability? I haven't let you drown yet, have I?' he countered and Ellie shot him an old-fashioned look.

'It's not the sailing that bothers me,' she retorted drily and he smiled.

'Worried I'll have my wicked way with you? Well, maybe I will, but only if that's what you want, Ellie. Nothing will happen unless you want it to. So, what's it to be? You know you love getting out on a boat. Can I tempt you?'

He could and that was the major drawback. However, he was right, she did love mucking about on boats. This might be the only opportunity she would get this summer, and she was loath to refuse. So, what to do?

Ellie knew that to agree was to go against all the advice she had given herself about not getting involved with Jack, but the time for non-involvement was long past. She was already involved, but how far and how fast that involvement developed was up to her. She had control, and his offer was tempting. It could do no harm to go, providing she kept her head.

'OK, you've talked me into it,' she told him and, as if he had been waiting on her answer, Jack smiled.

'You won't regret it, I promise you.'

A quirky smile curved her lips. 'I wouldn't get your hopes up too high if I were you. I'm agreeing to the sailing, that's all.'

He laughed huskily. 'I believe you, Angel,' sounding far from convinced.

His reply left her feeling mildly exasperated. 'But you think it's only a matter of time before I end up in your bed, don't you?'

Jack shrugged a shoulder. 'A man has to dream.'

Ellie poked a finger at that shoulder. 'Some dreams become nightmares.' She should know. Her relationship with Luke had been a classic example.

'Whilst other dreams drive the nightmares away,' he countered softly, turning her heart over in the process.

Oh, how she would like that. To have such good memories that the bad ones never returned to haunt her.

'Can anyone join in, or is this a private affair?'

Since neither of them had heard the other couple return, Luke's joking comment from above made them both look up with a start.

Jack held his brother's gaze steadily. 'It's a private affair,' he confirmed lazily, then looked down at Ellie and smiled meaningfully. 'Very private,' he added huskily, then sighed heavily. 'However, as we've been rudely interrupted, we'll have to put it on hold.'

Luke looked hard at Ellie as she and Jack sat up. 'I thought you were going to sleep.'

Jack drew Ellie into the vee of his legs and draped his arms loosely about her. 'We were, but then Ellie decided to seduce me, so sleeping was out of the question,' he returned humorously.

Andrea looked as appalled as Jack had meant her to do. 'You should save that kind of thing until you're somewhere private.'

Ellie couldn't resist responding to that. 'There was nobody here but us and the birds, and they didn't appear to be too bothered. So, what brought you back so soon?'

'Luke started complaining we'd gone too far,' Andrea explained snappily as she sat down.

'Yes, my brother and exercise are only nodding acquaintances,' Jack confirmed. 'He'd rather exercise his charm than his body.'

'I prefer the results,' Luke admitted as he joined them. 'I could never understand how you can inflict pain on yourself and call it fun. But I don't mind watching Andrea working out,' he added, jiggling his eyebrows suggestively at his fiancée. To her patent lack of amusement.

'Honestly Luke, I'm not a peep-show. You'd be fitter if you joined me,' Andrea pointed out, but Luke pulled a face and stretched out comfortably.

'Too much like hard work, darling.'

'Perhaps I ought to work out,' Ellie suggested, leaning back against Jack and casting a look up at him through her lashes.

'I love your body the way it is,' he told her silkily. 'In fact, I'd love to love your body any place any time.'

'Oh, pl…ease!' Luke exclaimed disgustedly. 'There's a time and place for everything.'

'We know. That's why Ellie and I are going off for a few days,' Jack revealed casually and, as Ellie's nerves jolted at the unexpected revelation, Luke's head shot up.

'What was that? You're going away? Where?'

'I'm hiring a boat. We're going to sail down the coast,' his brother obligingly explained.

Luke scooted round into a sitting position. 'Sounds like fun. We could go with you,' he suggested, and everyone looked at him in surprise.

Andrea was far from amused. 'Don't be silly, Luke. You know I hate boats,' she chided him. 'Besides, it's obvious they want to be alone. Two's company, four's a crowd. I think it's a great idea.'

To everyone's amazement, Luke promptly jumped to his feet. 'You wouldn't know a great idea if it bit you!' he exclaimed and stormed off.

Stunned, Andrea stared after him. 'Well, really!' she said, then rose with a set look to her face. 'He's been acting like a bear with a sore head for days, but that doesn't give him the right to speak to me like that!' she declared wrathfully, and went after him.

Ellie blew out a silent whistle. 'That went down well.'

'If I didn't know better, I'd say he was jealous,' Jack declared, frowning at his brother's disappearing back.

Ellie's heart skipped a beat as he came perilously close to the truth. Luke *was* jealous. Jealous that she could prefer anyone over him. Luke was backing himself into a pretty tight corner. If he wasn't careful he was going to be found out, and then the fat would surely be in the fire. When that happened he was likely to take his anger out on her. The woman he considered the source of the problem.

'There's never been anything for him to be jealous about,' she insisted, made distinctly uneasy by his behaviour.

'True, but he certainly doesn't like seeing us together. Now why should that be?' Jack mused and, because she didn't like the way his thoughts were turning, Ellie attempted to change tack.

'Maybe he doesn't think you're good for me.'

Jack tipped his head down and grinned lazily. 'What do you think?'

Looking up at him, Ellie felt an unexpected surge of emotion swell inside her. What did she think? There was no question of it. He was good for her. Oh so very good. Just days ago she would have thought differently, but she knew him better now. He wasn't the man she thought he was. These past days had shown her that. He was turning into someone she enjoyed being with. No, looked forward to being with. Not because he could turn her on with just a look, but because he made her feel good about herself. She was happy when she was with him, in a way she had never been happy with anyone else.

She smiled wistfully. 'I wish I hadn't been so blind all these years. I've missed being friends with you, Jack.'

He sighed heavily. 'It would have been more pleasant, but I have to admit I don't feel very friendly towards you now, Angel.'

Her brows rose at the flirtatious comment, and she admitted to herself that flirting with him was becoming addictive. 'No?'

Jack shook his head. 'No. Now I want you as a lover. I want the woman you are, not the child you were. I want your passion, your fire,' he told her with a depth of emotion that tightened invisible fingers about her heart. 'Nothing less will do. Does that scare you?'

It ought to. Lord knew, it should have—but it didn't. His words touched a core in her that she hadn't known existed. She knew she wanted nothing less from him. The knowledge filled her mind with wonder. She didn't know why she felt this so strongly, she only knew she did.

'Nothing about you scares me, Jack,' she told him boldly. 'But that doesn't mean I'm going to fall at your feet and say: take me I'm yours!'

Jack's eyes danced, and his smile was rueful. 'I always knew you'd be hell on wheels when you realised your full potential. Come on, we'd better go after the others and check that war hasn't broken out. I need to make a phone call about the boat, too,' he said, climbing to his feet and holding out a hand to help her up. 'With any luck I can arrange to have it tomorrow.'

That would be fine by her. If Luke was throwing a tantrum, she didn't want to be anywhere in the vicinity. Besides, she was secretly looking forward to being alone with Jack, despite the temptation he presented. Which only went to prove what a crazy world it was. She had been obsessed with Luke all those years, and never felt this depth of need or urgency. Which underlined how foundationless her feelings for him had been. If she had only known then what she knew now... But hindsight was a perverse thing. It showed you where you had gone wrong, but not the way to change anything.

That evening Ellie made a head start on her packing, gathering together the things she would need for a few days at sea, for they would be leaving early the following morning. Jack had managed to arrange to borrow a yacht from a friend and they would have the use of it for as long as they wanted. There was a fluttery feeling in her stomach at the prospect of being alone with him— totally alone—for the first time, but anxiety had little to do with it. She knew the feeling was anticipation. She wanted this time with Jack more than she could remember wanting anything for a long time.

Her packing was interrupted by a soft knock on the door and, when she went to open it, she found her mother outside. There was a tiny frown of concern on the older woman's forehead that caused Ellie to step aside to allow her mother in.

'Jack tells me you're going away for a few days,' Mary Thornton said without preamble as Ellie closed the door. Her gaze went to the open bag on the bed which mutely confirmed her statement.

Ellie wondered what was coming. Her mother hadn't looked this serious for a long time. 'Yes, we are. He's borrowed a boat. I'm hoping we can take in Naples. I want to see the Farnese collection again,' she responded as she turned to the chest of drawers.

Mary Thornton sat on the bed and watched her daughter sort through a pile of underwear. 'Is that wise, darling?'

Ellie tucked her finds into the bag and blew her hair out of her eyes. 'Well, I don't think they're cursed, so I should be safe enough,' she returned mischievously.

'You know perfectly well what I meant, Ellie,' Mary Thornton advised, shortly, and Ellie sighed.

'OK, I know what you mean, and no I don't think it unwise. We'll only be gone a couple of days.'

'You don't think going away with Jack is a little…premature?' her mother suggested and Ellie flushed, fully aware of what her mother meant by 'going away'.

'We're going sailing, nothing more,' she insisted, although she couldn't guarantee that that was how it would stay. Passions were running high between her and Jack, and that meant anything could happen.

'Sit down a moment, Ellie,' Mary commanded gently, and Ellie reluctantly sank onto the bed. 'Darling, are you in love with Jack?'

The question sent a jolt of electricity through Ellie's system, jangling her nerves and increasing the beat of her heart. 'What sort of question is that?' she gasped, not sure whether to laugh or not.

'A serious one, and I would like an answer please.'

There was a note in Mary Thornton's voice which her daughter well remembered from her childhood. It meant she had better give a straight answer. 'No, I'm not in love with Jack,' she said, but the minute the answer left her lips, she felt a strange queasiness settle in her stomach. 'I like him a lot. We like each other a lot,' she added hastily.

'Of course you do. Anyone can see that. The pair of you create enough wattage to light the island!' Mary agreed wryly. 'But…'

'But?' Ellie pursued, wondering what was coming next in this already startling interview.

Mary sighed and reached out to take her daughter's hand. 'Do have a care, darling. I know you wouldn't want to hurt a soul, but Jack's…vulnerable.'

Ellie was so surprised, she couldn't say anything for a moment or two. She had thought her mother was going to warn her about getting hurt by Jack, not warn her of hurting him! 'What are you trying to tell me, Mum?'

Her mother looked worried and uncomfortable by turns, but after a moment's hesitation she carried on. 'Don't allow him to think you feel more for him than you do, Ellie. Be kind.'

Ellie frowned, trying to make sense of the admonition, but failing. There was some hidden message here. Her mother knew she wouldn't deliberately hurt anyone, but why did she have to take care with Jack? It was a moment or two before a possible reason suddenly occurred to her. She thought she saw the light.

'Does this have something to do with the woman Jack

is in love with?' she asked, and her mother looked surprised.

'You know about her?'

'Jack told me,' Ellie nodded, certain she was on the right track.

'I see,' Mary Thornton said slowly.

'How do you know about her?' her daughter asked in turn, and Mary took a steadying breath, shifting about nervously before answering.

'He confided in me a long time ago,' she confirmed.

'You know who she is?' Ellie's curiosity was piqued.

Mary Thornton gave her daughter a steady look. 'I do, but don't ask me more, for I won't break a confidence. All I wanted to say was that whatever happens between you, don't play games with him. Be honest. Don't pretend what you don't feel. He's a good man and he deserves some good fortune for a change.'

Ellie had never guessed that her mother was so protective towards Jack, but it really shouldn't surprise her. She had taken the three motherless boys under her wing when she married their father and loved them unquestioningly. Jack's abortive love affair must have hurt him, and her mother knew it. Which was why she was warning her daughter not to cause him any more grief.

'I won't do anything to hurt him, Mum. Why would you think I would?'

Her mother captured both of her hands and squeezed them encouragingly. 'Because my darling, when it comes to men, you tend to go overboard. Look how you convinced yourself you were in love with Luke, and you weren't. Now, Luke being the type of man he is, that would not have hurt him in the long run, but Jack's another matter. He can be hurt. Think on that, darling, and be the gentle loving woman I know you can be.'

Ellie winced at the unwelcome reminder of her stupidity. Thank goodness her mother didn't know the true depth of it. As it was, what she did know was bad enough. 'I know I was foolish about Luke, but that's in the past. I've grown up—finally,' she added wryly, and Mary Thornton gave her a hug.

'I didn't mean to make you feel bad. I just thought you might not realise the damage you could do. I spoke from the best of intentions, for I do so want you both to be happy. Now I'll leave you to finish your packing,' she said as she rose and crossed to the door. There she paused and shot her daughter an impish grin. 'It doesn't sound very responsible and motherly to hope you enjoy yourself, when you're planning to spend a torrid few days alone with a handsome man, does it?' she laughed.

'Hey, it's going to be a totally innocent sailing trip!' Ellie exclaimed, not quite knowing how to respond without confirming the suggestion.

Mary laughed louder. 'And the moon is made of green cheese! I wasn't born yesterday you know. I had my moments. Your father and I…well, maybe I'd better save that for another day!' she tantalised as she went out, leaving her daughter in a state of bemusement.

What an amazing conversation! In a roundabout way, her mother had just given her blessing to whatever may or may not develop between her and Jack. Providing she didn't hurt him. Ellie shook her head in wonderment. It was hard to believe what had just been said.

Could her mother really be suggesting Jack could fall for her, given the right encouragement? It hardly seemed possible. Yet her mother seemed convinced he was vulnerable. She couldn't say she had seen any signs of it. They wanted each other, that was all. Any deeper feelings were out of the question. Jack knew that as well as she did.

Clearly her mother was overreacting because of what had happened in the past. This was different. There was no love involved, only passion. Jack wasn't about to fall for her nor she for him. Which was exactly the way she wanted it…wasn't it?

That was the question. Did she really know what she did want? Once it had seemed so clear, but now… The seed of doubt, once sown, took root, and slowly began to germinate in the recesses of her mind.

CHAPTER EIGHT

By late afternoon of the following day they were sailing steadily round the coast towards Salerno. Jack had promised they would drop in at Naples on the return trip. Now Ellie had the wheel whilst Jack dealt with the sails. She loved the feel of spray on her cheeks and the breeze in her hair, and felt like laughing for the sheer joy of it. Up ahead, Jack whistled happily. In deck shoes, black shorts and white T-shirt, he looked good enough to eat. Her heart did a crazy flip-flop in her chest and, for no reason at all, she started smiling.

'Something amusing you?' Jack asked as he made his way back and jumped down beside her.

'I was just thinking how handsome you looked,' she admitted and something flickered in his eyes.

'Now that deserves a kiss,' he responded and bent his head quickly, taking her lips in a short but nerve-tingling caress. Drawing back, he looked into her slightly dreamy eyes. 'Hungry?'

Ellie's stomach tightened as the glowing embers of desire sparked into life at the teasing question. Feeling reckless, she responded in kind. 'Depends what's on the menu.'

Laughing, he checked their heading before answering. 'Me or cold chicken and salad.'

'Mmm, decisions, decisions,' she teased back. 'What do I really fancy? I know. I'll have the chicken now and

132

save you for later. I've a feeling you'll improve with time.'

'Like a good wine,' Jack agreed, and she grinned.

'Or a ripe old cheese,' she riposted with a giggle.

Jack tipped his head as he watched her. 'You should do that more often,' he said, and she looked a query.

'What, call you an old cheese?'

Blue eyes narrowed playfully. 'No, laugh. You didn't look too happy at Christmas.'

She hadn't been, for she had been forced to follow a lead she was uncomfortable with. 'I probably had a lot on my mind.'

'You should have come to me for help,' Jack remarked, and she shook her head with a wry smile.

'You were the last person I would have turned to then,' she said wryly.

He picked up on the qualification. 'Then? Does that mean you'd turn to me now?' he asked curiously and Ellie sighed.

'Yes, I probably would,' she confirmed with a smile, and Jack nodded, his expression a curious mixture of satisfaction and something else.

'Good. Hold this course, there's a bay coming up we can spend the night in—unless you want to head for civilisation?'

Ellie darted him a quick look, knowing whatever she decided now would be important. If she told him to head for the nearest village, she would be saying keep your distance, and he would respect that. But, if she was honest with herself, she didn't want to say that at all. She wanted him, with a need that seemed to be growing daily. Why was she denying them what they both wanted? It was the fear that she was making another mistake. She had trusted Luke and he had used her. Yet Jack was everything Luke was not. Honest, strong, kind, trustworthy. He had said he wouldn't let anything bad happen to her, and she believed him. An affair with Jack need not be a mistake. It was time to take a risk.

'The bay sounds perfect,' she said huskily, and then the strangest thing happened. The instant her decision was made, all doubt seemed to vanish. Something inside her said this was right. That nothing which involved Jack would be wrong. She had never felt so sure of anything in her life before.

Jack said nothing just nodded but, as he passed her, he touched her briefly on the shoulder. It was the merest caress, yet it made her feel warm and bubbly inside and brought a smile to her lips.

She turned and looked after him in a kind of wonder, searching for what it was about him that made the difference, but he was just Jack. No different from the man who had plagued her life with his criticisms. It was she who had changed, seeing things as they really were, not how she had thought them to be. Which meant the man she had thought she loved, she now disliked, and the man she had hated, she now lov... The thought ended abruptly as she realised just what she was saying, but it couldn't be true. No, no, that was absurd.

Ellie turned her concentration back to sailing the yacht, feeling confused and unsettled. She wasn't going to think along those lines. She wanted Jack in a passionate way, but that was all. That had to be all.

They sailed on for another hour, then dropped anchor in the tiny secluded bay. Whilst Jack stowed the sails, Ellie, once more in control of her thoughts, went below and began preparing the food. As Jack had promised there was chicken and salad, plus wine and other tasty tidbits the housekeeper had supplied for their trip. They certainly weren't going to starve.

She was cutting bread into chunky wedges when Jack called down to her.

'I'm going for a swim before supper. Care to join me?'

Ellie didn't even have to think about it. She abandoned the bread and headed for the steps. The thought of a cool swim after the heat of the day was music to her ears. She had been wearing her bikini under her shorts and T-shirt, and it was the work of a moment to strip them off when she was back on deck. Jack was already down to the minuscule trunks he preferred to wear for swimming, and as ever the sight of so much tanned, muscular flesh set her pulse tripping along.

Jack didn't miss the way her eyes ate him up, and it brought a sultry look to his eyes. 'Of course, we don't have to swim if you'd rather do something else,' he suggested but, tempting as the offer was, Ellie shook her head.

'I think we've got time for a swim as well,' she pointed out with a quirky grin.

'As well as what?' he queried, and she laughed.

'Why, supper, of course. What else?'

Blue eyes glittered dangerously. 'So that's how it's going to be, is it? Something tells me I'm going to have to assert my authority or you'll be walking all over me,' Jack declared, advancing on her.

Her brows rose, though she was careful to retreat. 'Oh, yes, and how do you propose to do that?' she wanted to know, just as her legs struck the side.

'Like this,' Jack grinned, and swooping he picked her up in his arms and promptly tossed her over the side.

Ellie just had time to take a deep breath before she disappeared under the water. Arching her body, she gave a quick flick of her feet and shot to the surface. Brushing the hair from her eyes, she trod water and glanced round. Jack surfaced a few feet away, still grinning.

She shook her head at him. 'Bad move, Jack. Very bad move. You'll pay for that.'

'Threats, Angel?' Jack mocked, slowly beginning to circle her.

'Promises,' she countered. 'You're going to be sorry.'

'Mmm, can't wait,' he laughed softly, and she smiled back.

'What do you imagine I'm going to do to you?'

'Plenty—with any luck.'

Ellie circled too, maintaining the distance between them. 'It's supposed to be a penance. You aren't supposed to enjoy it!'

That brought another of those sultry smiles he did so well. 'I doubt very much if there is anything you could do that I wouldn't enjoy, so do your worst, Angel.'

'You don't think I could hurt you?' she taunted, though she knew she wouldn't even attempt to. It wasn't in her nature to be deliberately cruel.

'Not physically, no,' Jack agreed, and she frowned.

'But I could hurt you in other ways?' she probed, no longer teasing. 'Mum hinted the same last night.'

'Really?' Jack sobered too, and looked around him. He pointed to some rocks not far off. 'Let's go sit over there, then you can tell me what she said.'

He set off using a long lazy stroke that got him to the rock just ahead of her. Climbing out he reached down to help her up. The rock was still warm, and Ellie stretched out, enjoying the early evening sun. Jack made himself comfortable resting on his elbow looking down at her.

'So, what did Mary have to say about me?'

Sighing, Ellie looked up at him. A lock of damp hair had fallen over his forehead, and she reached up to comb it back, and even that small gesture made her fingertips tingle. She debated whether to tell him the truth or not, but knew she didn't want to lie to him if she could help it. There were too many lies already. 'She asked me not to hurt you.'

Jack's brows shot up, registering his surprise. 'How does she imagine you would do that?' he asked, capturing her hand and linking his fingers with hers.

Their connected hands were sending a wave of heat up her arm, centring deep inside her. 'It had to do with the woman you love. She was worried that I might…mislead you into thinking I feel more for you than I do.'

Understanding flashed in his eyes, and a rueful smile curved his lips. 'I see. She needn't worry. I know exactly what you feel for me.'

Her eyes rounded, and her heart knocked suddenly. 'You do?'

'Oh, yes. You want me.'

For no reason at all, the answer made her throat close over. It was so bald—so lacking in any kind of warmth. She felt disappointed for some reason, and it must have showed on her face.

'Unless I missed something?' Jack queried, and Ellie slowly shook her head.

'No. No, you didn't,' she confirmed, but there was a

nagging feeling inside her that something was wrong. She just didn't know what.

'So, is that all she had to say?'

Dragging herself away from her muddled thoughts, Ellie produced a grin. 'Actually she wanted to make sure I knew what I was doing, going away for a torrid few days with you.'

He laughed and smiled lazily. 'Torrid, hmm? Well, do you?'

There was that certain something in his smile which set her heart tripping. 'Oh, I think so.'

Some emotion flashed into his eyes, but was quickly hidden. 'You can always change your mind, Angel. I've never compelled a woman to do anything against her better judgement, and I don't intend to start with you.'

'Would you be disappointed if I did?'

'Very. I've been looking forward to this.'

'Then it's just as well I have no intention of backing out,' she told him, holding his gaze so that he would be in no doubt. Then, quick as a flash, she pulled her hand from his and gave him a shove. As he fell backwards, she jumped to her feet and shot him a grin. 'Race you back,' she challenged and dived in.

Ellie was a decent swimmer but, even giving herself a head start, she knew he would soon catch her up, which he did when she was no more than halfway back to the boat. Jack was waiting on deck to help her up the ladder when she climbed out of the water.

'I should tan your hide for that,' he threatened, wrapping a towel around her, but instead of drying her off, he used it to haul her closer.

Ellie placed her hands flat against his chest and looked up at him. 'Is that really what you want to do?' she asked breathlessly, knowing it wasn't from the aroused state of his body. Feeling his desire for her set her own body pulsing with need.

He didn't answer, instead his head swooped and he took her mouth in a kiss that demanded a response. She gave it, welcoming the sensual thrust of his tongue, matching it with her own. He touched her in no other place and, for sheer eroticism, it was mind-blowing. It was a greedy, hungry kiss that fed off its own passion and left her aching when he finally lifted his head.

Without a word Jack dropped the towel and picked her up in his arms. Equally speechless, Ellie wrapped her arms around his neck and buried her face against his shoulder. She had thought he was taking her to the main cabin, but instead he set her down beside him in the shower. He disposed of their clothes in a few brisk moves then clean water was washing away the sticky salt. Ellie closed her eyes as he turned her so her back was to him and ran soapy hands over her sensitised skin, gasping when he found her breasts, then groaning when he abandoned them again to trail lower. It was delicious torture, but she couldn't allow him to have it all his own way. Turning, she took the soap and proceeded to give him a taste of his own medicine. It was music to her ears to hear him catch his breath as her hands roved over the muscled planes of his chest but, when she attempted to go further, his hands fastened on her wrists. Their eyes met.

'I only have so much control,' he growled, reaching past her to turn off the water. Then he was picking her up again, this time heading for the bedroom.

Jack dropped her damp body on the bed and followed her down, one powerful male thigh settling between her own. Ellie groaned with satisfaction as his body moulded itself to hers. This was what she had ached for ever since she had set eyes on him again, and her arms went round him, her hands caressing every inch of silky male flesh she could reach. Jack's hand stroked in one long scorching caress from her shoulder to thigh then back again as his lips plundered the sensitive skin of her neck.

When his mouth trailed lower to the soft foothills of her breasts, Ellie caught her breath, waiting for the touch she longed for. Yet it was not his lips which claimed the peak, but his hand and, when she blinked her eyes open and looked down, it was to find him watching her through eyes heavy with barely controlled passion. As her breathing grew more ragged she watched him look down to where his thumb was grazing her turgid flesh, teasing her nipple into a hard nub. Pleasure arced through her, down to the aching centre of her passion, and helplessly her body arched upwards, seeking more. Jack's head bent, his tongue flickered out, and as she cried out his mouth closed hotly around her flesh, suckling her towards the point of insanity. Ellie's fingers blindly sought the dark tangle of his hair and clung on as she was battered by delicious sensations. When he transferred his attention to her other breast, a low moan was forced from her throat as he dealt it the same nerve-tingling pleasure.

'Oh, Jack,' she sighed, but got no further because he was moving on.

Hands framing her hips, he laid a trail of kisses down her body. His tongue found her navel and circled it lazily before pressing onwards, past the curve of her hips until he reached the juncture of her thighs. There, with the gentle pressure of his hands, he urged her to open to him, and with infinite care his lips and tongue sought and found the moist core of her. Ellie's fingers clutched at the covers beneath her as Jack's deft caresses ravaged her senses, tightening the spiralling coil inside and brought her to a swift climax.

As she lay trembling in the aftermath, Jack came up beside her. Taking his weight on his arms, he settled himself between her thighs and looked down at her.

'That's what I wanted to do,' he growled huskily, dropping ever more passionate kisses on her mouth. 'You were so sweet, so responsive, I nearly lost it,' he confessed.

Instead he had made sure that she did. Ellie had never known such an unselfish lover, a man intent on giving a woman pleasure before taking his own. It was a revelation. She held on to his shoulders, not really surprised to feel the desire mounting in her again so soon.

'I wanted us to lose it together,' she breathed, kissing him back, and felt his lips curve.

'We will, Angel. We will,' he declared and began to make love to her all over again.

This time they each took it in turns to arouse the other. Limbs entangled, they rolled back and forth across the bed, lips and hands driving each other crazy. The silence of the cabin was punctuated only by their moans and sighs of pleasure and their pleas for more. Ellie moved beneath Jack restlessly and there was an urgency to their caresses which was fast breaking the bounds of their control. Their sweat-slick bodies were burning up with need, and she knew that if he did not end this soon, she would die.

'Please, Jack, now!' she urged brokenly, and with a

groan his hands fastened on her hips lifting her to receive him.

With one powerful thrust he was home, and through her own sense of satisfaction at having him buried so deep within her, she could feel him battling for control. Yet control was the last thing she wanted. She wanted his passion and she wanted it now. Locking her legs around him, she moved against him in an invitation that destroyed the last vestiges of restraint.

Groaning, he began to move, every thrust driving them ever nearer to the goal they sought. There was no thought of holding back on either part. Then she was there, reaching heaven and shooting out into space on an explosion of pleasure that had her crying out. Seconds later Jack joined her, and all they could do was hold on to each other and ride the waves of passion until they reached the safety of the farther shore and came to rest.

Spent though he was, Jack's hand came up to gently cup her flushed cheek. 'Eleanora,' he sighed softly, and for the first time ever the name sounded beautiful to her ears.

Ellie found the energy to comb her fingers into his sweat-damp hair, sighing with a profound sense of satisfaction. What had just happened was…indescribable. She had reached peaks she hadn't known it was possible to climb. Jack had taken her there in a way she knew no other man ever could.

She knew that it signified something important, but her eyes felt as if they had lead weights in them. Sleep was calling her, and she didn't have the strength to fight it. Closing her eyes, she wrapped her other arm around him. She would think about whatever it was tomorrow.

*   *   *

It was dark when she woke, and she was alone in the bed. Coming up on one elbow, the cover which had been draped over her fell away. Jack must have covered her over when he left. She could hear noises coming from the galley and it made her realise that she was hungry too. Clambering from the bed, she gathered a brightly coloured sarong from the chair where she had left it and wrapped it around herself before padding out to find him.

Jack was indeed in the galley and, having arrived unheard, Ellie leaned against the doorframe and watched him. He was setting out the salad ingredients she had sorted earlier, on a tray, whistling tunelessly to himself as he bustled about. A fond smile curved her lips as she noted he was eating as much as he was putting on the plates.

'Hi,' she greeted softly, and he looked up with a start, his surprise turning to a look of pleasure when he saw her.

Wiping his hands on the shorts he had put on, he took the few steps necessary to join her. 'Hi, yourself,' he returned, taking her chin between finger and thumb and raising her head so that he could kiss her thoroughly. There was a warmth in his eyes when he raised his head that matched the glow in her chest.

Ellie's hands had gone to his waist to steady herself, and now she slid them slowly up his chest. 'I missed you,' she confessed as he pulled her into his arms and hugged her close.

'I planned to be back before you woke. This was supposed to be a midnight snack,' he said, inclining his head towards the food.

'Is it midnight?' she asked in surprise and he grinned.

'It's closer to two in the morning. I didn't intend to sleep so long, but you wore me out.'

Her eyes danced. 'Perhaps we ought to limit the amount of loving you get,' she suggested.

'Don't even think about it,' Jack rejected the idea immediately. 'Are you hungry?'

There was no doubt this time he was referring to food. 'Famished,' she confessed, and her stomach growled to add the full stop to it.

Jack picked up the tray. 'Do you want to eat up on deck? It's still warm out there.'

'Oh, up top. No question,' she decided and led the way outside.

They sat out under the stars, Jack leaning back against the seat and Ellie leaning on him. For a while they said very little as they quickly demolished the chicken and salad. Only when her initial hunger was satisfied did Ellie sit back with a sigh.

'You know, I never thought we'd end up like this,' she mused, picking up an apple and taking a bite out of it.

'On a boat?' Jack teased, and she elbowed him in the ribs, causing him to grunt at the unexpected impact.

'No, as lovers,' Ellie corrected as Jack fastened his arms about her waist, his chin coming to rest on the cushion of her hair.

'Strange things happen at sea,' he joked and she groaned at the tired adage.

'That isn't what I mean.'

It might not be the most appropriate time to talk about his brother, but the truth was beginning to weigh on her conscience now that she and Jack were involved. Never mind her pride. He ought to know, and she should be the one to tell him.

'Luke was always between us. I think we need to talk about him, Jack.'

'No, we don't,' Jack denied forcefully, angling her head so that he could look down into her eyes. 'I'm declaring this boat a Luke-free zone. This is our time, Angel. I don't want to think about anything but us. Forget Luke.'

She probably ought to have insisted, but the intensity of his gaze caused her to back off. It was incredibly heady to know he wanted nothing to intrude into their private world, and as a consequence she could do nothing but comply. 'OK,' she breathed. 'No Luke. He wasn't the only reason I never saw us as lovers anyway,' she went on huskily.

'No?'

Maybe she couldn't tell him the truth, but she could hint at it. 'My last relationship wasn't a happy experience,' she confided, and that was putting it mildly, but was all she could tell him about her and Luke. 'I made up my mind I wasn't going to get involved again for a long time.' Especially not with another Thornton.

'So why are you here with me?' he wanted to know, and she sighed.

'I couldn't resist you. Oh, I tried, but in the end I just didn't want to fight it any longer.'

'Which was what I was hoping for,' Jack responded, planting a kiss on her hair.

Ellie finished her apple and tossed the core onto the tray. 'So you have your wish. What happens now?' Only as she asked the question did she realise how important it was for her to know where she stood. She had to know what his intentions were now.

'Who knows,' Jack shrugged. 'We're at the beginning of something even I don't know the end of. I do know I'm in no rush to get there.'

That was good. She needed to hear that, but... 'How long do your affairs usually last?' she asked, and from the way he went still, she could sense him frowning.

'You make it sound as if I've had hundreds of affairs.'

'Maybe that's an exaggeration, but you've had more than me. I just wanted to get some idea as to how quickly you get bored.'

'That would rather depend on the woman. You can breathe easy, Angel. You haven't bored me yet,' he returned sardonically.

'That's a comfort,' Ellie quipped back wryly. They had been lovers for only a few hours, so the gloss was hardly likely to have worn off.

'You're worrying too much. Can't you just accept that we're here together now?' Jack suggested, and she knew that she was being foolish. There were no guarantees on relationships such as theirs. Passion that sprang up so swiftly, could just as easily vanish overnight. The sensible thing to do was enjoy it while it lasted—however short a time that might prove to be.

Ellie tugged at his hands until he relaxed his grip then twisted in his arms. Coming up on her knees, she straddled his legs and placed her hands on his shoulders. 'You're right. I'm just being silly. Put it down to the fact that nobody has ever made me feel the way that you do, and it's made me a tad paranoid about losing it.'

Jack's hands had come to rest on her thighs, and now began a slow glide upwards to her hips. Fastening on her slim behind, he urged her closer to him, so that she could feel the stirrings of his arousal. 'I told you this wasn't going to go away. Trust me, we have plenty of time,' he told her with that wicked glint in his eye that set her heart tripping faster.

Her own response was instant, her body coming alive again as desire quickened in the core of her. Holding his gaze, she moved against him, and was delighted when he let out a soft groan.

'Minx,' he accused her, and she laughed huskily.

'You never asked me if I got bored easily,' she told him, still moving against him, and arousing herself as much as him, so that she had to bite down on her lip to withhold a moan of her own.

Jack's hands trailed up her ribcage, his thumbs finding the slopes of her breasts and gliding up them to the stiffening peaks. 'God, I hope not, I want you too much.'

Ellie's head went back as his hands claimed her breasts, her fingers clamping onto the flesh of his shoulders. When she looked down at him again, her eyes were clouded with need. 'Perhaps we can keep boredom at bay between us. Want to give it a try?'

His smile was wolfish. 'I'm game for anything,' he declared, and that was all the encouragement she needed to untie the knot of her sarong and let it fall to the floor.

Eyes flashing a warning of her intent, she lowered her head and found one flat male nipple, teasing it with her tongue and teeth until she forced another groan from him, then she transferred her attention to its mate, dealing it the same fate. When she had gained the same result, she raised her head, tossing her hair back so that she could look into his eyes.

'Are you still with me?' she taunted and he laughed.

'Angel, I'm way ahead of you.'

Her fingers fluttered down to the fastening of his shorts and hovered there. 'Do you want me to stop?'

Jack shook his head, eyes dancing with amusement, yet behind it was a burning desire. 'You do, and I might just be forced to do something desperate.'

Ellie flicked open the snap. 'Well now, we can't allow that to happen, can we?' she said laughingly, and very very slowly began to lower the zip.

'Were you a torturer in a former life?' Jack groaned, raising his hips as she tugged the offending shorts down. He barely had time to kick them aside before her hand closed around him and her head lowered. Then he had to grit his teeth as he watched her doing to him what he had done to her earlier.

Ellie had no intention of going too far, but Jack stopped her anyway by tangling his fingers in her hair and bringing her head up to his. 'Hey!' she protested gruffly.

'Enough,' he ordered, rolling sideways and taking her with him so that she ended up beneath him. With one smooth move he was sheathed inside her once more. Braced above her, he looked down into her flushed face. 'Witch. What you do to me! I can't get enough of you.'

Ellie reached up and pulled his head down to hers, taking his mouth. 'Last I heard, rationing was over,' she breathed and he groaned.

'Thank God for that,' he muttered and kissed her.

It was the last intelligible thing either said for some considerable time.

CHAPTER NINE

THE three days that followed were, in Ellie's opinion, magical. They just sailed down the coast and back again, only putting into a harbour when their supplies finally ran low. The remainder of the time they spent together, either talking, swimming or, most often, making love.

If she had thought that by becoming lovers, the desire they had for each other would begin to lessen, she was mistaken. In fact, the opposite happened. The more they made love, the deeper the need grew. Ellie had never experienced such an empathy with another human being. It was as if she had found a lost part of herself. Jack made her feel complete for the first time in her life.

She was happy.

On the third day, as promised, they stopped off at Naples so that Ellie could see the Farnese collection. The paintings were magnificent, and she could have spent hours wandering around, studying them from all angles. Eventually, they were forced to leave because the museum was closing. They stayed on in the city for dinner and ate at a harbour-side restaurant noted for its seafood and relaxed dress code, and lingered over coffee. Consequently, it was quite late before they finally returned to the yacht.

'Do we really have to go back tomorrow?' Ellie asked as she emerged from the shower with a towel wrapped around her, using another to dry her hair.

Jack had already showered, and was lounging on the

bed. He rose, leaving the towel he wore hitched low on his hips. He took the towel from her and continued the job of drying her hair. ''Fraid so. It's the engagement party tomorrow night, remember?'

She grimaced. 'I'd forgotten. I must have had other things on my mind,' she returned wickedly, and he laughed.

'Such as?' he probed, casting the towel aside and combing his fingers through the damp gold strands.

His touch on her scalp sent shivers down her spine. 'Oh, I'd guess it would be six foot odd of handsome, sexy male.'

'Been thinking about me, Angel?'

Only all the time, she acknowledged wryly. 'Now and again,' she told him with an offhand shrug. 'You know, when I can't find a good book to read.'

'Are you telling me I'm not as interesting as a book?' Jack growled, and she giggled.

'I would never be so rude,' she denied, eyes dancing as she waited for his response to that. 'But you are closer to forty than I am. You can't expect to be as…vigorous as you once were.'

'That does it,' Jack declared menacingly. 'Nobody questions my manhood. Especially not a little squirt like you,' he added, spinning her around. 'Apologise or take the consequences.'

Ellie looked up at him from beneath her lashes, nerves thrilling to the glint in his eye. 'I can't. It's against my religion.'

Teeth flashed whitely as he smiled wolfishly. 'Then I guess I'm going to have to show you how wrong you are,' he pronounced, swinging her up in his arms and carrying her to the bed.

A long time later, Ellie lay in Jack's arms and smiled. 'I take it back. You're much better than a book,' she said, running her hand in lazy circles over his chest.

'And my manhood?' Jack queried.

'Is in good working order, I'm happy to say.'

'Good. Let that be a lesson to you,' he retorted, and she could feel the rumble of laughter in his chest.

'You know, there are some lessons that have to be repeated often for the message to get through,' she teased. 'You might have to jog my memory from time to time.'

'It will be my pleasure, Angel. Now get some rest, we have an early start tomorrow.'

Ellie frowned, wishing he hadn't reminded her of why they had to leave early. She had been trying not to think about it ever since he had brought up the subject of the party over dinner. A cloud had appeared on her horizon, because it had dawned on her that time was running out—literally. She had realised that by going back, the end of the pretence was approaching.

The thought of it then, as now, made her go cold inside, yet there was no avoiding the truth. After the party it would only be a matter of a few days before she had to go home, and she knew what would happen then. The real world would impinge on this magical one she inhabited. Icy fingers tightened on her heart as she accepted the blunt truth of it. Jack had his own life to live and so did she. However real this was here, it didn't exist in their other lives.

Which was a problem because she didn't want it to end. The imminence of their departure was forcing her to be honest with herself. It was too soon. She wanted more. She wasn't ready to end it. Yet it had only ever been a ruse. OK, the affair had become real, but nothing else was. It was a game, never meant to be taken seriously. Not that she was taking it seriously exactly, she just didn't want it to end so soon. Yet there was nothing she could do to change things.

She sighed heavily, feeling foolishly close to tears. Which was ridiculous because she had always known it was a game. It just didn't feel like one, that was all.

'What's up?' Jack asked softly.

There was no way she was going to tell him why she suddenly felt so maudlin. She was going to be as civilised about it as he would be. 'Oh, nothing really. I just don't want to go back tomorrow—or is it today now?' She didn't know what time it was, but it had to be after midnight. 'Do you think they'd miss us if we played truant?' she tried to make light of it but didn't sound too convincing to her own ears.

Jack's hand caressed the curve of her shoulder. 'It's a tempting thought, but we'd never get away with it. Your mother and my father would have plenty to say. Much as I'd rather sail off into the sunset with you, we'll have to go back.'

She knew he was right. 'Oh, well, they say all good things come to an end,' she said stoically, knowing it was far too soon for her.

Jack raised himself up enough to squint down at her. 'Who says it's the end?'

Ellie rested her chin on his chest and looked at him regretfully, determined to play it cool. 'My boss. I only had two weeks' holiday and most of that has gone already. I'll be flying home in a few days.'

'Is there some law I haven't heard of that says we can't continue seeing each other back in England?' he countered and Ellie was so surprised, she forgot to breathe for a second or two. Then she tried to act calm, though her heart was racing like fury.

'But once we leave here, the pretence will be over,' she reminded him, and he shook his head sadly.

'Funny, but it's all felt very real to me.'

Ellie grimaced, for it was very real to her too, only... 'You know what I mean. This was an act for Luke's benefit.'

'Luke has nothing to do with it. I still want you. Or are you saying you don't want me?' His blue eyes were suddenly narrowed and watchful.

'Of course I want you,' Ellie exclaimed, her mood lifting as she realised it didn't have to be over yet.

'Then that's settled,' Jack declared with satisfaction, and he lay back down again.

Ellie gave herself a mental shake, taking it all in. The relief was heady. It wasn't over. Jack wanted their affair to continue. Happiness bubbled up inside her. She felt like laughing, but bit it back. There was time. Time for what, exactly, she couldn't say. She only knew that far from being the end, this was only the beginning.

Ellie sat in the stern and watched Jack as he kept the yacht headed into the wind. They needed to make up time because they hadn't started on the homeward journey as early as Jack intended. She smiled to herself. It had been his own fault. He shouldn't have kissed her like that. One thing had led to another and, hey presto, it had been closer to lunch than breakfast when they set off.

He was very easy on the eye, and just watching him brought a smile to her lips and a warm glow to her chest.

He was just about perfect, she supposed, and that was probably why she loved him so much.

The thought just slipped into her consciousness with all the force of a hurricane. Ellie was staggered by it. Loved him? She loved him? The world seemed a little unsteady but it had nothing to do with the swell. She couldn't love Jack—could she? The answer came back loud and clear. She could. She did.

Everything she felt, everything that had happened between them, pointed to the truth of it. I love him, she told herself silently and, in the saying, all the things she had been feeling coalesced into a huge swell of emotion inside her. Her heart lurched, then raced on, and she pressed faintly trembling fingers to her lips. Of course she loved him. It was the only thing that made sense.

She could see it now very clearly. He was her destiny. All of her life had been leading to this moment. She loved him—had fallen in love with him there on the dock, when he had appeared to her out of the heat haze.

'Jack.' His name was little more than a breath on the breeze.

No wonder she hadn't wanted this affair to be over. It was because she was in love with him. He had, without her knowing it, become the centre of her world. Everything which was good in her life was connected to him. No other men had been able to make her feel what he had made her feel, because she hadn't loved them. It was Jack. Only Jack.

And then she remembered the woman he loved.

Ellie felt as if she had had heaven within her grasp and had just had it snatched away. She might well love Jack, but he could not love her. His heart belonged to another, and the irony was that part of what made her love him was his steadfast heart. The very thing she loved him for, would keep him from loving her.

Her heart started to ache with an unquenchable pain. As she sat there in the grip of something approaching despair, she knew it wouldn't take much for it to break in two. For to love Jack was to want all of him, and yet she better than anyone knew there was one part of him she could never have—his heart.

Had it been anyone else she might have hoped one day to win his love, but not with Jack. The most he would ever have to offer was affection. At the present, so far as he was concerned, all that was between them was a powerful sexual attraction. If it lasted, he might want a more permanent relationship, but the odds were against it. In all these years he hadn't found anyone he wanted to spend the rest of his life with. Why should she prove any different to the rest? Which left her with only what they had now—for as long as it lasted.

Could she accept that? Did she have any choice? Something always had to be better than nothing, but would a small amount of something fill the void of a whole future with nothing? It would have to, for the alternative was unthinkable. She wouldn't walk away from him. In fact, she doubted that she could do it. He would have to tell her to go. Only then would it finally be over.

'Come back, Ellie,' Jack's gentle command broke through the wall of her thoughts and she blinked at him.

'What?' she asked vaguely then, seeing the concern in his eyes, her heart turned over.

Jack was still frowning. 'You looked lost and sad,' he observed, and Ellie felt colour wash into her cheeks, for that was exactly how she had been feeling.

Licking her lips nervously, she produced a smile, though it was a travesty of the real thing. 'Was I?'

He nodded. 'What were you thinking?'

She shrugged diffidently. 'Oh, that life can play tricks on you.'

'The thing with life is that sometimes you have to look it squarely in the eye and dare it to do its worst,' Jack advised. 'Things have a way of turning out for the best then.'

Her smile widened a little. 'You're speaking from experience? Did it work?'

He grinned. 'The jury's still out, but I've a gut feeling they'll find in my favour.'

Ellie swallowed a painful lump in her throat. 'I hope they do, Jack. I really hope they do.'

For a moment he said nothing, merely looked at her, then he held out a hand to her. 'Come over here. You're too far away and I want to hold you.'

Putting her gloomy thoughts aside, Ellie went to him. 'The last time you held me, we lost all track of time,' she reminded him of just that morning.

Jack pulled her in front of himself so that his arms were around her even as he held the wheel. 'I'll be on my best behaviour. The last thing I want to do is capsize the boat and lose you just when I've caught you.'

Ellie laughed as he intended her to, but unseen by him her eyes glittered with unshed tears. She didn't want him to lose her either, but she knew that fate, that fickle creature, still had its last cards to play.

The party was going with a swing. Everyone was having a wonderful time. At least, all the guests were.

From her position by the window Ellie could see that

Andrea was looking bored, whilst Luke had barely spoken a word. So much for being 'The Happy Couple', she thought wryly. Not that she was in much of a party mood herself, but at least she was making an effort to enjoy herself.

She had spent most of the early evening helping in the kitchen. Jack and his father had been in charge of making room for dancing and seeing there were enough chairs for those who wanted to sit down. Consequently she had seen very little of him. Which had given her time to put things in perspective. The sky hadn't fallen in just because she'd discovered she loved Jack. It was one of those things she had to have the grace to accept. Railing against it certainly wasn't going to get her anywhere. In the meantime, she was going to make the most of what she did have.

Starting right now.

She looked for Jack and found him talking to her mother. He looked devastatingly handsome in his dinner suit. Not to mention downright sexy. The music playing was slow, and she could think of nothing she'd rather be doing than slowly circling the dance floor in his arms.

The thought being father to the deed, she began to make her way towards him, but someone walked directly into her path, forcing her to stop. Stepping back, Ellie found herself staring into Luke's angry eyes. He was the very last person she wanted to be talking to, and her first instinct was to attempt to step round him.

'Excuse me,' she said coolly, but he quickly stepped in front of her again.

'Not so fast,' he commanded. 'I want to talk to you. Let's dance.'

Ellie stood her ground. 'I don't think we've anything

to say to each other, and all things considered, I'd rather dance with a toad than you. So, if you don't mind...'

Luke's smile appeared but failed to reach his eyes. 'Oh, but I do mind. I mind about a lot of things. For instance, I mind very much about you and my brother getting all cosy.'

She had known he would. Luke was a sore loser. 'Our relationship has nothing to do with you, Luke,' she told him firmly.

'It is when I find him poaching on my territory. I won't have it, and I intend to put a stop to it,' Luke declared nastily, and Ellie's stomach lurched, for she knew he was a dangerous man to cross.

Still, she wasn't about to show he was making her anxiety level hit the roof. 'Oh, yes, and just how do you plan to do that?' she challenged scornfully, and he smiled.

'Come outside with me and I'll tell you,' he proposed, and Ellie debated whether to comply or not. She didn't want to but she needed to know his intentions.

Shrugging as if the whole business was unimportant, she nodded. 'Very well, I'll listen.'

His amusement was far from encouraging. 'Thought you might,' he mocked, and taking her by the arm led her out onto the terrace. Several people were chatting outside, but off to the left there was a private area. Luke headed for it.

Ellie turned on him then, trying to shake off his hand but he held on and placed his other hand on her shoulder, successfully trapping her. Unwilling to create a scene with others nearby, she was forced to grit her teeth and bear it. 'You had something to tell me,' she reminded him.

'Ah, yes, my brother,' he murmured, allowing his hands to glide down her arms and up again.

His touch made her flesh crawl and she tensed, bristling. 'Stop that!'

'Prefer other hands now, do we?' Luke sneered. 'Just what did you and Jack get up to on that boat?'

Ellie finally managed to prise his hands away by dint of digging her nails in—hard. 'Keep your hands to yourself in future. I'm not your property. I never was. Leave us alone, Luke.'

'Do you love him, Funny Face?' Luke asked, then proceeded to answer his own question. 'Of course you do. You're here right now because you're worried that I might hurt him, aren't you?'

She stared into his angry eyes and knew trouble was brewing. She just didn't know what form it would take. 'I won't let you hurt him,' she warned icily.

He laughed. 'Ah, the power of love. Well, relax, I'm not going to do anything to Jack. He's my brother after all. But you, Ellie, you aren't family at all. You shouldn't have left me, you know. It made me angry, and I really can't let you get away with it.'

Her chin went up, though her heart quailed at the thought of what he could do. He was a very vindictive man. 'You can't do anything to me, Luke.'

'Oh, yes I can. I can take away the one thing you really want. My brother. Call it tit for tat. If I can't have you, then I intend to see Jack doesn't have you either. Perfect.'

If he thought that, he didn't know his brother very well. Jack wasn't easily swayed by outside forces. Knowing it, Ellie shook her head. 'You won't succeed,' she said confidently.

'Care to put a bet on it?'

'You're missing the point. He doesn't love me.' Though it hurt to say it, her defence was strengthened by the truth of it.

To her surprise Luke threw back his head and laughed. 'No, it's you who's missing the point, Funny Face.'

She frowned. 'What do you mean?' A knot settled in her stomach.

'A funny thing happened whilst you were gone. I was out here on the terrace and just happened to overhear a conversation between our parents. Do you want to know what I heard?'

'Not particularly,' she denied, though her heart rate had increased along with a feeling of dread. He was going to tell her, and intuition told her she wasn't going to like it.

'I'll tell you anyway. The parents were talking about you and Jack, and you'll never guess what?'

Ellie gritted her teeth, hating the amusement he was getting from this. 'Either tell me or shut up. I'm not interested in your mean little games, Luke.'

'You'll be interested in this one. Remember the woman I told you Jack had fallen for all those years ago? Brace yourself, darling. Turns out it was you!'

He couldn't have handed her a more profound shock. Ellie stared at him uncomprehending for what seemed like aeons, but was barely a second in reality. She could feel the blood leaving her cheeks as the stunning message got through. 'What did you say?' she asked incredulously.

Luke was enjoying himself. 'I know. Hard to take in, isn't it. You're the mystery woman. Jack loves you. But what you have to ask yourself is this, will he still love you when I tell him about us? Hmm? What do you think?'

Ellie felt the ground sway under her feet. Jack loved her? Had loved her for years? It couldn't be true. She knew it couldn't, and yet... So many things suddenly began to make sense. Things which, separately, meant nothing, but put together pointed to one thing. That Luke was telling the truth. He had no reason to make it up, for as the truth it had untold power. Power to cause pleasure and pain. For whilst there was nothing she wanted to hear more than that Jack loved her, she had no way of knowing how he would react to the news of her affair with Luke.

'Ellie?'

Jack's voice saying her name made Ellie spin round. She could feel his eyes on her face and knew she looked as pale as she felt.

'Hey, Jack!' Luke greeted his brother cheerily. 'We were just talking about you.'

Jack didn't smile as he came closer, for he would have to be an insensitive clod not to pick up on the atmosphere. 'What's going on here?' he demanded to know, looking from one to the other questioningly.

The question was all the opening Luke would need and, recognising that, Ellie pulled herself together in a hurry. At all costs she had to prevent Luke from carrying out his threat. Which meant getting Jack away from there fast. Hurrying to his side, she took his arm.

'Nothing's going on. Let's go back inside,' she urged, mentally willing him to do as she wanted, but Jack didn't move.

Freeing himself, he took Ellie by the shoulders, compelling her to meet his eyes. 'You're lying. You're as white as a sheet. What did he say to you?'

Silently, grey eyes begged him to let them leave. 'Nothing important. Please, Jack, I want to go back now.'

'Don't run away on my account,' Luke put in mockingly, and Ellie shot him a look of pure scorn.

'You're despicable,' she said coldly. Licking her lips nervously, she turned back to Jack. He was looking grim, and her nerves jangled. 'If you come with me, I'll tell you what you want to know, but we have to go now,' she insisted, and could feel the tension in Jack's arm.

He gave her one final look, then took a deep breath and nodded. 'Very well.'

Ellie breathed a sigh of relief as they turned to go back inside, but it was short-lived.

'By the way, Jack,' Luke spoke to their backs. 'You never told me how good she was,' he drawled, and Ellie caught her breath in a horrified gasp.

Jack slowly faced his brother, a deep frown creasing his forehead. 'What was that?'

Luke grinned. 'I wondered how good she was. Just idle curiosity, seeing as I was the one who taught her all she knows. From what I can remember, as lovers go, she was hot!'

Beneath her fingers, Jack went utterly still. 'Say that again,' he commanded in a voice so frosty, Ellie shivered.

Luke was enjoying himself too much to take heed of the undercurrents. 'Didn't she tell you we were lovers? Tut, tut, Ellie, you really should have told him. She was an enthusiastic learner. In fact—'

What he would have said then was a matter for pure

speculation, for at the precise instant Jack knocked him down with one powerful punch. As his brother crumpled at his feet, Jack turned and looked at Ellie. He didn't say a word, but he didn't have to, his silence was eloquent. Ellie's heart twisted painfully in her chest.

Finally he raked a hand through his hair, and shook his head slowly. 'Any denials?'

She swallowed painfully. 'No.'

Spinning on his heel, he went to walk away, pausing beside her for a second. 'He was right about one thing. You should have told me,' he said, then brushed past her and disappeared inside.

Ellie stared after him helplessly, knowing she had been a fool. She had done everything wrong, and now she didn't know if she could put it right. She shivered, feeling cold despite the balmy night air. Of course she was going to try, because she loved him. This was not the time to be faint-hearted. He deserved the truth, no matter how bad it made her appear. Then maybe, if he loved her as Luke said he did, he would understand and forgive her. Lord, she hoped so, because if he didn't, Luke would have his victory.

She gave Luke's unconscious figure one last look, then hurried after Jack. As luck would have it, she bumped into Andrea in the doorway.

'Have you seen Luke?' the other woman asked, in that superior tone that instantly put Ellie's back up. In no mood to suffer in silence, she nodded her head towards the terrace.

'You'll find him out there. Throw a bucket of water over him and give him a couple of aspirin. Then when he's feeling better, ask him what he did to make Jack knock him down. It will make interesting listening!'

With a tight smile she left Andrea gaping and made her way through the gyrating dancers to where her mother and Tom were having an animated conversation by the door.

'Have you seen Jack?' she asked without preamble, and Tom Thornton hiked a thumb towards the stairs.

'He went through here looking like a thundercloud. Last I saw of him he was taking the stairs two at a time.'

'Have you two argued?' her mother asked, searching her face for clues, and Ellie winced.

'Not exactly,' she squirmed, then looked apologetically at her stepfather. 'You might want to go outside and see how Luke is,' she advised, and his brows shot up questioningly. 'Jack hit him,' she elucidated, and drew gasps from the pair of them. Then, to her surprise, Tom started to laugh.

'Well, that's been a long time coming. No doubt Luke deserved it. He must have said something pretty nasty to stir Jack to violence,' he said, and looked another question.

Ellie braced herself, but didn't flinch from telling the truth. 'You might as well know. Luke told Jack we'd been lovers, and Jack took exception to it,' she explained, and met her mother's eyes briefly before glancing away.

'Oh, Ellie!' Mary Thornton exclaimed softly.

Ellie shrugged diffidently. 'Not my only mistake, but the biggest.' By saying it out loud, the enormity hit her hard, and her bottom lip showed an alarming tendency to quiver. She pressed her lips together hard to stop it. 'Trouble is, I know I never did love Luke, but I do love Jack. Which is why I have to go after him and try to explain. Do you think... No, don't answer that. I'll know either way soon enough,' she said with an expressive grimace and headed for the stairs.

Ellie approached Jack's bedroom door with a hollow feeling in her stomach. This was not an interview she was looking forward to, but it had to be done. She knew he had a right to be angry with her, but if he loved her... That was the hope she clung on to as she knocked on the door. Without waiting for an answer, she opened the door and stepped inside, closing it firmly behind her.

Jack lay on the bed, his jacket and tie discarded, shirt sleeves rolled up to the elbow and several buttons opened at his throat. He looked round as the door opened but said nothing until she closed it behind her.

'You weren't invited in,' he told her bluntly.

Ellie rested back against the solid wood and took a deep breath. 'I knew better than to wait for an invitation. You're angry,' she observed and he laughed hollowly.

'Hell, yes, I'm angry. Which is why you shouldn't be here right now,' he shot back, eyes glittering a warning.

'You won't hurt me,' she returned simply and he glared at her.

'Really? Didn't you just see me floor my brother?'

'You were provoked,' she countered, and Jack laughed.

'And you think you aren't provoking me? I don't want you here, so I'd advise you to get out whilst I still have control of my temper,' he ordered, looking away from her.

Ellie held her ground. 'I came to explain about everything, and I'm not leaving until I have.'

'And if I don't want to hear it?' he charged, angry eyes swinging back to her face.

That was the problem. If he really didn't want to hear

anything she had to say, all he had to do was get up and leave. She wouldn't be able to prevent him. She had to say something that would make him stay and hear her out. Whatever it was, it had to be bold, and she had to think of it fast.

'Will you at least tell me why you're so angry?'

Jack came to his feet in one lithe movement and rounded the bed to face her. 'I'm angry, Angel, because I thought you had more sense than to sleep with my brother!'

'Obviously I'm not as bright as you thought I was!' she said gruffly.

A muscle in his jaw clenched. 'You were clever enough to tell the whole family a pack of lies.'

'I know, but there were reasons.'

Jack dragged a hand through his hair. 'There always are. Look, I really don't care to hear about it right now.'

Her nerves jangled as she realised he was about to end the discussion. These were desperate times and called for desperate measures. She knew of only one thing she could say to make him listen. It could open her up for more heartache than she had ever experienced, but she could see no other way.

'You're right, I was a fool, but at least my relationship with Luke taught me what love wasn't, so that I could recognise the real thing when it came along. And it did come along. If you won't let me tell you anything else, at least hear this. I love you, Jack,' she admitted in a voice thick with emotion, and held her breath for his answer.

The confession stunned him into silence for a moment or two, then he gave his head a shake. 'What was that?'

Ellie swallowed hard and kept hold of her courage. 'I

said I love you. It probably won't help, but I just wanted you to know.'

Jack's hands settled on his hips as he looked at her incredulously. 'Damn you, Ellie, you certainly know how to pick your moment!'

She spread her hands in entreaty. 'All I want is a chance to explain.'

He grimaced and rubbed a hand around his neck as if to ease out the kinks. 'OK, I'll listen, though I don't know what you hope to gain.'

She could have told him in a few short words. What she hoped for was that he would tell her he loved her. That at least would tell her all was not lost. What she would settle for... Well, that would depend on the outcome of the next half-hour.

CHAPTER TEN

Now that she had been given the opportunity to explain her actions, Ellie found she didn't exactly know where to start. Jack had walked over to the open window and was staring out into the night sky, his hands shoved into the pockets of his trousers. He looked distant and unapproachable, and those icy fingers tightened their grip on her heart.

From some way away they could still hear the sounds of the party going on downstairs. It seemed to be mocking them.

'Cat got your tongue?' Jack taunted from across the room, and she jumped, realising she was wasting precious time.

She took a couple of hesitant steps towards him, then stopped again. 'I was wondering where to begin,' she confessed.

He laughed humourlessly. 'Trying to work out which version of the events will get the best results?'

That stung, as it was clearly meant to, but at least it had her chin lifting. 'There is only one version—the truth,' she told him firmly, and he shot her a mocking look over his shoulder.

'But with you being such an adept liar, Angel, how am I to know the truth is the truth, hmm?'

That brought colour to her cheeks, for she knew she had made things difficult for herself by all the lies she had told, and then perpetuated. 'I guess I deserve that.

All I can do is tell you the truth as I believe it to be, and let you use your own judgement.'

'This being the judgement that believed you the first time, and has clearly been proved faulty,' he jibed, quirking one lazy eyebrow at her.

Ellie stared at him, knowing she deserved to be given a hard time, but hurting anyway. 'You're determined to make it difficult.'

'Give me one good reason why I should make it easy?' he countered, and she bit her lip.

There was a good reason—because he loved her—but she wouldn't use it. She couldn't use against him something he hadn't told her himself. She believed it to be the truth but, until he said it in as many words, it simply didn't exist. It hadn't come from his heart.

Folding her arms to hide the fact that her hands carried a visible tremor, Ellie crossed the floor to the window and looked out.

'I'm sorry,' she apologised in a soft voice made thick with emotion. 'I never meant to hurt anyone. I just didn't want you all to know how stupid I'd been. It seemed…easier to say nothing. The crazy thing is, the affair didn't even last long. I knew I'd made a mistake almost from the beginning. You remember I told you I'd lost those rose-tinted glasses I'd worn for so long? Well, you don't know how much I wish I'd lost them a lot earlier,' she admitted ruefully. She could feel Jack's eyes on her, but resisted the urge to look round. 'I never knew how selfish Luke was. How incapable he was of being faithful, and how much he enjoyed playing games and manipulating people.'

'It's his favourite pastime,' Jack observed grimly.

She nodded, knowing it now. 'That's what he was doing last Christmas.'

'You were lovers then?' he asked in disbelief, and she nodded.

'Yes.'

'My God!' Jack gritted through his teeth and she knew he was remembering what had happened then.

'Believe me, I had no idea until you told me that he'd asked everyone's advice on what to do about me. You see, he'd insisted we kept the affair secret. At first I thought it was because he didn't want to share what we had with anyone, and that was fun. But then I realised he was never going to say anything. He thought it was a great joke to lead you all down the garden path, and because I'd agreed to it in the first place, I was trapped. I went along with it, but I hated making fools of you all. I just didn't know how to put things right so I decided to say nothing.'

'Something of a habit of yours,' he responded sardonically, and Ellie glanced round at him.

'I hated myself for being used, and for letting down the people I cared about. I knew I'd disappointed you all, and that made me a coward. I've had to live with it, and believe me I'm not proud of myself.'

If she hoped to see a softening of his expression, she was disappointed. Jack's face could have been carved from stone. She had no idea what he was thinking. Confession was good for the soul, and she was glad she was telling him now, but it was doing nothing for her heart.

'So,' Jack said coldly. 'Having discovered what a louse my brother really is, what did you do next?'

Ellie looked at him steadily. 'I ended the affair of

course,' she replied, and at last saw something flicker in the depths of his blue eyes.

'That couldn't have gone down well. Luke prefers to be the one in control,' he observed, and Ellie shrugged.

'It was another thing we disagreed on. Needless to say he didn't accept it. He still thinks he can get me back with a click of his fingers! I've done everything but take out an ad in the newspapers to make him understand it's over. I don't want him. I certainly never loved him. I was Trilby to his Svengali for too many years, but the magic eventually wore off, and I saw him for what he was.'

'Ah, now I understand your change of heart the other day. So you finally decided to use me to prove to him that you didn't want him, didn't you?' he charged, fixing her with a gimlet eye, and she knew she hadn't done her cause any favours.

'It seemed appropriate to try and kill two birds with one stone,' she expanded, but Jack looked sceptical.

'The only trouble with that, Angel, was that there was really only one bird so far as you were concerned. You must have found it vastly amusing to have me insist on you proving to everyone that you had finally got over your crush when you planned to do it all along!' he returned scornfully, and Ellie grimaced, knowing she had been right about how much her behaviour would hurt her family.

She looked at him with regret. 'I never laughed at you, Jack. I used the situation, that was all. You were using it too, remember and you were the one that suggested everything in the first place!'

'At least I was open about my intentions,' he pointed out, and Ellie shook her head at the double standard.

'So it's honourable for you to try and get me into bed, but not for me to have an affair with your brother?' she argued, only to have Jack come right back.

'Everyone could see what I was doing. You and Luke made a point of hiding it. You lied to us. You played us all for fools, and that isn't something we're going to forgive you for too easily.'

That was what she was afraid of. It would be bad enough coming from her mother, but what she really feared was that Jack would not forgive her. 'Surely I'm allowed one foolish mistake?'

Jack's laugh was mirthless. 'True, but you made two. The first one was to get involved with Luke in the first place. The other was lying about it,' he counted off on his fingers, and Ellie felt her heart constrict.

'So you'll allow me the foolishness of falling for Luke, but not the other? I thought you would be kinder.'

Jack's eyes flashed angrily. 'Unluckily for you, Angel, I'm not feeling too kindly right now.'

She should have expected that. 'And what I said makes no difference?' she simply had to ask.

Something glittered in Jack's eyes as he folded his arms and stared down at her. 'You've said quite a lot, so you'd better remind me what you consider significant.'

Ellie caught her breath, discovering for herself that it was impossible to take a pound of flesh without drawing blood. 'I told you I loved you,' she reminded him huskily.

'Oh, that,' he said carelessly. 'Tell me, is there any reason why it should mean anything? It isn't as if the feeling is reciprocated, now is it? Or did you think that because I'd taken you to bed, I loved you?' he went on, and tutted. 'Come on, sweetheart, you should know from your own experience it's possible to sleep with someone without loving them.'

Only then did she truly appreciate just how angry he was. If she told him that she knew he loved her, she would only make things worse. Right now the last thing he wanted her to know was how he felt about her. She would have to hope that in a few days he would see things differently. He would come round in the end. She had to believe that or the future would look incredibly bleak.

Licking trembling lips, she rubbed her hands over her arms uneasily and began to move towards the door. 'I see. In that case I won't disturb you any longer. Thank you for listening to me.' She reached the door but kept her back to him, afraid he would see the gleam of tears in her eyes. 'Will you at least do one thing for me?' she asked as she opened the door.

'Depends what it is,' he responded shortly.

'Just remember I do love you, Jack. Goodnight.'

She didn't wait for a response, but went out and closed the door behind her. Unable to take another step, she pressed a hand to her mouth to hold back a sob. Oh, God, he was so angry, and it was the kind of anger that could make him steel his heart against her. It was possible to push love to its limits, to where forgiveness was impossible. Had she done that? Had she destroyed the one thing that really mattered to her? She really feared that she just might have done.

The thought of rejoining the party right now made her wince, so she walked the few metres to her own room. There was enough light from the moon to illuminate the room, so she didn't bother to switch on the light, merely kicked off her shoes and made herself comfortable on the bed.

What a mess. How had things become so complicated? There was no simple answer, nor a simple solution. Either Jack would come around or he wouldn't. He was angry with her, and he had a right to be. She shouldn't have lied in the first place. But what was done was done. Now all she could do was wait and hope. Never the two easiest things to do, but if there was an alternative, she didn't know about it.

It was going to be a very long night.

Having taken for ever to fall asleep, Ellie woke late the following morning feeling less than refreshed. Her first instinct was to go to Jack, but she knew that would be a mistake. She had to give him time. Steeling herself to what lay ahead, she showered and dressed in a cool cotton sun dress and headed downstairs to face the family. By now everyone would know the main details, but she knew she would have some explaining to do.

Paul was in the kitchen raiding the fridge when she stopped off there to get a cup of coffee. He grinned when he saw her.

'Some party!' he teased, deciding on a chicken drumstick left over from yesterday.

Ellie shuddered and poured herself the coffee. 'I'd rather not think about it.'

'For what it's worth, I'm on your side. Someone should have given Luke a black eye a long time ago.'

Her face mirrored her surprise. 'He has a black eye?'

'A real beauty. Jack sure didn't pull his punch any. I wish I'd seen it.'

His grin was infectious, and Ellie couldn't help laughing. 'He did go down as if he was poleaxed. Mind, it wasn't funny at the time.'

'I guess not. Anyway, it had one result. Luke and Andrea left right after the party, and I can't say I was sorry to see them go. He's a pain and she's a pill. They ought to do well together!' Paul added with a roll of his eyes. 'You'll find Mum and Dad out on the terrace.'

'I'd better go and make my peace with them. Why do I feel about ten years old?'

Paul wagged the half-eaten drumstick at her. 'The price of a guilty conscience. Try grovelling, that generally works.'

Ellie thanked him for the advice and they parted company. She found her mother and Tom where Paul said they would be, but there was no sign of Jack. She didn't know if that was a good sign or not.

'Good morning,' she greeted, kissing them both on the cheek before taking a chair opposite them. 'I hear Luke and Andrea have gone. I'm sorry if what happened caused problems for you.'

Tom Thornton amazed her by looking amused. 'It didn't. Most of our friends were intrigued by the unexpected fight. We could probably dine out on it for the next six months.'

Ellie smiled as she was supposed to do, but her eyes sought her mother's and saw the questions there. 'I guess Jack told you everything,' she sighed, and was surprised when her mother shook her head.

'He hasn't said a word. Other than to say it was up to you to explain.'

That was unexpected but, on consideration, she probably should have guessed. Jack was never one to tell tales. 'Then I'll start at the beginning. Just keep in mind that your daughter is a fool, OK.' So saying she started to tell the whole story about her involvement with Luke, and all the lies she had told. It wasn't a pleasant tale to tell, but it was cathartic. At the end she felt better, if still guilty.

'I don't come out of it very well, do I?' she said ruefully.

'Luke comes off worse. I had no idea my son could be quite that devious,' Tom declared grimly. 'No wonder he left in such a hurry. He knew the truth was bound to come out, and he didn't want to face the music. Never mind. I'm a patient man. I'll catch up with him eventually, and I will have a thing or two to say that he definitely isn't going to like.'

Ellie reached across the table to take his hand. 'I didn't tell you to put all the blame on him. I was at fault too. I'm sorry.'

'No wonder Jack was furious,' Mary Thornton said with a frown. 'He wouldn't have been expecting Luke's confession.'

Which brought Ellie to something important she wanted to ask. She sat forward and chose her words carefully. 'There was one other thing that Luke said, and I need to know if he told the truth. I think he did, but only you can confirm it. He said that Jack loved me. He had overheard the two of you talking about us, and that you said I was the mystery woman he was in love with. Is it true? Please tell me. I have to know.'

Mary gave her husband a significant look. 'I told you I thought I heard someone outside,' she tutted. Turning back to her daughter, she sighed. 'There doesn't seem to be much point in denying it, does there? Yes, Jack loves you, and he's waited a long time for you. This thing with Luke…well, it must have been a blow. And now you know you love Jack, who I've always thought was the perfect man for you, and it's all blown up in your face. Ellie, my darling, you do make things difficult for yourself.'

Ellie smiled ruefully. 'I know. But I told him I love him, and I'm hoping that soon he'll stop being angry with me. Then perhaps he'll admit he loves me. I need him to tell me.'

Her mother's brows rose. 'He doesn't know you know, does he?' she exclaimed in surprise, and Ellie shook her head.

'No. I couldn't do that to him. If he wants me to know, he'll tell me. If not…' she left that hanging. If he didn't want her to know. If he couldn't forgive her deception, then it didn't make any difference what she knew. Love had to be unconditional. Freely given and freely returned, otherwise it meant nothing.

There was a look of pride in Mary's eyes. 'That's very brave of you, darling.'

Ellie shook her head. 'I'm not brave, I'm terrified, but I love him enough to let him go, if what happened has pushed him too far. I made a fool of him, and that hurts a man's pride.'

'Pride is all very well, but it can't hold you and love you, and keep you warm at night,' Tom argued. 'Which I will be happy to point out to him the next time I see him.'

'Tom!' Mary cautioned much too late. Sighing, she looked ruefully at her daughter.

Ellie's heart lurched. 'When you see him? But, I thought… Where is Jack?' she demanded in sudden alarm.

'He left on the first ferry this morning. We did try to make him change his mind, but he was adamant.'

Ellie glanced at her watch and closed her eyes helplessly. He had been gone hours. He would be almost back in England by now. Swallowing hard, she smiled wanly. 'Well, that's that then.'

'Darling it doesn't mean he's made a decision, just that he had to get away for a while. You have to keep your chin up,' her mother said reassuringly, worry written plainly on her face.

Ellie did her best not to look downhearted. 'I bet you're right, but if it's all the same with you, I think I'll go home too.' There really didn't seem to be any point in staying if Jack had gone.

'You must do what you think best, darling,' Mary comforted. 'We'd love to have you stay longer, but if you must go, then so be it.'

'Would you like me to make the arrangements?' Tom offered, and Ellie nodded gratefully. He went off to use the telephone, and Ellie was left facing her mother.

'I'd better go and pack,' she said, getting to her feet.

Mary smiled at her fondly. 'Don't give up. Jack hasn't loved you this long to lose you now. He'll realise it soon enough.'

Ellie took the thought with her as she went upstairs again. She was going to do her best to look on the bright side, but it wasn't going to be easy. If only Jack were still here she wouldn't feel so ill at ease. Although there was an upside to the situation. At least in England she would be nearer to him, so, if he wanted to get in touch, she wouldn't be hundreds of miles away. But, if he didn't call, a few miles would feel like a hundred to her heart.

*   *   *

London was basking in a mini-heatwave. Normally heat didn't bother Ellie, but this time she found it enervating. She had been home for two weeks now, and had heard nothing from Jack. The heat was making it hard for her to keep her hopes up. She kept telling herself fourteen days was no time at all, but as each day passed her heart ached a little more.

Ellie couldn't count the number of times she had actually picked up the phone, intending to call Jack, only to put it down again with the number half punched-in. She longed to hear his voice, but had promised herself she would not pressure him. He had to come to her. It had to be his decision.

Today she had arrived home from work feeling limp and drained. The job she was working on was more intricate than most, and for some reason she had been all fingers and thumbs, so that she had had to unpick what she had done several times. In then end she had decided to call it quits for the day, and hope that tomorrow her concentration would be back.

Her first task when she arrived home, as always, had been to check the answer phone and her computer for messages, but there were none. Dispirited, she had showered and slipped into an old baggy T-shirt, then padded into the tiny kitchen of her flat and glanced through the meagre contents of her fridge. Nothing tempted her, but she made herself eat a yoghurt. Her appetite had vanished along with Jack.

Flicking on the TV, she listened to the news, which all seemed to be depressing, then surfed desultorily through the channels, trying to find something that would occupy her mind. The telephone rang, and she reached for it automatically.

'Hello,' she greeted, wondering if it could be her mother calling. She had done so several times since Ellie had returned home. When nobody answered immediately, she frowned, not in the mood for crank calls. 'Who is this?' she demanded to know.

'Ellie?' The surprise in the voice at the end of the line had her sitting up like a Jack-in-the-box.

'Jack?' she breathed back, knocked for a loop, but knowing it was his voice. 'Jack is that you?' she asked in a stronger voice when only silence followed her query. She had opened her mouth to say more when she heard the sound of the receiver going down. 'No! Wait!' she called out, but it was too late, the connection was severed.

Ellie stared at the useless lump of plastic in her hand in a state of shock. Jack had called her. No matter that he hadn't said more than one word. No matter that the surprise in his tone suggested that he hadn't intended to call her. Something had directed his fingers to punch in her number. Could he be as lonely and miserable as she was? Could he secretly want to contact her but his pride was getting in the way?

Her thoughts whirling, Ellie fumbled the receiver back into its rest. Her hands were trembling and she pressed them together to stop it. After two weeks of silence, the sound of his voice had sent her heart soaring. If only he hadn't rung off. If only he would call again. She stared at the phone, willing it to do just that, but it remained stubbornly silent.

Ellie shot to her feet and began pacing the room as the minutes passed and turned into half an hour. This was awful. He had to call again. He just had to. As she approached the phone again, she glared at it.

'Ring, damn you! Ring!' she commanded the silent machine, then positively jumped out of her skin when the front doorbell peeled instead.

Pressing a hand to her wildly thumping heart, Ellie gathered her composure and went to answer the summons. Expecting it to be one of her neighbours come to borrow sugar or coffee, she plastered a smile on her face and opened the door. The smile disappeared when she saw who stood on her doorstep.

Jack's tall, broad-shouldered figure filled the doorway. He was still in the dark suit he must have worn for work, but he carried no briefcase. In fact his hands were stuffed into his trouser pockets, and he was frowning.

'Tell me what the hell I'm doing here,' he growled at her, and Ellie blinked, her jaw dropping at his unexpected arrival, and less than gracious question.

Something told her that if she said the wrong thing, he might just turn and walk away again, so she pulled herself together in a hurry. He clearly needed an answer and, with a mind gone blank, she said the first thing that entered her head.

'You missed me and couldn't stay away a moment longer?' she suggested, then cringed at what had to be the very worst thing she could have said. He was going to leave. He was…

'You got it in one, Ellie,' Jack grunted, surprising her yet again. 'Well, are you going to ask me in?' he charged, staring down at her.

Not sure that she hadn't fallen asleep and was dreaming, Ellie stepped out of his way. 'Come in,' she invited, totally bemused. He stepped round her and headed for her sitting room. Ellie was left to close the door and follow, slowly absorbing the knowledge that he had missed her. Hope fluttered its tiny wings.

She had no idea what was going on, and his mood hardly appeared lover-like, but her heart had leapt at the sight of him and, no matter that he was behaving oddly, she was so very pleased to see him. Jack, meanwhile, was wandering around the room inspecting her books and CD collections. She watched in silence as he picked things up, studied them for a while, then put them back again.

Folding her arms in a protective gesture, Ellie cleared her throat. 'I didn't expect you. I mean, I wanted you to come, but didn't expect you would. After all, it's been two weeks.' The longest two weeks of her life.

'Fifteen days, eleven hours and—' he glanced at his watch '—thirty-seven minutes, to be precise,' he told her.

Her jaw showed a tendency to drop again, and she closed it with a snap. 'You kept count?'

'Didn't you?' he asked, and she nodded, suddenly feeling a great need to smile, but not knowing if she should. Jack removed his jacket and tossed it onto a chair, then proceeded to remove his tie and unbutton the neck of his shirt. 'I intended to stay away longer, but as you can see, here I am.'

A smile did escape her then at the disgust in his voice. 'Yes, here you are,' she agreed softly.

'I've waited for you all this time, so you'd think I could stay away for a few more days!' he railed at himself, and Ellie found her smile turning into a grin. Jack saw it, and his hands settled on his hips as he sighed heavily. 'I know, I know. Unfortunately for my intentions to make you suffer a little longer, I spoke to your mother this evening and she casually informed me that you knew I loved you before you came to plead your case that night. Why didn't you say anything?'

Ellie sobered instantly, though to hear him finally admit that he loved her brought a lump to her throat. 'Because I couldn't do that to you, Jack. Love shouldn't be used as a tool to get what you want from somebody. I want you to love me. It's broken my heart to know I've hurt you and let you down. If I could change it I would, but I can't.'

Jack came to her then, reaching out to cup her face in his hands. 'Thank you for saying nothing. I couldn't have told you I loved you that night because I was too angry, but I can say it now. I love you, Ellie. I've loved you for a long time, and God willing, I intend to love you till the end of for ever,' he said softly but firmly, and the warmth and love in his eyes was suddenly there for her to see.

The declaration brought tears to her eyes. 'So you forgive me?' she asked in a wobbly voice, and he smiled.

'Of course I forgive you, Angel. I love you.'

Ellie closed her eyes, made almost speechless by the emotions welling up inside her. Yet there was one important thing she had to ask him before she could allow herself to believe that everything was going to be all right.

'And Luke?' she probed gruffly. 'Do you mind very much about him?'

Jack sighed and pulled her into the haven of his arms, resting his cheek on her hair. 'I wish he had never been a part of your life, Ellie, but I know he means nothing to you. Like I told you once, the past is another country. We won't go there again.'

Relief made the tears overflow, and for a minute or two Ellie could do nothing to stop them flowing. Eventually though she sniffed and looked up at him. 'Just how long had you intended to make me wait?' she demanded to know in a stronger voice, and Jack had the grace to look shamefaced.

'Another week,' he admitted. 'Although I doubt very much if I would have got beyond tomorrow. I knew I was in trouble when I found myself dialling your number when I meant to order Chinese,' he added wryly, and she laughed.

'Oh, I do love you!' she exclaimed, hugging him tightly.

'Ellie?' Jack's use of her name in that tone made her look up again. 'I'm sorry I put you through hell these last two weeks,' he apologised and she lifted one hand to stroke his cheek.

'I might forgive you in a couple of weeks,' she teased, and brought a glint to his blue eyes that sent shivers down her spine.

'Sooner than that, I hope. I've come to claim my prize,' he told her, and Ellie frowned.

'Prize?'

Jack grinned. 'I bet you, you'd have forgotten all about Luke by the end of the summer. The winner was to name their own prize.'

She remembered, and this was one bet she was happy to lose. 'And just what prize are you claiming?'

'Your hand in marriage just as soon as it can be arranged,' he declared, taking her breath away.

She was so happy she could have burst. 'Is that the only proposal I'm going to get?'

'Take it or leave it,' Jack confirmed, and Ellie threw her arms about his neck and kissed him.

'Oh, I take it! You're mine now, Jack Thornton, and don't you forget it.'

Jack brushed her lips with his. 'I've always been yours, Angel, but now we both know it,' he murmured, and anything more she might have said was lost beneath his lips as he kissed her.

PASSION IN SECRET

by

Catherine Spencer

Catherine Spencer, once an English teacher, fell into writing through eavesdropping on a conversation about romances. Within two months she changed careers and sold her first book to Mills & Boon in 1984. She moved to Canada from England thirty years ago and lives in Vancouver. She is married to a Canadian and has four children – two daughters and two sons – plus a dog and a cat. In her spare time she plays the piano, collects antiques and grows tropical shrubs.

CHAPTER ONE

EVEN without the bitter wind howling in from the Atlantic, the hostile glances directed at her as she joined the other mourners at the graveside were enough to chill Sally to the bone. Not that anyone said anything. The well-bred residents of Bayview Heights, Eastridge Bay's most prestigious neighborhood, would have considered it sacrilege to voice their disapproval openly, before the body of one the town's most socially prominent daughters had been properly laid to rest.

No, they'd save their recriminations for later, over tea, sherry and sympathy at the Burton mansion. Except that Sally wouldn't be there to hear them. The blatant omission of her name from the list of guests invited to celebrate a life cut tragically short, was an indictment in itself, and never mind that her name had been officially cleared of blame.

"Earth to earth, ashes to ashes, dust to dust...." The minister, his robes flapping around him, intoned the final burial prayers.

Penelope's mother, Colette, gave a stifled sob and reached out to the flower-draped casket. Watching from beneath lowered lashes, Sally saw Fletcher Burton clasp his wife's arm in mute comfort. Flanking her other side and leaning heavily on his cane, Jake stood with his head bowed. His hair, though prematurely flecked with a hint of silver, was as thick as when Sally had last touched it, eight years before.

Seeming to sense he was being observed, he suddenly glanced up and caught her covert scrutiny. For all that she

5

knew she was encouraging further censure from those busy watching *her,* she couldn't tear her gaze away. Even worse, she found herself telegraphing a message.

It wasn't my fault, Jake!

But even if he understood what she was trying to convey, he clearly didn't believe her. Like everyone else, he held her responsible. He was a widower at twenty-eight, and all because of her. She could see the condemnation in his summer-blue eyes, coated now with the same frost which touched his hair; in the unyielding line of his mouth which, once, had kissed her with all the heat and raging urgency perhaps only a nineteen-year-old could know.

A gust of wind tossed the bare, black boughs of the elm trees and caused the ribbon attached to the Burtons' elaborate wreath to flutter up from the casket, as if Penelope were trying to push open the lid from within. Which, if she could have, she'd have done. And laughed in the face of so much funereal solemnity.

Life's a merry-go-round, she'd always claimed, *and I intend to ride it to the end, and be a good-looking corpse!*

Remembering the words and the careless laugh which had accompanied them, Sally wondered if the stinging cold caused her eyes to glaze with tears or if, at last, the curious flattening of emotion which had held her captive ever since the accident, was finally releasing its unholy grip and allowing her to feel again.

A blurred ripple of movement caught her attention. Wiping a gloved hand across her eyes, she saw that the service was over. Colette Burton pressed her fingertips first to her lips and then to the edge of the casket in a last farewell. Other mourners followed suit—all except the widower and his immediate family. He remained immobile, his face unreadable, his shoulders squared beneath his navy pilot's uniform. His relatives closed ranks around him, as if by doing so, they could shield him from the enormity of his loss.

Averting her gaze, Sally stepped aside as, openly shunning her, Penelope's parents trekked over the frozen ground to the fleet of limousines waiting at the curb. She had attended the funeral out of respect for a former friend and because she knew her absence would fuel the gossip mills even more than her presence had. But the Burtons' message set the tone for the rest of the mourners following close behind: Sally Winslow was trouble, just as she'd always been, and undeserving of compassion or courtesy.

That being so obviously the case, she was shocked to hear footsteps crunching unevenly over the snow to where she stood, and Jake's voice at her ear saying, "I was hoping you'd be here. How are you holding up, Sally?"

"About as well as can be expected," she said, her breath catching in her throat. "And you?"

He shrugged. "The same. Are you coming back to the Burtons' for the reception?"

"No. I'm not invited."

He regarded her soberly a moment. "You are now. As Penelope's husband, I'm inviting you. Your friendship with her goes back a long way. She'd want you there."

She couldn't look at him. Couldn't bear the cool neutrality in his voice. "I'm not sure that's so," she said, turning away. "Our lives had gone in separate directions. We didn't always see eye to eye anymore." *Especially not about you or the sanctity of your marriage.*

Unmindful of the buzz of speculation such a gesture would surely give rise to, he gripped her arm to prevent her leaving. "It would mean a lot to me if you'd change your mind."

"Why, Jake?" she felt bound to ask. "You and I haven't been close in years, either, and under the circumstances, I can't imagine why you'd want to seek me out now."

"You were the last person to see my wife alive. The last one to speak to her. I'd like to talk to you about it."

"Why?" she said again, stifling a moment of panic. "The police report spells out the events of that night pretty clearly."

"I've read the police report and also heard my in-laws' account of what took place. It's what you have to say that interests me. *They* know that an accident occurred, but you're the only one who knows how or why."

The panic stole over her again. "I've already told everything there is to tell, at least a dozen times."

"Humor me, Sally, and tell it once more." He indicated the cane in his left hand. "They released me from the military hospital in Germany less than twenty-four hours ago. I got home early this morning, just in time for the funeral. Everything I've learned so far has come to me secondhand. Surely you can understand why I'd like to hear it from the only person who was actually there when Penelope died."

"What do you expect to accomplish by doing that?"

"It's possible you might remember something that didn't seem important at the time that you gave your statement. Something which would fill in what strike me as gaping holes in the accounts I've so far received."

In other words, he suspected there was more to the story than the nicely laundered official version. She'd been afraid of that. Afraid not of what he might ask, but that he'd discern the painful truth behind the lies she'd told to spare his and the Burtons' feelings.

"Sally?" Margaret, her older sister, bore down on them, her slight frown the only indication that she found Sally's fraternizing with the widower, in full sight of the bereaved family, to be totally inappropriate. "We need to leave. Now."

"Yes." For once glad of her older sister's interference, Sally put a respectable distance between herself and Jake.

"I was just explaining that I can't make it to the reception."

"Well, of course you can't!" Margaret's expression softened as she turned to Jake. "I'm very sorry about your loss, Jake, as are we all. What a dreadful homecoming for you. But I'm afraid we really do have to go. I need to get home to the children."

"You and Sally came here together?"

"Yes. She hasn't been too keen on driving since the accident. It shook her up more than most people seem to realize."

"Did it?" His glance swung from Margaret and zeroed in again on Sally with altogether too much perception for her peace of mind. "At least, you escaped serious injury."

"I was lucky."

"Indeed you were. A great deal more than my wife."

A trembling cold took hold as memories washed over her: of the protesting scream of the brakes, the smell of burning rubber as the tires left tracks on the road. And most of all, of Penelope, flung out of the car and lying all broken in the ditch, mumbling with a spectral smile on her face, *Silly me. I fell off the merry-go-round before it stopped, Sal.*

With an effort, Sally shook off the painful recollection and, aware that Jake continued to scrutinize her, said, "Yes, I was lucky. But not all injuries appear on the outside. Watching a friend die isn't something a person easily gets over."

"Not as a rule."

Although polite enough on the surface, his words rang with such searing contempt that, ignoring her better judgment, she burst out, "Do you think I'm lying?"

"Are you?"

"Good grief, Jake, even allowing for your understandable heartache, that question is uncalled-for!" Margaret seldom approved of anything Sally did, but when it came to outside criticism, she was all mother hen protecting her young. "My sister was—*is!*—devastated by Penelope's death."

Something shifted in his expression. Not a softening, exactly, but a sort of resignation. "Yes," he said. "Of course she is. I apologize, Sally, for implying otherwise."

Sally nodded, but her sigh of relief was cut short when he continued, "And I'll be glad to arrange a ride home for you after the reception."

"Thank you, Jake, but no. I've already inconvenienced Margaret. I wouldn't dream of imposing on you as well, especially not today."

"You'd be doing me a favor. And if you're afraid—"

"Why should she be?" Margaret interjected sharply. "Penelope's death was ruled an accident."

"I'm aware of that, just as I'm equally aware that not everyone accepts the verdict at face value."

"Then perhaps you're right. Perhaps taking her to the reception isn't such a bad idea." Margaret pursed her lips in thought, then gave Sally an encouraging poke in the ribs. "Yes. Go with him after all, Sally. Face the lot of them and prove you've got nothing to be ashamed of."

Rendered speechless by Margaret's sudden about-face, Sally groped for an answer which would put a definitive end to the whole subject. She had enough to cope with; she wasn't up to dealing with the unwarranted antagonism she'd face by agreeing to Jake's request.

"No!" she finally spluttered. "I don't have to prove anything to anyone!"

But the only person paying the slightest attention was Jake. Having issued her decree, Margaret had cut a brisk path among the graves to that section of the road where she'd parked her car a discreet distance away from any other vehicles, and was already climbing behind the wheel.

"It would seem," Jake murmured, clamping his free hand around Sally's elbow before she bolted also, and steering her toward the sole remaining limousine, "that you have no choice but to prove it. Let's not keep the driver waiting. I can't speak for you, but I'm in no shape to hike the four miles back to my in-laws', especially not under these conditions." He glanced up at the leaden sky pressing coldly down on the treetops. "We're lucky the snow held off this long."

Thankfully the last car was empty except for a couple from out of town who didn't seem to know that the passenger accompanying Jake was the woman whom popular opinion held responsible for rendering him a widower. Grateful that they showed no inclination to talk beyond a subdued greeting, Sally huddled in the corner of the soft leather seat and welcomed the blast of heat fanning around her ankles.

She'd be facing another round of chilly displeasure soon enough. In the meantime, she might as well take comfort wherever she could find it.

Lovely Sally Winslow was lying through her teeth. It might have been years since he'd last seen her, but Jake remembered enough about her to know when she was covering up. The question buzzing through his sleep-deprived mind was, for what purpose?

She'd been formally cleared of blame in the accident. So why couldn't she look him straight in the eye? Why was she instead staring fixedly out of the window beside her so that all he could see of her was the back of her head and the dark, shining cap of her hair. What was with her sitting as far away from him as she could get, as if she feared grief might prompt him to grab her by the throat and try to choke the truth out of her?

The chauffeur drove sedately along the broad, tree-lined

avenues of Bayview Heights, turned onto The Crescent and past various stately homes sitting on five acre lots, then hung a left through the iron gates guarding the Burton property. Except for the gleam of lamplight shining from the main floor windows and casting a soft yellow glow over the snow piled up outside, the massive house, built nearly a hundred years before from blocks of granite hewn from the quarry just outside town, rose black and brooding in the early dusk.

The limo barely whispered to a stop under the porte-cochère before Morton, the butler, flung open the double front doors. At the sight of Sally climbing the steps, a flicker of surprise crossed his face. "Ahem," he said, extending one arm as if to bar her entry.

"Miss Winslow is here as my guest," Jake informed him, taken aback at the surge of protectiveness he felt toward her. Whatever else she might not be, Sally had always been able to fend for herself. She hardly needed him playing knight errant.

With fastidious distaste, Morton relieved her of her coat. "The family is receiving in the drawing room, Captain Harrington," he said. "Shall I announce you?"

"No need. I know the way." Jake handed the manservant his cap, brushed a few snowflakes from his shoulders and cocked his head at Sally. "Ready to face the fray?"

"As much as I'll ever be."

He thought of offering her his arm, and decided she'd have to make do with his moral support. No point in rubbing salt into his in-laws' wounds. They were suffering enough.

The drawing room, a masterpiece of late nineteenth-century craftsmanship with its intricate moldings and ornately coffered ceiling, hummed with the low buzz of conversation. Every spare inch of surface on the highly polished furniture was filled with photographs of Penelope framed by huge, heavily scented flower arrangements.

Under the tall Arcadian windows overlooking the rear gardens, a table held an assortment of fancy sandwiches, hot canapés and French pastries. A fat woman whom he didn't recognize presided over the heirloom sterling tea service and priceless translucent china. At the other end of the room, a Chippendale desk served as a temporary bar with his father-in-law in charge. Colette, an empty brandy snifter at her elbow, perched on the edge of a silk-upholstered chair, accepting condolences.

Fletcher Burton saw him and Sally first. At six foot one—only an inch shorter than Jake himself—he stood taller than most of the rest grouped about the room. About to pour sherry for the weepy-eyed woman at his side, he thumped the heavy cut-glass decanter back on its silver tray and cut a swath through the crowd. "I don't know how this young woman managed to get past Morton—!"

"I brought her here, Fletcher."

"What the devil for?"

"She and Penelope had known each other from childhood. They were friends. Sally was the last person to see your daughter alive. I'd say that gives her as much right to be here as anyone."

"For God's sake, Jake! You know Colette's feelings on this. We're trying to put the past behind us."

"With altogether more speed than decency, if you ask me."

"Nevertheless, under the circumstances, I hardly think—"

"I agreed to your taking charge of all the funeral arrangements because I couldn't be here in time to handle them myself," Jake cut in. "But may I remind you, Fletcher, that although you were Penelope's parents, I was her husband. I believe that entitles me to invite whom I please to this reception honoring her memory.''

''No, it doesn't. Not if it adds to anyone's grief.'' Sally, who'd been edging back toward the foyer, spoke up. ''I came to pay my respects, Mr. Burton, and now that I have, I'll leave.''

''Thank you.'' Poor old Fletcher, henpecked to within an inch of his life, cast an anxious glance across the room to where Colette held court. ''Look, I don't mean to be offensive, but I'm afraid you're no longer welcome in our home, Sally. If my wife should see you, she'd—''

But the warning came too late. Colette *had* seen them and her outraged gasp had everyone looking her way. Handkerchief fluttering, she fairly flew across the room. ''How dare you show your face in our home, Sally Winslow? Have you no sense of decency at all?''

''She came with me.'' Not only was he beginning to sound like a broken record, Jake was growing thoroughly tired of repeating the same old refrain. It was his own fault, though. He should have stood his ground and insisted on postponing the funeral until he could have taken over. A few more days wouldn't have made any difference to Penelope, but if he'd hosted her wake in the house they'd shared as a couple, he might have been able to circumvent the present scene.

''How could you do that, Jake?'' Colette wailed, her baby blues swimming in tears. ''How could you hurt me by desecrating Penelope's memory this way? I've suffered enough. I need some closure.''

''We all do, Colette,'' he said gently, moved despite himself by her anguish. Colette Burton might be a diva of the first order, but she'd truly adored her daughter.

''And you expect to find it by bringing that woman here?'' She let out a tortured sob. ''What kind of son-in-law are you?''

Fletcher would have caved at that line of attack, but Jake wasn't about to. "One trying to put back together the pieces of his life."

"With the help of your wife's murderer?"

The shocked reaction brought on by that remark—because there wasn't a soul in the room who hadn't heard it, including his parents—bounced back from the walls in a throttling silence broken only by a faint whimper of despair from Sally.

Caught again in the urge to leap to her defense, he said, "Perhaps you'd like to retract that accusation, Colette, before it lands you in more trouble than you're able to handle right now."

"No!" Sally overrode him, her voice thick with emotion barely held in check. "Don't blame her." She turned to Colette, and touched her hand contritely. "Please forgive me, Mrs. Burton. I shouldn't have come. I just wanted to tell you again how very sorry I am that Penelope's life ended so tragically. I truly feel your pain."

Colette snatched her hand away as if she'd been singed by a naked flame. "Do you really, Sally Winslow! Are you trying to tell me you've walked the floor every night since she was killed, wondering what that strange noise is and realizing it's the sound of your own heart breaking, over and over again?"

"No, but I've—"

"Of course you haven't! You're probably glad Penelope's dead, if truth be known, because you always resented her for being prettier and smarter than you. But now, you don't have to live in her shadow anymore, do you?"

"Colette, that's enough." Fletcher tried steering her away, to no effect.

"Leave me alone! I'm not finished with her yet." Like a wild thing, she flung him off and rounded on Sally again.

"Do you have any idea how it feels to see your child lying dead in her box? Do you know what it's like to finally fall asleep from sheer emotional exhaustion, and do so praying that you'll never wake up again? *Do you?*"

Sally, pale enough to begin with, blanched alarmingly and pressed her lips together to stop their trembling. Perspiration gleamed on her brow. Her eyes, normally dark as forest-green pools, turned almost black with distress.

"That's what you've done to me, Sally Winslow." Colette's voice rose shrilly. "I'll never know another moment's peace, and I hope you never do, either! I hope what you've done haunts you for the rest of your miserable days!"

Again, Fletcher moved to intervene. "Hush now, Colette, my darling. You're overwrought."

She'd also fortified herself with more than one brandy and was three sheets to the wind, Jake belatedly realized. Her breath was enough to knock a man over. But it was Sally who suddenly fell limply against him and, before he could catch her, crumpled to the floor at his feet.

Drowning out the chorus of shocked exclamations, Colette teetered in Fletcher's hold and shrieked, "I hope she's dead! It's what she deserves!"

"Sorry to disappoint you," Jake said, stooping to feel the pulse, strong and steady, below Sally's jaw. "I'm afraid she's only fainted." Then, although he shouldn't have, he couldn't help adding, "Probably too much hot air in here. Where can we put her until she comes to?"

"The library," Fletcher said, handing a sobbing Colette over to one of her hangers-on. "She can lie down in there."

"I'll take her, Jake." His father materialized at his side. "You'll never make it with that injured leg."

"I'll manage somehow," he muttered, wishing his parents hadn't had to witness the scene just past. There'd never been much love lost between his family and the Burtons, and he knew they'd be upset by Colette's attack on him.

"You don't always have to be the iron hero, you know. It's okay to lean on someone else once in a while."

"Can the advice for another time, Dad," he said, a lot more abruptly than the man deserved. But cripes, his leg *was* giving him hell, and that alone was enough to leave him a bit short on tact. "It's my fault Sally's here at all. The least I can do is finish what I started. If you want to help, get Mom out of here. She looks as if she's seen and heard enough."

Clamping down on the pain shooting up this thigh, he scooped Sally into his arms and made his way through the crowd, which parted like the Red Sea before Moses. There might be some there who felt sorry for her, but no one except possibly his relatives dared show it. Colette had cornered the market on any spare sympathy that might be floating around.

The library was a man's room. Paneled in oak, with big, comfortable leather chairs and a matching sofa flanking the wide fireplace, some very good paintings, a Turkish rug and enough books to keep a person reading well into the next century, it was Fletcher's haven; the place to which he retreated when things became too histrionic with the women in his household. Jake had joined him there many a time, to escape or to enjoy an after-dinner drink, and knew he kept a private supply of cognac stashed in the bureau bookcase next to the hearth.

Just as well. Sally needed something strong to bring the color back to her face. Come to that, he could use a stiff belt himself.

Depositing her on the couch, he covered her with a mohair lap rug draped over one of the chairs. She looked very young in repose; very vulnerable. Much the way she'd looked when they'd started dating during her high school sophomore year. He'd been a senior at the time, and so crazy in love with her that he hadn't been able to think straight.

Even as he watched, she stirred and, opening her eyes, regarded him with dazed suspicion. "What are you doing?"

"Looking at you," he said, using the back of the sofa for support and wondering how she'd respond if he told her she had the longest damned eyelashes he'd ever seen, and a mouth so delectable that he knew an indecent urge to lean down and kiss it.

Get a grip, Harrington! You've been a widower less than a week, and should be too swamped with memories of your wife to notice the way another woman's put together—even if the woman in question does happen to have been your first love.

Her glance shied away from him and darted around the room. "How did I wind up in here?"

"I carried you in, after you fainted."

"I fainted?" She covered her eyes with the back of one hand and groaned in horror. "In front of all those people?"

"It was the best thing you could have done," he said, limping to the bureau and taking out a three-quarter-full bottle of Courvoisier cognac and two snifters. "You upstaged Colette beautifully. Without you to lambaste, she was left speechless." He poured them each a healthy shot of the liquor and offered one to her. "This should put you back on your feet."

"I don't know about that," she said doubtfully. "I haven't eaten a thing today."

"I wondered what made you pass out."

"I haven't had much of an appetite at all since…the accident."

"Feel up to talking about that night?"

She sat up and pushed her hair away from her face. "I

don't know what else I can say that you haven't already heard.''

Cautiously lowering himself into the nearest chair, he knocked back half the contents of his glass and, as the warmth of the brandy penetrated the outer limits of his pain, said, ''You could try telling me what really happened, Sally.''

The shutters rolled down her face, cloaking her expression. ''What makes you so sure there's more to tell?''

''You and I were once close enough that we learned to read each other's minds pretty well. I always knew when you were trying to hide something from me, and I haven't forgotten the signs.''

She swirled her drink but did not, he noticed, taste it. Why was she being so cagey? Could it be that she was afraid the booze might loosen her tongue too much and she'd let something slip? ''That was a long time ago, Jake. We were just kids. People grow up and change.''

''No, they don't,'' he said flatly. ''They just become better at covering up. But although you might have fooled everyone else, *including the police,* you've never been able to fool me. There's more to this whole business than anyone else but you knows, and I'm asking you, for old times' sake, to tell me what it is.''

Just for a moment, she looked him straight in the eye and he thought she was going to come clean. But then the door opened and Fletcher appeared. ''I expect you might need this, Jake,'' he said, brandishing the cane. ''And I wondered if Sally felt well enough for one of the chauffeurs to drive her home, before the cars fill up with other people.''

Masking his annoyance at the interruption, Jake said, ''Can't it wait another five minutes? We're in the middle of something, Fletcher, if you don't mind.''

''No, we're not,'' Sally said, throwing off the blanket

and swinging her legs to the floor. ''If you can spare a car, I'd be very grateful, Mr. Burton. I'm more than ready to leave.''

Frustrated, Jake watched as she tottered to her feet and wove her way to the door. Short of resorting to physical force, there was nothing he could do to detain her. This time.

But he'd see to it there was a next time. And when it happened, he'd make damn good and sure she didn't escape him until he was satisfied he knew the precise circumstances which had finally freed him from the hell his marriage had become.

CHAPTER TWO

YOU'VE never been able to fool me, he'd said, but he couldn't be more wrong. She'd fooled Jake about something a lot more momentous than the events leading up to Penelope's untimely end. She was very good at keeping secrets, even those which had ripped her life apart, both literally and figuratively.

Guarding this latest would be easy, as long as she didn't let him slip past her guard. And the only way to avoid that was to avoid him. Because, in her case, the old adage *Out of sight, out of mind,* had never applied to Jake Harrington. Just the opposite. No matter how many miles or years had separated them, he'd never faded from her memory. If anything, distance had lent him enchantment, and seeing him again had done nothing to change all that. The magic continued to hold.

He looked older, of course—didn't they all?—but the added years sat well on him. The boy had become a man; the youthful good looks solidified into a tough masculine beauty. Broader across the shoulders, thicker through the chest, he cut an impressive figure, especially in his military uniform. A person had only to look at him to know he'd seen his share of trouble, of tragedy, and emerged stronger for it. It showed in his manner, in the authority of his bearing.

This was not a man to shy away from the truth or crumble in the face of adversity. And she supposed, thinking about it as she made her way along the crowded halls of Eastridge Academy on the following Monday morning, in that respect at least he wasn't so very different from the boy who'd stolen her heart, all those years ago, in this very same school. Even at eighteen, he'd possessed the kind of courage which was the true mark of a man.

Still, Sally couldn't imagine telling him about Penelope. Male pride was a strange phenomenon. It was one thing for a man to climb behind the controls of a fighter jet and risk life and limb chasing down an anonymous enemy. And quite another to confront betrayal of the worst kind from the woman he'd married, *especially* if he discovered he was the last to know about it.

The senior secretary called out to her as she passed through the main office on her way to the staff lounge. "Morning, Sally. You just missed a phone call."

"Oh? Any message."

"No. Said he'd try to catch you later on."

He? "Did he at least give a name?"

"No." The secretary eyed her coyly. "But he had a voice to die for! Dark and gravelly, as though he needed a long drink of water which I'd have been happy to supply. Sound like anyone you know?"

Premonition settled unpleasantly in the pit of Sally's stomach but she refused to give it credence. Plenty of men had dark, gravelly voices. That Jake could be numbered among them was pure coincidence. "Probably someone's father calling to complain I give too much homework. If he happens to phone back, try to get a number where he can be reached. I'm going to be tied up with students all day."

"Will do. Oh, and one more thing." The secretary nodded at the closed door to her left. "Mr. Bailey wants to see you in his office before classes start."

Oh, wonderful! A private session with the Academy principal who also happened to be her brother-in-law and definitely not one of her favorite people. The day was off to a roaring start!

"You asked to see me, Tom?"

Tom Bailey looked up from the letter he was reading, his brow furrowed with annoyance at the interruption of Very Important Administrative Business. "This isn't a family gathering, Ms. Winslow. If you're determined to ignore professional protocol, at least close the door before you open your mouth."

"Good morning to you, too." Without waiting to be invited, she took a seat across from him. "What's on your mind, *Mr. Bailey?*"

"Margaret tells me you managed to get yourself invited to the reception at the Burtons' on Saturday."

"I prefer to say I was coerced—as much by your wife as anyone else."

He leaned back in his fancy swivel chair and fixed her in his pale-eyed stare, the one he used to intimidate freshmen. "Regardless, let me remind you what I said when all this mess with Penelope Harrington started. Our school prides itself on its fine reputation and I won't tolerate its being sullied by scandal. Bad enough you've been on staff less than a month before your name's splashed all over the front pages of every newspaper within a fifty-mile radius, without any more shenanigans now that the fuss is finally beginning to die down. I did you a favor when I persuaded the Board of Governors to give you a position here, because—"

"Actually," Sally cut in, "I'm the one who did you a favor, Tommy, by stepping in at very short notice when my predecessor took early maternity leave and left you short one art teacher."

He turned a dull and dangerous shade of red. Subordinates did not interrupt the principal of the Academy and they particularly did not challenge the accuracy of his pronouncements. "You showed up in town unemployed!"

"I *came home* looking forward to a long-overdue vacation which I cut short because you were in a bind.'' She glanced pointedly at the clock on the wall. ''Is there anything else, or am I free to go and do what the Board hired me to do? I have a senior art history class starting in ten minutes.''

If it hadn't been beneath his dignity, he'd have gnashed his perfectly flossed teeth. Instead he made do with a curt, ''As long as we understand one another.''

''I've never had a problem understanding you, Tom,'' she said, heading for the door. ''My sister's the one I can't figure out. I've never been able to fathom why she married you.''

As soon as the words were out of her mouth, she regretted them. She'd been known as a wild child in her youth, but she liked to think she'd matured into a better person since—one for whom taking such cheap shots wasn't her normal style. But ''normal'' had been in short supply practically from the minute she'd set foot in town again, beginning with the morning she and Penelope Burton Harrington had happened to run into one another in the Town Square.

''Sally!'' Penelope had fairly screamed, rushing to embrace her as if a rift spanning nearly a decade had never crippled their friendship. ''Oh, it's wonderful to see you again! It's been like living in a tomb around here lately, but now that you're back, it'll be just like old times, and we can kick some life into the place.''

The cruel irony of her words had come back to torment Sally during the long, sleepless nights since the accident. But thanks to Tom's having hired her, at least her days were too busy to allow for much wallowing in useless guilt, which made her parting remark to him all the more unforgivable. To satisfy her own sense of fair play, the least she could do was seek him out later and apologize.

She had a full teaching load that day, though, plus a

meeting at lunch with the nit-picking head of the Fine Arts department, and an after-school interview with a furious student who didn't understand why copying an essay on Henri Matisse from the Internet was plagiarism and warranted a big fat *F* on his midterm report.

Somehow, the events of first thing slipped to the back of her mind and she forgot about Tom. She forgot, too, about that morning's phone call from the man who hadn't left a message.

But he didn't forget about her. He came to her classroom just as she was stuffing her briefcase with the assignments she planned to mark that evening. By then it was after five o'clock and the building was pretty much deserted except for the cleaning staff. In fact, when she heard the door open, she was so sure it was the janitor, come to empty the waste bins and clean up the sinks, that she said, "I'll be out of your way in just a second," without bothering to look up from her task.

The door clicked closed which, in itself, should have alerted her to trouble. "No rush. I've got all the time in the world," came the reply, and there it was: the dark, gravelly voice which had so captivated the school secretary earlier.

It didn't captivate Sally. It sent shock waves skittering through her. The stack of papers in her hand flipped through her fingers and slithered over the floor. Flustered, she dropped to her knees and began gathering them together in an untidy bundle.

"I'd no idea teachers put in such long hours," Jake said, his cane thudding softly over the floor as he came toward her. "Let me help you pick those up."

"No, thank you!" Hearing the betraying edge of panic in her voice, she took a deep breath and continued more moderately, "I don't need your help. In fact, you shouldn't be here at all. If Tom Bailey finds out—"

"He won't. His was the only car in the parking lot and he was leaving as I arrived. We're quite alone, Sally. No one will disturb us."

She was afraid of that! "Oh, really? What about the cleaning staff?"

"They're busy in the gym and won't get down to this end of the building for at least another hour." His hand came down and covered hers as she scrabbled with the pages still slipping and sliding from her grasp. "You're shaking. Are you going to faint again?"

"Certainly not!" she said, scooting away from him before he realized how easily his touch scrambled her brains and stirred up memories best left untouched. "I just don't like people creeping up and taking me by surprise, that's all."

"I'm not 'people,' and I didn't creep." He tapped his bad leg. "It's a bit beyond my capabilities, these days."

"No, you're the wounded hero come home to bury his wife, but if you insist on being seen with me at every turn, you're going to lose the public outpouring of sympathy you're currently enjoying, and become as much of a pariah as I have."

"I'm not looking for sympathy, my lovely. I'm looking for information."

My lovely…that's what he'd called her in the days when they'd been in love; when they'd *made* love. And the sound of it, falling again from his lips after all this time, brought back such a shock of déjà vu that she trembled inside.

Late August, the summer she'd turned seventeen, just weeks before he started his junior year at university, two hundred miles away…wheeling gulls against a cloudless sky, the distant murmur of the incoming tide, the sun gilding her skin, and Jake sliding inside her, with the tall grass of the dunes whispering approval in the sea breeze. "I miss you so much when we're apart," he'd told her. *"I'll love you forever."*

But he hadn't. Thirteen months later, she'd spent two months studying art in France. When she returned, she found out from Penelope that he'd been seeing a college coed while she'd been gone.

She'd been crushed, although she really shouldn't have been. As her weeks abroad passed, there'd been signs enough that trouble was brewing. His phone calls had dwindled, become filled with long, awkward pauses. He wasn't there to meet her as promised, when she came home again. He didn't even make it back for Thanksgiving. And finally, when there was no avoiding her at Christmas, he'd shamelessly flaunted her replacement in her face.

"Jake Harrington's a two-timing creep," sweet sympathetic Penelope told her, *"and you're too smart to let such a worthless jerk break your heart. Forget him! There are better fish in the sea."*

But she hadn't wanted anyone else. As for forgetting, it was a lot easier said than done for an eighteen-year-old who'd just discovered she was pregnant by the boy she adored and who'd passed her over for someone new.

The spilled assignments at last cradled in her arms, Sally struggled to her feet with as much grace as she could muster and crammed the papers into her briefcase. "We went over all this on Saturday. I've told you everything there is to know."

"Okay." He shrugged amiably. "Then I won't ask you again."

Elation flooded through her. "I'm glad you finally believe me."

"Of course I do," he said. "You're not the kind of person who'd hold out on me about something this important, are you?"

Guilt and suspicion nibbled holes in her relief. "Then why did you come here to begin with?"

"Mostly to find out if you've forgiven me for landing you in such a mess an Saturday. If I'd known Colette was going to go after you like that—"

"You had no way of knowing she'd react so badly. Consider yourself forgiven."

"A lot of women wouldn't be so understanding," he said diffidently. "But then, you never were like most women."

Diffident? Jake Harrington?

She'd have laughed aloud at the idea, had it not been that the hair on the back of her neck vibrated with warning. He was up to something! She could almost hear the wheels spinning behind that guileless demeanor! "And?"

"Hmm?" Doing his best to look innocently virtuous, he traced a herringbone pattern over the floor with the tip of his cane.

"You said 'mostly'—that you were here *mostly* to find out if I'd forgiven you. What's the other reason?"

He tried to look sheepish. Would have blushed, if he'd had it in him to do such a thing. "Would you believe, nostalgia got the better of me? When I heard you were on staff here, I couldn't stay away." He leaned against one of the cabinets holding supplies and sent her a smile which plucked unmercifully at her heartstrings. "This is where we met, Sally. We fell in love here. I kissed you for the first time next to the lockers right outside this room. You had blue paint on the end of your nose."

"I'm surprised you remember," she said, warmth stealing through her and blasting her reservations into oblivion.

"I remember everything about that time. Nothing I've known since has ever compared to it."

The warmth turned to melting heat. Against her better judgment, she found herself wanting to believe him. "You don't have to say that. You *shouldn't* say it."

"Why not? Don't I have as much right to tell the truth as you do?"

He sounded so sincere, she found herself wondering. *Was* he playing mind games with her? Trying to trip her up? Or was she seeing entrapment where none existed?

Deciding it was better to err on the side of caution and put an end to the meeting, she indicated the bulging briefcase and said, "I should get going. I've got a full evening's work ahead."

He eased himself away from the desk. "Me, too. I'm still sorting through Penelope's stuff and deciding what to do with it, and the house. I don't need all that space."

Watching as he limped to the door, she knew an inexplicable regret that he accepted his dismissal so easily. So what if his smile left her insides fluttering? They weren't teenagers anymore. First love didn't survive an eight-year winter of neglect to bloom again at the first hint of spring.

Still, having him show up so unexpectedly had unsettled her almost as badly as seeing him at the funeral. He stirred up too many buried feelings.

His voice, the curve of his mouth, the latent passion in his direct blue gaze, made her hungry for things she shouldn't want and certainly couldn't have. So, rather than risk running into him again, she waited until his footsteps faded, and the clang of the outside door shutting behind him echoed down the hall, before she ventured out to retrieve her coat from the staff cloakroom.

The sky had been clear when she left for work that morning and she'd enjoyed the two-mile walk from the guest cottage at the end of her parents' driveway and through the park to the school. Sometime since classes ended, though, the clouds had rolled in again and freezing rain begun to fall. The ramp beyond the Academy's main entrance was treacherous with black ice.

Twice, she'd have lost her footing, had it not been for

the iron railing running parallel to the path. But the real trouble started when she gained the glassy sidewalk and found it impossible to navigate in shoes not designed for such conditions.

Turning right, as she intended to do, was out of the question. Instead, with her briefcase rapping bruisingly against her leg, she lurched into the dirty snow piled next to the curb, three days earlier, by the road-clearing crews.

It was the last straw in a day which had started badly and gone steadily downhill ever since. Exasperated, she gave vent to a stream of unladylike curses which rang up and down the deserted street with satisfying gusto.

Except the street wasn't quite as deserted as she'd thought. A low-slung black sports car, idling in the lee of a broad-trunked maple not ten feet away, cruised to a stop beside her, with the passenger window rolled down just far enough for Jake's voice to float out. "Faculty members didn't know words like that when I was a student here," he announced affably. "Come to think of it, I'm not sure I knew them, either."

"Are you stalking me?" she snapped, miserably conscious of the fact that she cut a ridiculous figure standing there, ankle-deep in snow.

"Not at all. I stopped to offer you a ride home."

"No, thanks. I prefer to walk."

"Oh," he said. "Is that what you were doing when you came sailing into the gutter just now?"

"I temporarily lost my balance."

"Temporarily?" He let out a muffled snort of laughter. "Dear Ms. Winslow, if you insist on wearing summer footwear in the kind of winter which Eastridge Bay is famous for, it'll be anything but temporary. Stop being stubborn and get in the car before you break your neck. I'd come round and hold the door open for you, except I'm having enough problems of my own trying to get around in these conditions.''

She debated telling him what he could do with his offer, but her frozen feet won out over her pride. ''Just as well you're not inclined to play the gentleman,'' she muttered, yanking open the door and climbing in to the blessed warmth of the car. ''I might be tempted to knock your cane out from under you!''

''Now that,'' he remarked, stepping gently on the gas and pulling smoothly out into the road, ''is why some people—people who don't know you as well as I used to—talk about you the way they do.''

''And how is that, exactly? I'm living in the guest cottage on my parents' estate, by the way. You turn left on—''

''I remember how to get there, Sally,'' he said. ''I've driven you home often enough, in the past. And to answer your question, unflatteringly. They say you came back to town and brought a bagful of trouble with you. Are they right?''

''Why ask me? You'll find listening to their version of the facts far more entertaining, I'm sure.''

''As a matter of interest, where *have* you been for the last several years?''

''At university on the West Coast, and after that, down in the Caribbean.''

He didn't quite snicker in her face, but he might as well have. ''Doing what?'' he inquired, his voice shimmering with amusement.

''Well, not weaving sun hats from coconut palm fronds or singing in a mariachi band, if that's what you're thinking!''

''You have no idea what I'm thinking, Sally. None at all. And you haven't answered my question. What kept you in the sunny Caribbean all this time?''

"The same thing that's keeping me occupied here. Teaching, except the children down there were so under-privileged that working with them was pure pleasure."

"Very commendable of you, I'm sure. How long did you stay?"

"Two years in Mexico, and two years on the island of St. Lucia after that."

"Why that part of the world?"

"They needed teachers as badly as I needed to get away from here."

"What?" His voice quivered with silent laughter. "You never yearned to settle down in picturesque Eastridge Bay? To follow in your sister's footsteps and marry a fine, up-standing man of good family?"

Once upon a time I did, but you chose to put a wedding ring on Penelope's finger, instead! "Not all women see marriage as the be-all and end-all of happiness. Some of us find satisfaction in a career."

"But not everyone runs away to a tropical island to find it."

"I was trying to escape the winters up here. But this town is my home and I was happy to come back to it—until everything started going wrong." She shivered inside her coat. The rain, she noticed, had turned to snow and was sliding down the windshield in big, sloppy flakes. She noticed, too, that they'd passed the turnoff for Bayview Heights blocks before, and were speeding instead along the main boulevard leading out of town. "You're going the wrong way, Jake!"

"So I am," he said cheerfully.

"Well, turn around and head back! And slow down while you're at it. I've spent enough time stuck in a snow-bank, for one night."

"No need to get all exercised, Sally. Since I've missed

the turn anyway, we might as well enjoy a little spin in the country.''

''I don't want to go for a spin in the country,'' she told him emphatically. ''I want to go home.''

''And you will, my lovely. All in good time.''

''Right now!'' She reached for the door handle. ''Stop this car at once, Jake Harrington. And stop calling me that.''

He didn't bother to reply. The only sound to register above the low hum of the heater was the click of automatic door locks sliding home and the increased hiss of the tires on the slick surface of the road.

Stunned, she turned to stare at him. There were no street-lights this far beyond the town limits, but the gleam of the dashboard lights showed his profile in grim relief. ''Are you kidnapping me?''

''Don't be ridiculous.''

''Then just what *are* you doing?''

''Looking for a place where we can get something hot to drink. It's the least I can do, to make up for keeping you out past your bedtime.''

The words themselves might have been innocuous enough, but there was nothing affable or benign in his tone of voice. The man who'd beguiled her with his smile and tender memories not half an hour ago, who'd offered her a ride home to spare her walking along icy streets, had turned into a stranger as cold and threatening as the night outside.

''You had this planned all along, didn't you?'' she said, struggling to suppress the fear suddenly tapping along the fringes of her mind. She'd accepted a lift from her one-time lover, the local hero come home from doing battle and with the scars to prove it, not from some faceless stranger, for heaven's sake! To suspect he posed any sort of threat was nothing short of absurd. ''This is what you intended, from the minute you showed up in my classroom.''

"Yes," he said.

"Well, you didn't have to go to such extremes. I'd have been happy to stop for coffee at a place in town."

"Too risky. Think of the gossip, if we'd been seen together. The widower and the wild woman flaunting their association in public! Better to find some out-of-the-way place where the kind of people we know wouldn't dream of setting foot. A place so seedy, no respectable woman would want to be seen by anyone she knew."

Seedy? What on earth would prompt him to use such a word?

Numbly she stared ahead, once again in the grip of that eerie unease. By then, the snow had begun to settle, turning the windows opaque except for the half-moons cleared by the windshield wipers. She could see nothing of the landscape flying past, nothing of where they'd been or where they were headed.

Then, off to the side, some hundred yards or so down the road, a band of orange light pierced the gloom; a neon sign at first flashing dimly through the swirling snow, but growing brighter as the car drew nearer, until there was no mistaking its message. Harlan's Roadhouse it read. Beer— Eats—Billiards.

And her premonition crystalized into outright dismay. She'd seen that sign before. And Jake was well aware of the fact!

He slowed to turn into the rutted parking area, nosed the car to a spot close to the tavern entrance and turned off the engine. Immediately the muffled, relentless throb of country and western music filled the otherwise quiet night, its only competition the equally brutal pounding of Sally's heart.

He climbed out of the car and, despite his earlier claim that he was too lame to play the gentleman, came around and opened the passenger door. When she made no move to join him, he reached across to unclip her seat belt and grasped her elbow. "This is as far as we go, Sally," he said blandly. "Hop out and be quick about it."

"I'd rather not."

"I'd rather you did. And I'm not taking you back to town until you do."

Odd how a man's mood could shift so abruptly from mild to menacing; how smoldering rage could make its presence felt without a voice being raised. And stranger still that a person could find herself responding hypnotically to a command she knew would result in nothing but disaster.

Like a sleepwalker, she stepped out into the snow, yet felt nothing of its stinging cold. Was barely aware of putting one foot in front of another as she walked beside Jake, past the rusted pickup trucks and jalopies, to the entrance of the building.

"After you," he said, pushing open the scarred wooden door and ushering her unceremoniously into the smoke-filled interior.

At once, the noise blasted out to meet her. The smell of beer and cheap perfume, mingled with sweat and tobacco, assailed her senses.

Stomach heaving, she turned to Jake. "Please don't make me do this!"

"Why ever not?" he asked, surveying her coldly. "Place not to your liking?"

"No, it's not," she managed to say. "I'm insulted you'd even ask."

"But it was good enough the night you came here with Penelope, the night she died, wasn't it?" he said. "So why not now, with me?"

CHAPTER THREE

SHE didn't reply, nor had he expected she would. He'd outmaneuvered her too thoroughly. Instead she hovered just inside the door, uncertain whether to flee or surrender. Since he hadn't a hope in hell of catching her if she tried to make a run for it, he eliminated the possibility by marching her to a booth on the other side of the dance floor.

"Cosy, don't you think?" he said, sliding next to her on the shabby vinyl banquette so that she was trapped between him and the wall. Too bad he had to put his mouth to her ear for her to hear him. He didn't need the dizzying scent of her hair and skin making inroads on his determination to wring the truth out of her.

"What'll it be, folks?" A giant of a man, with beefy arms covered in tattoos and a head as bald as an egg, came out from behind the bar and swiped a dirty cloth over the tabletop.

Without bothering to consult her, Jake said, "Beer. Whatever you've got on tap. And nachos."

"I don't drink beer and I don't like nachos," she said snootily, the minute the guy left to fill their order.

"No?" Jake dug in his hip pocket for his wallet. "What did you have the last time you were here—champagne and oysters on the half shell?"

"What makes you think I've been here before?"

"I read the police report, remember?"

She slumped against the wall, defeated. "Why are you doing this, Jake?" she asked, raising her voice over the din from the jukebox. "What do you hope to accomplish?"

"I want to know why my wife made a habit of frequenting places like this while I was away on combat duty, and if *you* won't tell me, I'll find someone here who will."

"You're wasting your time. Penelope and I were here only once, and when I realized the kind of place it was, I insisted we leave."

He scanned the room at large. On the other side of the dance floor, a woman much the worse for wear had climbed on a table and was gyrating lewdly to the applause of the patrons lining the bar. Swinging his gaze to Sally again, Jake asked, "Was it your idea to stop here to begin with?"

"Certainly not!" she snapped. Then, realizing how much she'd revealed with her indignation, added, "We'd decided to drive out to a country inn for dinner that night, it started snowing on the way home, the roads were even worse than they are tonight, and we were looking for a place to wait out the storm. Why is that so hard for you to believe?"

"It's not, Sally. But nor does it explain what made you change your minds and venture back on the road anyway, before the weather improved. One look out the door, and you must have known you were taking your lives in your hands by getting back behind the wheel of a car."

"I already told you. We didn't like the…clientele here."

The tattooed hulk returned just then. "Where's your gal pal tonight?" he asked, sliding a tankard of beer across the table to Sally. "The regulars miss seein' her around the joint. She knew how to party."

"You know what they say," Jake cut in, before Sally could answer, even assuming she could come up with anything plausible after having just been exposed as a blatant liar. "Three's a crowd."

The server's face split in a grin. He had a scar running down one side of his massive neck and was missing three front teeth. Probably got the first from a knife wound, and lost the rest in a brawl. "Little old Penny-wise wouldn't horn in on your date for long, dude. Plenty of guys around here'd be only too willing to take her off your hands.''

''I think,'' Sally said, in a small, despairing voice, as the oaf lumbered off to collect their nachos, ''I'm going to be sick.''

Unmoved, Jake knocked back half his beer. ''That tends to happen when a person's attempt to hide the truth blows up in her face. I'd bet my last dollar you'd feel a whole lot better if you'd spit out the load of rubbish you've been feeding me.''

''It would serve you right if I did!'' she cried with surprising passion. ''But since truth's so all-fired important to you, try this on for size—I don't know what happened to turn the boy I used to know into such a hard-nosed bully, but I do know I don't like the man you've become.''

He didn't much like it himself. Browbeating a woman—*any woman*—wasn't his style. Traumatizing Sally to the point that she looked as bewildered as an innocent victim caught in enemy crossfire filled him with self-loathing. He hadn't come home to continue the inhumane practices of war. He'd come looking for a little peace.

Trouble was, he was no closer to finding it here than he had been on the other side of the world, and it was eating him alive, though not for the reasons Sally might suppose.

Hardening his heart against her obvious distress, he said, ''I'm not especially enamored of you, either. I'd hoped by now that you'd outgrown the habit of taking the easy way out of whatever tight spot you happen to find yourself in.''

She picked up her tankard of beer and, for a second, he thought she might fling it in his face. But at the last minute, she shoved it away and spat, ''I resent that, and I refuse to sink to the level of the company in which I find myself. I might be all kinds of things, but I've never lied to you in the past.''

"Never, Sally? Not once? Not even to spare my feelings?"

She opened her mouth to reply, but at the last minute appeared to think better of it. Her eyes grew huge and haunted, and filled with tears.

He wanted to wipe them away. Wanted to take her in his arms and tell her he was sorry; that raking up the distant past wasn't his intent because it didn't matter—not any of it. He wanted to tell her that he could forgive her anything, if only she'd free him to live in the present and be able to face the future without guilt weighing him down and souring each new day. And the depth of his wanting staggered him.

His wife was barely cold in her grave, for Pete's sake, and all his suspicions aside, common decency demanded he at least observe a token period of mourning.

Slamming the door on thoughts he couldn't afford to entertain, he drained his beer. "I don't know who it is you think you're protecting, Sally," he said, "but to prove I'm not completely heartless, I'll make a deal with you. Instead of badgering you to betray secrets you obviously hold sacred, I'll spell out what I believe happened, the night Penelope died. All I ask of you is that you tell me honestly whether or not I'm on the right track. Agree to those terms and, after tonight, I'll never bring the subject up again."

She moistened her lips with the tip of her tongue and stared stubbornly at her hands, but he could see she was wavering.

"I'll give you some time to think about it," he offered, levering himself away from the table and grabbing his cane, "but don't take too long. I'll only be gone a few minutes."

He wove his way through the couples squirming up against each other on the dance floor, knowing she was watching him the entire time. The men's room lay at the end of a long, badly lit corridor toward the rear of the building. A boy no more than eighteen swayed in the doorway, vacant-eyed and decidedly green about the gills. The squalor in the area beyond defied description.

Cripes! Jake had known his share of dives, but this one took some beating!

"Hey, pal," he said, catching the kid just in time to stop him doing a face plant on the filthy floor, and propelling him toward the back exit. "How about a breath of fresh air?"

The snow had tapered off, and a few stars pricked the sky. A clump of pines bordering the parking lot glowed ghostly white in the dark. Somewhere across the open fields to the west, a pack of coyotes on the hunt howled in unison. Under different circumstances, it would have been a magical night, peaceful and quiet, except for nature's music.

Propping the boy against the wall, Jake rubbed a handful of snow in his face. The poor guy gasped and shuddered. Doubled over. Recognizing the inevitable was about to occur, Jake stood well to one side.

"Feel better?" he asked, when the kid finally stopped retching.

"I guess."

"What's your name?"

He wiped the back of his hand across his mouth. "Eric."

"You of legal age to be hanging around bars, Eric?"

"No," he moaned miserably, sagging against the wall.

"Didn't think so. You live far from here?"

"Down the road some." He swallowed and grimaced. "A mile, maybe."

Jake weighed the options. He had problems enough of his own, without taking on someone else's. And a mile was no distance at all. The kid was young and strong; he could walk it in a quarter of an hour. Less, if he put his mind to it and didn't get sidetracked by the next bar he passed along the way.

But the temperature had dropped well below freezing, and he wasn't in the best shape. Jake's playing Good Samaritan would take all of five minutes. He could be back before Sally had the chance to miss him.

More important, he'd be able to sleep that night with a clear conscience. He'd been young and stupid himself, at one time, and felt for the poor kid whose troubles had only just begun. By morning, he'd be nursing one mother of a hangover!

He zipped up his jacket and fished the car keys out of his pocket. "Come on," he said. "I'll drive you."

"That's okay. I can walk."

"You can barely stand, you damn fool!"

The kid started to cry. "I don't want my mom to see me fallin'-down drunk. She's not gonna like it."

"If you were my son, I wouldn't like it, either." He jerked his thumb over his shoulder at the building behind. "But I'll bet money she'd rather have you passing out at home, than winding up as roadkill when that lot in there decide to hit the highway."

If she hadn't been so preoccupied, she might have noticed the man sooner. But by the time she realized she'd become the object of his attention, he'd lurched onto the bench beside her and slung a sweaty arm around her shoulders. "Lookin' for company, babe?"

"No," she said, recoiling from the foul breath wafting in her face. "I'm with someone."

He made a big production of swinging his head to the left and right, and then, with a drunken guffaw, peering under the table. "Don't look that way to me," he snickered, lifting his smelly T-shirt to scratch at the hairy expanse of blubber underneath. "Looks to me like you're all on your little ol' lonesome, and just waitin' for Sid to show you a good time."

"No, really! I'm with…my boyfriend. He's just gone…." *Where,* exactly, that it was taking him so long?

"To take a leak?" Sid chortled and reached for her untouched beer.

Good grief, could the clientele possibly have sunk even lower than the last time she'd set foot in this place? Revolted, she shrank into the corner of the booth, as far away from him as she could get, and made no effort to disguise her abhorrence.

Big mistake! Sid's eyes, close-set and mean enough to begin with, narrowed menacingly. He slid nearer, pressed his thigh against hers. "Wha'samatter, honey? Think you're too good for a stud like me?"

"Not at all," she said, averting her face. "I'm sure you're a very nice man."

"Better believe it, babe." His hand clamped around her chin, and forced her to turn and look at him again. He shoved his face closer, licked his lips. The fingers of his other hand covered her knee. Began inching her skirt up her leg. "Better be real friendly with Sid, if you know what's good for you."

Oh, God! Where was Jake?

Sid's fingers slid under the hem of her skirt. Crawled over her knee. Someone plugged another selection in the juke box: Patsy Cline singing "Crazy."

How appropriate! Unable to help herself, Sally giggled hysterically.

Sid squeezed her thigh. "Tha's better, babe! Treat me right, and I'll make you feel *real* good."

By then, so unnerved that she could barely breathe, she seized on the first escape possibility that occurred to her. "Dance with me," she said, praying he wouldn't hear the terror crowding her voice. Praying that he was too clumsily drunk to realize until it was too late that the only thing she wanted was to get out of the confining booth and put some distance between him and her.

"Sure thing, babe!" He grinned evilly and, with bone-crushing strength, hauled her bodily off the seat and into his arms, and pinned her like a butterfly against him.

At least, though, his hand was no longer creeping up her thigh! At least she stood a better chance of distracting him long enough to wriggle free. And if that didn't work, she could scream for help and stand a reasonable chance of being heard by the other bodies crammed on the dance floor.

"Start enjoyin', babe," Sid grated. "Ain't no fun dancin' with a corpse."

If he'd left it at that, she might have survived unscathed. But as added inducement, he stuck his tongue in her ear. Repelled beyond endurance and unmindful of the consequences of her action, she responded by lifting her knee and ramming it full force in his groin at the same time that she raked her fingernails down his face.

He roared like a wounded bear, reared back and landed a vicious slap to the side of her head. The grimy silver ball rotating from the ceiling swung crazily in her line of vision. The faces of the people around her tilted; their voices merged with coarse laughter into a cacophony of unintelligible sound.

Dazed, she lifted her head and saw his fist coming at her again. Pain cracked against her cheek in a burst of fire. She crumbled to her hands and knees on the filthy floor. Tasted blood, warm and salty on her tongue. Felt him grab her by the hair. Savagely yank her to her feet again.

Then, as suddenly as he'd latched on to her, he backed away, felled by a blow from behind. Jake, his face a distorted mask of white fury, his eyes blazing, swam into view.

A woman nearby screamed, someone else swore. Needing no better excuse to start a fight, half the men in the room joined in the fray, indiscriminately landing punches on whoever happened to be handy. But they gave Jake a wide berth. Drunken hoodlums though they might be, they had no wish to tangle with a man wielding a cane like a shillelagh and clearly willing to crack the skull of anyone foolish enough to challenge him.

Weaving his way to her through the pandemonium, he reached an arm around her waist and pulled her against him. Up to that point, she'd been too focused on defending herself to give in to the terror screaming along her nerves. Surviving the moment had been the only thing of import. But at his touch, at the cold, clean scent of him and the solid reassurance of his body shielding hers, she fell apart completely.

"I thought he was going to kill me!" she sobbed, burying her face against his neck.

He stroked her hair, murmured her name, and oh, it felt so good to be held by him again. So good to hear the old tenderness creep into his voice. Despite all the chaos and din pulsing around them, he created a tiny haven of safety she never wanted to leave.

He was of a more practical turn of mind. "Let's get out of here while we still can," he muttered, hustling her toward the door. "Things are going to get uglier before the night's over."

Just as they reached it, though, the door flew open and half a dozen police burst into the room, making escape impossible. "Hold it right there. Nobody leaves until I say so," the officer leading the pack ordered, and even in her shocked state, Sally recognized him as one of those who'd been first on the scene, the night Penelope had died.

He recognized her, too, which was hardly surprising, given the amount of publicity the accident had received in the local news. "Not you again!" he said, on an exasperated breath, as his colleagues set about restoring order. "Gee, lady, how many times does it take before you learn your lesson and stay away from places like this?"

"Never mind the clever remarks," Jake said. "She needs to see a doctor right away."

The officer eyed her appraisingly. "As long as she's still on her feet and able to walk, it'll have to wait," he finally decided. "I'm taking you both in, along with every other yahoo in the place."

"I'm the one who called you to begin with, you fool!" Jake snapped. "If you want to harass someone, go after the guy behind the bar who makes a habit of serving liquor to minors. Or the lout over there, with the bloody nose, who gets his kicks out of beating up women half his size. We'll be pressing assault charges against him, in case you're interested, but not before the morning."

"You'll do it now, and keep a lid on your temper while you're at it," the other man cautioned. "I'm ticked off enough as it is."

"It's all right, Jake," Sally said, sensing the anger simmering in him. "I don't mind going down to the station and making a statement. I've done nothing wrong."

The patrolman rolled his eyes wearily. "That's what they all say."

"Maybe *they* all do, but in my case, Officer," she told him, staring him down with as much dignity as she could drum up, considering one eye was swollen half-shut, "it happens to be the truth."

Jake touched his finger lightly to her cheek. "All it'll take is a phone call to my lawyer to have things postponed until morning, Sally. You've been through enough for one night."

And she'd have done it all again if, at the end of it all, he looked at her as if she held his heart in her hands, and cushioned her next to him, prepared to defend her to the death, if need be. It made her wonder if she was hurt more than she realized, had even suffered minor brain damage, that she was so ready to forget the terrible price she'd paid for loving Jake in the past.

Steeling herself not to weaken, she said, "I'd rather get it over with, if you don't mind."

He shrugged. "Wait here, then, while I collect your coat, and we'll be on our way." He tipped a glance at the police officer. "Is it okay if I drive us in my own vehicle, or are you going to insist we get carted off in the paddy wagon?"

"How much have you had to drink?"

"Half a beer."

"Okay. Take your own vehicle. But just in case you're thinking of pulling a fast one, I'll be following right on your tail."

It was past ten by the time they'd signed their statements at the police station and Sally had been checked over in the Emergency Room of Eastridge Bay Hospital, and closer to half past before Jake finally drew up in front of the guest cottage. By then, the pain in her face and the throbbing headache which accompanied it had subsided to a dull roar, thanks to the medication prescribed by the doctor on duty.

"Come on," Jake said, shutting off the engine and flinging open his door. "Let's get you inside and into bed."

"Jake" and "bed" were not a combination she could handle with equanimity at that point. "I can manage on my own," she informed him, feeling as if her mouth were stuffed with absorbent cotton balls.

He laughed, not very kindly she thought. "You're doped up to the eyebrows, honey. I doubt you can even stand unassisted."

"Oh, really?" Determined to prove him wrong, she managed to open her door and swing both feet out. Not very gracefully, to be sure, but they landed in the snow more or less where she intended they should. "Watch me!" she said, and tried to lever the rest of her body out, only to discover her legs possessed the vertical stability of tapioca pudding.

"Lucky for you that I am," he said, hauling her upright before she made a complete fool of herself. "Where's your house key?"

"Behind the passenger seat of your car...in the front pocket of my briefcase."

"That figures." He strode up the steps to the covered front veranda and propped her against the railing. "Think you can hold on long enough for me to go back and get it?"

"Do I have any choice?" she muttered, far from certain, but fortunately he made short work of the job and soon returned with her briefcase and keys.

He propelled her into the cottage, booted the door closed and waited while she flicked on the switch to his left. The twin sconces on either wall filled the front hall with mellow light and flung soft, welcoming shadows across the floor of the living room.

She'd never been so happy to come home, never so ready to climb onto the big feather bed in the room at the back of the house, and sink into sleep. "You can go now," she told him.

"Sure thing, Sally. Just as soon as you're tucked in for the night."

Marching her into the living room, he dumped her on the sofa in front of the fireplace. "Stay put. I'll be back."

As though from a great distance, she heard him moving about the house. Heard the furnace growl to life in the basement, and water running in the kitchen. Saw through the window the glimmer of stars between the bare branches of the ancient elms bordering her parents' property. Smaller stars than those in St. Lucia, and not hanging nearly as close to earth. But spinning…spinning…in lazy, hypnotic circles….

Her bedroom was large and elegant, like everything else to do with the Winslow estate, including quarters intended for short-term occupancy only. Satin smooth oak floors, rich Oriental rugs, some sort of silk paper the color of old parchment on the walls, and woodwork painted glossy white weren't too tough to take. Jake had spent the night in far less luxurious surroundings, and with a lot less desirable company.

Not that Sally knew he was there, or that he'd stripped her down to her underwear before putting her to bed. The pills she'd swallowed at the hospital had finally kicked in and she was about as dead to the world as was safe, given her condition.

"She can't be left alone tonight," the E.R. doctor had warned him. "Someone has to wake her every couple of hours and if she doesn't respond, get her back here on the double. The X rays didn't show any fractures, but I'm not ruling out a possible concussion. She's very lucky she got off as lightly as she did."

So was the savage who'd used her as a punching bag. Damned lucky!

A comfortable armchair with a footstool, both on casters, stood beside the window. Rolling them over the rug to a spot next to the bed, Jake eased himself into the chair and, with a grimace, lifted his leg onto the stool. Packing a semiconscious woman up a flight of steps to the front door, and from one room to another—even a featherweight like Sally—wasn't part of his rehab program, and he was paying dearly for it.

On the other hand, he ought to be grateful. If he hadn't been hampered by injury, he'd probably be behind bars now. The blind urge to kill the brute who'd gone after her had been tempered not by prudence but by his own physical limitations.

Even now, thinking back to the moment he'd returned to the roadhouse and realized who it was being smacked around the dance floor, filled him with such a flaming rage that he could taste it. It would be a long time before he was able to erase the image of that hamlike fist raised above her head, before he could forget his first sight of Sally's battered face. And a whole lot longer before he forgave himself for being the one most responsible for what had happened to her.

This wasn't how the evening was supposed to end, with him no nearer finding the answers he sought, but altogether too close for comfort to finding himself caught up again in a web of feelings for Sally Winslow. He didn't want to care about her. As a couple, they'd been over for a very long time.

But watching her breathe, seeing the gentle rise and fall of her small, perfect breasts, and recalling how she'd felt beneath his hands when he'd undressed her, a few minutes earlier, filled him with restless yearning. And too many memories.

She'd always had skin like cream. Always been so slender, he could span her waist with his hands. Always smelled like a meadow full of wild flowers under a summer sky, even tonight, after she'd put in a full day teaching, and been rolled around that stinking roadhouse floor.

But that's all they were: memories of a yesterday that could never be recaptured. Because they weren't the same people anymore. Too many years and too many mistakes had come between them. So how crazy was he to want to lie beside her now, and hold her safe in his arms until a new and better tomorrow dawned?

She stirred and moaned softly, bringing him upright in the chair. He lowered his bad leg to the floor with gingerly care and bent over her. Smoothed the dark, silky hair away from her brow, and winced again at the purple bruise discoloring her face. "Sally?"

She opened her eyes and smiled at him, a soft, unfocused smile that stabbed him as sharply as a knife. It was how she used to smile at him after they'd made love. "Hi," she murmured fuzzily.

What's your life been about all these years we were apart, Sally? he wondered. *How many men have there been since me? How many broken hearts littered along the way?*

She drifted back to sleep with the smile still on her lips. Would that he could've shut off his thoughts so easily! But the door had been opened a crack, and it was enough for all the questions he'd suppressed for so long to come rushing through.

What happened to change things between us, Sally? he asked her silently. *Was the French guy who replaced me a better lover? Did he promise you more than I did? Is that why you put such a definitive end to us? Or we were both too young to realize how fragile love is, and just didn't know enough to take care of it properly?*

CHAPTER FOUR

RELUCTANTLY, Sally struggled through befuddled layers of sleep, loath to forfeit the dreams still chasing her, of a voice—*his* voice, deep and gravelly—murmuring endearments as his hands moved over her limbs and along her shoulders, soothing...healing...captivating. But the flat, white light from outside, a sure sign that yet more snow was falling, splashed insistently against her closed eyelids, telling her it was morning and long past the time to be indulging in dreams.

How could that be? On school days, she awoke at six-thirty, hours before sunrise. Even stranger, how come the aroma of freshly brewed coffee floated on the air?

Puzzled by the amount of effort it took, she turned her head and squinted at the digital clock on the nightstand. *Nine forty-five?* Couldn't be! Classes started at eight-thirty. Academy policy dictated that faculty arrive on campus no later than eight, and good old Tom Bailey put a black mark next to the names of those who didn't observe the rules. Quite what punishment he'd mete out to a teacher who missed the first two classes of the day was enough to boggle even the clearest mind.

Wondering why so slight a movement tugged painfully at one side of her face, why she felt as if she'd been run over by a truck, why the alarm hadn't wakened her at the usual hour, she ventured another glance at the clock just as the display rolled over to nine forty-six. Despite her oddly blurred vision, there was no mistaking the number.

Appalled, she threw back the covers and swung her legs to the floor, intending to make a dash for the bathroom and

51

let a very brief but very hot shower chase away the peculiar fog still swirling in her head. But all that washed over her was a river of pain so ferocious that she sank back on the mattress with a stifled moan.

She hurt everywhere. *Everywhere,* from her head to her feet. Even her teeth ached. And as she fought to contain the myriad pinpoints of agony assaulting her, memories of the previous evening rushed in with equal brutality and left her gasping all over again.

Tentatively she touched her face. Her left cheek was as puffed up as the little lemon cakes which Edith, her mother's housekeeper, sometimes baked for afternoon tea, and felt shiny-smooth as if the skin were stretched too tightly.

Trying not to jar her tender flesh any more than was absolutely necessary, she staggered to the dresser at the foot of the bed, looked in the mirror and almost fainted. The face peering back was barely recognizable: swollen, discolored, and with one eye so bloodshot that she cringed at the sight.

Just then, the faint squeak of wheels approaching down the hall drew her attention. A second later, Jake appeared, pushing the brass tea wagon normally kept in the dining room. He was barefoot, his blue shirt hung open over his navy slacks, his hair was damp and his jaw newly shaved. In short, he looked as casually polished and perfect as she looked damaged and unkempt!

"Uh-uh, none of that," he admonished, parking the trolley to one side and turning her away from the mirror. "Get back into bed, right now, and that's an order."

If it hadn't been for the fact that he was less interested in looking at her ravaged face than at the rest of her, she'd have told him she didn't take orders from anyone, not even a man of his elevated military status. But the attentive way his gaze swept her from head to toe brought home the fact that she was standing there practically naked, and had no memory at all of having undressed herself, the night before. That her bra and panties barely covered the parts he found most engrossing was all the incentive required to send her scurrying back to bed as nimbly as possible.

"How did I get like this?" she asked suspiciously, pulling the covers up to her chin.

He regarded her gravely. "Are you saying you don't remember being at the roadhouse, or the guy who—?"

"Not that," she interrupted. "Of course I remember *that!* I'd have to be brain dead not to! I'm talking about how I came to be here with hardly any clothes on."

"I took the rest off."

Oh, good grief! "When?"

"While you were passed out."

The mere idea almost gave her an aneurism. "Isn't that a bit kinky, especially for a recently bereaved husband?"

He rolled the tea wagon up beside the bed and tried to hand her a glass of orange juice. "No need to fret, sweet Sally. I didn't peek at any naughty bits, if that's what's got you all in a lather. But what if I had? It's not as if I haven't already seen the way you're put together, more times than I can count—although I must admit you've filled out a bit since the last time, and in all the right places and to exactly the right degree, I might add."

"I really don't care what you think," she said, stifling the tingle of delight inspired by his words. "And I don't want any juice, so please stop shoving it at me. What I *do* want is an explanation of just what you're still doing here in my house."

"Juice first, conversation later. And swallow this while you're at it." He pushed the glass at her again, along with a little white pill.

She inspected it skeptically. "What's this?"

"Not an aphrodisiac, if that's what you're hoping. It's

bona fide pain medication prescribed by the doctor who treated you last night." Then, sensing she was still inclined to balk, he added, "Don't give me grief on this, Sally. I'm not in the mood for it. You're not the only one who had a lousy night. That chair might be comfortable enough for an hour or two of reading, but it's not designed for sleeping."

"I didn't ask you to stay here and baby-sit."

"Now that," he said, sounding decidedly testy, "is what I call ingratitude! A second ago, you made light of not being brain dead, but it's nothing to joke about. You came very close to being badly injured last night."

"And whose fault is that?"

"Mine," he said. "And I feel like a big enough jerk, without you rubbing it in."

She looked away, ashamed. Not everything that had happened last night was crystal clear in her mind, but the fury and horror she'd seen on his face when he came to her rescue was etched indelibly on her memory. "Sorry. That was uncalled-for."

He shrugged. "Down the pill and the juice, Sally. Breakfast is getting cold."

She saw then that, in addition to juice and coffee, he'd brought in poached eggs and toast, and that he'd made enough for two. "I appreciate all the trouble you've taken, Jake, but I really don't have time for this. I've already missed my morning classes. Tom Bailey will be fit to be tied."

"And you'll be missing this afternoon's, too. In fact, he's going to have to manage without you for a few days, as I made clear when I phoned the school first thing this morning—and those are doctor's orders, not mine." He touched her bruised cheek with a gentle fingertip. "In any case, you've seen how you look. What sort of a stir do you think you'll create, showing up with a black eye and half your face swollen to the size of a balloon?"

Of course, he was right. Even if her students didn't mind her appearance, she was pretty sure Tom would. A member of his staff showing up looking as if she'd gone ten rounds with a heavyweight boxing champion was hardly something he'd condone and, in all truth, she didn't feel up to challenging him on it.

Still mindful of her state of undress, she poked one arm out from beneath the covers. "Will you at least hand me my robe? It's hanging on the back of the bathroom door."

He did as she asked, helped her slip her arms in the sleeves so that she looked reasonably decent and fluffed the pillows at her back. A stranger looking in the window might have mistaken him for a devoted husband caring for his ailing wife.

"That's more like it." He nodded approval as she washed down the pill with a mouthful of juice, and tackled her poached eggs. "You'll feel a whole lot better with something in your stomach. You're kind of skinny overall, you know. Do you eat properly, or are you one of those women who live on tofu and celery?"

"I eat like a horse," she informed him, enjoying the food more than she was prepared to admit, even though chewing caused her some discomfort. "And I thought you said I'd filled out in all the right places."

The way he smiled at her spelled trouble she couldn't afford. "It's not where you've filled out that I'm talking about, Sally. It's the rest of you."

"That's what comes of living on a tropical island for years," she said lightly.

"You were short of food?"

"No, but I led a pretty active life. Lots of swimming, scuba diving, beach volleyball and tennis, in my time off."

He poured their coffee, then eased himself onto the side of the bed and started in on his own eggs. "You had plenty of friends, then?"

''A fair number. The ex-pat community was quite large.''

''Men friends?''

''Some.''

''Any serious involvements?''

''That stopped being any of your business a very long time ago.''

''Yes,'' he said. ''There was never much doubt about that, was there?''

Curiosity had her wanting to ask him what prompted him to look so grim as he spoke, but prudence told her to leave the matter alone. Revisiting their shared past was a pointless and dangerous pursuit, threatening not just to open old wounds but also to expose secrets she could never share with him. Better to stick to more neutral territory. ''I wasn't lucky enough to find anyone who made me want to exchange the single life for married bliss.''

He shrugged. ''Marriage has its drawbacks. Not everyone's cut out for it.''

But you were, Jake! You just didn't want to share it with me. And even now, it hurts to think how easily you passed me over for someone else.

She pushed aside her plate, her appetite fading a lot faster than her memories. ''Thank you for making breakfast. I'm sorry I can't do it justice.''

''You're welcome. More coffee, before I clear everything away?''

She shook her head and blinked, horrified to find his kindness sweeping her to the brink of tears. The medication must be playing havoc with her emotions; she hadn't wept for him in years.

Watching her altogether too closely, he said, ''Is there anything else you'd like?''

To rewrite history, perhaps, but it would take a miracle to achieve that.

"A bath." She ran her fingers through her hair. Felt the grit against her scalp, and shivered with revulsion. "I want to scrub away the grime from last night."

"Understandably." He leaned toward her and went to pull back the bedcovers. "I'll give you a hand."

"You will not!" she said, clutching them against her breast. "I can manage perfectly well on my own."

She thought he was going to argue the point, but after a moment's indecision, he contented himself with, "Fine— as long as you leave the bathroom door open."

"Forget it! You're not—"

"It's not negotiable, Sally. Either the door stays open, or you stay in bed. And in case you're harboring any ideas about thwarting me on this, you should know I helped myself to a shower this morning, while you were still sleeping, and happened to notice the lock on the door can be opened from the outside."

She glared at him, frustrated. "Isn't there some other place you should be? Some tiny detail elsewhere that desperately requires your immediate attention?"

"Nothing that can't wait," he said implacably. "So, are we agreed we'll do things my way?"

She capitulated from sheer exhaustion. "Whatever! Anything for a peaceful life."

"Good girl." He limped over to the dresser. "Tell me where to look and I'll get you a clean nightgown."

"No, thanks! I don't want you fiddling around in my drawers."

He didn't offer a verbal reply. But the glance he cast over his shoulder—long and enigmatic—conferred a provocative subtext to her words which made her blush. She could only pray her multicolored bruises disguised the fact.

To give him credit, he didn't intensify her embarrassment further. "Suit yourself," he said mockingly, wheeling the tea wagon to the door. "While you're cleaning up, I'll don my little apron and do the same to the dishes. Call if you need help.''

The minute he disappeared, she crawled out of bed, collected fresh underwear and a soft cotton nightshirt and fled to the bathroom. She turned on the faucet and tossed a generous handful of aromatic bath salts into the jetted tub—a long, deep luxurious affair designed for leisurely soaking—and, while it filled, stepped under the shower to shampoo her hair and scrub away the worst of the grime.

Then, feeling halfway presentable again, she set the timer on the spa controls, climbed into the tub and immersed herself up to the chin in water so hot she'd probably look like a boiled lobster when she got out. But she didn't care. With her inflatable daisy pillow supporting her neck, and the soothing pulse of the power jets massaging her aching muscles, she'd have been happy to spend the next several hours in such splendid isolation.

Too soon, though, Jake's voice intruded from the other side of the door, an unpleasant reminder that she wasn't entirely in charge of her own destiny at that moment. "You've been in there long enough, Sally," he said, raising his voice to be heard over the noise of the spa motor. "Time to hop into bed again."

"Go away," she told him irritably. "I'll come out when I'm ready, and not before."

He rattled the doorknob, a signature warning that her defiance would exact a price she might not care to pay. "Don't push your luck!"

As if in cahoots with him, the timer control gave a little *ping,* and the jets dwindled into the same expectant silence emanating from the other side of the door. Recognizing that, in this instance at least, he had the upper hand, she let out a long-suffering sigh. "Oh, all right! You win this round."

Surprisingly, instead of crowing over his victory, he accepted it without further comment. She heard his uneven tread as he crossed the bedroom, followed by the sound of the door closing and his footsteps fading as he made his way back to the kitchen wing.

She didn't wait to find out how long he'd be gone, or what he planned to do when he returned. Seizing the moment, she hauled herself out of the tub, toweled herself dry and dressed as quickly as possible.

Just as well she didn't waste any time. She'd barely finished doing up the buttons on her nightgown before the bedroom door was flung open again. "I'm just about ready," she called, flicking a comb through her hair. "If you'd given me another minute instead of being so impatient, I'd have been back in bed again and you'd have nothing to complain about."

The silence which greeted that remark was, she thought, rather ominous. And as soon as she came out of the bathroom, she discovered why. Jake was not the only one waiting for her to put in an appearance. Her mother and sister were there, too, and it was obvious from the latter's scandalized expression that she'd leaped to all the wrong conclusions about exactly what was going on.

Her all-encompassing gaze darted from Sally's attire, to the rumpled bedcovers, to Jake's sweater lying on the floor next to the armchair and, finally, on a heaving breath of indignation, to Jake himself. "Did you spend the night here?"

"Not in the sense that you're implying," he replied coolly.

"And what sense is that, may I ask?"

"As if you'd barely missed finding your sister and me rolling around between the sheets and going at it like a pair of demented rabbits."

Margaret was unaccustomed to being confronted so bluntly and, at the look on her face, Sally couldn't repress a little chirp of laughter. If she'd thrown a lighted match into a can of gasoline, the result couldn't have been more explosive.

Margaret rounded on her in fine fury. "You'll be laughing on the other side of your face when word of your latest escapade reaches certain quarters! I managed to keep it from Tom at breakfast, but he's sure to have heard about it by now, and if you think it's not going to cost you your—"

Distressed, their mother said, "Will you, for heaven's sake, stop fussing about things that aren't important and pay attention to what matters, Margaret? Frankly I'm grateful to Jake. Any fool can see Sally needed someone to look after her through the night, and since none of us knew she'd been hurt, I'm glad he was here to take on the job." She touched her hand lovingly to Sally's bruises. "I'm so sorry, darling. I didn't know what had happened until I saw this morning's paper."

"I made the news?"

"Oh, you did more than that," Margaret huffed, waving the *Eastridge Daily News* under her nose. "It wasn't enough that you made the front page last week, with the daughter of one of this town's leading families winding up dead because of it. No, you had to do it again this week— and involve her husband, if you please!—just to remind everyone how much you enjoy creating a sensation. Once again, you've humiliated all of us with your outrageous behavior and I, for one, have had enough of it. Don't expect me to rush to your defense again, Sally Winslow. This time, you're on your own."

"Which is exactly what I'd like to be right now…left on my own."

"Well, never let it be said I don't know how to take a hint!" Margaret made a grand exit, slamming the front door behind her as a final exclamation point to her annoyance.

Their mother, though, didn't budge. "Either you convalesce up at the main house, Sally, or I'm sending Edith down here to play nursemaid. But you will *not* be left alone until I'm satisfied you're on the mend and able to look after yourself again."

"Glad you're taking that attitude, Mrs. Winslow," Jake said, scooping up his sweater. "Someone needs to crack a whip around this daughter of yours. The hospital staff were adamant that she be watched for twenty-four hours, but she's a difficult patient, as I expect you already know."

"Oh, yes!" She rolled her eyes. "The tales I could tell, if we only had the time. But I can see you're anxious to be off."

Anxious? Desperate was more like it, judging from the way he was edging toward the door. "I do have a few things to take care of," he said.

"I'm sure. What a terrible homecoming you've had, Jake. But thank you for everything you've done. We're very grateful, aren't we, Sally?"

"Yes," she said meekly, willing to agree to just about anything, if it put an end to being badgered. In truth, her head was pounding again and the prospect of crawling back into bed growing more attractive by the minute.

"Then I'll leave you to it." He bathed her in a smile so reminiscent of the old days that she went weak at the knees. "Try to behave yourself, okay?"

"Such a nice man," her mother observed, straightening the sheets and ushering her back to bed as the front door thudded closed behind him. "When you're feeling better, you'll have to tell me what possessed you to go out with him last night, and to that disreputable roadhouse, of all places, because you know, darling daughter, Margaret *does* have a point. It really doesn't enhance your reputation to be seen frequenting such an establishment."

"Yes, Mom. I'm sure you're right. It won't happen again."

Not up to another lecture so soon after the first, Sally closed her eyes, and found it surprisingly easy to slide back into that other, dreamlike world of drifting clouds and deep, restful silence.

A few times in the hours which followed, she sensed that Edith hovered nearby. Once, she was aware of the house-keeper's arm supporting her, of sipping a cool drink and swallowing another pill. But mostly she slept, while her body healed itself.

Sally wasn't the only one targeted for criticism. Colette Burton showed up at Jake's door shortly after he got home, and voiced her displeasure loud enough for half the neigh-borhood to hear.

"How could you be so disrespectful?" she howled, shak-ing the morning paper in his face as she stormed past and took up a position in the middle of the opulent foyer. "My daughter adored you, Jake. You were her whole life. It would break her heart if she knew how soon you'd taken up with someone else a *mere week after her death!*" She dissolved into noisy sobs. "And with *that woman,* of all people! Do you have any idea of the damage you've done to your reputation?"

Given what he suspected and the little bit he'd learned the night before, he'd have liked to tell her that the repu-tation most in danger of being irreparably tarnished was Penelope's. He took no pleasure in inflicting pain, though, so he contented himself with saying mildly, "Things aren't always as they seem, Colette. My reasons for being with Sally Winslow last night were strictly business."

"At some low-class tavern?" She sniffed scornfully, and he could hardly blame her. It *was* a pretty lame reason. "What kind of fool do you take me for?"

He shrugged. "If you choose not to believe me, there's not much I can do about it."

"You can try behaving in a manner befitting a man recently widowed. It might lend more credibility to your protests. Your whole attitude since you came back from overseas is creating comment, Jake. You've been cold and distant to the point of outright cruel. You didn't shed a single tear at the funeral. You ignored my express wishes and flaunted Sally Winslow in our faces afterward." She shook the newspaper again and stared at him, hollow-eyed. "And now, only three days later, we're presented with this! What are we supposed to think?"

"That there might be more to the situation than you realize."

Her tears stopped abruptly, replaced by a shifty wariness. "What do you mean? What are you trying to do?"

"Find some peace of mind."

"At my daughter's expense? I'll see you hung out to dry, first!"

"Don't put words in my mouth, Colette. And don't threaten me."

Her expression slid from cunning to soulful. "Threaten you? Jake, I'm trying to help you!"

"Concentrate on helping yourself," he said. "We each deal with tragedy differently. Accept that your way isn't necessarily the same as mine."

"We should be supporting each other through this terrible time, not struggling through our grief in isolation. There must be something I can do."

"There is," he said. "You can explain why you saw fit to come here and remove Penelope's personal items, instead of leaving me to take care of them. And you can tell me why the coroner's office was directed to send the autopsy results to Fletcher's office, instead to me."

"Why, to spare you, of course! You've been through so

much in the last six months, Jake, and coming home at last, only to be faced with so many sad reminders, didn't seem fair. We wanted to take as much off your shoulders as possible. It's not as if there's any secret about how Penelope died, so why expose yourself to the unpleasantness of the coroner's report? And as for her things, well, sorting through a woman's clothing and deciding what to do with them isn't something most men would want to tackle. If it's her jewelry you're worried about—?''

"I'm not," he said. "I have no use for it or her clothes. What I'm trying to say, as tactfully as I know how, is that you're interfering in matters which are not your concern."

"Penelope was our daughter!"

"Yes. But as you keep reminding me, she was also my wife."

Nostrils flaring with indignation, she pulled on her gloves and wrenched open the front door. "I'm sorry you see it that way, Jake. I had thought we were family and, as such, deserving of the privileges that entails. Obviously I was wrong. I'll stay out of your way, in the future."

He knew what he was supposed to do next: refuse to let her leave; beg her forgiveness; tell her she'd always be an important part of his life and prove it by giving her free run of the house. It was the kind of price she exacted from poor old Fletcher, any time he dared disagree with her or exert a little independence. But she'd picked the wrong man, this time.

"Regrettable, but perhaps unavoidable," he said, standing aside so as not to impede her exit. "Goodbye, Colette. I'll be in touch if there's anything else we need to discuss. Give Fletcher my best."

She didn't quite snort in his face. She'd have thought that beneath her. Instead she spat, "You'll be sorry you've taken this tack with me, Jake—you and Sally Winslow, both! You've been away more than you've been home over

the last few years, so you may have forgotten how much
influence I wield in the upper echelons of this town's social
hierarchy. You'll find flouting convention a lot more costly
than you seem to realize. Doors which, in the past, have
been wide-open to you will be slammed shut in your face.
You'll become as much a social outcast as your tacky little
tart.''

Not about to get involved in further mud-slinging, he
inclined his head dismissively and closed the door on her.
No point in retaliating by acquainting her with the knowledge that, from everything he'd so far uncovered, the only
tart in the picture appeared to be the one he'd married. Even
he drew the line at burdening his in-laws with that kind of
information.

But his speaking so bluntly had undoubtedly landed Sally
in more trouble than that in which she already found herself. He harbored no illusions about the roasting they'd both
receive, the next time his mother-in-law got together with
her martini-swigging lady friends.

In all fairness, he had to warn Sally. But not yet. Not
until she was on the mend. And definitely not until he'd
wormed out of her the information she was so bent on
keeping from him.

Oh brother! Landing a fighter jet on the deck of an aircraft carrier was a piece of cake compared to navigating
the minefield he'd found waiting for him at home. It was
enough to make a guy wish he'd signed up for another tour
of duty.

Honorable military discharge might have a fine illustri-
ous ring to it, but it was no guarantee of peaceful retire-
ment. He was still up to his ears in war!

CHAPTER FIVE

HE WAITED four days then, after dark so as not to give rise to any more scandal, went back to the Winslow guest house. A single-story structure designed along the same turn-of-the-century lines as the main mansion, it sat about forty feet inside the driveway, clearly visible to passing traffic or anyone on foot. Not that there was ever much of either in that secluded section of The Crescent, but he deemed it wiser not to draw attention to his presence by driving through the double gates and parking outside her front door.

Instead he left his car on the road, and passing through a smaller side gate set in the wall enclosing the five acre property, approached the cottage. A faint light from the living room to the left spilled out over the garden. His arrival muffled by the snow underfoot, Jake veered off the path leading to the covered porch and looked through the undrawn drapes at the sight within.

Although the rest of the room hovered in shadows, the flickering flames in the hearth and a small table lamp in the corner showed Sally crouched in a chair in front of the fire, with her knees drawn up under her chin. She wore what appeared to be a dark green robe and fluffy white slippers, and even though her hair had swung forward to obscure her face, he sensed her despondency.

As it had at the Burtons' the day of the funeral, and again at the roadhouse the other night, an almost feral urge to rush in and chase away her demons swept over him. Suppressing it, he mounted the steps and pulled the old-fashioned bell chain hanging on the wall beside the door.

When she answered, he waved a large paper sack under her nose. "Before you tell me to take a hike, get a whiff of this. Takeout from the Japanese restaurant on Beach Street, guaranteed to chase away the winter blues."

She sniffed obediently and cast him a glance from beneath her lashes. "Did you bring saké, too?"

"Naturally."

Without another word, she took the bag, gestured him across the threshold, and made tracks for the kitchen.

He tossed his jacket over a brass hook on the coat stand, shucked off his boots, and followed her. "I didn't expect you to capitulate quite that easily, Sally."

"I can't afford to be choosy about the company I keep. Friends are in short supply right now."

"Should I take that to mean you've had another run-in with your sister?"

"Sister and brother-in-law both!" she said, opening the various cartons of food. "Oh, goody! Sticky rice, sauces and chicken yakatori—and shrimp tempura, too! Yum yum!"

Not bothering to hide his grin, he said, "I take it you haven't eaten dinner yet?"

She wrinkled her nose. "It's not that I didn't have the chance, but if I never see beef broth again, it'll be yet too soon. I emptied the last batch down the sink."

"Ungrateful wench!" he chided, breaking the seal on the bottle of rice wine. "Don't suppose you happen to own a set of those little Japanese serving sets for this stuff?"

"Naturally," she said, mimicking the tone of his reply when she'd asked if he'd brought saké, and reaching into the back of a cupboard, brought out a porcelain flask and two little cups etched with graceful white cranes in flight on a celadon background. "This kitchen is nothing if not well-stocked for every occasion. Will you get the tea wagon? We might as well cart everything through to the living room and eat by the fire.''

She turned toward him as she spoke, and in the brighter light of the kitchen, he saw that although the swelling on her face had subsided, the bruises were still livid. Stunned at the fresh uproar of fury to which they gave rise, he did as she asked, glad of any diversion which provided a chance for him to wrestle his emotions under control again.

''You might like to know that the brute who attacked you is behind bars and likely to stay there,'' he told her, rolling the wagon from the dining room to the kitchen counter, and loading the food and plates while she heated the wine. ''He was refused bail—too many previous assault charges. He'll get the book thrown at him, this time.''

''I'll try to draw comfort from that as I figure out my next move.''

He'd have preferred not to acknowledge how uncomfortably depressing he found her answer, but it refused to go ignored. ''Don't tell me you're thinking of leaving town again.''

She tilted her shoulder in a delicate shrug. ''That wasn't exactly what I meant, but now that you mention it, why not? It would seem that, all my good intentions notwithstanding, I'm a source of annoyance or embarrassment to everyone I keep trying so hard to please. What's to keep me here?''

''There's me,'' he heard himself say, before the folly of such an admission could make itself felt. Sheesh, what was it about being near her that brought out the idiot in him? And how come he wasn't fighting harder to conquer it?

''You've got enough to deal with.''

''I've always got time for an old friend.''

Her mouth drooped again in melancholy and he'd have touched her, if she'd let him. Slung a platonic arm around her shoulder and given her a bracing, brotherly hug, as much to convince himself he was in charge of his emotions as to comfort her. But she edged away from him to pour the hot saké into the flask which was, perhaps, a wise move on her part. Touching her under any pretext was as risky as playing football with a live bomb, and he'd be a fool not to admit it.

"Really?" She gave him a blast from those incredible green eyes which never had known how to hide her innermost feelings. "Is that why I neither saw nor heard from you in the last four days?"

"It wasn't from lack of interest on my part, Sally," he said, aching to cup her jaw and trace the sweet, sad curve of her mouth with his thumb. "I thought it best to wait until the ruckus died down some before I came calling again."

"It isn't going to die down, Jake," she said on a quiet sigh. "People in this town have long memories and they don't forgive easily. I was labeled years ago as an incorrigible teenager who abused the privileges to which she was born, and events of the last two weeks have merely confirmed public opinion that I haven't matured into anything much better."

"So you're going to run away?"

She grimaced at the teasing scorn he injected into the question. "Call it that, if you like."

"I *don't* like, Sally!"

"What would you have me do instead? Offer to stand in front of the courthouse, and let the sanctimonious residents of Eastridge Bay pelt me with rotten tomatoes as punishment for my sins, both real and imagined?"

"No," he said, nurturing the anger usurping the maelstrom of less admissible emotions churning his innards. "Prove everyone wrong, instead. Stop groveling for approval and start demanding respect, for a change."

"That won't be easy."

"I never said it would be. Striking out in a new direction takes guts, and I ought to know."

On her way to hold open the kitchen door, she ran her finger over the polished head of his cane, propped against the Welsh dresser, and nodded at his leg. "That's put paid to your military career, then?"

"Yeah. My days flying F-14 Tomcats are over," he acknowledged, managing to steer the loaded tea wagon past her and down the hall to the living room without incident, "but at this rate, I'll make a damn fine butler."

Her laugh, the first genuine sign of amusement he'd heard since he'd met up with her again, floated out to enfold him in memories. They'd laughed a lot in the old days, sometimes freely in pure enjoyment of the moment, and sometimes in the quiet, intimate way that lovers do when only the stars are there to hear.

"Who are you trying to fool, Jake? Our families' roots are as firmly dug into the refined soil of The Crescent as the foundations of their mansions. They don't *produce* servants, they *hire* them."

"Times change, Sally, and we have to change with them."

"Not quite that much! Your father's serving his sixth term as mayor, and your mother's as famous for her elegant soirees as her charity fund-raising." She eyed him thoughtfully as he threw another log on the fire. "And then there's you, a decorated war hero, fresh from the Persian Gulf. Somehow, after all the excitement *that* must have involved, I can't see you settling for the mundane."

He pulled another chair close enough to hers that they could both help themselves from the tea wagon, and poured the saké. "Not so. If war's excitement, I've had enough of it to last me a lifetime. I'm tired of violence." He shot another glance at her bruised face. "I'm tired of seeing innocent victims being subjected to men's brutality."

Ignoring the reference to her own injuries, she said, "You sound burned-out, Jake, and small wonder. Perhaps you just need to do nothing but recover for a while. It's not as if you can't afford it."

He extended his leg and patted the section of thigh just below his hip. "This won't be a problem much longer, and money never has been. My military pension alone's more than enough to keep me afloat, and never mind the investments I made with what I inherited when I turned twenty-one. But I'm not geared for idleness. Once I've got my affairs in order, I'll be ready to take on new challenges."

She dipped a chunk of shrimp tempura in sauce. "And what shape are these challenges going to take? Politics? Law? Finance?"

"Uh-uh." He shook his head. "I'm looking at something a bit more hands-on and down-to-earth than the kind of undertaking my family usually gets involved in."

Her eyebrows shot up in surprise. "Break with tradition, you mean? Good grief, you'll become as much of an outcast as I am!"

"I don't care." Astonished at how easily his thoughts flowed, how ideas which had been fermenting vaguely at the back of his mind for days suddenly took shape and direction, he went on, "I want to build, instead of destroy. Create lucrative jobs for men who don't have much but are willing to put in an honest day's work to earn a dollar. Be remembered as someone who made a difference to ordinary people, instead of that rich guy up on the hill who didn't give a damn about how the other half lived." He flung her an ironic grin. "Feel free to laugh anytime."

"I don't feel like laughing," she said soberly. "You've touched a chord in me. My conscience bothers me in exactly the same way. I've never known want. Never had to wonder where my next meal's coming from, or if, come nightfall, I'd have a roof over my head. Making a difference to people who've never enjoyed the privileges to which I was born is what made working in the Caribbean so rewarding.''

"And you don't find the same kind of satisfaction teaching at The Academy?''

She made a face. "I guess you haven't heard. I've been relieved of my duties there. Tom stopped by yesterday and delivered the news in person. The Board of Governors doesn't care for the kind of notoriety I bring to the school.''

"I'm sorry, Sally. I'm afraid I'm mostly to blame for that. If I hadn't dragged you to Harlan's Roadhouse—''

She waved aside his apology. "I'd have found some other way to offend. I don't fit the sort of image they like to project.''

"Maybe not, but that's no reason to let them chase you out of town. There must be other schools looking for teachers.''

"I don't want any other school, any more than I ever wanted The Academy, because I'm not really cut out for teaching. It's something I drifted into because there was a need on St. Lucia for something I could offer, but I'm not passionate enough about it to want to pursue it here. It doesn't inspire me.''

"Funny you should say that. I never could imagine you as a schoolmarm, though I doubt your students would agree with me. I imagine they found you to be an excellent teacher.''

She shrugged and popped a sauce-smeared fingertip into her mouth, then slowly drew it out again, oblivious to the innate sensuality of her action. But he was overwhelmed with stunning recall of the time at the country fair that they'd shared a huge ball of cotton candy and, afterward, she'd licked away the grains of spun sugar sticking to his chin, then let her tongue trace a leisurely path down the length of his throat. He'd been left painfully aroused, and felt the same stirrings threatening his self-control now.

Dragging his gaze away, he shifted in the chair, tried to look unmoved, and said, "So if teaching doesn't light a fire under you, what does?"

She selected a skewer of chicken and regarded it pensively. "Fighting for the underdog," she said at last. "Defending the right to be different of those who don't fit the conventional mold, or who aren't able to defend themselves."

"Pretty lofty ideals, Sally."

"No more so than yours."

"I guess not, but then, we always were on the same wavelength."

Sudden tense silence exploded as palpably as if an unwelcome third party had crashed through the door and cast a paralyzing spell on everything in the room. Even the flames in the hearth seemed to lose their energy.

"No, we weren't," she said, shattering the brittle atmosphere. "Not always."

"If you're referring to the summer you went to Paris, we never did talk about it, and I've often—"

"I see no point in harking back to the distant past."

The warm, animated woman who'd shared his ambitions a moment before changed before his eyes, morphing into a stranger in less time than it took to blink. Just as well. He hadn't come to her house to dig up old bones; they had more current skeletons to uncover.

"Then how about if we clarify a few points about the *recent* past, specifically the events of the other night?" he suggested coolly.

Her eyes grew as secretive and guarded as a forest glade. "To my mind, the only thing that's unclear is how you can justify leaving me to fend for myself in that swill-pot of a bar."

"I can't," he said, "and you've got to know I've cursed myself a thousand times since for what happened to you."

"More to the point, Jake, what happened to *you?* Where did you disappear to?"

"I found a kid of eighteen, drunk out of his mind in the men's room, and drove him home. I figured I'd be back before you had time to miss me. Only problem was, he passed out in the car and his mother thought I was the one who'd been feeding him liquor. By the time we sorted that out and I helped her get him upstairs to bed, it took me fifteen minutes instead of five. But if I'd known that you—"

"There was no way you could have," she interrupted softly. "You did the right thing, helping that boy, and if I didn't forgive you before, I do now."

"But I haven't forgiven myself, and I don't know that I ever will. I was ready to commit murder when I saw what that brute was doing to you. Might have given in to the urge if the police hadn't shown up when they did. Just as well I called them after I left the boy's house to report them serving underage kids." He returned his half-finished meal to the tea wagon, his appetite killed by the ongoing wretchedness which had haunted him for the last four days. "All my fine talk about despising violence doesn't amount to much when the chips are down, does it? I'm still a savage when it comes to defending the woman I l—"

What? *The woman I love?* Is that what he'd almost said? He must be crazy! He hadn't been in love with any woman for years.

Flabbergasted, he leveled a glance at her, expecting to see amusement mirrored on her face, and instead surprising such a look of raw vulnerability that it was all he could do not to leap up and haul her into his arms.

As though she realized she'd betrayed too much of what she was feeling, the color flooded her face. But it was too late for evasive action. Some things time couldn't change, and that instinctive, deep-down knowledge of each other was one of them.

He hadn't needed to finish his sentence for her to figure it out. If uncertainty existed as a result, it was his, because he had no idea why she should find his near-admission so painful.

"What I should have said," he began, stumbling over the words.

But she, recovering more quickly, cut him off. "Is that the built-in male instinct to protect the weaker sex ruled the moment."

"Something like that," he said, and decided it was high time to change the subject. "I went back to the roadhouse yesterday. It's been temporarily shut down for violation of the liquor law, but I tracked down the owner and showed him a photo of Penelope. It took a bit of fiscal persuasion, but he finally admitted she'd been a regular there for months—long before you came back to town."

Sally stared at her bowl of rice as if she feared it might jump up and bite her. "Did he indeed?"

"Mmm-hmm." He watched her closely, but unlike the moment before, she was no longer giving away anything of what she was thinking, so he decided to pull out all the stops. "He went so far as to call her 'a regular little sex terrier in heat.' Not a term I'm familiar with, I admit, but you have to agree, it does paint a telling picture."

"Yes," she said, her voice as flat and unrevealing as the drab winter landscape outside. "I suppose it does."

"You surprise me, Sally," he said mildly. "I expected you to refute any such allegation—and with a lot more vigor than you're presently exhibiting. Which begs the question: Why? How much more do you know that you're not willing to tell me?"

That brought about the results he'd been looking for!

Agitated, she flung down her rice bowl, hurled herself out of her chair, and circled around the furniture to the window, so that he was left staring at her back.

"Why should I know anything?" she said. "She didn't confide in me."

"The pair of you were inseparable once. You knew her better than anyone."

"That was before."

"Before what?"

She pinched her mouth shut, as though she regretted having spoken so rashly, and chose her next words more carefully. "Before we drifted apart. We weren't in regular contact while I was away. I have no idea which places she normally frequented. We went out together only the one time, to catch up on each other's news, and you already know how the night ended. You're a widower because of my recklessness."

"Am I?" he said, hoisting himself to his feet and going after her. "Do you really hold yourself to blame for my wife's death?"

She shied away from him like a nervous foal. "Who else? I was the one driving the car."

"You were driving *her* car which isn't quite the same thing. Care to tell me why?"

"No," she said stubbornly.

"Then I'll tell you. She was too drunk to drive, so you took over. She didn't like the idea. Probably fought you for the keys. How am I doing so far, Sally?"

She didn't reply, nor did she need to. The pallor creeping over her face and made all the more noticeable because of her bruises, said it all.

"You probably had to pour her into the passenger seat," he continued. "And either you didn't notice she hadn't done up her seat belt, or she refused to buckle it, which is why, when you wrapped the car around that power pole, you emerged virtually unscathed, but she was thrown out of the car and killed.''

He'd finally found the key to breaking her silence and once she started talking, she couldn't stop.

''She didn't want to leave the bar,'' she said, her voice as lost as that of a child trying to outrun a recurring nightmare. ''Oh, it was horrible…embarrassing! She made a terrible scene, crawling around on her hands and knees, and swearing. She was like an animal. I hardly recognized her. Didn't want anyone to know I knew her. When I finally got her outside, she dropped her purse and that's how I managed to get the car keys. I had to fight to get her into the car. She was furious…out of control. Lunging to grab the keys out of the ignition. Trying to grab the steering wheel. The car started skidding…I thought the tires would never stop screaming…and I couldn't…I couldn't…!''

''I know you couldn't,'' he said, hating himself for what he was doing to her, but too driven by his own demons to let the matter rest. ''I've been through the same thing with her, more times than I care to count.''

''But you didn't end up killing her.''

''It was an accident, Sally—one she caused. If you'd let her get behind the wheel of that car, you'd both be dead—and that I couldn't live with.''

''I should have stopped her from drinking so much. You must hate me for what I let happen.''

Without considering the repercussions to such a move, he closed the remaining distance between them, and reached out to stroke her hair. A blameless enough gesture in itself and intended only to soothe her misery, it backfired disastrously. The strands slipped between his fingers like polished silk, and he found his hand caressing her face instead.

At that, all the restraint, all the tight, unspoken caution between them, disintegrated into ashes, seared by a jolt of awareness so acute that she flinched at its impact. Her hands shot up, as if to shove him away, but she turned toward him instead and clutched at the front of his sweater. She closed her eyes, and let out a stifled moan.

Of defeat? Surrender? It didn't matter. What happened next was beyond her control or his. Their lips came together, guided by tacit yearning, and it was as if yesteryear had never happened. The floodgates opened and let the pent-up longing run free. One second they stood at arm's length from one other, and the next she was crushed against him, and he was punctuating short, frantic kisses with words he had no business thinking, let alone speaking aloud.

"I could never hate you," he muttered, anguished that she'd even entertain the idea. "You were my first love...my best love."

"Don't!" she cried. "You can't say things like that! You just buried your wife."

"I know...I know."

And still he kissed her, stealing his mouth along her jaw and down her throat. And still she let him. Her arms stole around him. Her head fell back, leaving her long, lovely neck exposed to his domination. She trapped his knee between her parted legs, and tilted her hips against him with a desperation which matched his.

She was crying the whole time, and she was beautiful. So beautiful, he could hardly breathe.

"You'll hate us both, tomorrow," she whispered, the tears seeping out from beneath her closed eyelids. "You'll feel such remorse...!"

He raised his lips to trace fleeting kisses over her bruises. "Nothing I've done before or ever might do in the future can equal a tenth of the remorse I feel for what I let happen to you on Monday."

"It wasn't your fault."

"It was my fault." He stroked the ball of his thumb over her tears, tasted the salty tracks they left behind. "And I wanted so badly to make it up to you. Wanted to lie beside you in your bed. Hold you all night long. Keep you safe and never let you go."

"It's because you're in denial over Penelope," she sobbed. "You don't want to accept that she betrayed you. That's why you're saying all this. You just need someone to hold on to, and I happen to be here."

He wished it were so. It would make everything so much easier. But he was tired of pretending to be grief-stricken. Tired of trying to preserve a charade which had played itself out years ago.

"Not just anyone, Sally," he said, rocking her in his arms. "Only you. When we're together, I believe in tomorrow. You make me *feel* again. You make me want to live."

She melted against him, her protests dying on a sigh as he covered her mouth again with his. He stroked his hand down her throat, over the fabric of her robe—some sort of dense silky fabric with a raised, uneven texture. And beneath it, infinitely softer, a thousand times silkier, her skin, smoother than cream.

The scent of her, light, with a trace of vanilla, owed nothing to perfume and everything to the essence of the girl she'd once been and the woman she'd become. He'd have recognized that fragrance anywhere. It beckoned to him just as the aroma of rich, warm food would lure a starving man.

Who knew what might have happened next, if a too-bright light hadn't splashed against the window from outside and revealed them in blatant contravention of everything society held decent?

"What the devil…!"

He swung her behind him, aware that although he could shield her from further physical exposure right then, he could do nothing to prevent the further damage to her reputation later. Whoever had come sneaking up to the house had found what they'd been seeking and he doubted they'd keep it to themselves.

Trying to apprehend the intruder was futile. As swiftly as it had pierced the dim ambience of the room, the flashlight was extinguished. A figure scurried across the snow-covered lawn and down the drive toward the gates. Seconds later, the sound of a car racing down the road split the silence of the night.

''Hell's bells!'' Cursing, he yanked the drapes across the window.

''Thank you,'' she murmured on a frail breath.

''For what? Talk about too little, too late!'' He turned back to find her cowering against the chair with her fingers pressed to her lips. ''I'm sorry, Sally. I'm afraid whatever problems you thought you had before I showed up here tonight have just multiplied a thousand times over.''

CHAPTER SIX

STUNNED, Sally stared at him. "Why do you say that?"

"Think about it," he said, limping to the hall and pulling on his jacket and boots. "What kind of person shines a light through a window to spy on someone, then takes off without explanation? He—or she—wasn't collecting donations for the SPCA, Sally, you can bet on that! They had an ulterior motive in mind."

She trailed after him, still struggling to come to grips with the situation. "Like breaking and entering, you mean?"

He shrugged. "Could be."

"Oh, I don't think so! This is just a guest cottage with nothing much in it worth stealing. Why would anyone bother with it, when there are far richer pickings to be found all over the neighborhood?"

"I rather think the fact that it's *your* cottage is the real issue."

A flutter of alarm quivered up her spine. "That doesn't exactly reassure me, Jake!"

"Sorry. Forget I said anything. I'm as much in the dark as you are." He stepped out onto the front porch. "To be on the safe side, though, lock the door behind me and stay put while I take a look around to make sure whoever it was isn't still hanging around. Might be as well to check all the other doors and windows as well, while you're at it. I'll be back shortly."

She'd never been afraid of living alone before; never seen the guest house as anything but a charming cottage safely set within the grounds of her parents' estate, in an area regularly patrolled by security guards. Petty crime was almost unheard-of in that neighborhood.

Since coming back to town, though, she seemed to be a magnet for trouble. It had dogged her wherever she went, and the strain was beginning to tell. As she made her way from room to room, she found herself jumping at shadows and listening, with her nerves on edge, for any unfamiliar sound.

Suddenly the French doors in the dining room seemed too flimsy to deter an intruder; the low sill of the long window in her bedroom too easily straddled. No fence separated the patio at the back of the house from a thicket of dwarf pines set so closely together that a dozen pairs of eyes could be watching her every move from between the dense branches. And the furnace—had it always made that odd clicking sound, or was someone tampering with the latch at the laundry room window?

A sudden sharp rap at the front door caused her heart to miss a beat, then race with erratic relief when Jake called out, "It's me again, Sally."

She hurried to let him in. "Did you find anything?"

"Just footprints in the snow. The bad news is your uninvited guest tramped over those dwarf shrubs out front. The good news is, he doesn't have very big feet and won't have done too much damage."

"And that's all?" She leaned out and lifted the lid of the mail box hanging on the wall beside the door. "No nasty anonymous note left behind? No brick ready to be thrown through the window?"

"Nothing. Which leads me to deduce this was a spur-of-the-moment sort of thing—most likely some kid showing off for his buddies. It's the kind of thing teenagers do for kicks." He pulled his keys from his pocket and turned up the collar of his jacket. "No big deal, really."

More dismayed than she cared to admit, she said, "And that's it? You're leaving, just like that?"

"Might as well. I'm pretty sure you won't be bothered again tonight, but set the house alarm before you go to bed, just to be on the safe side."

"That's not why I asked." She raised her hands, palms up. "Jake, before we were so rudely disturbed, you and I—"

"Were playing with fire," he said flatly. "You should be grateful we were interrupted. My coming here tonight was a big mistake."

Well, he'd certainly learned how to get his point across plainly! No subtle hints or gradual lessening of interest designed to spare her feelings this time around, just blunt, outright rejection, and to hell with whether or not he left her bleeding!

"I know," she said, injecting her voice with chilly pride. "In fact, if you recall, I tried telling you that, but you wouldn't listen."

"Well, I'm listening now. And I thank you for the reminder."

He deigned to look her squarely in the face then, and just fleetingly she thought she saw pain in his eyes. But if so, it was probably because his leg was hurting. Or his conscience. "Don't forget your cane," she spat, running to the kitchen to retrieve the damned thing and practically throwing it at him. "I'd hate to think you might find a reason to come back again. And who knows, you might need it the next time you have to rush to the defense of a woman you've coerced into accompanying you to the seediest dive in the county."

She was panting for breath by the time she'd finished her tirade. Not that it seemed to impress him any!

"I'm sorry if I've upset you," he said calmly. "You've

had more than enough to deal with lately, without my making things worse.''

"You haven't made things worse, so don't flatter yourself." Furious to discover she'd learned *nothing* from past experience, she almost shoved him back onto the porch. "If anything, I'm grateful to you for reminding me why we didn't last as a couple before. You always had a talent for getting things started, but you never were very good at carrying them through to any sort of decent conclusion.''

"What the devil do you mean by that?"

"Figure it out for yourself," she snapped, and without waiting for him to reply, slammed the door shut in his face and turned off the outside light.

So what if he fell down the steps and broke the other leg? It was no less than he deserved! Not that there was much chance that he would. The moon shone so brightly, it cast shadows over the lawn. If he hadn't rendered her half-blind with passion, she'd have seen the prowler approaching long before he'd had the chance to shine his flashlight through the window and catch her on the verge of making the second biggest mistake of her life.

Jake was right on that score: she *was* lucky they'd been interrupted, and in more ways than he could begin to imagine! Being around him made her reckless. She was far too inclined to let things slip—things she'd kept secret for years.

By fair means or foul, he managed to infiltrate her defenses. He brought the past alive again, as vividly as if it had taken place just yesterday. But worse—much worse!—he glossed over the bad parts and persuaded her to remember only the good. In short, he made her forget to be careful.

Seething at the realization, she turned away from the door, intending to go back to the living room to throw out the remains of their meal and anything else which migh remind her of him. But as she passed by, she happened to catch sight of herself in the hall mirror.

Appalled, she stared at the vacant-eyed creature confronting her; at her kiss-swollen mouth and the faint red traces of whisker burn along her jaw and down her throat. Her hair lay in wild disarray. The zipper of her robe had slipped down far enough to bare one shoulder and reveal the swell of her cleavage.

In short, she was shown exactly for what she was: weak, contemptible, stupid, and so mired in old misery that she hadn't a hope of outrunning the painful memories chasing her....

Things had started to unravel between her and Jake the September she left for her semester at the Sorbonne in Paris. He'd turned twenty the previous spring, and was half-way through the undergraduate degree required for admission to Naval Aviation Officer Training School. She'd been just eighteen, newly graduated from high school and still glowing from a summer spent with the man she adored with every particle of her being.

Saying goodbye to Jake hadn't been easy, but she'd accepted the opportunity to perfect her French while she pursued her interest in art, in the most romantic city in the world, as fair compensation for being so far away from him.

It wasn't as though they'd have spent much time together if she'd stayed home. The four hundred miles separating them ever since he'd gone off to university, two years earlier, meant they weren't able to see each other very often during the academic year. And although other long-distance relationships might falter, theirs had grown stronger. They had never been more deeply in love. So she'd gone off with an easy mind, sure nothing Europe had to offer could change that.

Nor had it. The changes had come from him—little

things at first, creeping in so subtly that she refused to acknowledge the intuitive dread slowly poisoning her mind.

If he sounded remote and strained over the phone, it was because she was half a world away. If he sometimes wasn't at his apartment when she called him, it was because of his heavy third-year course load and he was probably still at the campus library.

When he suggested cutting back their twice-weekly conversations and relying on email instead, she agreed it would be more convenient, because she didn't want to come across as possessive and insecure. After all, they trusted one another. Implicitly. Didn't they?

If he sometimes took days to acknowledge her messages and then sent only a few noncommittal lines in reply, it had to be because he didn't want anyone else accidentally coming across what he'd written. Either that, or he was preparing for midterm exams and was preoccupied. Understandable enough. Good grades were essential if he was to achieve his career ambitions.

So she continued making excuses and living in a make-believe world, until the day that reality caught up with her.

"The reason your cycle isn't normal has nothing to do with illness, my dear," the kindly French doctor told her when, alarmed by two consecutive months of spotty menstrual bleeding, she finally sought medical advice. "You're about ten weeks pregnant. It happens sometimes with a woman that there's a little show of blood at the time she'd normally have her period. It usually stops after the first trimester and becomes a matter for concern only if the flow increases significantly and is accompanied by cramping."

Her life was spiraling out of control, yet still she tried to delay coming to terms with it. She couldn't tell Jake about the baby. Not yet. It wouldn't have been fair to burden him with news like that by email or telephone. Very soon now, she'd be going home, and they'd be together again.

He'd promised he'd be waiting to meet her flight, that they'd spend the Thanksgiving holiday together, and she'd clung to that. The news could wait until then; until he was holding her in his arms again, and she could see for herself the passion in his eyes which he'd never been able to hide.

But he hadn't been there when she got home, and suddenly there was no longer any denying what her heart had been trying to tell her for weeks. Shattered, she'd confided in Penelope.

"Something's terribly wrong between me and Jake," she'd said, and poured out all her misgivings in the desperate hope that her best friend would laugh and tell her she was imagining things.

Penelope hadn't laughed. She'd looked deeply regretful and said, "Yes, something's wrong. Better brace yourself, Sally."

"Why? What is it?" Fear had clutched at her throat and made it near-impossible for her to breathe. "Is he ill?"

"Hardly! He's seeing someone else. A freshman coed."

It had been as if someone had struck a hammer blow to her heart. For a few seconds, she'd done more than stopped breathing; she'd stopped living. "Where did you hear such a thing?"

"From my cousin Thea. She lives in the same college dorm as his new girlfriend, and she told me when I went to visit her. As a matter of fact, I saw him while I was there, as well. We had lunch together."

"I don't believe it!" Sally had cried, all the while knowing at some deeper level that it was the truth. "I trust him. He'd never cheat on me."

"He's been cheating on you for weeks, Sal. Why else do you think he stopped phoning?"

"Trans-atlantic calls are expensive."

"Don't make me laugh! He could afford to call you three times a day, if he wanted to."

"The time difference makes them inconvenient. We decided we'd write to each other, instead."

"And how long did that last before he grew tired of it?"

She'd clamped a hand to her mouth, afraid she'd become physically ill as the suspicions she'd harbored crystallized into a mass of huge, unmanageable certainty. The tears had rolled down her face in rivers.

Oozing a convincing mixture of sympathy and outrage, Penelope had handed her a box of tissues. "He's such a jerk, Sally. You're well rid of him."

"No, I'm not!" she'd wept. "I love him! And I have to talk to him. There's something he needs to know."

Penelope had sighed. "Talking isn't going to do any good. He won't listen."

"He has to!" Despair getting the better of her, she'd spilled out the awful truth. "Penelope, I'm pregnant!"

"Oops!" Penelope's eyes had opened wide in mock horror. "Is he the father?"

If she hadn't been so devastated, she'd have slapped Penelope for asking such a question. "Of course he's the father!"

"Well, you can't blame me for wondering. You *have* just spent three months in Paris, after all—more than enough time to enjoy a little fling on the side with someone else."

"You know I'd never do that! Jake's the only man I've ever been with."

"Pity he wasn't smart enough to use a condom then, is all I can say."

"He did." She'd laid her hands lightly against her abdomen. "That's why I didn't suspect there'd be a baby in here."

"And you think saddling him with the news now will bring him back? Dream on, girlfriend! These days, men aren't shackled by such old-fashioned notions of honor.

He'll either deny any responsibility for the blessed event, or else cut you a check and tell you to get an abortion."

By then beside herself, she'd wailed, "You're wrong. He'd never leave me to deal with this alone."

"He'll wash his hands of you. Face it, Sally, he's moved on to someone else and you can't count on him for anything anymore." She'd slipped an arm around Sally's shoulders. "But you can count on me. I'll stand by you."

Inconsolable, she'd sobbed, "But I want Jake!"

"Well, he doesn't want you," Penelope told her briskly, "so you'd better learn to live with it."

She'd rather have died than accept such a painful truth, but fate wasn't done with her yet. That night, she started bleeding again, in earnest this time, and by morning she was doubled over with cramps. Heartbroken and ashamed, she'd turned again to Penelope because she couldn't tell her parents. She couldn't have borne their sorrowful disappointment.

Penelope drove her to a hospital in the next town, and waited while she underwent surgery to finish what nature hadn't managed to complete on its own. Penelope comforted her afterward and promised she'd never tell a soul. Penelope took care of everything.

But she couldn't mend a broken heart. Nor could she spare Sally the pain of seeing Jake over the Christmas holidays. She hadn't known he was home, and froze with shock when she bumped into him outside a downtown shop.

He looked wonderful. *Wonderful!* So tall and dark and handsome that she couldn't drag her gaze away. "Oh!" she said, the word puffing out of her mouth on a cloud of chilly condensation. "Oh, hi! What a surprise, running into you like this."

"Yes," he said, and might as well have been a total stranger, he spoke so coldly. "How was Paris?"

"Very French," she replied, somehow managing to smile, even though his attitude left her heart in shreds. "Very exciting. I learned a lot."

"I think we both did—a hell of a lot more than we bargained for."

How could he be so distant? So unmoved? As if she were just a girl he'd known in high school and whose name he barely remembered? "I'm not sure I know what that means," she said, her voice breaking despite herself.

At that, a shadow had crossed his face, and for one insane moment, she thought she'd managed to pierce his formidable reserve and find the boy she used to know.

Elated, she hung on the edge of hope, but too soon crashed down to earth again as the shop door to her left opened, and a petite brunette wearing a scarlet beret and cape came out.

"Sorry to keep you hanging around in the cold, sweetie," she chirped, dangling a beribboned box under Jake's nose, "but I want your gift to be a surprise." Then, noticing Sally, she smiled prettily and said, "Oh, hello! Am I interrupting something?"

"No," Jake said, making a big point of tucking her hand in the crook of his elbow.

Bright-eyed as a baby robin, she glanced from his face to Sally's. "But you know each other, yes?"

"Not anymore," Sally choked, and brushing roughly by them, hurried away.

Concerned by their daughter's despondency over what they believed to be nothing more than a bad case of first love gone wrong, her parents sent her to college in California in January, hoping year-round sunshine and a change of scene would revive her spirits.

She'd been glad to go; glad to get away from all the reminders of the things she'd lost. She'd mourned for a year—for the baby who'd never had a chance to live, and for being gullible enough to believe Jake had ever really cared for her.

Rather than risk running into him again, Sally came home seldom over the next three years, and then stayed only briefly. Penelope, meanwhile, flitted from one exclusive eastern college to another. Weakened by the miles separating them, their friendship dwindled and eventually died.

It didn't matter. New friends eventually replaced the old, and if she didn't entirely forget her previous life, Sally believed the scars had finally healed over. Until she was in the final year of her undergraduate degree, that was, and Margaret sent her a newspaper clipping announcing the marriage of Lieutenant Jake Harrington.

She realized then that she hadn't healed at all. The wound ripped open with a vengeance made all the more painful by the knowledge that his bride was none other than her erstwhile friend, Penelope Jessica Burton....

And now Penelope was dead.

Sally Winslow and Jake Harrington were both in the same town again.

She was as susceptible to him as ever.

And he was still as untrustworthy and heartless.

Impulsively, Sally raised her fist and smashed it against the mirror, wanting to break it and not caring if she cut her hand to ribbons in the process. Wanting only to get rid of the foolish twenty-six-year-old face staring back at her from haunted eyes.

But the mirror only swayed a little on the hook holding it in place. The thick beveled glass didn't crack. And the face reflected in it remained as it was before.

Some things never changed, no matter how much time went by or how much wisdom a person thought she'd acquired.

Disgusted with herself, she turned her gaze aside. What kind of warped individual was she, that she allowed him to

wield such power over her? What did she have to do to cut
the ancient ties which persisted in holding her to him?

As though it had been lying in wait for just such a moment to reassert itself, the familiar answer rang through her
mind, clear as a church bell tolling across the frozen coun-
tryside: *She had only one option. She had to run away
again because, as long as their paths continued to cross,
she'd never be free of him. He would continue to play
havoc with her emotions, her life, her peace of mind.*

The decision made, she ran to the bedroom and flung
open the closet and the dresser drawers, anxious not to
waste another precious moment. She could pack and be on
her way before he had time to realize she was gone.

She'd find another place to put down roots. One far
enough removed from his shadow that it couldn't reach out
to touch her, ever again.

The next morning, she received a subpoena to appear as
chief witness for the prosecution, in the case against Sidney
Albert Flanagan, charged with assault and battery. His trial
date had been set for the beginning of April. Six long weeks
away.

Escape wasn't going to be as quick and painless as she'd
thought, after all.

He knew she was hurt at the way he'd taken off and left
her hanging like that, as if he was glad he'd been given an
excuse to escape. But he'd been so bloody furious at what
he'd discovered when he went outside that he'd hardly been
able to contain himself, and telling her what he'd found
would have upset her more than his running out on her.

If he cared for her at all—and he knew now that his
feelings ran deeper than he'd ever realized, despite everything she'd done in the past—he had to stay away from her
until he'd taken care of a problem which he'd created but

which she was paying for. Because it was pretty clear that he was the reason she'd been targeted the night before.

The tire tracks skimming alongside his car had gouged deep furrows in the snow. Whoever had spied on them had been in one hell of a hurry to leave. Enough that they'd sideswiped his right front fender and left it flecked with scrapings of dark maroon paint.

Nor was that the only clue he'd come across. He'd told Sally the truth when he said he'd discovered footprints on her front lawn. What he didn't disclose was that only a woman with very expensive tastes would wear a winter boot so delicately fashioned and with such a narrow, pointed heel.

He hardly needed supernatural powers to figure that someone had recognized his Jaguar, and stopped to investigate the reason he'd left it parked in the shadow of the wall surrounding the Winslow estate. Or that the someone in question was a rotten driver and owned a dark maroon car. And he'd have had to be brain dead not to be able to put two and two together, and come up with four. Which was why, the next morning, he paid a call on his mother-in-law.

Colette was in the breakfast room when he arrived, shortly after half-past nine, and his most charitable thought when he saw her was that she looked like hell. Wearing a filmy, pale yellow negligee to match her complexion, she drooped over the black coffee poured by the faithful Morton as if she couldn't summon up the strength to lift the delicate china cup.

Jake knew a hangover when he saw one; he'd had plenty of practice with Penelope. Nor had he served six years' active duty in the military without recognizing panic when it was staring him in the face. As soon as she set eyes on him, Colette just about had a stroke!

He slid into the chair opposite hers and helped himself

to coffee. "Sorry to bother you so early, Colette, but I wanted to catch you before you went about your day."

"Why? What do you want?" she inquired faintly, peering at him from bloodshot eyes.

"Well, it's like this," he said, and pasted on his most soulful smile. "I'm planning to send most of the furniture in the house to auction or give it to charity, but if there are any pieces you'd like—"

Colette's eyes welled with tears. "Couldn't you wait a decent interval before you wipe every trace of my daughter from your life?"

"I don't need things to remind me, Colette," he said. "I have other, less tangible souvenirs. And since I plan to move soon—"

"You're selling the house Penelope loved so much?" Outrage left spots of color on Colette's otherwise sallow cheeks. "The house her father and I gave you as a wedding present?"

"It isn't mine to dispose of," he said, with what struck him as admirable restraint. Though a generous gift, the pretentious mansion two blocks away had always been a bone of contention between him and Penelope. He'd never felt at home there and was relieved to be free of it. "It's yours to do with as you see fit. I'm simply moving to something more suited to my needs."

"Whatever they might be!" she shot back nastily.

"Yes," he said. "Whatever they might be—which brings me to the reason I'm here now. My car's been involved in an accident."

"What's that got to do with me?"

"I wondered if you'd thought to check yours," he said, staring idly out at the snow-covered terrace. "I imagine it's a bit banged up, too."

"I haven't the foggiest idea what you're talking about,"

she said loftily. "The only place I went last night was to play bridge at the club."

He swung his gaze back to her and waited a moment to let her absorb what she'd let slip, then said, "Did I specifically mention last night, Colette?"

Her hand started to shake so badly, she had to replace her cup on its saucer. "What I meant is that last night was the *only* time I went out yesterday."

He forbore to add that he hadn't specifically mentioned "yesterday," either, and merely repeated, "To play bridge at the country club."

"I already told you that I did."

"From here," he said conversationally, "the only way to get to the club is to drive along The Crescent."

"Well, yes, Jake," she snapped, and directed an emphatic glance at the carriage clock on the mantel. "Is there a point to all this? I'm in rather a hurry."

To do what, he wondered uncharitably. Fall back into bed and try to sleep off the effects of last night? "Then I'll cut to the chase. I believe you when you say you spent the evening playing bridge at the club."

"Thank you, I'm sure!"

He fixed her in the sort of stare guaranteed to reduce a junior officer to babbling incoherence. "I also believe that, on the way home, you came across my car parked outside the gate to the Winslow property and decided it was your business to find out why. You saw lights in the guest cottage, came sneaking up to see what kind of mischief might be going on, discovered me with Sally, and elected to teach us both a lesson. So you went back to your car, shone a flashlight through the window to leave us in no doubt that we'd been caught misbehaving, and hoped it would be enough to scare her into shutting me out of her life for good."

"That's the most preposterously far-fetched idea I've

ever heard. If you're worried about what to do with your time now that you're no longer with the military, Jake, you should think about writing children's fairy tales.''

"If I've jumped to the wrong conclusions, there's an easy enough way to prove it.''

"And how's that?''

"Show me your car.''

"I will not!'' She tried, but her attempt to project righteous indignation fell badly short of the mark.

"You do realize there's nothing to stop me going to your garage and taking a look for myself?''

"I'll have you thrown off the property first!''

He sighed, his patience at an end. "I'm not enjoying this any more than you are, so allow me to speak plainly. I waited until I knew you'd be alone before I confronted you because I didn't think you'd want Fletcher knowing what you've been up to. But either we settle this now, or I go straight from here to his office—with a side-trip to the police first, to report a hit-and-run incident incurring several hundred dollars of damage to my very expensive automobile. I don't imagine they'll have any trouble tracking down the perpetrator. Yours, I believe, is the only maroon Lincoln Town Car in the area. It's your call, Colette.''

Her face crumpled and suddenly she looked seventy instead of only fifty-six. "It's your own fault!'' she said bitterly. "You and that bitch who killed my daughter deserve to be shown up for the liars and cheats that you are. So go ahead and report the damages to your precious car. Tell the police I'm the one who caused them. I don't care! I can afford the increased premium on my insurance. But one way or another I'll drive Sally Winslow out of this town, if it's the last thing I do.''

"If anyone should be driven out of town, it's you, for impersonating a pit viper! And not that I owe you any explanations, but I went to Sally's house uninvited. *I'm* the one who got carried away. If it were up to her, she'd be happy never to have to set eyes on me again.''

Colette let out a harsh, ugly laugh. ''Who do you think you're trying to fool? I saw her. She had her tongue half-way down your throat. Another five minutes, and I'd have been treated to the sight of her lying on the floor with her legs spread.''

''I had no idea you were capable of such vulgarity, Mother-in-law,'' he said, coldly furious. ''Did you perhaps learn it from your daughter? I understand she was pretty good at spreading her legs for any man who took her fancy.''

She reared up from her chair, her expression wild. ''You'll be sorry you ever said that, Jake Harrington,'' she shrieked, saliva spraying from her mouth. ''And if I ever hear of you repeating it to another living soul, Sally Winslow isn't the only one I'll run out of town. You'll never again be able to walk down the street again with your head held high, either!''

CHAPTER SEVEN

"PLEASE don't act hastily," Martha Winslow begged, when Sally told her mother about the incident with the intruder and said she was thinking of leaving town as soon as the trial was over. "We're your family and we've seen so little of you since you left university. You've no idea how thrilled your father and I are at the thought of you settling down here at last, and perhaps getting married and having babies who'll live close enough for us to watch them growing up. It means so much to us, Sally."

"I hardly think Margaret and Tom would agree with you. They find me an embarrassment."

Her mother made a face. "Tom's always been a little...conservative. He's more comfortable living by a strict set of rules. That's what makes him such an excellent school principal. But you're different. Margaret knows that and loves you for it. As Tom's wife, though, she's in a difficult position. Her first loyalty is to her husband, and rightly so. But don't assume for a moment that that means she isn't happy you've come home again."

Sally paced to the wide windows in her mother's garden room and looked down the hill to the crescent-shaped bay for which the town was named. At that time of year, with the late winter winds still howling, the surf-capped waves rolled and heaved with furious, restless energy but, under a summer sun, the water turned from glacial green to deep blue, and lapped ashore with leisurely, seductive indolence.

She loved the changing seasons; they were one of the things she'd missed most, living in the tropics. Coconut palms and coral lagoons had their place, but nothing quite compared to beach combing here, after a fierce Atlantic storm, or wading through milk-warm tidal pools in August, with wild blueberries hanging ripe on the bushes just beyond the dunes.

"It's not that I want to go," she said on a sigh, turning to face her mother again. "I really was eager to come home. I just hadn't expected I'd create such a stir practically from the day I set foot in town."

"You've been unlucky and perhaps a little unwise, but all that will blow over in time." Her mother shot her a telling glance. "Frankly I'm surprised you're giving in so easily. I thought you had more backbone than to let some anonymous prankster rob you of your dreams."

"There's more to it than that, Mom. It's Jake, as well."

Her mother leaned forward and stroked her cheek. "You think I don't know that, my darling? You and he share a lot of history and were very close at one time. It's natural that he tugs at your sympathy when he's coping with such grievous loss. He needs plenty of support—but I'm not sure he needs it from you. At least, not yet. Not until all the furore surrounding Penelope's death simmers down. Even then, there might not be any going back to what you once had together. You've changed, and so has he. But there's enough room for both of you in this town. Your life doesn't have to coincide with his."

Her mother wasn't telling her anything she hadn't already told herself. Constantly running away didn't resolve anything. Eventually a woman had to stop and confront her demons. Had to fight for the kind of life she wanted—and she'd wanted so badly to prove that the once-headstrong teenager, more concerned with Jake Harrington than any well-brought-up girl should be, had matured into a steady, responsible woman. She wanted to be accepted into that segment of society she'd once thumbed her nose at.

"I know you're right," she said. "About everything. I

would like to have children and a husband and, yes, a house with a picket fence and roses climbing up the wall. And if all that makes me a cliché, at least I've grown up enough to admit it. But for heaven's sake, Mom, I can't make a career out of snagging a man and dragging him to the altar. I have to have something else to strive for—something that will bring me satisfaction even if I never marry. The problem is, I don't have the first idea what it is I'm looking for."

"Maybe because you're trying too hard to find it. Sometimes the best ideas come when you least expect them."

"But I need something to occupy me until then."

Her mother smiled impishly. "The annual fund-raising gala's coming up at the end of June, and even though the planning committee's been working on it for months, we can still use all the extra help we can get. The whole affair's grown so much from what it used to be that you'll hardly recognize it. You *will* be attending this year, of course?"

"I don't think so, Mom. I don't have a date."

"You won't need one. You're going to show up wearing the most gorgeous dress this town's ever seen, and have every eligible man in the county flocking around you, begging for a dance. Not only that, Tom's brother, Francis, is joining our party, and I'm sure he'd be happy to stand in as your official escort for the evening." She caught Sally's hands and squeezed them pleadingly. "Don't disappoint me, Sally. You can spare me one evening, surely?"

Surprisingly, upon consideration, Sally found the whole idea quite appealing. It had been a while since she'd dressed to the nines and sipped champagne from wafer-thin crystal flutes. Life in the Caribbean had tended to be more casual; a sun dress, sandals, and piña coladas in a coconut shell were more the style.

"All right." She smiled at her mother, her mood lightening. Maybe she *had* been overreacting by allowing a silly, juvenile prank to derail her plans.

"Just as well," her mother admitted, on a sigh of relief. "I've already bought the tickets and reserved a table for six. Now, about helping out beforehand, we hold the event in the drill hall attached to the old naval training base, these days. The hall itself's not the most glamourous venue, but the gardens around it are lovely, and the officers' club is perfect for predinner drinks, or a quiet place to sit for those who want a break from dancing. Turning the main area into a fairyland is a major headache though. But you're so creative, you'd probably come up with a hundred ideas. If you're willing to volunteer your time and don't mind taking on a challenge, I can keep you busy twelve hours a day for the next month."

"I'll do my best not to let you down," Sally said, wrapping her mind around the idea and finding it, too, rather appealing. "If nothing else, at least no one could fault me for not putting my time to good use."

"On the contrary, the planning committee will welcome you."

"I don't know why."

"Because," her mother said, her eyes misting over suddenly, "regardless of what mistakes you might have made along the way, you're one of us. This is your home. You belong here, Sally."

After a while, Sally actually felt as if she did. Once they got past their initial reservations and realized she was in for the long haul, the other women on the planning committee were thrilled with her ideas for dressing up the stark, unlovely drill hall, and disguising its cold cement floor and bare walls. They approved her sketches, gave her a generous budget to work with, and free rein on how she spent it.

March roared in on an icy blast, but drifted away in a flurry of mild, sun-splashed days. The snow melted and the first crocuses poked their heads above the ground. The incident with the trespasser faded from Sally's memory, along with her bruises.

She appeared at Sid Flanagan's trial and not only managed to avoid Jake who, she'd learned, had also been subpoenaed, but also gave clear and convincing testimony which not only helped convict the accused, but also showed her to be a woman of courage not about to be intimidated by the aggressive cross examination of the defense lawyer.

Suddenly her days were full and rewarding. People smiled acknowledgment when they passed her in the street. A flattering commentary on her volunteer efforts received notice in the newspaper. If Jake himself made no attempt to contact her, other men, including Francis Bailey, Tom's surprisingly nice brother, did. She went out for dinner, to the theater, to house parties.

Then, just when she began to believe her mother had been right and there really was room in town for both of them, she literally ran into Jake one afternoon at a coffee parlor in the Old Mill Arcade, a one-time derelict cavern of a building on the north side of town, which had been turned into a trendy shopping mecca. Like her, he was loaded with purchases, neither was paying attention, and they collided with an almighty bump which sent half her shopping bags flying.

She could hardly pretend she hadn't seen him nor, after he'd recovered her packages and offered to buy her a coffee, could she come up with a plausible reason to refuse. She was too undone by the sight of him.

He wore black cords and a tan leather jacket, a cream shirt and black loafers. The lines around his eyes and mouth were less pronounced. He seemed younger, more rested. Never more attractive, and never more taboo. He threatened everything she'd worked so hard to achieve. He made a mockery of her hard-won independence of him.

When he pulled out a chair for her, she sank into it thankfully, before her legs gave way beneath her. "Espresso," she said, when he asked what she'd like. She needed a jolt of something strong to redeem her from the pitiful weakness attacking her.

"So," he said, frankly appraising her, once they were settled at a table, "you're looking better. No bruises."

"You, too," she replied. "No cane."

He laughed and she wished he hadn't. She didn't need him drawing her attention to his perfect, even teeth. She didn't need to be reminded how talented and versatile his mouth was.

"Not much of a limp left, either," he said. "I guess we're both as good as new, though you carry it off better than I do. You look wonderful in purple—like a crocus in bloom."

"Thank you." She played self-consciously with the single button on the jacket of her linen suit. His gaze followed the movement of her fingers, then traveled slowly up her neck to her face. She felt the color flow into her cheeks and knew he noticed.

Desperate to find some neutral topic, she dragged her avid gaze away from him and brought it to bear on his assorted bags and packages. "You've been shopping, I see."

"A few little extras to make my new place feel like home."

"You've moved?"

If he'd said he'd taken up residence on another planet, she couldn't have sounded more unhinged. Embarrassed, she took a mouthful of her scalding espresso. The pain as it burned its way down her throat made her wish she'd tasted it before she spoke. Maybe then she'd have kept her mouth shut altogether.

"Only to the other side of the hill," he said easily. "I was ready for a change, so I shopped around, found a house I liked, and took possession a couple of weeks back. How about you? Still staying at the guest cottage?"

"For now. I was called to testify against Sid Flanagan, but I dreaded it, and held off making any long-term plans until after the trial. The boy you drove home that night gave evidence, too, against the tavern owner."

"I know."

"You've kept in touch with him?"

"Yes."

How typical! He'd take up with perfect strangers, and ignore her. "Is he staying out of mischief?" she asked lightly.

"Yes. I gave him a job, and he's shaping up well." He paused, and for a second, she thought he was going to elaborate, but he turned the conversation back to the trial. "I'm glad they found enough evidence to put Flanagan away for a good, long time."

"Me, too."

He inspected her again, tilting his head to one side and squinting at her through the fringe of his long, dark eyelashes. "Guess you found it pretty hard, seeing him again?"

She averted her glance and pretended to worry a hangnail. "It was worth it."

"You should think about taking a couple of weeks' vacation, now it's over. Go someplace and soak up a little sun."

With you? she longed to ask, but clamped her mind shut on the unruly impulse and said only, "Even if I wanted to, I couldn't get away. I'm pretty busy with the fund-raising gala."

"So my mother tells me. From all accounts you've injected new life into a pretty tired old concept."

"I'm enjoying the challenge."

She dared to look at him again. The afternoon sun threw long shadows across the coffee parlor and bathed his face in a tawny glow. By what right had he cornered such a lion's share of masculine grace and beauty? she wondered resentfully. Once his period of mourning was over, he'd have every eligible woman under ninety chasing him around the block!

Refusing to give in to the senseless longing overtaking her, she asked, "How are *you* keeping busy when you're not fixing up your new house?"

"I'm taking over the reins of the family business."

The Harrington Corporation was one of the oldest and most prestigious in town, and Duncan Harrington, Jake's father, a force to be reckoned with in the business community. "Your father's retiring?" She shook her head in wonderment. "I can't imagine that."

"He'll stay on as board chairman, but he's kept pretty busy with his duties as mayor and needs someone else to take over the day-to-day running of the business."

"And you feel qualified to do that?"

The question emerged so loaded with venom that she cringed inside, but if he noticed, he gave no indication. He merely leaned back in his chair, hooked one arm over the back and said, "It'll be a learning curve, no doubt about that. But he's always there if I need advice. I'm planning to take the company in a new direction. We've talked things over and he likes my ideas. I'm pretty confident I can handle the job."

"You sound excited about it. I guess that means you've found the long-term challenge you were looking for."

"Yes," he said, and fixed her in another too-penetrating stare. "Have you found yours?"

"Not yet." She pushed aside her coffee cup and pointedly checked her watch. "My goodness, I had no idea it was so late. The arcade will be closing shortly."

"We've got a few more minutes before then."

"You might have, but I'm afraid I don't. I've got a lot of work ahead of me. Thank you for the coffee, and congratulations on your new career."

"I'll walk you to your car."

"No need," she said, collecting her shopping bags and doing her best not to allow the thought that, beside his certainty and sense of purpose, her recent accomplishments seemed little and trite. She *had* to get away from him, before she melted into a pool of unadulterated longing and despair.

He didn't bother to argue. Even less did he accept his dismissal. He simply commandeered half her stuff, gathered up his own, and waited for her to lead the way to her car.

The arcade itself was located in an area of abandoned warehouses. They loomed like dark skeletons all around the parking lot. Figures lurked in the shadows, young people with no apparent place to go, begging for money. It was a desolate scene as the day drew to a close, and Sally was rather glad not to be facing it alone.

They were at her car and she had unlocked the trunk when raised voices attracted their attention. Not far away, a girl, hugely pregnant and with tears running down her face, clung to the arm of a shifty-eyed boy.

"You've got to help me, Billy!" she cried thinly. "It's your kid, too."

"Yeah, *right!*" he sneered, shaking her off so roughly that she staggered. "Mine and who else's? Forget it, loser!"

The utter, wretched defeat on the girl's face and in her posture struck such a chord in Sally that she reacted without thought for the possible consequences to herself. Throwing her bags to the ground, she flew at the boy. "You rotten little creep!" she shrieked. "Don't you dare manhandle her!"

She'd have scratched his eyes out, if she'd had the chance. Yanked out his greasy hair by the roots, one miserable follicle at a time! But Jake's arms came from behind, bodily hauled her off her feet, and slammed her up against the solid wall of his chest with such force that the breath rushed from her lungs in a great *whoosh*.

The boy immediately darted to safety behind the nearest parked car. "Man, keep your rabid bitch on a leash," he yelled at Jake, interspersing every other word with his favorite four-letter obscenity. Then, his source of wisdom apparently exhausted, he took off. The last Sally saw of him, he was bobbing and weaving among the other shoppers returning to their vehicles, until he turned a corner and was lost to sight.

Furious, she thrashed to free herself from Jake's grasp and, in doing so, managed to land him a couple of well-placed elbow jabs to his ribs, which was no less than he deserved. "Why'd you do that?" she spat. "Why didn't you let me deal with him?"

"Because I'm not interested in testifying in another case of assault and battery," he said, calmly brushing himself off.

"He wouldn't have dared!"

"You don't know that. In fact, I begin to wonder if you know much of anything, Sally. Did it ever occur to you that that punk might have had a knife? That you could be lying in this back alley now, bleeding to death from a stab wound?"

"No, it didn't," she raged, "because it seemed to me there was someone else who needed protection more than I did. That poor child over there needed help."

"Which I was more than ready to offer—without starting a street brawl, I might add."

"So offer it now! Do something for her!"

His raised eyebrows spoke volumes of astonishment. "What do you suggest I do, Sally? She's safe enough, at least for now."

"And what about tomorrow, or the day after?"

"I'm afraid there's nothing I can do about that."

"Oh, how very convenient! You'll go out of your way to help a drunk find work, but you won't put yourself out for a girl in trouble. Why am I not surprised?"

"What would you have me do?" he said, almost as angry as she was. "Take her home with me? Adopt her?"

"She's alone and afraid! She needs an advocate."

"Unfortunately she's not alone. There are dozens like her. It's a major problem in this area. Ask my father, if you don't believe me. There's not a council meeting goes by that the subject doesn't come up of what to do about kids living on the street. But there are no quick-fix, easy solutions."

The girl had drawn a shabby sweater over her swollen belly and was pushing an old grocery buggy toward a warehouse close to the railroad tracks at the end of the alley.

"No quick-fix solution for babies having babies?" Sally said scornfully. "Well, there's one I can think of!"

Grabbing her purse, she raced after the girl. "Wait," she panted.

The girl turned, her eyes filled with suspicion, her expression so closed and wary that Sally's heart broke for her. Opening her wallet, she took out all the bills and loose change she had and stuffed them into the girl's hand.

"Take this," she said. "It's not much, but it'll help you buy a hot meal and find a motel room for the night."

When she returned to her car, Jake had picked up all her bags and belongings and stashed them in the trunk. "That was a kind and decent thing to do," he said, slamming down the lid, "but you do realize it's a bandage solution only, and won't fix the bigger problem?"

"Yes, Jake," she said, with heavy sarcasm. "I might be a fool, but that doesn't make me a congenital idiot."

"That's debatable." He opened her car door, helped her into the driver's seat then, before she had time to realize what he was up to, strode around to the passenger door and climbed in next to her.

"I don't recall offering you a ride home," she said.

"I don't recall asking for one."

"Then get out of my car."

"Not until you hear me out."

"I've heard enough already." She started the engine. "And I'm in a hurry."

He reached over and turned it off. "I'm not the one who got that girl pregnant," he said. "In fact, from where I stand, the only thing I did was keep you out of a hell of a lot more trouble than you could handle. That being so, would you mind telling me why it's my head you're ready to rip off? Are you perhaps taking out your frustration on me because your conscience is bothering you?"

"My conscience?" she echoed. "What's my conscience got to do with anything, unless it's the fact that, unlike that poor child out there, I've never known what it's like not to have a red cent to my name?"

"Precisely. You've always had money to buy your way out of any situation which didn't quite meet with your approval."

"And that's relevant now because?"

"Aren't you the one who claimed to want to defend the underdog? Well, here's your chance to put your money where your mouth is. If you really cared about that girl and others like her, you'd do something about it."

"Like what? Open a shelter for troubled teens?"

She tossed out the question with heavy sarcasm, yet even as she spoke, something clicked into place in her mind—as if, after stumbling around in the dark for years, she'd suddenly found a lamp and turned on the switch.

"It was just a thought." Jake shrugged dismissively. "Forget I mentioned it."

But though carelessly conceived, the idea had taken hold with such a wealth of logical certainty that she couldn't ignore it. "I don't want to forget it. You said yourself there are others like her out there, with no one to turn to and nowhere to go. Why not provide them with a safe haven? I *do* have the money. I could afford to take on such a project."

"Are you serious?"

"Yes," she said, marveling. "I absolutely am! Jake, I could make it work, I know I could. All I'd have to do is find suitable premises. Some big old house, with lots of rooms."

"Or a big old monastery that's been standing empty ever since the monks moved to their new digs across the bay."

"Are *you* serious?"

"You bet." His anger forgotten, he let his smile shine in the darkening afternoon like a lone ray of sunshine.

She knew the place he was referring to; a two-story stone building standing well back from the road about five miles east of town, on a slope above the river, with an apple orchard off to one side. "Is it for sale?"

"Has been for over a year, according to my father. It's too big for a private residence, and zoning laws won't allow it to be turned to commercial use."

"I'd need a permit—"

"You need to slow down and think about what's involved, before you go that far," he cautioned her. "You wouldn't just have pregnant girls on your doorstep. There'd be types like her charming boyfriend showing up, too."

"And I'd deal with them. I handled him, didn't I?"

"Yeah," he said, with a grin. "The whites of his eyes were showing and he looked about ready to wet himself!"

This time, she joined in his laughter. "I guess I did get a bit carried away."

"Then maybe you need to slow down and give all this more thought before you make any final decisions. It's easy to get swept up in the heat of the moment, and let's face it…if you do decide to run with the idea, you'd be taking on a huge commitment."

"I've never been afraid of commitment, Jake," she said, her enthusiasm suddenly eclipsed by futile regret.

The parking area was almost deserted by then. Being alone with him in a car, with dusk closing in all around, was altogether too intimate a setting. It stirred up memories best forgotten, of the times they'd driven to some out-of-the-way spot and made love in the back of the Jeep he used to drive. They'd never worried about being discovered. The windows had steamed up too quickly for anyone to see inside—and much the same thing was happening now, albeit for different reasons.

"What?" he said, watching her in the semigloom. "What took the light out of your eyes?"

"Old ghosts," she said, her gaze trapped in his. "And the cold. It's chilly in here now that the sun's gone down."

He leaned over and restarted the engine. "The last is easily rectified. Old ghosts, though…." He shook his head. "They're usually best left undisturbed. Let them go, and look to the future."

"How do I do that, Jake?"

"You chase them away," he said. "Like this."

She wasn't prepared for his kiss, or the surge of desire it inspired, which ran through her like a blowtorch. She wasn't prepared for the low moan of surrender which escaped her throat, or the way every inch of her skin came alive, with each pore opening to welcome him like buds unfurling beneath the seduction of the benevolent April sun.

Her only thought—and not a very coherent one at that—was that nothing would ever appease her hunger for him. Not time, and not another man. Regardless of what career path she might follow, or how rewarding she might find the journey, there would always be a part of her craving only him. The pain of the realization was so acute that she burst into tears.

"Stop hurting me!" she sobbed, tearing her mouth away.

He reared back, his eyes bleak with shock. "Hurt you? My God, Sally, I would never knowingly hurt you!"

Embarrassed by her outburst and the impossibility of trying to explain it, she fought to control it. "You do it all the time," she said, when she could speak again. "Whenever I see you, whenever you leave me, you steal a little bit more of my soul." Her voice sank to a whisper. She pressed a fist between her breasts. "I have to put an end to it. If I don't, I'll have nothing left in here. You'll eventually take all of me."

"And if I tell you I never want to leave you again?" His touch exquisitely tender, he framed her face in his hands and cradled her chin in the hollow formed by his palms. "What then, Sally? Would you let me stay?"

"No," she said, turning her head aside and refusing to allow temptation to get a foothold. "I wouldn't trust your reasons for being there. Apart from anything else, you aren't ready to make such a commitment. You've only been widowed a few months."

His sigh flowed over her, warm and coffee-scented. "Are we back to that again?"

"Yes," she said, staring determinedly through the windshield at the few cars remaining in the parking lot, because to look at him was to invite complete collapse of whatever moral scruples she still possessed. "I can't overlook it, even if you can."

"Would it make any difference if I told you that my marriage had been over for years? That the only reason it lasted as long as it did was the fact that I spent more time away than at home? That even absence had stopped making it bearable?" He cupped her jaw. "Look at me, and listen. If you believe nothing else, believe this—I was going to ask Penelope for a divorce as soon as I was discharged, and she'd have given me one."

"How can you be sure of that?"

"Because she was as miserable as I was." He laughed, a bitter, mocking sound bereft of amusement. "Do you think for a moment that I didn't suspect the kind of life she was leading when my back was turned? Why else do you think I harassed you about the night she died, if not to confirm what I've suspected for years?"

"Whatever Penelope's sins, she didn't deserve to die for them."

"I'm not suggesting she did. But in the end, she was the instrument of her own destruction, and I refuse to be governed by it any longer. It's time to move on, Sally."

He leaned toward her. Pulled her into the circle of his arms. Ran his hand inside the collar of her jacket. Stroked his fingers over her nape so artfully that a prickle of arousal chased down her spine.

"Do you remember how it used to be with us?" he murmured, nudging her mouth with his. "The way we'd never miss a chance to be alone together? How I used to make you laugh, and—?"

She snatched a breath from lungs rendered pitifully inadequate by his seduction. "You don't make me laugh anymore. You frighten me. What's made you so cold and merciless that you can dismiss a young woman's death so easily?"

"I revere life too much ever to dismiss it easily," he said. "That's one of the things war teaches a man. Nor do I hold Penelope solely to blame for the disintegration of our marriage. I was equally at fault."

"*You* cheated on *her?*"

"I didn't sleep with other women, if that's what you're asking. But if marrying her when I knew I didn't love her the way I should have is cheating, then yes. If infidelity of the mind amounts to the same thing as infidelity of the body, then yes again. I cheated on her."

"Why did you marry her, if you didn't love her?"

"Because I let pride come between me and the woman I really wanted. Because I never thought the day would come when I'd again get the chance for this."

His hand stole over her shoulder to the front of her jacket. Deliberately, he undid its solitary button and splayed his fingers over the silk shell she wore underneath.

"I can feel every beat of your heart keeping pace with mine, Sally. It's been so long since I did that."

She willed her breathing to remain even. Forced herself not to betray her body's screaming acknowledgment of his touch. But he mistook her silence for permission, and continued his voyage of rediscovery.

His hand slid lower, scorching over her breasts to her ribs, and past the flat contour of her stomach to the top of her thighs. His mouth scattered fleeting kisses along her jaw, nibbled a path from her ear to the base of her throat and from there, in one smooth sweep, to her nipple. She felt the heat and dampness of his mouth penetrate the thin fabric, and was helpless to prevent the puckering response of her flesh beneath.

"Stop!" she begged, knotting her fingers in his hair and wondering how the stern rebuttal she'd intended somehow emerged as a blessing.

"I will," he said. But he didn't. Instead his hand lingered

a moment at her knee, then trailed under the hem of her skirt and gently pried her legs apart.

Horrified by the abrupt flood of arousal dampening her underwear, she said with a lot more conviction, "Jake, I mean it! We can't do this!"

He leaned his head against the back of the seat, closed his eyes, and let out a mighty sigh. "I know, I know! You're afraid someone might see us. We're not teenagers anymore. You think it's too soon for me to be getting involved with you again. People will talk, and there's been enough speculation already." He expelled another long, frustrated breath. "You name it, I've thought about it. Why else do you think I've stayed away from you, except to spare you becoming the object of public censure and curiosity again? But, Sally, I've missed you. I ache to hold you again. Damn it, I want to let go of the past and start over. With you."

"I want that, too," she cried, the vehemence of his declarations spurring her to admit her true feelings, "but not sneakily, like this. Not fumbling around in some dark parking lot, as if the only thing that matters is sex when we both know there's so much more to a relationship. And not in plain view of the next person with a notion to spy through the window to see how much dirt they can dig up on us."

"You want me to date you? Come calling on a Saturday night, and take you to dinner and the theater? Broadcast to the whole world that we're a couple?" He flung out his hands, palms upturned. "I'm more than willing, if you are."

She shook her head, regret sweeping over her in long, cold waves. "No. Not yet. Not when I know it would create gossip. You might not understand this, but I like being regarded as a good woman, instead of a bad girl."

"Then what *do* you want me to do? Leave you alone for

another six months and pretend you don't exist? I've already tried that, sweetheart, and it doesn't work. Look what happened, the first time we found ourselves alone together.''

''There has to be another way, surely? Some middle ground?''

''A way for us to be together, without anyone being the wiser?'' He sat silently a moment, then slapped the flat of his hand to his forehead. ''There is! Of course there is! I have the perfect answer. Come to my new house.''

Be alone together, with no one and nothing to apply the brakes when passion threatened to run amok? ''Oh, I don't know about that! I can just imagine—''

''Think about it, before you reject the idea out of hand: no pressure, no demands, no conditions, just you and me getting to know one another all over again, at leisure and without any outside interference. Don't we deserve that much?''

Oh, the temptation he offered! But dare she agree? Dare she trust her heart, which heard only the promise in his voice, when her head was warning her that the chance of recapturing their enchanted past was slim at best, and not worth risking her future over?

''No one will ever know,'' he said. ''The house is hidden from the street. There's room for your car in my garage. It can be our secret hideaway, the place we escape to, to make the waiting more bearable.'' He reached for her hand and kissed each finger in potent persuasion. ''Come on, Sally. What do you say?''

CHAPTER EIGHT

SHE drove down the quiet lane just after eight the next night, and never would have suspected a house lay tucked behind the high hedge if he hadn't drawn her a map showing the unpaved driveway winding between a thick stand of maples.

"We'll have dinner," he'd said, "and talk. And if matters progress beyond that, it will be because you choose to let them."

Awash with hope and false confidence, she'd agreed. It had seemed, at the time, a reasonable enough suggestion. They were both mature adults, after all, and understood the principle of mind over matter. Only now, with the beam of her car headlights slicing across the front of a low-slung stone house set in a hollow above the cliffs, did the foolhardiness of the venture strike home.

But it was too late to change her mind. Even as she contemplated throwing the car into reverse gear and beating a fast retreat, the overhead door to the garage rolled up like a huge mouth waiting to swallow her. Caught between exhilaration and despair, she nosed her car into the empty space beside his.

No sooner had she killed the engine than the door rolled down again, and he stepped out of the shadows to welcome her. He squeezed her hands briefly, dropped a kiss on her cheek, and said, "Hi. I'm happy you're here."

Very nice. Very civilized. Very nonthreatening. So why were her legs trembling and her pulse leaping erratically?

"I didn't bring a housewarming gift," she babbled, desperate to fill the void following his remark. "I thought I'd wait to see what kind of decor you've chosen, first. There's nothing worse than having to pretend to like something you'd never have bought for yourself, is there—especially when it comes to knickknacks? They're a very individual, personal choice, don't you think? Some people can't get enough of them, and others can't abide them.''

"What I think," he said, drawing her gently through a side door into the house and guiding her down a narrow, softly lit hall, "is that you're afraid you've made a mistake in coming here, and are desperately trying to find an excuse not to stay.''

She attempted a laugh, but managed only a slightly hysterical giggle. "Is it that obvious?''

"Only to someone who knows you as well as I do." He stopped before an old-fashioned armoire and unwound the silk and Pashmina shawl from her shoulders. "You don't have to be afraid of me, Sally. I meant what I said yesterday. You set the pace of this, and every other meeting.''

All at once feeling foolish, she said, "Thank you for being so understanding.''

He hung her shawl in the armoire and led the way across a wider hall to a long living room with windows set on each side of a stone-fronted fireplace. The walls were painted white, and a faded, quite beautiful Turkish rug covered most of the dark oak floor.

Two plump armchairs and a three-seater sofa, upholstered in navy corduroy, curved around a glass-topped coffee table in front of the hearth. To one side was a wrought-iron wine rack, topped with a slab of dark green marble on which stood a pewter ice bucket and two tall champagne flutes. Above the mantel hung a painting in the Constable style, of grayhounds against a backdrop of dark, leafy trees. A large antique map in a carved frame graced the wall opposite.

He'd started a fire to banish the chill of the late April

evening. The flames leaped and crackled up the chimney and flung gaudy images over the polished brass andirons. The only other source of light came from several thick white pillar candles set in heavy brass holders placed strategically at various points around the room.

The total effect was so warmly inviting that Sally forgot to be nervous and exclaimed, "You put all this together by yourself?"

"Afraid so," he said, grasping the neck of the bottle chilling in the ice bucket.

"I think you've done a spectacular job!"

"I like it." He hoisted the bottle for her inspection. "Perrier Jouet okay?"

"Always!"

He poured the champagne, and lifted his glass in a toast. "Here's to old friends and new beginnings."

"Yes." She sipped from her glass, aware that although they both might pay lip service to the concept, the atmosphere hummed with a prophetic subtext far exceeding anything as straightforward as friendship. The evening had barely begun, and already she was floundering in the emotional undertow they were both working so hard to ignore.

Deeming it wise to maintain a little distance, she boycotted the chair he indicated and wandered about the room, stopping to admire a writing desk in one corner, and bending to inhale the delicate fragrance of a vase of scarlet and purple anemones on a side-table.

"I remembered they were your favorite flower," he said, watching her.

"Did you?" A wave of pleasure washed over her, sweeping her ever deeper into dangerous waters. "They're lovely, and so is your home."

"It's my kind of house. Unpretentious, solid and built to last."

"Is it very old?"

"About a hundred and fifty years. I'll give you the grand tour later, if you like."

"I'd like," she said, even though she knew it would be safer to decline. "I'd like it very much."

"Does that mean you're not sorry you didn't stand me up, after all?"

"Yes," she said, circling the room again. "I'm very glad I decided to come."

"Enough to relax and enjoy yourself?"

She glanced up sharply and found him leaning against the mantelpiece, his eyes unreadable. "I suppose so, but I wish you'd stop scrutinizing me like that."

"I can't help it. I find you very lovely."

"Actually, we look a bit like twins afraid of color," she said, drumming up a nervous smile at the coincidence of her having worn a long black skirt and ruffled white blouse to complement his black slacks and long-sleeved white shirt.

"I prefer to see us as an unfinished work of art," he replied, without a flicker of amusement. "The sketching's in place, but the harmony of color has yet to be decided. Are you hungry?"

The mere thought of forcing food down her throat almost made her gag. On the other hand, dining solely on champagne promised nothing but trouble she couldn't handle. "I am, rather."

"Good," he said. "So am I. But I'm not planning to eat you alive, Sally, so stop prowling like a caged animal, and come sit by the fire while I take care of a few things in the kitchen."

"May I help?"

He topped up her glass before heading for the door. "Not tonight. Next time, perhaps."

Would there be a next time? *Should* there be?

She was still debating the question fifteen minutes later, when he came back and announced dinner was ready.

"Good heavens!" She paused on the threshold, amazed at the sight before her. "What an unusual room!"

The dining area was circular, with a domed ceiling from which hung a delicate bronze chandelier. Floor to ceiling windows, topped by a painted frieze of exotic birds soaring against a pale blue sky, ran all around the room, except where built-in china cabinets flanked each side of the archway connecting it to the rest of the house.

Two chairs at a round table, centered on a fringed rug of the same shape, echoed the rotary theme. The only other items of furniture were another six chairs following the outer curvature of the floor, three to each side of a long, elegantly simple sideboard stationed on the far side of the room, parallel to the entrance. Candle flames flickered in here, too, but unlike those in the living room, were mirrored over and over in the night-dark glass of the uncurtained windows.

"An eccentric architectural feature," Jake remarked, ushering her forward. "One of many in this house."

"But charming, nonetheless. I love it!" She flung a wary glance at the windows. "At least, I think I do."

"If you're worried about anyone spying on us, don't be. There's nothing out there but ocean and sky. This part of the house sits at the edge of the cliffs. We won't be bothered by Peeping Toms tonight."

"That's a relief!" She took her seat, vividly aware of his presence as he pushed her chair a little closer to the table, then let his hand rest briefly on her shoulder before he assumed his own place across from her. "I'd hate to have an uninvited guest intrude and spoil yet another evening."

And nothing did. It was just the two of them engaged in conversation, with a Chopin nocturne playing softly in the background to absorb any awkward pauses which might arise. The combination of champagne and ambience worked a special magic, aided in no small part by the excellence of the meal. Vichyssoise, followed by lobster Mornay and baby asparagus, was no mean feat for anyone, least of all a man who claimed he knew next to nothing about cooking.

"I ordered it from a restaurant," he confessed, waving aside her compliments. "All I had to do was remember to turn on the oven. Steak on the barbecue is my only forte in the culinary department."

The pièce de résistance, though, and the one thing which reduced her to putty in his hands, was his choice of dessert. Layers of tangy orange mousse and whipped cream sandwiched between feather-light slices of sponge cake and decorated with curls of white chocolate, it had been the specialty of a little French bakery in the Square. They'd discovered it when they first started dating and it had come to symbolize everything that was good about their relationship.

"You remembered this, too," she marveled, overwhelmed.

"I remember everything about that time, Sally."

She sighed. "So do I. We celebrated every special occasion with this cake—our one month anniversary, our first Christmas together, Valentine's Day, our birthdays…" Thoroughly bedazzled, she ventured a glance at him.

"The first time we made love," he said, his blue eyes holding her prisoner. "And the last."

He spoke with such a world of regret that when she replied, her voice was embroidered with tears. "Please don't," she begged. "You said yourself, there's nothing to be gained by raking up old ghosts."

He shrugged assent. "All right. Let's talk about something else. What really triggered your response to that girl, yesterday afternoon, Sally? The fact that she was pregnant?''

''No. The fact that she was just a child and had no one to turn to.''

''If you follow through on your idea to open a shelter, it'll make a huge difference to others like her.''

''But it'll come too late to help her. Her baby must be due any day now, which means there'll be yet another homeless child out there.''

''Is that the only thing that's troubling you?''

''No,'' she said, her spirits dampened by painful memories of herself feeling every bit as afraid and alone, when she'd been of a similar age, and in a similar situation, to that girl.

''But you can't tell me what it is?''

''No. You wouldn't understand.''

''Try me,'' he said. ''You might find you've underestimated me.''

Was that possible? *Could* she learn to trust him enough to share the secret of her pregnancy with him?

''Perhaps, some day,'' she said. ''But not tonight.''

''All right.'' He didn't press the point. Instead, when they'd finished eating, he pushed back his chair and held out his hand. ''Come. We'll have coffee in the other room.''

''Let me help you clear away these dishes first.''

''You just want to check out the kitchen, to see what kind of a slob I really am,'' he teased.

Relieved at the lessening of tension, she laughed and said, ''How'd you guess?''

''You keep forgetting how well I know you.''

If anyone *had* been watching them through the window, they'd have appeared to be a couple enjoying good food, fine wine, and the simple pleasure of each other's company. But it was all an illusion. They might be interacting like

rational adults on the surface, but undercurrents of awareness swirled between them at a deeper level.

They were alone in a cosy, isolated house which carried
no bad associations for either of them; a private secluded
world all their own. And every accidental touch—fingers
touching fingers, as they collected the dishes, shoulder
brushing against shoulder, as they passed each other in the
kitchen—reinforced the fact.

The message, potent as forked lightning leaping from one
sensory point to another, was undeniable. And sooner or
later, she knew they'd have to acknowledge it. Not surprisingly, it caught up with them when, after they'd had
coffee, he took her on the promised tour of the rest of the
house.

Most areas presented no problem. When he showed her
the little atrium off the back of the house, her pleasure was
unfeigned. She sincerely admired the double-pedestal desk
in his office. "Very handsome," she remarked, tracing a
fingertip over its finely tooled, leather-inlaid top. "Do you
plan to do much work from home?"

"Why not? I'm away all day, but I don't have much of
a social life right now, so I'm here most evenings, and
there's still plenty to do with the company reorganization."

She looked at the rolls of blueprints stacked in an old
umbrella stand. "You never did explain what that involved.
Are you expanding the downtown premises?"

"What, and have the entire population of Eastridge Bay
coming down on me for tampering with a heritage building? Not likely!" He cupped her elbow and directed her
across the hall. "You're not far off the mark, though. I'm
planning to revitalize the north end of town. To my mind,
it's as much a part of local history as the Harrington
Building or the Burton Tower."

They were headed for the stairs. Trying hard not to hyperventilate at where they led, she said, "You mean the area we were in yesterday?"

"The very same. Ever since the fish packing company closed down, most of the buildings have fallen into disrepair, which is a shame. Now it's a shanty town for people like that girl we met."

"And you'd like to turn it into a money-maker again."

He threw open the door of the first room off the upper hall, and said reprovingly, "You make 'money' sound like a dirty word, Sally. It doesn't have to be, you know. It can do a lot of good when it's applied to a just cause."

"You call turning people out of the only home they know 'a just cause'?" she retaliated, less because she wanted to argue the point at that moment, than to distract herself from the sight of the big sleigh bed, with all its attendant connotations of intimacy.

"Never mind trying to pick a fight with me," he said, standing back to let her precede him into the room. "Think instead about us making love in here, when you're ready. When you trust me enough to share all of yourself with me."

She'd have told him that trust cut two ways and that once it was broken, it wasn't always possible to repair it. But her train of thought, already sadly impaired, collapsed altogether when she saw the photograph hanging on the wall above the bed.

It was a head shot of herself, taken during their last summer together. She was looking straight into the camera, her eyes wide and candid, her mouth tilted in a half smile.

"Yes," Jake said in a low, smoky voice, from his post at the door. "That's you—back in the days of your innocence."

"I wasn't so innocent," she said shakily. "We'd been lovers for over a year."

"And would be still, if we hadn't let other people come

between us.'' He came up behind and took her by the shoulders. ''How did that happen, Sally?'' he asked, planting a soft, spellbinding kiss on the side of her neck.

Hazy with encroaching pleasure and knowing she was fast losing her grip, she forced herself to say, ''You grew tired of dating a teenager and went looking for someone more sophisticated.''

She heard the hiss of his sharply indrawn breath, felt his grip tighten ominously, and found herself being spun around to face him. ''I did *what?*''

He wore such a look of wounded bewilderment that she almost let it deflect her from the truth. Almost! ''You took up with someone else,'' she said firmly.

''Not so!'' He shook his head, as if to clear away the confusing mists distorting his memory. ''*You're* the one who turned to someone else—the guy in Paris...your French roommate's older brother who appeared late on the scene to show you around the city and introduce you to its night life.''

''Night life—with *Emile?*'' She burst out laughing. ''Whatever gave you the idea there was anything romantic between me and Emile? He was a Roman Catholic priest, for heaven's sake, whose only passions were his religious calling and seventeenth-century French painters! Yes, he showed me around—the different museums. And yes, he introduced me to Nicolas Poussin—who, in case you're wondering, died in 1682!''

The thunderous silence with which Jake greeted that revelation defined his shock louder than a drumroll. He reeled away, paced to the window, braced his hands on either side of the frame, and stared out at the night, his spine rigid as iron.

When he finally whirled back to face her, she quaked inside. His face was white, his eyes dark as midnight, his mouth so compressed that if she hadn't known differently, she'd have thought it incapable of laughter or a smile. "A *priest?*" he repeated, his voice chillingly quiet. "I guess that's something Penelope forgot to mention when she regaled me with your doings."

There was no need to ask what he meant by that. Sally understood immediately, though she wouldn't have, eight years ago. Back then, she'd still thought Penelope was her friend.

His contained embitterment suddenly exploding into wild fury, Jake grabbed a book on the bedside table and flung it across the room. "That witch!" he ground out savagely. "I'd kill her with my bare hands, if she weren't already dead!"

"She's not the one who was to blame," Sally said, the enormity of Penelope's machinations seeming not nearly as reprehensible as their own stupidity. "We are. If we'd trusted each other—"

"Don't you dare make excuses for her!" he bellowed. "Don't you *dare* try to shift the blame to us!"

"Why not? If we'd believed in one another—"

"We were kids, for Pete's sake! Look at that picture hanging over the bed, if you don't believe me. You were the only girl I'd ever been with. I was your first...." He slammed his fist against the wall in impotent rage. "What the hell did we know about anything?"

"Not enough, obviously. If we had, we'd have reacted differently. But we can't go back and change any of it, so we might as well forget it."

"I don't think so, Sally! Not in this instance. Just because something's painful to remember doesn't justify denying it ever happened. You don't learn anything by doing that. You merely leave yourself open to being hurt again in the same way."

"I don't think I could ever be hurt like that again." For all her brave words, her voice broke when she continued,

"When we ran into each other, the Christmas after I came home from France, you were so cold. And that girl you were with…the way you looked at me, the way you flaunted her in my face…you behaved as if you hated me, Jake."

"I certainly tried hard enough to do just that." In three swift strides, he crossed to where she leaned against the bedpost and pulled her so hard against him that the breath flew out of her lungs. "But it didn't work. What you saw wasn't hatred, my lovely, it was anger and hurt pride. And the girl…" He kissed the top of her head, wound his arms around her tighter than ever. "She was just that—a girl, looking for a good time."

"She was so pretty, so animated. I felt nondescript beside her. Pale and uninteresting."

"Oh, honey, never compare yourself unfavorably to her or any other woman! She was fun, but neither of us was ever serious about the other. She was a diversion. A way to help me get over you."

"Were you lovers?" she asked, her throat constricting as she remembered the way the girl had looked at him; the way she herself once had looked at him. With private, intimate knowledge.

He pressed her face to his chest. "What does it matter, after all this time?"

"*Were* you?" she persisted, needing to know.

"Yes," he admitted on a sigh. "For a short while. Until the night I called her Sally, by mistake. Then it was over, for both of us." He held her at arm's length and looked at her searchingly. "I don't have the right to ask you this, but have there been other men for you?"

"No," she said, a tear slipping down her face. "I've wanted there to be. I've tried to make it happen—but at the last moment, I couldn't go through with it. You spoilt me for anyone else."

"Let me make it up to you now," he whispered hoarsely, drawing her down beside him on the bed and stringing a row of kisses across her eyelids and down her cheek to her mouth. "We've wasted so much time, my lovely Sally. Let's not waste any more."

He sounded so sure; so certain they could recapture all that they'd lost, and she wanted desperately to believe him. But there was more to their history than he knew.

How could she, in good conscience, exact information from him, yet keep secret the fact that she'd been pregnant? It had been his baby, too. And although she'd once thought he didn't deserve to be told, she now believed otherwise. He had a right to know the truth.

He might not take the news well. He might become angry and not want her anymore. But if that was so, better to find out before he broke her heart all over again, because such secrets almost always found a way to leak out, sooner or later.

"I don't think we should get carried away like this," she began. "I think we need to talk more. So much has happened—"

"Talk can wait," he muttered, rolling her onto her back and gazing down at her as if he'd never grow tired of the sight of her. "There's only one way to erase all those lost years, and that's for us to become one again. I want to feel you naked beneath me, Sally. I want to look at you—at all of you. I want to fall asleep with you in my arms and wake up beside you in the morning. And most of all, I want to lose myself inside you, again and again, because that's the only way I'll ever be able to forget what a damned fool I've been."

His words, his kisses, drained her of caution—and most important, of the will to resist him. She was putty in his hands. His to do with as he pleased. Whatever he asked of her, she would give.

Ask? That was a laugh! She was his willing slave. He didn't have to ask for a thing. She was his for the taking. She always had been.

Dimly, she was aware of him removing her blouse, her camisole, her bra. His lips blazed a trail over her skin and left behind a galaxy of sensation as dense as a shower of winter-spiked stars.

He touched her in the old familiar way. Rediscovered her with deft, tormenting brushes of his fingers and mouth until the sharp edge of desire sliced at her without mercy, and her flesh screamed for release. Heat, fluid and tempestuous, seared her.

Still, she could not silence the prompting of her conscience, and so she tried again to unburden herself. "You might not want me, if you knew—"

He took her hand and stroked it down his torso until she found that part of him grown so heavy with arousal that not even the barrier of his clothing could hide it. "You think I don't want you, my Sally?" he groaned, his eyes twin flames of blue fire as her hand closed around him instinctively, possessively. "Think again!"

"You don't fight fair," she whispered on a dying sigh, loving the burning strength of him against her palm.

"I fight to win," he replied. "I fight for what I believe in, and I believe in us."

"So did I, once upon a time, but something went wrong, Jake…!"

"Because we made mistakes," he said, "But now we'll make it right again."

She was in thrall to him, so drugged with mindless pleasure, that she was barely aware he'd almost stripped her naked until he slipped his thumb inside her panties and stroked it over the moist, satin fold between her legs. At that, she turned into a tigress, clawing at his shirt, wild to reacquaint herself with the smooth texture of his skin, and the long, strong muscles which had so captivated her before.

He uttered a low growl of triumph. With haphazard disregard, his fine cotton shirt landed on the floor next to her black crepe skirt. Her panties floated through the air, a silken, insubstantial parachute, and came to rest sprawled brazenly atop his briefs.

Then, it was as he'd said it had to be, with the two of them locked in a tight, urgent welding of flesh within flesh, and the race began. She clung to him, willing time to fly backward and let it be as if nothing and no one had never come between them. She gave herself up to the deep, desperate rhythm he imposed. Felt herself teeter achingly close to the brink of total surrender.

"Stay with me, sweetheart," he muttered tensely, his breathing deep and desperate as he battled to resist the completion threatening to overpower him.

She tried. But at the last, she could not. She was too oppressed with guilt. The best she could do was hold him close and mourn a little as he was swept to a place where she could not follow. And she realized that it wasn't the same between them and never would be again.

The tapestry of emotion was more richly textured, the design more intricate. Not a boy-and-girl thing at all, but a man-woman relationship with all the depth and complexity that implied.

They could never go back to the safe, idealistic state they'd known as teenagers. Too much had happened in the interim. Their only choice was to advance into the uncharted territory of an adult relationship, and hope they could evade the pitfalls littering their path.

Eventually, his breathing slowed and he lifted his head to look down at her. "You didn't come," he said, stroking the hair away from her face. "Have I lost my touch, sweet Sally?"

"No," she said miserably. "It was my fault. I was too tense…too preoccupied." Sorely troubled that they could have loved so deeply and still lost so much, she touched his cheek. "Oh, Jake, something happened that last summer we spent together…something I should have told you about at the time and didn't. I thought I could forget it, that it was in the past, but now that we've found each other again, it's preying on my mind. But I'm afraid to tell you in case it spoils…"

He kissed the tears pooling at the corners of her eyes. "Don't be afraid," he said. "There's nothing you can't tell me."

"Oh, but there is." Her voice sank to a whisper, and she clung to him. If she found the courage to confess, and he couldn't forgive her, this would be the last time she'd ever lie in his arms. Wouldn't she be better off learning to live with the burden of silence? Or would it taint this second chance to recapture heaven?

He tipped her face up to his and when she tried to turn away, held her chin between his thumb and forefinger so that she had no choice but to meet his gaze. How uncompromisingly direct his eyes were.

"Look at me, Sally, and stop putting yourself through all this unnecessary grief," he said sternly. "If it's the baby you're worrying about, there's nothing to tell. I already know. I've known about it for years."

CHAPTER NINE

THERE'D never been a more beautiful spring morning. Sunlight splashed on the polished wood floor of his kitchen, the coffeemaker burbled in harmony with the birds perched on the feeder outside the window, and Jake, wearing only blue jeans unsnapped at the waist, mixed champagne and orange juice for mimosas.

"We could make a habit of this," he said, dropping a kiss on the back of her neck. "You could move in and the three of us could live happily ever after."

"The three of us?"

"You, me and this." He tasted the Hollandaise sauce she was preparing for their eggs Benedict and smacked his lips appreciatively. "Don't worry, I was careful last night and used protection. You're not pregnant."

"We were careful before, and I got pregnant anyway."

"Accidents happen sometimes." He stroked her hair. "No point now in beating ourselves up about it."

"I was so afraid you'd be angry when you heard."

"I was, at the time," he said, a shade too grimly for her peace of mind. "Livid, in fact. But I got over it. You were young and afraid."

"How did you find out?"

"I'll give you three guesses, and the first two don't count."

"Penelope, of course." She rolled her eyes. "Why did I even bother to ask?"

"If she'd said something at the time, instead of waiting until after the fact, I've have been there for you. You wouldn't have gone through all that alone. But she didn't,

133

and neither did you, and I see no purpose in belaboring the issue at this late date.''

Again, the hint of something hard and cold in his voice, as difficult to pinpoint as a grain of sand trapped in molasses, cast a shadow over the bright morning. ''But it was our baby, Jake,'' she said softly. ''A little person created purely from love, the way all babies should be made, and I wish so much things could have turned out differently. Perhaps if I'd come to you—''

''But you didn't.'' Abruptly, he swung away and made a big production of checking the sliced ham and English muffins warming in the oven. ''Let it go, Sally. I have.''

''Are you sure? You don't sound like a man—''

''At the risk of repeating myself *ad nauseam,* we can't undo the past,'' he said curtly. ''The best we can do is make damn good and sure we handle things differently in the future, if we ever find ourselves in the same situation again. How are those eggs coming along?''

She didn't want to cloud the morning further by pointing out that, because the pregnancy had been doomed from the start, they couldn't have done things any differently the first time around, either. He was right. She had to move on— and she could, now that her conscience was clear and there were no more secrets between her and Jake. ''They're done,'' she said, drumming up a smile.

To her relief, he responded in kind. ''Then let's eat! A man needs to build up his strength after the kind of workout you gave me last night. By the way, did I mention how fetching you look this morning, Miss Sally?''

''Oh, I don't think so!''

Her hair was still damp from the shower, she was barefoot, and she wore one of his shirts. Hardly the most romantic way to greet the day, or face your lover across the breakfast table. Suddenly self-conscious, she pushed back the sleeves which, although she'd rolled them back, kept slipping down her arms. She wished she'd thought to put on her panties.

"You're blushing," Jake said wickedly. "You really shouldn't stand in the sun like that, my lovely. Everything you're trying so hard to hide is illuminated in perfect detail under that shirt, and it's driving me wild. Maybe we should forget breakfast and move this discussion back to the bedroom."

"After I've slaved over a hot stove to make you breakfast? Not a chance!" She spooned Hollandaise sauce over their eggs and passed the plates to him. "Here, make yourself useful."

He carried their meal to the breakfast nook, took a seat across from her, and clinked the rim of his mimosa glass against hers. "Thank you for last night, Sally. It meant a lot that you stayed."

"To me, too, though I don't know how I'll ever be able to look your mother-in-law in the face again."

It was entirely the wrong thing for her to say. As quickly as his voice had overflowed with warmth and tenderness, it turned cold again. "My mother-in-law doesn't enter into it. She has no bearing on us, and particularly not on you or your doings."

"That's not quite true. She's on the gala committee, and I can't avoid her. We've seen quite a bit of each other in recent weeks."

"I hadn't realized," he said, his surprise evident. "Is she giving you a rough time?"

"Not really. She's softened up quite a bit, probably because I follow orders without argument, generally make myself useful, and otherwise stay out of her way."

"That's Colette, all right. Happiest when she's dishing out commands and having everyone else jump to do her bidding."

"Well, you have to hand it to her, Jake. Whatever other

shortcomings she might have, she's good at organizing people—and keeping busy probably helps her cope with her grief.''

"I guess it beats her other pastime," he said cryptically, "but what's she going to do once this shindig's over?"

"I doubt she's thought of that. I guess, like the rest of us, she's taking things a day at a time. Will you be attending?"

"The gala?" He inspected his mimosa thoughtfully. "I hadn't planned to, but I will if you're going to be there."

"Even though we can't be seen together."

"You mean, we have to pretend we're not on speaking terms?"

She laughed, but it was an effort, because he clearly didn't find anything amusing about the prospect. "We don't have to go quite that far. We can be civil to one another but, for appearances' sake, Tom's brother, Francis, will be my official escort."

His mouth tightened ominously. "And you expect me to meekly go along with that? Fat chance!"

"You have to! It's just to spare both of us unnecessary criticism and gossip. After all, it was only a few months ago—"

"That I buried my wife. I know, and I'm growing tired of hearing about it. I'm sorry Penelope's dead—don't get me wrong about that—but I'm not sorry to be rid of her, and frankly, this whole mourning farce is wearing thin."

"But society expects it."

"Which society?" he exploded, flinging down his knife and fork, and shoving aside his half-finished meal. "Not the one I spent most of the last year in! The people there didn't have the luxury of observing polite niceties, and if I learned anything from them, it's this: life's too precious to be put on hold, and a damn sight too short to be wasted."

''We're not talking about forever, Jake,'' she said, striving to combat his anger with sweet reason.

''Then for how long? Six months? A year?''

''Somewhere between the two, yes.''

''And that's okay with you?'' He glowered. ''You might be prepared to skulk around that long, but I'm not. I'd rather be up-front about who I'm seeing, and take the flak that comes with it.''

''I'm not sure I would,'' she said, a shade wistfully. ''I rather like being accepted. It makes a nice change from being regarded as the town pariah.''

''What's it going to take for you to feel you've finally made the grade, Sally? Walking through the streets in sackcloth and ashes, and apologizing for being a normal woman with normal needs?''

''It beats proving I'm no better now than I was when I went slinking around, afraid people might learn I disgraced my family by being single and pregnant.''

''You're not the only one who paid dearly for that. A woman's lucky in some respects, if you ask me. There's no way a man's going to show up on her doorstep just when she's got her life back on track, and say, 'Hey, you had a baby no one ever told you about! How about that?' ''

''That's a rotten thing to say, and you know it!''

''What I know,'' he said bitterly, ''is that if kow-towing to outside opinion now matters more to you than I do, I have to question how much you really care about our being together again.''

''I didn't say I didn't care, so please don't twist my words! Do you think I'd have stayed here last night, or that I'd have made love with you, if I didn't cherish every single thing about us?''

''Don't ask me! I'm beginning to think I don't know the person you've become. You never used to be so hell-bent on pleasing everyone else.''

"Just because I choose not to fly in the face of convention all the time doesn't mean I'm not the same person inside. I've learned to choose my battles more wisely, is all."

"You've let this town's tight-ass upper-crust matrons subdue your zest for life."

"Or perhaps I've grown up." Disheartened by yet more evidence of this darker side of him, she tried to bridge the chasm threatening to separate them by reaching for his hand across the table. "Six weeks ago, I never thought I'd wake up to find your leg thrown over my hip and your arm anchoring me next to you in that big bed upstairs. I never thought I could fall into a sleep so sweet that if the future hadn't suddenly turned gloriously full of hope and promise, I'd have been happy never to wake up at all. Does that sound to you like a woman who's lost her zest for living?"

"Not as long as she can keep it a dark, dirty secret."

"Oh, Jake!" She sighed, at a loss. "Look, I understand your frustration at having to wait a decent interval before you can resume a 'normal' life. But the Burtons have lost their only child and regardless of whether or not Penelope brought her death on herself, for us to flaunt our affair openly when they're still in mourning goes beyond adding insult to injury."

"Is that what you call it—an *affair?* Gee, and to think I saw it as a time for responsible, unselfish lovemaking—a time for discovery, for unspoken commitment. Clearly I was wrong."

"That's emotional blackmail," she retorted, shaken, "and I refuse to be a party to it."

"And if I refuse to be a party to deceit?"

"Then I guess we've arrived at a stalemate," she said, her voice wobbling with distress.

"Finally we agree on something!"

Hollandaise sauce didn't sit well on a queasy stomach.

Swallowing, she pushed her chair away from the table. "I think this was a mistake, after all."

"This?" he said, his voice larded with scorn. "Are we talking about this morning's eggs, Sally, or last night's sex?"

Refusing to give in to the misery threatening to undo her, she said with superb composure, "I'm not the only one who's changed, Jake. You're different, too. I fell in love with a man who was both compassionate and even-tempered, neither of which quality you appear to possess."

"I'm sorry I've disappointed you," he said, sounding anything but. "Clearly pretense sits more easily with you than it does with me."

"It isn't a matter of pretense—!"

He dismissed her objection with a shrug. "It doesn't matter what name you put on it, it still comes down to the same thing for me. Putting on an act in public and pretending we're merely acquaintances is dishonest, whichever way you cut it."

"That's not what you said yesterday. Yesterday, you were all in favor of keeping our liaison under wraps."

"Call it the desperate act of a man who mistakenly thought he had nothing to lose when, in fact, he had nothing to gain but a load of aggravation he doesn't need." He raked a tired hand through his hair. "Sorry, Sally, but I've been living a lie for the last four years, and that's long enough for any man. I can't do it anymore. I won't."

"Then I guess there's nothing more to be said."

"Not a damned thing," he replied, with stunningly hurtful indifference. "If you want to wait until dark before you leave, rather than risk being seen in broad daylight, be my guest, but you'll excuse me, I'm sure, if I don't offer to keep you company?"

"I wouldn't dream of asking you to," she said. "I'll go

now, and be happy to do so. There's too much risk in my staying here.''

That afternoon, rain swept in from the sea and persisted for a week, beating down with such ferocity that the newly opened daffodils, too defeated to put up a fight, lay with their faces battered into the dirt. Much, Sally reflected, as she wished she could do, every time she allowed herself to think of how easily she'd fallen into bed with Jake and how quickly she'd come to regret it.

Another woman might have taken comfort in the knowledge that, for a few, brief hours, she'd known the wonder of connecting with him again, on every level. After that first, tension-fraught exchange, her inhibitions had fled and she'd responded to him with her old abandon.

There'd been no secrets between them; no issues still unresolved. So much of him had been as she remembered—loving, passionate, strong—that it had been easy to convince herself to ignore the other aspects of his personality which weren't the same.

Some of the time, they'd lain together, touching each other in the old, endearing way. She'd run her hand over the long, lean line of his flank. Kissed the scar disfiguring his thigh. Wept a little for the pain he'd endured. Quaked at the danger to which he'd been exposed, and admired the courage which had driven him to ignore his wound and concentrate only on piloting his damaged aircraft back to its home base.

They'd talked idly, trying to bridge the gap of the years they'd been apart.

''How did Penelope feel about your having kept that photo of me?'' she'd asked him, lying with her head on his chest and his arm around her.

''She didn't know,'' he'd said, walking his fingers down her spine with such exquisite finesse that she'd shivered with delight. "I'd forgotten I still had it. I found it when I started packing up my things to move out of the old house. It was stuffed inside a copy of an old high school year book. You wore your hair longer then. When did you cut it short?"

"When I went to California. I wanted to make a fresh start, with nothing to remind me of what I'd left behind."

He'd wound a strand around his finger. Tugged on it gently. "Did you forget me?"

She rolled onto her back. Feasted on the sensual pleasure of the way their bodies brushed teasingly against one another. "I tried to, but you're not easy to forget."

"Nor you."

And sweetly, trustingly, they'd made love again.

But it had all been a dream; a mirage which had disintegrated in the fresh, clear light of morning. Too soon she'd become vitally aware that she and Jake had been apart much longer than they'd ever been together, and that she'd plowed headlong into intimacy less with a lover she knew well than with a virtual stranger.

The boy had indeed become a man, and in the transition, had acquired a toughness, an impatience and an anger which were foreign to her. Worse still, she'd sensed all this beforehand, yet still she'd allowed him to blunt the finely tuned perimeters of her self-preservation. By giving in to unwise desire, she'd let him slip past her guard to reclaim his place in her heart.

The shame of it all tormented her to the point that she briefly considered running away again. Instead she dug in her heels, hid her misery from those around her, and kept busy with preparations for the gala. But she looked ahead, too, knowing that she needed a more permanent goal to pursue once the event was over.

The idea of opening some kind of youth shelter, which had fermented at the back of her mind for weeks, took on new and urgent life when she heard that Jake Harrington's plans to revamp the warehouse district had reached the point where a dozen homeless teens would soon be turned out on the street. She made inquiries into buying the abandoned monastery across the river, found she could well afford the asking price, and arranged to inspect the property.

The location was ideal: tranquil, pretty, and far-removed from the seamy section of Eastridge Bay which most of the town's well-heeled residents preferred not to recognize. The building itself would require some modification, but the general layout, with many small rooms upstairs and the large kitchen and living areas on the main floor, lent themselves well to her vision.

She spoke to a lawyer and, between them, they came up with a proposal which he presented before council. At the end of May, she received approval to go ahead with her plans and completed the purchase.

She told the family her news at a dinner hosted by her sister and brother-in-law on the Tuesday before the gala.

"We're so proud of you," her father said. "You've always been at your best when you've got something you can really sink your teeth into."

In typical fashion, Margaret saw only the possible drawbacks and pitfalls. "Let's hope you haven't bitten off more than you can chew," she chimed in. "The kind of people you're proposing to take in aren't kicked out of their homes for no good reason. Petty thugs and thieves are what you'll be dealing with more often than not."

Surprisingly Tom didn't share his wife's doubts. "I think she's onto something, Margaret," he said. "I've seen the way she interacts with teenagers. She knows how to handle them."

His brother, Francis jumped into the discussion. "I've

got some useful contacts in the hospitality industry. I'll be glad to put you in touch with them, if you like.''

''I look forward to taking you up on the offer, when the time comes,'' she said.

''Not nearly as much as I'm looking forward to Saturday night,'' he told her.

He was such a nice, self-effacing man, with none of the bombast which too often marked Tom's personality, and was very attractive, in his own quiet way. She'd enjoyed getting to know him better, and come to be very fond of him.

Maybe there was life after Jake Harrington, after all, she concluded. And maybe she'd needed one more night with him to find the closure which had eluded her the first time around. It had been an expensive lesson but, in the long run, might turn out to be worth the heartache it had entailed.

She'd been so busy, she never got around to finding something to wear to the gala but, buoyed with rare optimism, she talked her mother into going shopping with her. The next morning, they boarded the early train to the city, a hundred miles down the coast, and spent the day scouting the boutiques for the perfect outfit.

They struck gold almost at once, coming upon a gown newly imported from Europe. Strapless and made of white silk chiffon heavily embroidered with overblown white silk roses, it fell in diaphanous layers to a handkerchief hem which dipped almost to the floor on one side and rose to mid-calf on the other.

''You need shoes,'' her mother decided, as they celebrated over a lunch of fresh crab washed down with Chardonnay, at a charming seafood bistro on the waterfront. ''White peau de soie, with a heel. And jewelry. Great-aunt Miriam's diamond necklace and earrings, perhaps?''

''Just the earrings, I think. As I recall, they're practically the size of robin's eggs. Wearing the necklace as well would be overkill. What are you staring at, Mother?''

''You. I haven't seen you this happy in such a long time. The ghosts have gone from your eyes.''

''That's what shopping will do for a woman.''

''It's not the shopping that's done it, Sally, and we both know it. You're glowing from the inside out. Is Francis Bailey the reason?''

''No,'' she said honestly. ''It's got more to do with my being at peace within myself. It's been years since I've been able to say that and mean it. I've really come home finally, in more ways than one.''

''Will you ever feel able to talk about what it was that made you so eager to escape in the first place? Your father and I always supposed it was because things hadn't worked out between you and Jake, but I've often wondered if there was more to it than that.''

''There was.'' She smoothed her napkin over her lap, wondering how much she dared tell. ''We had more than just a simple boy-girl romance, Mom.''

''I know. You were lovers.''

Astonished, Sally met her mother's gaze and found it full of love and understanding. ''How did you know?''

''Even if you hadn't been the talk of the town, I'd have had to be blind not to see the way things were between you. But it didn't end there, did it?''

''No. While I was in Paris, I discovered I was pregnant.''

''Oh, my poor baby!'' Her mother looked out over the water, and when she turned back, her eyes were glazed with tears. ''I wondered at the time if that might be the case. Why didn't you come to me?''

''I miscarried shortly after I came home. There seemed no point in burdening you with something you could do nothing about.''

''You must have been devastated.''

"I was. And ashamed, too, at having let you down. You'd given me everything a girl could possibly want— love, security, freedom—and look how I repaid you."

"A parent's love doesn't hinge on approval of everything a child does, Sally, and if you thought it did, your father and I didn't do nearly as good a job as you give us credit for."

"You're right. I should have had more faith in you." She gave a little shrug. "But all things considered, things probably turned out for the best. Jake and I weren't right for one another."

"Are you sure?"

"I wasn't, for the longest time, but I am now. It's been eight years, Mom, and time hasn't stood still for either of us. He and I have grown apart. We're set on different paths now."

"He's creating quite a stir in the business community, I'll grant you that. When his father was at the helm, the Harrington Corporation stuck pretty much to the traditions which made it successful in the first place, but things have changed since Duncan handed over the reins to Jake. He's striving with a vengeance to fulfill all his ambitions."

"I'm not surprised. He was always single-minded and never believed in half-measures. With him, it was always a case of all, or nothing." She finished her wine and set down the glass with a delicate but decisive thump. "I'm happy he's discovered an outlet for his energy. I wish him every success and hope he's finding civilian life full and rewarding."

She was able to speak with utter conviction because she truly believed every word she said.

Her ideas for decorating the drill hall translated into a reality which surpassed even her high expectations. Yards of billowing, semisheer fabric the color of cherry blossom, draped the walls and hung in swags from the raftered ceilings. Hundreds of tiny foil stars sprinkled over the imported dance floor glimmered in the light of an enormous antique chandelier rescued from the attic of the oldest residence in town. Banks of gardenias and roses perfumed the air. Pink and white candles glowed on the linen-draped tables.

"You've worked a minor miracle!" people exclaimed.

"Fabulous!" others gushed. "Incredible!"

Even Colette Burton favored her with a nod of approval. "Very nice," she murmured, as she passed by. "And your dress is quite lovely, my dear. You do us all proud."

Overhearing, Francis said, "In case I haven't already made it clear I second that opinion, let me say again that you're easily the most beautiful woman in the room, Sally." He offered her his arm. "Shall we take a tour of the silent auction before we sit down to dinner? I want to make sure no one outbids me on your dance card."

"Tell me you're joking!" she exclaimed, still too flabbergasted by Mrs. Burton's compliments to take him seriously. "The suggestion was tossed around that all the ladies involved in pulling this affair together put themselves on the block to raise more funds, but I didn't think anyone actually followed through on it."

"Come and see for yourself," he said. "Not only has the idea evolved into a reality, it's such a hit that it'll probably become a tradition."

Dazed, she followed him to the officers' club where items donated for auction were arranged on long, velvet-covered tables lined up against the walls. As always, people had given generously. Everything, from heirloom jewelry to modern art, restaurant vouchers to weekend retreats, spa memberships to theater tickets, was offered. And, astonishing though it might be, dance cards printed with the names of every woman who'd given of her time and effort to make the evening a success.

''I see I have competition,'' Francis said, eyeing hers and scribbling a figure and his signature below the last bid. ''Half the men in this town are giving me a run for my money.''

But it was the *amount* of money they were willing to spend which left Sally speechless. Although the minimum bid had been set at a modest fifty dollars, the sum had risen to four figures already. Nor was she the only one reeling in the cash. Every other dance card showed similar sums.

''No one in his right mind should pay over two thousand dollars for a five-minute waltz,'' she blurted out. ''This is crazy, Francis!''

''Not when it comes to supporting worthy charitable causes,'' he reminded her. ''And not when the people bidding have deep enough pockets that they can afford it.''

''Well…!'' Flattered and more than a little relieved that she'd splurged on a new dress, she smoothed her hand over the filmy skirt of her gown. ''I'm flabbergasted, to say the least.''

''And the evening's only just begun,'' Francis said, giving her hand a purposeful squeeze. ''Who knows what else lies in store?''

She certainly didn't! If she'd had any idea of the next big surprise awaiting her, she'd have sneaked out of the nearest side door and gone home. But by the time she remembered it never paid to become overconfident, it was no more possible to avoid the man observing her from across the room, than it was to ignore the woman hanging on to his arm as if she were afraid to let it go.

Sally could hardly blame her. Jake in white tie and tails was dashing enough to make any woman stop and look twice. But his impact on Sally dealt a blow which ran far deeper than mere appearances could achieve.

It had been almost ten weeks since they'd seen or spoken to each other—time enough, she'd believed, to overcome

her distressing tendency to suffer a relapse at the sight of
him. Yet one glance into those inscrutable blue eyes and
she was floundering in a morass of hopeless yearning, all
over again.

"Is everything all right, Sally?" Francis inquired, re-
garding her solicitously. "You're looking rather pale all of
a sudden."

She clenched her fists hard enough to leave nasty little
dents where her nails bit into her palms. "I'm perfectly
fine."

Of course, she wasn't. She was a mess, and it was all
Jake's fault. Why couldn't he have stayed away, and left
her delusions of immunity intact?

But wishing he and his lady friend would disappear in a
puff of smoke wasn't going to work. Much though she'd
have preferred to do otherwise, Sally had no choice but to
pin a smile on her face and confront the situation head-on.

CHAPTER TEN

HE'D come prepared, knowing they were bound to run into each other sooner or later, and certain that he'd carry off the occasion with so much flair that she'd drool with regret for having walked out on him.

Cripes, much he knew! The minute he clapped eyes on her, his brain froze and his tongue stuck to the roof of his mouth. *Where did she find that dress and what the devil was holding it up?*

"Hello," she said stiffly, fixing her glance on a spot just beyond his left shoulder. Her mouth—that mouth he'd fantasized about altogether too often since the last time he'd tasted it—was as puckered up as if she'd accidentally swallowed a pint of vinegar, instead of the champagne everyone else was drinking. "How very nice to see you again."

Yeah, right, Sally! About as nice as discovering you've got head lice! Who do you think you're fooling?

"You, too," he replied, his attempt at blithe indifference putrefying into an inarticulate grunt.

Dismissing him with a faintly pitying lift of her elegant brows, she switched her attention to Ursula. "You look familiar. Have we met before?"

"Only about a thousand times," Ursula said. "We went to school together, Sally. Grade nine. I'm Ursula Rushton, though you knew me when I still went under the name Phillips."

"Of course! How silly of me not to remember." She bent a winsome smile on Ursula and fluttered her hand at the man by her side. "Let me introduce you to my very

149

good friend, Francis Bailey. Oh, and this is Jake Harrington, Francis. I went to school with him, as well.''

"I'd say we did a bit more than that," Jake spat, barely able to shake the man's hand, so peeved was he at the way she tacked him on as an inconsequential afterthought. "Once upon a time, Sally considered me a very good...*friend,* too."

She didn't miss his deliberate hesitation, or the inflection in his voice. The color ran up her face, deepening her skin to warm honey, and just for an instant she looked him directly in the eye. "You're right," she said. "Once upon a time, I did."

He held her gaze, such a hollow ache gouging his gut that he winced inwardly at the pain of it. "But we move on, don't we, Sally?"

"Indeed we do." She took a deep breath and smiled at the man by her side. "And on that note, I think we should move on, and find the rest of our party, don't you, Francis?"

"Absolutely," he said, his gaze so worshipful on her that Jake just about choked.

She tucked her hand more securely under Bailey's arm and inclined her head at Ursula. "It was lovely talking to you, Ursula. Perhaps we'll see each other again some time. Enjoy your evening."

"So that's the way things stand," Ursula said, staring after her. "After all these years, you've still got something cooking with Sally Winslow."

Regret bitter on his tongue, Jake said, "No. That implies a mutuality which no longer exists between us. But old habits die hard, as you already know. Do you care for more champagne?"

"Yes." With a last glance at Sally's departing figure, she handed him her glass. "I need something to wash the taste of envy out of my mouth. No woman has the right to be so utterly irresistible to men. Did you see the way Francis looked at her?''

"I saw," he said grimly.

"What's she got that I don't have, Jake?"

"I'm not sure," he said, putting a different spin on the question as he watched Bailey place an altogether too-familiar hand in the small of Sally's back. But before the evening drew to a close, he intended to find out.

Although the winning bids were kept secret until the band began its last set for the night, the silent auction closed just before dinner. In the interval, Sally managed to recover something of her poise.

It helped that Jake and Ursula, who were sitting four tables away with the Burtons, left midway through the meal, after a waiter handed Ursula a slip of paper.

It helped, too, that over the course of the evening, Sally became reacquainted with a number of other people she'd known at school. Between catching up on news of who'd married whom, and dancing just about every dance, some with Francis and others with men she'd last known as boys, she found she was enjoying herself after all, and quite able to put Jake out of her mind.

What turned out to be the biggest hit of the evening finally took place just before midnight, when the women whose names were on the dance cards were called up to the podium to be claimed by their partners.

Sally's card was among the last to be announced. Francis had kept such a close eye on the competition that, certain he'd posted the final bid, she paid little attention to the sudden mild flurry of movement as people stepped aside to admit someone coming in through a side door. In fact, she was halfway down the steps to where Francis waited expectantly, when the emcee stopped her in her tracks by declaring that the winning bid had gone to Captain Jake Harrington.

"It can't have," she said sharply. "He left hours ago."

The emcee pointed across the room. "But he came back to claim his prize," he informed her, and to her mixed annoyance and trepidation, she saw Jake weaving a path through the crowd, toward her.

"Stop looking as if someone shoved a broom handle up the back of your dress and try to smile, my lovely," he murmured, drawing her down the last two steps, and pulling her firmly into his arms. "They're playing our song."

If she hadn't known that every eye in the room was on them, she'd have ground her heel on his instep and told him to keep his distance. Instead, she was forced to follow as he swept her into the middle of the dance floor and led her in a flawless foxtrot.

"I hope you find this is worth whatever it cost you," she said, in a low, furious voice. "But just for the record, I am not enjoying it one little bit."

"Sure you are," he replied flatly. "You're wallowing in every second of it and probably hoping I'll try to sneak a look down the front of your dress. But that would be a bit pointless, wouldn't it, considering I already know exactly what's holding up that delectable froth of strapless silk?"

"Don't be vulgar!"

"Vulgar? That's not a very friendly thing to say." He made an unexpected reverse turn which brought her up against his chest so snugly that she could feel the buttons of his shirt pressing against her skin. "And we were once such good friends, weren't we, Sally?"

By then so discombobulated she could hardly think straight, she said, "We could be still, if you weren't so wrapped up in your own wants that you never give a thought to anyone else's."

"That's not true," he countered mildly. "I've followed

the progress of your latest venture with a great deal of interest.''

''Meaning?''

''Meaning I'm very proud of you for sticking to your guns about helping out kids who've never known the kind of privilege or luxury to which you and I were born.''

''Well, someone has to step in on their behalf and from everything I hear, it's not going to be you. Couldn't you at least wait until I have my place up and running before you turf them out of your precious warehouses?''

''It's for their own protection. At present, half those buildings are potential death traps. Not that I'm able to impress that message on the kids in question. As fast as I board up access in one area, they find a way to get in somewhere else, and that, my dear, keeps me awake at night even more than thoughts of you do.'' He indulged in a bit more sudden fancy footwork which had her clinging to him for dear life. ''So you see, Sally, I'm not entirely self-obsessed.''

''I didn't mean to imply that you were.''

The band changed tempo and segued into something slow and dreamy. The lights on the big antique chandelier dimmed to near-nothing. The floor grew crowded as more couples joined in the dancing.

Absently, as if he wasn't really aware of what he was doing, Jake slid his hand up the low back of her dress to caress her skin. ''Didn't you?'' he said. ''I must have misunderstood.''

Determined not to betray the shameful flood of awareness he excited, she said, ''You're doing this out of spite, aren't you?''

''I'm not sure I know what you mean.''

''Sure you do! The only reason you're putting the moves on me in full view of everyone in this room is to feed your own ego.''

"You think so, do you?"

"Yes," she hissed. "You knew very well that I wanted to dance with Francis, but you just can't stand to lose out to another man."

He dropped his arm. Released her hand. Stepped away from her. "If that's what you believe, then go to him. If he's who you really want, I won't try to stop you."

She fought the truth, but it wouldn't be silenced. "He...isn't," she admitted, her voice sinking to a defeated whimper.

"Then I feel sorry for the poor sod. He's so far gone on you that he'd donate both his kidneys to keep you happy, if you asked him to."

"Whereas you cared for me so little that you couldn't wait to replace me with someone else."

He caught her in his arms again. "If you're referring to Ursula, I'm merely the understudy for the man she hoped would be her escort tonight. She and her husband split up recently."

"Because of you?"

"No, Sally," he said soberly. "Because of another woman. Contrary to what you might choose to believe, I revere the sanctity of marriage and have never chased another man's wife—or cheated on my own. But nor am I averse to lending a friendly shoulder to lean on, once in a while."

"So why did Ursula leave early tonight, then? Did you have a falling-out?"

His voice quivering with devilish laughter, he said again, "No, my lovely. You're the only woman who makes a career out of picking fights with me. She was called home because one of her children became ill."

"I'm sorry. I hope it was nothing serious."

"A case of too many strawberries for dessert, I understand. Why don't we change the subject and talk about us?''

''What's the point? There is no 'us.' You made that clear enough, the last time we were together.''

''Because temper got the better of me. I tried to see things your way, Sally, but feelings I thought I could control rose to the surface and took me by surprise. I told myself they were wrong. Indecent. Unforgivable. But the only indecency lay in ignoring them, the only thing unforgivable, lying to myself and you.''

She was so mesmerized by his words that she hardly noticed he'd waltzed her out of the drill hall and into the gardens, until her heels sank into the lawn and caused her to miss a step. At that, a flutter of alarm winged its way up her spine. ''Why have you brought me out here?''

''Because I'm going to kiss you, and I didn't think you'd appreciate having everyone watch me do it.''

She swatted feebly at his hands as they came up to cup her face. ''I don't want you to kiss me,'' she said.

His mouth grazed hers. ''Why do you even bother telling such lies when neither of us believes you?''

Oh, he was arrogant—bold—dangerous! So sure all he had to do was exert a little charm, and she'd forget how coldly he'd sent her packing before, and fall eagerly into his arms again.

Injecting considerably more starch into her voice, she said, ''*I* believe me. I find I'm quite liking life without you.''

''Are you?'' he said, undeterred, and ran the tip of his tongue lightly over her lower lip. ''I quite detest mine without you.''

''What you detest, Jake,'' she said, warming to the subject, ''is not getting your own way. You detest that I didn't come running back, begging for yet another chance to make things work between us. You detest that I wouldn't settle for an illicit affair. For being your mistress in secret.''

He slid his hands down her arms, sank his fingers into the filmy clouds of fabric clinging to her hips, and jerked her close. ''Tell me you haven't missed this,'' he said, his voice suddenly raw and his meaning unmistakable. ''Dare to tell me again that you haven't missed *us*.''

And just that swiftly, the warmth of her indignation turned to searing, sensual heat. She sagged against him, every pore, every nerve ending, reaching out to absorb him. She lifted her face, parted her lips on a sigh, and let him in.

At first, it was enough. To be in his arms again, to indulge in the magic he wove with his mouth, with his tongue, to hear the muttered endearments he couldn't contain—they sufficed. For a little while. But just as puffs of cloud could billow and boil without warning into a storm, so a deeper hunger, a stronger need, suddenly roared to life.

With a muffled growl of frustration, Jake tore his mouth free. ''This is too damned public, even for me,'' he muttered, glaring at the open door of the nearby drill hall. And before she had time to anticipate his next move, he grabbed her wrist and dragged her down the sloping lawn to where a trellis, heavy with wisteria blossoms, offered a screen of privacy.

She should have been outraged; should have resisted. Instead, she surrendered. Exulted in the bruising strength of his grip, in the harsh, impatient rasp of his breathing. And quivered all over with shameless anticipation for what she knew would happen next.

The grass was velvet soft, perfumed with early summer, dotted with tiny daisies. ''I don't want to hurt your dress,'' he said, pulling her down beside him and plucking impatiently at the delicate fabric. ''I don't want to hurt you. But Sally, I need you so badly, I'm afraid I'll do both.''

"The dress doesn't matter," she whispered, and closed her mind to the voice of caution warning her that his other misgiving posed a far greater risk.

"You shouldn't have worn it. All this skin...." He groaned and bent his head to nip gently at her bare shoulder. "Did you do it on purpose, Sally, to torment me? Did you choose it because it showed only a glimpse of one leg when you move, and you knew I'd go crazy wanting to see more?"

"Yes," she said, the ugly truth vaulting out of nowhere to slam her into startled awareness. "I wanted you to notice me."

Less gently, he tugged at the strapless bodice. The silk resisted briefly, then slithered down to expose her breasts. "Did you want me to do this, as well?" he rumbled, his mouth plucking at her nipples and stirring them into electrifying sensitivity.

"I wanted you!" she cried, in an agony of despair. "Everything I do, everything that I am, *always* comes back to my wanting you! But I didn't think you felt the same. You sent me away...you were so angry with me."

"I know," he said, raising his head to cover her face with butterfly-light kisses. "And I'm sorry. I tried telling myself that you were young and afraid and it was as much my fault as yours. If I'd known, if *you'd* known you could count on me, everything would have been different and you wouldn't have cared about what other people thought. We let each other down then, but when you still refused to be seen with me after we'd finally found each other again...hell, Sally, I couldn't take it a second time."

Had he drunk too much wine, she wondered, confused by the disjointed context of his words, or were they simply talking at cross purposes? Uncertain, and knowing only that she couldn't bear the river of pain flowing through his voice, she said, "All I've ever wanted is to be with you, Jake."

"Then come back to the house with me," he urged, adding persuasion to his plea by running his fingers under her skirt to caress her thigh and press the heel of his hand against the passion-dampened swath of satin between her legs. "Let me love you all night long."

The potent intimacy of his touch left her so beside herself with longing that she'd have gone with him in a flash, had a burst of laughter from the other side of the trellis not brought her to her senses as bracingly as a pail of cold water splashed in her face.

What was she thinking of, to be rolling around on the ground, within hearing and seeing range of the hundreds of people who, only a short time before, had applauded her? Why was she leaving herself wide-open to criticism and censure, after she'd worked so hard to redeem her reputation?

Horrified, she pushed his hand aside and clamped her legs together. "I can't!"

"Why not?" The question hung in the air, smoky with passion.

"Because," she said, scrambling to her feet, "it wouldn't be the right thing to do."

He lay spread-eagled on the grass and closed his eyes. "Oh, for Pete's sake, are we back to that again?"

"Yes," she said, hardening her heart against the weariness she heard in his voice. "Anyone could find us here including the man who's supposed to be my escort."

"Perhaps it would be a good thing if he did. It'd spare him getting ideas of his own about where his relationship with you is headed."

"It would be shameful, and I refuse to subject him to that kind of humiliation."

"What you're really saying, then, is that he comes first."

"Don't make this about him, when it's really about me. It might not seem important in your eyes, Jake, but I like being respectable—and respected. I like being able to look Mrs. Burton in the eye without blushing, and knowing she no longer regards me with such hostility."

"That's because Fletcher made her read both the police and the autopsy report on Penelope, and she can't hide her head in the sand any longer. She's seen irrefutable proof of the kind of life her daughter was leading behind everyone's back, and realizes she can't go on blaming you for the accident."

"I don't care what made her change her mind. It's enough that she did."

"Very decent of you, Sally, I'm sure." He bounded to his feet in one lithe leap and brushed his hands over his jacket. "Tell me, is there any room at all for me in this rosy little picture?"

"Only if we can arrive at some sort of compromise."

"Compromise? Pity that didn't enter into your thinking when you decided to get rid of my child. If it had, my son or daughter would be turning eight pretty soon, and we wouldn't be having this conversation."

Sure she couldn't have understood correctly, she stared at him. "What did you say?"

"You heard."

"You're accusing me of...*aborting* our baby?" She could barely bring herself to utter the words, let alone give them any credence. "Is *that* what you were rambling on about, a few minutes ago?"

"You didn't think Penelope settled for telling me only half the story, did you, when it gave her so much pleasure to relate every last disgusting detail, right down to her having to nurse you back to health because you didn't want your family to know you'd visited a back-street abortionist in another town?"

"But it's not true!" she gasped.

"What, that you weren't pregnant? Too late, Sally! You already admitted you were."

"I miscarried through no fault of my own."

"Sure you did," he sneered.

"Ahh!" She pressed both hands to her mouth, cut to the quick by his unadorned cynicism. "And to think I was ready to trust you yet again with my heart! To think I was fool enough to believe that your feelings for me were strong enough to overcome any obstacle!"

"Yeah," he said bitterly. "And to think I was, too."

"Check the records at St. Mary's Hospital in Redford, if you don't believe me. They don't lie."

He must have heard the incontestable ring of truth in her voice because, for a second or two, he stared at her in silence, his gaze so intense, it almost drilled holes through her skull. Then, mouthing an obscenity of self-loathing which made her flinch, he swung away and looked out at the glimmering lights of the boats anchored in the harbor.

The silence following his outburst was hard enough to bear, but when a selection from *Les Miserables* drifted out of the drill hall, beginning with the hauntingly beautiful "I Dreamed A Dream," it epitomized the entire spectrum of their history so poignantly that her heart broke.

His voice floated on the still air, in melancholy counter-point to the music. "I took you to see this show, the year I graduated from high school."

"I remember."

"You cried all the way through."

"Yes."

"Are you crying now?"

"Yes."

Another second ticked by, and then another, before he spoke again. "Why can't things ever be easy for us, Sally?"

"Because we care too much," she sobbed.

"Do we? Or is it that we never manage to care quite enough to trust each other completely?"

A terrible hopelessness took hold of her then. It would always be like this for them: the potent, simmering sexuality that never slept; the frantic, mindless greed which always gained the upper hand. And, sadly, the regret which always followed.

She looked down at her dress; at the pretty handkerchief hem, soiled now, and at the delicate silk embroidery stained with grass. It was ruined. Just like them.

"You're right," she said. "We never did."

"Will we ever learn?"

"I don't think so."

"So where do we go from here?"

"Nowhere," she said. "The merry-go-round's stopped, Jake. It's time to get off."

CHAPTER ELEVEN

"No," HE said. "I refuse to give up on us. I won't let Penelope win."

But the only reply was the sound of her walking away, her footsteps falling soft and light across the dew-damp lawn.

It took every ounce of grit he possessed not to go after her, but what little sense he still had told him this was not the time. Not while they were both reeling from shock and pain and grief.

Grief…God, how often had he experienced it over the last year, and when was it going to stop? Children mutilated and orphaned by war. Hospitals blown sky-high. Refugee camps crowded with the sick and the dying. A buddy whose jet didn't come back. Another who went home with both legs missing. And a girl he'd loved all his life, and whose heart he'd crushed under his heel, because he was such a damned fool that he'd listened to the one woman he'd known for years he couldn't trust.

The lights across the harbor misted over and he blinked furiously, not because grown men didn't cry—he knew that wasn't true; he'd seen them with their faces buried in their hands and their shoulders heaving, and heard the primeval sobs tearing them apart as they mourned a fallen comrade—but because he didn't deserve the cleansing release of tears. He deserved the big, ugly chunk of frozen misery lodged in his throat and clogging his airway.

Looking up, he saw the sky was covered with a shimmer of stars. Was she looking at them, too, and thinking of him? Was she still crying? Was Bailey lending her his handkerchief and holding her? Perhaps telling her he loved her and, if she'd let him, he'd make sure no one ever made her unhappy again? Would he, Jake, one day pick up the morning paper and find a wedding announcement on the social page: *Mr. and Mrs. Byron Winslow are pleased to announce the forthcoming marriage of their youngest daughter, Sally Elizabeth, to Francis Bailey, who deserves her a hell of a lot more than Jake Harrington ever did?*

Oh, no, not that! Not as long as he had breath in his body! "It isn't over," he told the quiet night. "Not by a long chalk. I don't care if it takes another eight years, I'll win her back, one way or another."

Keep busy. She didn't know who'd first dished out such advice, but it was the lifeline to which Sally clung in the days following, and it saved her sanity. She threw herself into the renovations needed on the monastery and if nothing quite managed to ease the persistent ache in her heart, at least she found some comfort in the support she received, as word of her endeavors spread throughout the county.

The redevelopment permits she required were issued promptly. The various municipal inspectors who came to assess the repairs and upgrades needed, were helpful, directing her to the most competent electricians, plumbers, stone masons and carpenters in the area.

Francis carried through on his promise. As a result, a discount outlet in the next town offered her fifteen new mattresses and bed frames; another, dishes, cutlery and cooking utensils. A restaurant going out of business sold her stainless steel commercial-quality kitchen appliances at a fraction of what it would have cost her to buy them new.

Friends and strangers alike donated furniture, clothing, linens, pillows, books, television sets. A local nursery promised to prune the neglected fruit trees and clean up the gardens.

A couple in their fifties, the husband a social worker used to dealing with troubled teens, the wife a nurse, applied to be resident house parents.

Sally had begun with a seed of an idea, generated by a chance meeting with a pregnant girl who had no home, and although it remained unalterably *her* project, as the weeks passed and the momentum grew, so did community involvement. And she welcomed it. What mattered was not who was in charge, but that there would be a safe house staffed with caring adults, to which teenagers living on the streets of Eastridge Bay could turn.

What she would not do, however, was accept help from the Harrington Corporation, even though a truck arrived one day with a load of bricks she sorely needed to repave the courtyard at the front of the building. "Take them back," she instructed the dumbstruck driver who could clearly see the ruined state of the area in question. "I don't want them."

A week later, another truck showed up, this time with enough imported Italian tiles to cover the kitchen and laundry room floors. "No, thanks," she said. "I'll shop somewhere else."

Most of all, she refused to take Jake's phone calls. She couldn't. She'd had enough. The pain that came from knowing him just wasn't worth it. They'd crossed a line, the night he'd accused her of aborting their child, and this time there'd be no going back.

It wasn't just the things they'd said to one another in the heat of the moment, which defeated her. It was the much deeper hurt of his having entertained, even for a moment, the idea that she'd willfully destroy the life of his, or anyone else's, child. How did they go about healing such a mortal wound? How could they repair the damage to the very foundations of their relationship?

Francis remained a pillar of support during those difficult

weeks. He never pushed for too much, the way Jake had. He never issued ultimatums.

"I would tell you I love you," he said, one day when he'd persuaded her to take the afternoon off and go for a picnic with him along the river. "But I don't think you want to hear the words, at least not from me."

She could have wept for both of them. He was kind, perceptive, steady, loyal, handsome—all the things any woman could ask for in a mate, and more. Why weren't they enough to make her love him back?

"I wish that weren't true," she said sadly. "I wish it could be otherwise."

"But that's not how it works. We don't choose love, it chooses us. So there's nothing to be gained by lying about your feelings because, in the end, you just end up punishing yourself. Better to settle for nothing, than try to make do with second best."

"But I don't want to lose your friendship. It means the world to me."

He took her hand and pressed a kiss to her palm. "It's yours for however long you want it."

August arrived, and with it, a rash of complications no one had anticipated. The tail end of a hurricane sweeping up the coast brought gale-force winds lasting nearly three days, and dumped over two inches of rain in the region.

Before the storm passed inland, it brought down a hundred-year-old copper beech, causing major damage to the back wing of the monastery and breaking the main sewer line running in from the road. In another area, the roof had sprung a huge leak. Three of the upstairs rooms suffered substantial water damage as a result.

Mice found a way into the cellar and from there, up the inside walls into the attic. In the evening, when the workmen had left and the place was quiet, Sally could hear the scurrying patter of little feet racing between the rafters. Within a very short time, she discovered evidence of them in the big walk-in pantry which she'd already stocked with staples like flour and cereal. Everything had to be thrown out.

She'd hoped to have the shelter ready for occupancy by the end of the month, but she was forced to postpone the official opening until the problems were fixed. They took longer than expected.

One day toward the end of the month, as she was sorting through the mail in the room she'd set aside as an office, she heard a vehicle draw up in front of the house. Expecting it was yet one more tradesman come to work on the repairs, she paid no attention until, several minutes later, she heard footsteps pause in the hall outside the room. She looked up to find Jake standing in the open doorway, watching her.

The shock of seeing him was so acute, she could barely function. The letter opener slipped out of her hand and landed on the floor with a clunk.

She tried to reach down for it, and couldn't. Couldn't stand. Couldn't run. Her body seized up—except for her heart. It staggered and leaped so erratically, she thought she was on the verge of cardiac arrest.

Finally, she managed to croak, "You're trespassing."

"So sue me," he said, stepping across the room and leaning over her as she sat frozen behind her desk.

"You think I won't?"

"I think you can do anything you set your mind to. But you're not Superwoman, and right now, you've got trouble. What I can't figure out is why you'll accept all kinds of help from total strangers, but you won't let me or my workers get a foot in your door."

"Your foot is altogether too far in my door right now, Jake, and I'd appreciate it if you'd remove it."

He straightened and shoved his hands in the back pockets

of his blue jeans—hardly what she'd have expected the new CEO of the Harrington Corporation to wear to work. She doubted his father would ever have appeared in public in anything but a custom-tailored business suit, silk tie and starched shirt. The way Jake was dressed though, he might have been a lowly company employee so far down on the totem pole that he didn't merit notice, even if he did come blessed with the looks and self-assurance to leave most women panting in his wake.

Most! she reminded herself sternly. She would not become one of them. Not again.

"You know, Sally," he said conversationally, strolling around the office as if he owned it, and inspecting the blueprints tacked on the wall, "I credited you with more brains than this. Which matters more: that you get this operation up and running with all due speed, or that you keep punishing me for my many past and grievous sins?"

"What makes you think I can't do both at the same time?"

"You're cutting off your nose to spite your face."

"But it's my nose, and my face."

He looked at her long and thoughtfully. "Maybe so," he finally said. "But I love them where nature intended they should be. I love you."

"No, you don't!" she cried, the emotions she'd struggled to contain boiling up to the surface again. "A man doesn't harbor unfounded anger and resentment against the woman he loves. He doesn't believe her capable of aborting his child just because someone tells him she did. He goes to her and asks for the truth, confident that he can believe whatever she tells him."

"We were young and naive, Sally. We both made mistakes. You could just as easily have come to me."

"Fine! Then we're even. Consider the score settled and go away."

"I'm sorry you're taking things this way. I hoped you'd see my offer to help for what it really is—an attempt to put things right between us."

"Oh, please!" Strength flooding back into her body, she hauled herself out of the chair. "You think I don't know why you really came here today? You don't give a rap about whether or not I've got problems. The only reason you want to help me get this place finished is so that you can be rid of all those pesky young people presently cluttering up your precious warehouse."

He took another turn about the room. Stopped in front of the window. And finally spun back to face her. "What do I have to do to prove myself worthy of another chance, Sally?" he asked bitterly. "Throw myself off the nearest cliff?"

"You can burn in hell, for all I care," she said, steadfastly refusing to admit how badly she wanted to believe one more chance might be enough to mend what was broken between them.

"I already am, my lovely." He stretched out his hand. Traced his fingers across her cheek, over her mouth, and down her throat. "For me, hell is life without you."

His touch was light, fleeting, but it left behind such an uproar of sensation that her skin puckered from the impact. He stood close enough that she could have counted every long, silky lash framing those unforgettable blue eyes. Every breath she took left her filled with the essence of him…clean, virile. Every inch of him was so powerfully attractive that it took every ounce of willpower she possessed not to fall into his arms.

But although submitting to temptation now might be easier on both of them in the short run, it would be so much more painful in the end. She knew because that was the pattern they'd established. Ecstatic highs followed by soul-destroying lows.

So she pushed him away and said firmly, "Don't! It's over between us, Jake. It has been for a long time. We just weren't smart enough to read the signs."

"I'll never accept that."

"I already have. Please don't make this any harder than it has to be. Please, just go away."

"Tell me you don't love me," he said, hypnotizing her with his low, compelling voice and the burning intensity in his eyes, "and I will."

She took another breath, and drew on her dwindling self-possession. "I don't love you."

He stared at her a moment longer, watching for a crack in her defenses—as if, by the sheer force of his will, he could make her change her mind.

She held his gaze. The tension flowed around them, filling the room to bursting with a high, silent scream.

"I hope you don't live to regret saying that, Sally," he said at last.

And then he turned and left her.

When a man couldn't stand to be alone with his thoughts, or bear to look down the road to see what tomorrow held, there was only one remedy, and that was to drive himself to such a point of exhaustion that, come night, he fell into bed practically comatose. Which probably explained why, by the middle of September, at 2:32 in the morning, it took Jake a while to realize the din which had woken him came not from the alarm on his clock radio, but from the phone standing next to it.

"'Lo?" he muttered groggily, raking a hand through his hair.

It was the police. One of his warehouses was on fire. They thought he'd want to know.

The days were bad, but the nights were worse. She'd come home worn out, make something quick and easy for dinner, and be so tired by nine o'clock that she'd climb into bed and be asleep within minutes. Then, around one, she'd wake up, her mind alive with thoughts of Jake, and that would be it until four, sometimes five the next morning, when she'd finally fall asleep again.

It was a ruinous pattern which Sally seemed unable to break. Finally, those bleak, dark, empty hours became such hell to endure that, to get through them, she took to watching a local television channel which ran old movies throughout the night.

They did the trick. Within an hour, her eyelids grew heavy. Sometimes, she made it back to bed. Others, she fell asleep on the couch in the living room, and awoke at sunrise, chilled and sore from lying too long with her neck at an awkward angle, to hear the TV set blasting out the morning news. It wasn't an ideal situation, but it beat insomnia.

One night, in the middle of September, just two days before the shelter opened, she was debating whether or not she had the energy to turn off the set and stagger upstairs, when the flickering, slightly fuzzy black and white movie abruptly disappeared from the screen and was replaced by live coverage of a reporter speaking into a hand-held microphone.

The scene behind him was chaotic. Fire trucks, police cars and ambulances littered the area. Flames licked over the roof of the building in the background. People ran madly in all directions, or huddled together in horrified groups. Sirens split the night, distorting the reporter's words.

She didn't need to hear what he was saying, though, to interpret his message. She recognized the location, and what was happening spoke for itself. One of Harrington Corporation's recently acquired warehouses was going up in smoke. She recognized, too, both the man to the left of the screen, and the girl he held pinned in his arms and was doing his best to comfort.

And Sally knew, with preternatural foreboding, why the girl—no longer pregnant—was so distraught, and why the man looked over at the burning building with such despair. And a horror like nothing she'd ever known before filled her.

She had no memory of how she came to be in her car, or how long it took her to speed across town along streets mercifully deserted at that hour. She didn't care that when she arrived on the fringe of the warehouse district, she had to abandon her vehicle two blocks away and run the remaining distance in her slippered feet.

She knew only a terrible, suffocating sense of urgency— and dread of what she'd discover when she finally reached her destination.

She found the girl at once. The poor child, on the verge of hysterical collapse, was being tended to by a paramedic.

"Her name's Lisa," an ambulance driver told Sally. He jerked his head at the burning building. "She and a bunch of other kids have been living in there for months. Seems they made a fire to keep warm through the night, but set it too close to a pile of dry lumber. They woke to find the place full of smoke and got out just in time. Trouble is, she's got a baby, a little boy, only a few months old. In the confusion, she thought her friend had taken him. Bottom line, though, is the poor little tyke's still in there somewhere."

It was as Sally had feared. "But someone's gone in to find him, surely? They're not just standing around doing nothing?"

She learned then that, bad as things were, they could get worse. "Oh, someone's gone in, all right. The damn fool who owns the place bulldozed his way past the barricade and went charging in."

"You mean Jake Harrington?" Her voice sounded thin and foreign to her ears. "And no one tried to stop him?"

"Nobody could. He was like a wild animal gone mad." The driver shook his head. "As if our guys don't have enough to deal with already, without having to go searching for him, as well."

She let out an involuntary wail of anguish.

The man eyed her sympathetically. "You don't look so hot, all of a sudden. Is he someone you know?"

"He's someone I know," she managed to say, and clutched at the air as she felt her knees buckle beneath her.

"Whoa!" He caught her before she hit the ground. "You'd better sit in the ambulance with the mother, while we wait for news."

"No. I have to be there when he comes out," she whispered, her eyes searching for that familiar, beloved face…and finding only strangers and the awful, hot, red glow of fire. Yet all she felt was a bitter, penetrating cold which started deep within her and spread until she was shaking all over from it.

"Look at you," the driver chided. "You're not dressed for a night like this. You're not even wearing proper shoes."

His concern was genuine, but she shut him out. Trapped in a nightmare of her own making, she heard only the specter of her own voice coming back to haunt her again. It echoed repeatedly through the empty cavern of her mind.

You can burn in hell, for all I care…burn in hell…!

CHAPTER TWELVE

SHE found a blanket. Draped it around herself and the over-wrought girl. They clung together, two strangers caught up by chance in the same bottomless pit of despair, both of them praying aloud for a miracle to save the life of a lost baby and the man who'd risked his to find it.

Time was measured in heartbeats; a race which never ended but ran in endless circles, driven by the tormenting refrain of all the things Sally had said to him. Untrue things, intended only to hurt.

You just want to be rid of all those pesky teenagers cluttering up your precious warehouse…consider the score settled…go away…it's over between us….

And the worst lie of all, I don't love you!

"I didn't mean it, Jake," she whispered. "I'll love you forever. Please come back so that I can tell you…show you…"

But the memory of how he'd looked when last they'd confronted each other, tormented her. His words filled her with a dread which went beyond fear for his physical safety.

For me, hell is life without you, he'd told her and, at the time, she'd dismissed it as just another ploy designed to worm his way back into her good graces.

Now, though, it assumed a different, deadlier context. He was a brave man. He'd faced danger and bodily injury before without flinching. But if his will to survive was extinguished, what then?

A shout went up from the crowd. Afraid to see why,

afraid not to, she slipped her arm around the girl and half-dragged her out of the ambulance to where the driver stood.

"They've brought someone out of the building," he said.

Someone?

Frantic to find out more, she'd have rushed forward if he hadn't prevented it. "You'll only be in the way," he said. "Stand back and let the experts do their job. We'll find out soon enough how things stand."

"Is it my baby?" Lisa asked piteously. "Did they find my little boy?"

"I hope so, darling," Sally said. But although she craned her neck and strained her eyes trying to make out what was happening, all she could determine was a paramedic racing toward the ambulance. Only as he drew close enough for her to hear a baby crying did she realize he carried a small bundle in his arms.

He climbed into the ambulance, wrapped the child in an insulated blanket and slipped an oxygen mask over the tiny face. "You're lucky," he informed the sobbing mother. "He seems to be in pretty good shape. No burns, just a couple of minor scrapes and bruises. Being on the floor probably spared him from the worst—less danger of smoke inhalation down low—but we'll have him checked out in Emergency to be sure. Hop aboard, honey. We're going for a ride."

Aware of Sally hovering anxiously to the rear, the driver asked, "Shall we wait for the guy who went in after her?"

"Uh-uh." The paramedic shook his head and reached back to close the door. "There's no hurry on him. The rest of the team can handle it."

At that, the world tilted and no matter how hard she flailed her arms, Sally couldn't retain her balance. The stars fell in a shower of tiny sparks, and blurred with the receding tail lights of the ambulance. She hit the ground with a thump which knocked the breath out of her.

There's nothing to be gained by lying about your feelings, Francis had said. *The person you end up punishing is yourself.*

He was right about so many things, but he'd failed to mention that, in punishing herself, she'd ended up hurting the person she loved most in the world. Why hadn't he thought to tell her that, too?

A grubby hand swam into her line of vision, and she looked up to find a boy bending over her. One of those who'd been living in the warehouse, probably. He was no more than fifteen and behind the tough facade with which he confronted an uncaring world, she saw the face of a frightened child. "You okay, lady?" he asked.

"No," she said. "I'll never be okay again."

He was used to dishing out orders, not taking them, and if they didn't quit poking at him and shoving him around, he was going to punch somebody's lights out.

"I don't need a hospital," he wheezed, swatting aside the mask they kept trying to put on his face, and sending it flying. "Go play Florence Nightingale to somebody else. God knows, there are enough kids around here who could use a bit of care and attention."

The one in charge stood back and tucked his stethoscope into his pocket. "They're often like this," he said, full of his own importance. Cripes, put a man in a uniform, and he thought he ruled the world! "Strap him down, if you have to, and ship him off. He's inhaled a fair bit of smoke."

"Much you know," Jake tried to bellow, but wound up coughing too hard to make himself clear.

"Take it easy, buddy," wannabe Dr. Know-It-All advised him. "The kids all got out of there in one piece. The only real casualty is your warehouse. It's had the biscuit."

Damn good thing, too! First chance he got, he'd have

the whole lot of them burned to the ground. Some things weren't worth saving.

And others, not worth fighting, he decided, as they finished trussing him up like a Thanksgiving turkey and rolled him toward the waiting ambulance. Sick to death of the sight and sound of everyone and everything, he conceded defeat and closed his eyes. Let them do their worst. He was past caring.

He smelled her before he heard her. Came swimming up out of the most restful sleep he'd known in weeks, and recognized her scent, despite the lingering taste of smoke distorting his senses. Diva had been her favorite perfume for as long as he could remember. She'd been wearing it the last time he'd taken her to bed. She'd worn it the day she kicked him out of her life for good.

Why was she here now? Surely there was nothing left to be said?

Her voice tremulous, she murmured, "Jake, can you hear me?"

Oh yeah! And he'd have told her so if he thought she was going to say anything he wanted to hear.

"Open your eyes, Jake," she begged, and wrapped his hand in both of hers.

He could feel her, too, and that was good. That was very good. He'd known too many men who'd woken up in a hospital bed, unable to feel a damn thing because bits of them had been blown off in combat, or hacked off by a military surgeon.

"There's such a lot I have to tell you," she went on, and she must have leaned on the side of the Gurney, or whatever it was they had him laid out on, because it shifted slightly to one side under her weight.

He thought again about replying but decided it was safer to play possum.

"Jake…?" A sob threatened, but she swallowed it on a long, indrawn breath. He could imagine how she looked at that moment, fighting to control her trembling mouth. Glaring defiantly through a haze of tears.

"*Damn you,* Jake!" The words shot out like bullets…*ping, ping, ping!* "Open your eyes and look at me! I love you, do you hear? I believe in us. *Us!* Don't you *dare* deprive me of the chance to prove it." She punctuated the order with a thump on his shoulder. She actually hit him while he lay on his sick bed, the little weasel! *"Don't you dare!"*

Slowly he lifted his lids. Focused on the ceiling fixture from which a pleasantly dim light shone, and the pale green curtain surrounding him on three sides. Rolled his eyeballs to the right until she swam into view.

"Oh, you're awake!" Although she stuffed her fist to her mouth to smother a spate of giggles, her voice swam with tears. "And you look drunk as a skunk!"

He wet his lips and blinked. "And you look ridiculous," he said, trying to lighten the atmosphere. "What's that thing you've got on?"

She pulled self-consciously on the faded hospital gown she wore over a short pink nightshirt printed with purple frogs which most definitely was *not* hospital issue. "I didn't take time to dress. When I heard about the fire, I just came running to find you." She stroked his hair. "You remember there was a fire, don't you? At the warehouse?"

"Yeah," he said. "And I found the baby. I might be all kinds of a fool in your eyes, Sally, but I'm not mentally defective!"

"You did more than find the baby, Jake." Her hand drifted down his face, rasped over the day-old stubble of beard on his jaw. "You saved his life."

"That's good, isn't it?"

"Of course it is! It's the best news possible."

"So how come you're looking so tragic?"

"Because the paramedics said there was no hurry to get you to the hospital." Her mouth quivered all over again. "I thought they meant you were dead."

"And you're ticked off that I'm not?"

"I'm ticked off with myself," she said, losing the battle with the tears. They splashed down her face in rivers. "I lied to you and to myself, and almost left it too late to put things right."

At that, he gave up. He'd have liked to play the tough guy a bit longer, as payback for what she'd put him through, but the tears undid him. Too many had been shed already. It was time they came to an end.

"I haven't been completely honest with you, either," he said. "I heard everything you said when you thought I was still out cold. And just in case you spoke out of guilt, I want you to know I won't hold you to any of it. We all say and do things we don't really mean when we're under stress."

"But I did mean them," she said. "With all my heart. And if you had died last night without hearing them, I would have died with you. You are my life. You always have been."

He caught her hands and never wanted to let them go. "Do me a favor," he said. "Go find my clothes and somebody to discharge me from this joint. We're getting out of here before I make a spectacle of myself."

"I'll do no such thing," she scolded. "You need rest."

"I need you."

"You have me."

"Then prove it and go find my clothes. We have some serious making-up to do, and it's not going to happen here."

"Are you sure you're up to it?"

He tried to look serious, but his mouth twitched and gave

him away. "Take a peek under this sheet, my lovely Sally, and find out for yourself how very much I'm up to it."

It was enough to persuade her, but it took quite a bit more to convince the uniforms. When they realized he'd leave the hospital anyway, they grudgingly gave him his walking papers and a load of advice he had no intention of following.

Within the hour, he was in the passenger seat of her car and feasting his eyes on her as she drove him home. She still wore the tacky hospital gown over her nightshirt, and fluffy white slippers a lot the worse for wear.

She didn't have a speck of makeup on her face, nor a single piece of jewelry anywhere. A far cry from the vision she'd presented at the gala. Yet every male hormone he possessed was screaming for release and urging him to have at her with all due speed.

Her skin smelled of Diva body lotion, she looked luscious as the golden pears hanging on the tree in his garden, and he'd never found her more lovely or more desirable.

The sun was just peeping over the horizon as she pulled into his driveway. "You want to park in the garage?" he asked her.

"No," she said, turning to look at him from eyes as deep and mysterious as priceless jade. "My priorities have shifted. It no longer matters if anyone sees me here."

He leaned over and with exemplary restraint, kissed her cheek. "I've waited months to hear you say that, Sally, but now that you have, it's been worth every minute of it."

She held his hand and followed him into the house. "Are you hungry? Shall I make you breakfast?"

"Oh, yeah!" he said, pulling her at last into his arms, where she'd always belonged and inching her toward the stairs. "I'm hungry all right—but not for breakfast."

*   *   *

They began with a shower. A long, hot, lovely melding of skin against skin, and big, fat soapy sponges to chase away the bleak, terrifying reminders of the night just past. She scrubbed his back; he shampooed her hair. She flattened her hands over the strong, beautiful contours of his chest. He cupped her bottom. Pressed her against him.

"I love you," he said, against her mouth.

A current of joy ran through her. "I've missed you saying that to me," she sighed.

"If I promise to spend the next fifty years making up for it, will you marry me?"

She burst into tears. It seemed to be the thing she did the most often, lately. "Yes," she said. "Oh, yes!"

He wrapped her in a big, fluffy towel, draped another around his waist, and carried her to his bed. The September sun washed over the tumbled sheets and filled the room with mellow light.

"I don't have champagne or roses," he said, lowering her to the mattress. "I don't have a ring or violins. I don't even have fresh sheets on the bed. They'll have to wait until another time when I'm better prepared. Right now, my love, the only thing I have to give you is me."

"You're all I need or want," she said dreamily, opening her arms to him. "My only regret is that I almost had to lose you forever to realize how precious what we share is."

He came to her in a rush of urgency and heat that melted the chilly isolation which had reigned so long in her heart. He came to her with passion and tenderness and love. In a union of mind and body and soul, he restored her to a tempestuous joy of living she hadn't known in years.

Afterward, with the aching hunger sated for a while, they lay quietly together. The blood no longer raced through her veins, but flowed with a sweet and heavy harmony. Here at last was the bliss which had been missing in their previous encounters: the mutual aftermath of *making* love which promised a tomorrow of *being* loved.

She turned to him, her eyes drowsy with passion. "We made another baby, Jake," she said softly. "I'd swear my life on it."

"I wouldn't be surprised," he said, pulling her to rest against his heart. "But this time, we'll do it right."

EPILOGUE

SHE called the shelter The Haven, and although the formal ribbon-cutting ceremony with Mayor Harrington and the town dignitaries didn't take place until the end of October, Sally opened the doors five days after the fire.

Lisa and her son, David, were the first residents and, by the end of that week, five more girls and two boys, ranging in age from fourteen to seventeen, had joined them. The monastery, which had stood silent and empty for so long, was suddenly filled with the clatter of feet and the cautious laughter of young people who, until then, hadn't known much in the way of happiness or acceptance.

One crisp, frosty morning shortly before the official opening, a farmer from down the road brought over a cart full of the biggest, fattest, most brilliantly orange pumpkins imaginable. "For the kids," he said. "Bet they can't remember the last time they had a real Halloween."

He gave them two black Labrador-cross puppies, as well, "because a house ain't a home without a dog or two in it. And I'll have kittens for you, come the spring. That'll put an end to the mice in your attic."

By sunset, some of the teens had carved enough jack-o'-lanterns for one to glow from every window, and the rest to line the front steps and the driveway. Under the guidance of the housemother, those who didn't want to carve filled the house with the scent of roasted pumpkin seeds, and pumpkin soup, and spiced pumpkin loaves.

Just before dinner that night, one of the girls, a fragile, tentative waif of fifteen, set aside the biggest jack-o'-lantern, plunked Lisa's baby in it so that his sweet little face poked out of the top, and borrowed Sally's Polaroid camera to take a photo. Meanwhile, the puppies chewed up a pair of shoes, and left little calling cards on the living room carpet.

Nobody was upset. Things like that happened. It was what being a family was all about.

In between watching her project blossom into a success beyond anything she'd ever hoped for, Sally tried to keep her breakfast down—because she'd been right; she and Jake had made a baby—and planned her Christmas wedding.

"Don't sew up the side seams of that dress until the last minute," her mother ordered the seamstress making the bridal gown. "We want to be sure she'll fit in it."

"Really, Sally, you and Jake took long enough to sort yourselves out," Margaret scolded, dusting off the heirloom cradle their great-grandfather had made. "Couldn't you have held out a bit longer, and waited until you had a ring on your finger before you got pregnant?"

"I have a ring," Sally said serenely, flashing her diamond. "And it's beautiful."

"It's certainly big enough—and considering you're not even three months along yet, so are you. Are you sure you're expecting only one baby?"

Just after Thanksgiving, she found out that she was carrying two.

"How'd you feel about asking Colette and Fletcher to be godparents?" Jake asked, when he'd recovered from the shock. "It's the closest they'll ever come to having grandchildren of their own, and I'm all they've got left of family."

Considering how wholeheartedly the Burtons had accepted her engagement to their son-in-law, Sally was happy to agree. But then, she was happy about everything, these days. How could she not be, with the tangled uncertainty of her previous life finally straightened out, the future shining with promise, and the man she adored chafing at the bit to make her his wife?

"This is cruel and unusual treatment for a man in my condition," he moaned, when he had to kiss her good-night at the door and spend the night alone at his own house.

But he had no other choice. "There'll be none of that!" her parents decreed, the day he proposed and suggested they set up house together before the wedding. "You're moving back home until you're decently married."

They became husband and wife by candlelight, in an evening ceremony, on December the fifteenth, in the biggest church in town, because just about everyone within a twenty mile radius wanted to be there to wish them well.

It snowed the entire week before the wedding. Eastridge Bay always had snow in December. On the big day itself, though, the clouds scattered and left the sky studded with icy stars, which was as it should be: a perfect night on which to begin a marriage which promised to be as close to perfect as anything to be found this side of heaven.

MILLS & BOON

Romance

On sale 3rd August 2007

*An Italian toyboy, a marriage of convenience,
five adorable babies, and a love lost and found…*

THE ITALIAN'S WIFE BY SUNSET *by Lucy Gordon*

The Rinucci brothers are back! Della's affair with sexy
toyboy Carlo wasn't meant to last, but this is one Italian
determined to win himself a bride…

REUNITED: MARRIAGE IN A MILLION *by Liz Fielding*

Belle's perfect life and gorgeous husband are the envy
of many. But underneath, the truth of their marriage
of convenience is tearing them apart in this first of the
stunning *Secrets We Keep* trilogy.

HIS MIRACLE BRIDE *by Marion Lennox*

Shanni doesn't 'do' family, but when she is faced with *five*
little babies to care for – and one extremely handsome helper
– she begins to change her mind…

BREAK UP TO MAKE UP *by Fiona Harper*

Nick and Adele thought their marriage was over – until a
romantic evening by a twinkling fire shows them that the
wonderful thing about breaking up…is making up!

0707/06

MILLS & BOON

Blaze

On sale 3rd August 2007

IF YOU COULD READ MY MIND...
by Jeanie London

What if your lover knew your every fantasy? Michael Landry has discovered he can read his wife's mind. And now he knows her secret desires, he knows *just* how to rekindle their spark!

MINUTE BY MINUTE
by Jo Leigh

Meg Becker thinks Alex Rosten is the perfect online boyfriend – clever, sexy and five thousand miles away! But he's sent her a ticket to a gorgeous island resort. Can their virtual fantasies live up to reality?

MIDNIGHT TOUCH
by Karen Kendall

Blue-blooded Kate Spinney is branching out on her own when she meets the raw, sexy Alejandro Torres, who seems determined to take her on a sexual adventure she'll never forget...

MY ONLY VICE
by Elizabeth Bevarly

Rosie Bliss has a *big* thing about the police chief. But when she propositions him, his hands say yes, while his mouth says no. Lucky for Rosie she's hard of hearing...

THE ROYAL HOUSE OF NIROLI

...International affairs, seduction and passion guaranteed

Volume 1 – July 2007
The Future King's Pregnant Mistress by Penny Jordan

Volume 2 – August 2007
Surgeon Prince, Ordinary Wife by Melanie Milburne

Volume 3 – September 2007
Bought by the Billionaire Prince by Carol Marinelli

Volume 4 – October 2007
The Tycoon's Princess Bride by Natasha Oakley

8 volumes in all to collect!

THE ROYAL HOUSE OF NIROLI

...International affairs, seduction and passion guaranteed

Volume 5 – November 2007
Expecting His Royal Baby by Susan Stephens

Volume 6 – December 2007
The Prince's Forbidden Virgin by Robyn Donald

Volume 7 – January 2008
Bride by Royal Appointment by Raye Morgan

Volume 8 – February 2008
A Royal Bride at the Sheikh's Command by Penny Jordan

8 volumes in all to collect!